INCLUSIVE EDUCATION TWENTY YEARS AFTER SALAMANCA

Disability Studies in Education

Susan L. Gabel and Scot Danforth
General Editors

Vol. 19

The Disability Studies in Education series is part of the Peter Lang Education list.
Every volume is peer reviewed and meets
the highest quality standards for content and production.

PETER LANG
New York • Bern • Frankfurt • Berlin
Brussels • Vienna • Oxford • Warsaw

INCLUSIVE EDUCATION TWENTY YEARS AFTER SALAMANCA

EDITED BY FLORIAN KIUPPIS
AND RUNE SARROMAA HAUSSTÄTTER

PETER LANG
New York • Bern • Frankfurt • Berlin
Brussels • Vienna • Oxford • Warsaw

Library of Congress Cataloging-in-Publication Data

Inclusive education twenty years after Salamanca /
edited by Florian Kiuppis, Rune Sarromaa Hausstätter.
pages cm. — (Disability studies in education; vol. 19)
Includes bibliographical references and index.
1. Inclusive education. 2. Educational equalization.
3. Children with disabilities—Education. 4. Children's rights.
I. Kiuppis, Florian, editor of compilation.
LC1200.I543 371.9'046—dc23 2014040424
ISBN 978-1-4331-2697-0 (hardcover)
ISBN 978-1-4331-2696-3 (paperback)
ISBN 978-1-4539-1464-9 (e-book)
ISSN 1548-7210

Bibliographic information published by **Die Deutsche Nationalbibliothek**.
Die Deutsche Nationalbibliothek lists this publication in the "Deutsche Nationalbibliografie"; detailed bibliographic data are available on the Internet at http://dnb.d-nb.de/.

The paper in this book meets the guidelines for permanence and durability of the Committee on Production Guidelines for Book Longevity of the Council of Library Resources.

29 Broadway, 18th floor, New York, NY 10006
www.peterlang.com

Printed in the United States of America

Dedication

In memory of Irving Zola (1935–1994)

Table of Contents

Acknowledgements

We wish to express our deep gratitude to Susan L. Gabel and Scot Danforth for inviting us to publish in the series "Disability Studies in Education". We are also grateful to the team at Peter Lang in New York. Moreover, we thank all authors and anonymous reviewers, as well as Edina Fidelis for providing us with an illustration for our cover.

In addition, Florian would like to express a heartfelt thanks to Rosemarie Garland-Thomson and Benjamin Reiss, as well as to the collective of graduate students, affiliated faculty, steering committee and support staff in context of the Disability Studies Initiative at Emory University (USA) for their hospitality, collegiality, and inspiration.

Florian Kiuppis	Rune Sarromaa Hausstätter

Foreword: The Salamanca Declaration:

Still Our Guide for the Future

EMILY VARGAS-BARÓN

I met Lena Saleh in UNESCO before she became the skilled architect of the process that culminated in the development of the *Salamanca Statement and Framework for Action* of 1994, known widely as the *Salamanca Declaration*. It was clear then that Lena was firm and decisive in her dedication to promoting fully inclusive education of high quality.

It is often said that no one individual is truly indispensable. Generally this is true. But once in awhile there is an exceptional leader who proves to be truly indispensable. This was the case with Lena both before and after the *Salamanca Declaration* was adopted. Lena faced mandatory retirement from UNESCO not long after the adoption process had been completed. Had she been allowed to remain in her post for a longer period of time, I believe that the people she represented in her heart would have benefitted far more from the *Salamanca Declaration,* and later related normative instruments, than has been the case.

THE IMPORTANCE OF THE SALAMANCA DECLARATION

The *Salamanca Declaration* marked the first focused international recognition of the right of each child to achieve his or her full potential from birth onward. Since the *Salamanca Declaration* was established, the *Convention on the Rights of the Child* (CRC), *General Comment 7 of the CRC for Implementing Child Rights in Early Childhood*, and the *Convention on the Rights of Persons with Disabilities* (CRPD) have been adopted. These normative instruments reaffirmed the importance of inclusive education for children with developmental delays and disabilities. In addition, they further refined the parameters of inclusive education and ensured full United Nations support for early intervention and inclusive education.

Incredibly enough, many development managers who work in today's UNESCO have forgotten about the *Salamanca Declaration*. This year, I was appalled to find that a long list of UNESCO normative documents compiled by UNESCO did not include the *Salamanca Declaration*! Yet this incredibly important instrument provided a first road map for achieving improved educational opportunities for all children, youth and adults with developmental delays or disabilities.

It must be observed that now in 2014 we are still at the beginning stages of developing inclusive education in most countries of the world. So much remains to be done. As Dr. Ulf Janson[1] said to me in 2013, "As yet no country has developed a fully inclusive system of education."

In addition, early childhood intervention (ECI) services for children from birth to three or five years of age with developmental delays and disabilities are only now becoming known in low- and middle-income countries. Many early educators and maternal-child health specialists in the world still do not know what ECI is, and what constitutes an effective and sustainable national ECI system!

Furthermore, many persons with disabilities still do not understand the benefits of ECI. Most parents with young children who need ECI services have never heard of them. And they will not learn of them if we do not work assiduously from this point forward to develop national ECI systems in all countries.

As many authors note in this book, the field of inclusive education that was called for in the *Salamanca Declaration* has become highly diffuse and even misunderstood on occasion. It is essential, of course, to use the term 'inclusive education' to refer to educational services that ensure the full inclusion of children with developmental delays and disabilities and also the inclusion of children from ethnic minority groups, lower social castes, under-represented genders, refugees and internally displaced persons, and children living in poverty and other difficult circumstances.

Inclusive education should ensure that all children receive culturally derived and culturally appropriate education. The mother tongue should be used as the language of instruction during all of early education and up to the fourth or fifth grade at a minimum (Ball, 2011).

However, the *Salamanca Declaration* clearly focused mainly on ensuring the provision of inclusive education for children with developmental delays and disabilities. Increasingly, programmes for inclusive education in various countries have left out these children, either by omission or commission. When this has occurred, the very essence of the *Salamanca Declaration*, the *CRC*, *General Comment 7* and *CRPD* has been abrogated.

Furthermore, many educational leaders have tried to label the provision of separate schools or separate classrooms in schools as "inclusive education" when clearly these services are not inclusive. I can attest to the fact that the concept of inclusive education as suffused throughout all classrooms of preschools, primary and secondary schools is still a foreign approach in many nations' public and private educational systems. Much work remains to be done to ensure each child has every opportunity from birth onward to achieve her or his inborn potential through inclusive educational practices of high quality.

TOWARD DEVELOPING COMPREHENSIVE NATIONAL FRAMEWORKS FOR ACHIEVING THE OBJECTIVES OF THE *SALAMANCA DECLARATION, CRC, GENERAL COMMENT 7*, AND *CRPD*

We have now established a strong international normative basis for promoting and implementing education systems that are fully inclusive. Indeed, some countries have established national laws, policies or strategies for inclusive education. However, many nations have not done so as yet. Furthermore, few countries have developed and successfully implemented Action Plans (Operational Plans) for achieving the objectives of inclusive education. Few "roadmaps" have been developed that outline the phases required to develop fully inclusive education systems.

To achieve equitable child development and fully inclusive education systems, countries need to establish strategic priorities for:

- Ensuring full educational equity and child rights;
- Establishing multisectoral coordination and programme integration;
- Addressing remaining national needs for normative guidance, through laws, policies or strategies;
- Setting service standards and programme policies and procedures;
- Ensuring quality improvement and resource development through universal design for curricula that is linked to pre-service training and continuous in-service training;
- Developing systems of accountability through supervisory support, monitoring and evaluation;
- Expanding investment in early childhood and inclusive education services until nationwide coverage is achieved; and

- Developing effective policy advocacy focused on parents and communities as well as on national, regional and community leaders. (Adapted from Vargas-Barón, 2013).

In addition, from the point of view of lifelong education and development, greater attention is urgently required to prevent developmental delays and disabilities, to identify infants and young children needing early intervention, and to ensure a continuity of high-quality services for child development and parental education and support, with effective transitions to inclusive preschool, primary and secondary schooling.

The following content areas especially require attention for nations to provide a full set of comprehensive and continuous services for young children and their parents.

Preconception, prenatal and neonatal education and care

To prevent disabilities and to improve birth outcomes and parenting knowledge and skills, preconception, prenatal and neonatal education and care are needed. However, many nations still lack preconception education and adequate prenatal education and care. High-risk pregnancies often are not well identified and treated in a timely manner. Many infant deaths still occur during the critical hours and days after birth; therefore, neonatal education and care is also essential along with ensuring good parent-child bonding.

Early childhood intervention

To establish a strong developmental foundation for all children, early childhood intervention (ECI) services are required for children from birth to three or five years of age with fragile birth status, developmental delays, malnutrition, chronic illnesses, disabilities, and atypical behaviors, such as the autism spectrum and attention deficit and hyperactivity disorders. To be effective, these services are usually provided in the child's natural environment: the home and/or daytime nursery or preschool. They seek to build on each child's abilities and each family's strengths. They focus on the child's next steps for good development as identified by the parents and their service partners (usually early intervention specialists).

Abundant research has shown that it is essential to identify and support parents whose children have developmental delays or disabilities. In the years since the signing of the *Salamanca Declaration*, early childhood intervention activities have expanded and have been greatly improved. From their early beginning in the 1970s in Colombia, Germany and the United States, ECI services have expanded to cover all states of the United States, all provinces of Canada, most nations of Western Europe, at least 12 countries of Eastern Europe, three countries of the Middle East, three countries of Africa, and in the Asia-Pacific region at least Australia, New Zealand, India, Singapore and China. Currently, the International Society on Early Intervention, the Early Childhood Program of The Open Society Foundations, and The RISE Institute are conducting an international survey that will give us a better overview of the current presence of ECI services in nations.

It is clear, however, that these services need to be scaled up in several countries, and they are yet to be designed and developed in many other nations. Millions of young children currently are not developing to their full potential due to the lack of these essential services. In nations with high levels of poverty, child abuse and neglect, community violence, depressed parents, or other difficult and stressful situations, the rate of children needing ECI services can range from 20% to 45% of the cohort of children from birth to five years of age. Within countries, some provinces reveal high levels of developmental delays and disabilities while other provinces have relatively lower rates. No country is exempt from the need to develop ECI services.

Early education and support for vulnerable children and families

For children from birth to five years of age, a continuum of services is needed in each country from: 1) the most intensive and individualized services that are given to children and parents with the greatest needs; 2) to moderately intensive but still individualized services; and to 3) the least intensive and most general of services for children and parents (Vargas-Barón, Janson and Mufel, 2009).

ECI services represent the most intensive and individualized services. They include frequent visits in the natural setting of the child.

The intermediate level of programming addresses needs for early education on the part of high-risk and vulnerable children and families, with a strong attention given to infants and children with mild developmental delays. Without early intervention, there is a high likelihood that such children would require ECI services in the future.

The least intensive services for early education and support assist low-risk children and families. All parents and children require some level of education and support that can be provided through online learning, group sessions or reading materials.

Emerging results from neuroscience and child development research confirm the fundamental importance of the period from preconception and birth to three or five years of age. However, as yet few countries have taken this comprehensive approach to ensuring that all children and parents are adequately supported in culturally appropriate ways.

Inclusive preschool education

Ensuring a good transition from comprehensive ECI and early education and development services to inclusive education services at the preschool level is critically important.

Inclusive preschool education will help children of all ability levels to develop a strong foundation for learning and will help to ensure lifelong social inclusion. By playing and learning with children of all abilities, children develop friendships, empathy, improved senses of self, and new communication skills that will stay with them all of their lives.

Transition from inclusive preschool to inclusive schooling

The transition from inclusive preschool education to inclusive primary and secondary education is also exceedingly important. Children need to gain a good level of self-regulation and learn to share and interact well with others of all ability levels before entering primary school.

Preparing children and parents for inclusive primary school is the main goal of a good transition programme. As yet, few nations have developed such comprehensive transition programmes.

FUTURE CHALLENGES

In summary, the normative foundation for inclusive education has been established but the systems for developing equitable, high-quality and accountable early learning for all are still lacking in most nations.

In reality, after 20 years from the adoption of the *Salamanca Declaration*, our work has only just begun. We must help nations ensure they provide the best possible start in life for ALL of their children.

I am profoundly convinced that once policy leaders are given the opportunity to understand the very real and often dramatic needs of the children in their nations, they will work to improve national systems for child development. I believe they will create effective and more equitable services for preconception, prenatal and neonatal education and care, early childhood intervention, early education and development, and inclusive preschool, primary and secondary education. I believe this because I have seen well-informed policy leaders of several nations establish policies and programmes for inclusive education and expand their investments in programmes for their most vulnerable children.

To achieve improved child development for all, multisectoral and integrated approaches will be needed. Skilled policy planners will be required and dedicated national leaders must be identified, trained and supported. Hopefully, these prerequisites will occur in all countries during the next twenty years.

If this vision is accomplished, we shall not have laboured in vain in our attempt to ensure all children will fulfill their inborn potential.

NOTE

1. Dr. Ulf Janson, an outstanding researcher of the University of Stockholm and a great leader of inclusive education, passed away in December 2013.

CHAPTER ONE

Inclusive Education for All, and Especially for Some?

On Different Interpretations of Who and What the "Salamanca Process" Concerns

FLORIAN KIUPPIS AND RUNE SARROMAA HAUSSTÄTTER

In June 1994, the World Conference on Special Needs Education, held in Salamanca (Spain) and organized by UNESCO (United Nations Educational, Scientific and Cultural Organization) in cooperation with the Spanish Ministry of Education and Science, was attended by more than 300 people. The participants included representatives from 92 governments, along with education officials, policy-makers, administrators and members of 25 international organizations, including the United Nations (UN) and its specialized agencies, other IGOs (international government organizations), NGOs (national government organizations), and donor agencies. The conference participants collectively adopted the Salamanca Statement and Framework for Action on Special Needs Education (see Appendix A), which reflects high ideals of progress (e.g., to end all forms of discrimination and to foster social cohesion), thereby making it quasi-obligatory for national delegations to implement the objectives contained within the Statement. The principal element of this text was a "new thinking" in special needs education, and the Statement called on all governments to "adopt as a matter of law or policy the principle of inclusive education" (paragraph 3) and, in this connection, to reorient educational strategies to meet special needs in mainstream education.

WHAT DOES MEETING SPECIAL NEEDS IN MAINSTREAM EDUCATION MEAN?

Arguably, the "new thinking" associated with inclusive education has been interpreted in different ways (Kiuppis, 2014b). In the literature, three main agendas can be roughly distinguished:

1) Many actors and theorists, evidently the majority of whom are from the USA, understand the concept of meeting special educational needs in mainstream education (as well as the term "inclusive education") as primarily concerned with people with disabilities, either in the sense of "schools for all" or in the sense of education in integrated settings as an alternative to education in segregated settings (Baglieri et al., 2011). The association of inclusive education with disability makes sense due to the notion of inclusion that arose in the mid-1990s from UNESCO's Special Education Unit and its representatives' communications with their peers and competitors (Kiuppis, 2014a). Recently, the way in which people with disabilities are considered the primary focus group of inclusive education has been strongly fuelled by contributions pointing to the UN-Convention on the Rights of Persons with Disabilities adopted in 2006, which—primarily with reference made to Article 24 of the convention (see Appendix B)—suggests that inclusion is a conceptual advancement of integration and is thus first and foremost intended for people with disabilities (Rieser, 2012). The readers of the present volume may empathize with this thinking, since the book deals with inclusive education and is published in a disability studies series in the USA.

2) Other researchers may interpret meeting special needs in mainstream education as an objective to widen the focus of special needs education in terms of the target group, for example by understanding inclusive education as an approach to address the issues of *access to*, as well as of *participation* and *achievement in education* for various groups (Westwood, 2013). Understood in that sense, inclusive education is framed as a concept that is directed to all, but in practice focuses especially on particular populations that are considered the most vulnerable (e.g., working children, those belonging to indigenous groups and linguistic minorities, nomadic children, and those affected by HIV/AIDS), marginalized (e.g., children from households in rural or remote communities and children in urban slums), or that have "special educational needs," that traditionally have been attributed to people with disabilities (e.g., Riehl 2000). Understood in this way, inclusive education can be described as a "developmental approach seeking to address the learning needs of all children, youth and adults with a specific focus on those who are vulnerable to marginalization and exclusion" (UNESCO, 2004, quoted in Westwood, 2007, p. 3).

3) A third common understanding of inclusive education found in the literature is connected with approaches that are inspired mainly by the work of

change agents in ordinary schools in the UK to reach out to the heterogeneity of learners—in other words, approaches that take diversity as a starting point for educational theory and practice (Ainscow and César, 2006) and aim at answering the question of "whether the population [of special needs education—the authors] was to be defined in terms of children in special schools or the wider population of children experiencing learning difficulties for any reason" (Mittler, 2010, p. 175). Studies that deal more broadly with the heterogeneity of learners have highlighted a non-categorical approach to inclusive education and argued that the objective that was agreed upon in connection with the 1994 World Conference on Special Needs Education, according to which special educational needs potentially should be met in the mainstream, implied a widening of the target group of special needs education and thus the tendency to renunciate the focus on particular groups, such as people with disabilities. According to the wider understanding, inclusive education is considered a non-categorical, all-embracing approach characterized by "ensuring a basic minimum standard of education for all" (Ainscow, 2012, p. 290; OECD, 2007) and deals with heterogeneous learning populations in which individual differences are not classified according to categories such as race, religion, gender, or disability (Booth, 1996; Dyson and Millward, 2000).

Depending on the question of which group is considered the intended recipient of inclusive education (if *any*, given that the non-categorical approach that focuses on the heterogeneity of learners avoids the classification of students according to attributable features), measures of *how* to arrange education that is "inclusive" change accordingly. Differences remain between contexts in which the same group is in focus: for example, regarding how "inclusive education systems," as imagined in the 2006 UN-Convention (cf. Appendix B), are organized. That is the reason why national reports on inclusive education, such as those published in context of the most recent International Conference on Education (held in 2008, in Geneva) declare all of the following settings as "inclusive": "schools for all" with heterogeneous classes; schools with integrative settings; schools with special classes; and special schools as part of "general" education systems.

However, it is readily apparent that the Salamanca Statement reflects the idea of overcoming the divide between regular and special (needs) education. While in the literature and in political statements there are quite different positions to be found regarding the question of whom *inclusion* addresses, there is overall agreement on the point that educational *integration* (which was the predominant paradigm prior to the 1994 World Conference in Salamanca) is first and foremost concerned with the question of how children with disabilities can ideally participate in mainstream schools. However, there are also different understandings regarding the question of what *inclusion* as "new thinking" in special needs education is replacing:

> For example, some researchers view inclusive education as an ongoing development of special education. Others believe that what we refer to as inclusion is, and should be, derived from mainstream approaches to instruction and school organization, creating an alternative to special education knowledge and practices.
>
> (Ballard, 1999, p. 1)

While there is broad consensus that inclusion is associated with "schools for all," arguably there are differing agendas regarding the questions of how to frame the student population of inclusive education (including people with disabilities) theoretically, as well as conceptually (Kiuppis, forthcoming). How can we think of appropriate ways for education that on the one hand take into account the universalistic character of the notion of inclusion and on the other hand the particular situations people with disabilities are both embedded in and facing when looking at their future, while experiencing barriers for access to and participation within education?

Studies of inclusive education published to date can be roughly differentiated according to their aims and objectives. Some contributions are mainly descriptive (e.g., Miles, 2002), some are explanatory and seek to clarify the meaning of inclusive education (some with a rather rhetorical use of theory) and place emphasis on a certain way to perceive it (e.g., Hinz, 2004), and some are more emphatic, and develop concrete ideas for how to implement it (e.g., Ainscow and César, 2006; for a critique of "finished solutions," see Sarromaa Hausstätter, 2013) or have been written in an ideological tone (for an overview see, e.g., Brantlinger, 1997). By contrast, relatively few studies have provided a historical context for inclusive education, including recognition as to how and why the principle of inclusion and the inclusive education approach have morphed and been transformed during their diffusion, adoption, and hybridization (Artiles et al., 2011, pp. 3ff.). To our knowledge, no contribution to date has *bridged* different notions of inclusive education in the way that the present volume does by providing a frame in which contrasting understandings find place and are interrelated. However, at stake here are the consequences of the World Conference in Salamanca and the impact of different meanings of inclusive education for Disability Studies in Education and for the practical education of people with disabilities.

INCLUSIVE EDUCATION 20 YEARS AFTER SALAMANCA

It is our contention that in order to move research, policy, and practice forward along the lines of the 1994 Salamanca Statement and the 2006 UN-Convention there needs to be clarity regarding what is meant by inclusive education. The chapters of this book reflect a broad range of different understandings of inclusive education, drawing from a wide variety of uses of the word *inclusion*, and thus mapping the diverse meanings of this issue, or in other words a "heterogeneous inclusivity" (Kiuppis, 2014b) that emerged in various contexts: spatially, temporally, academically, as well as practically.

A book titled *20 years after Salamanca* could take very different vantage points. It could outline various understandings or it could support one understanding by putting particular emphasis on a certain way of perceiving it. This book reflects on the consequences of the World Conference in Salamanca for the education of people with disabilities. In particular, this contribution to Disability Studies in Education aims to explore the role played by inclusive education in this context during the last 20 years, since UNESCO and the Spanish Ministry of Education and Science organized the Salamanca conference. The book includes theoretical considerations, analyses, as well as relevant case studies from perspectives within applied sciences. Hence, it enters the "Salamanca Process" (Kiuppis, 2014a) from different angles. We have aimed to bridge the various approaches to the study of inclusive education and disability by highlighting the differences in narratives of inclusive education in a multiplicity of contexts. However, we do not favor one understanding of inclusive education over another but rather take a lateral view and present the heterogeneity of meanings of inclusive education in its broad spectrum.

Readers might wonder that we chose to publish the book in a Disability Studies series. Although the book contains chapters by authors who share an interest in mainstreaming the rights of children with disabilities into international development cooperation, and particularly advancing the educational rights of that group, we do not imply here that inclusive education is an approach that necessarily needs to focus on disability (Kiuppis and Peters, 2014). Moreover, we do not state that inclusive education is just for marginalized and vulnerable groups, congruent with the "Education for All" agenda. Particularly, valorizing the non-categorical approach would have somewhat prohibited the publication of this book in a Disability Studies series. However, concurring with any one of those three agendas identified in the literature review would be to neglect intersectionalities, for example with race, gender, and class. In sum, this book encompasses a new area within the inclusive education debate in context of Disability Studies in Education. We developed it in memory of Irving Zola who died twenty years ago, in December 1994.

SECTION ONE

Actors and Their Role in the Salamanca Process

CHAPTER TWO

Salamanca as a World Conference:

The Role of International Development Organizations

COLETTE CHABBOTT

Over its 74-year history, the recommendations issued by the annual or bi-annual International Conference on Education (ICE)[1] reflect many shifts over time in the concerns and practices of the international education community.[2] The recommendations of the 1936 and 2008 ICE illustrate particularly dramatic changes in best practices with respect to special needs education. The 1936 session recommended the organization of "special schools" for the "physically and mentally defective." In contrast, the 2008 session recommended an "inclusive education approach in the design, monitoring and assessment of education policies as a way to further accelerate the attainment of Education for All."

Recommendations like these from other, general education conferences like ICE, such as UNESCO's regional education conferences and, more recently, the 1990 World Conference on Education for All in Jomtien (EFA or Jomtien) and the 2000 World Education Forum in Dakar (WEF or Dakar), reflect some success in bringing global and national education discourse into line with the international human rights agreements since the end of World War II.

This chapter suggests that earlier world conferences may have provided not simply an impetus for the Salamanca Conference, but also a blueprint to promote special needs education beginning at the global level. The blueprint for world conferences was largely developed and popularized by international development organizations and the professionals in them over the last 50 years and has served to extend the *de facto* jurisdiction of those organizations and professionals (Abbott,

1988) from the international to the national and local levels. As nation states accede to international human rights protocols they face pressure from international organizations to make and then implement ambitious national plans of action consistent with those protocols. The chapter also examines the role of international and national non-governmental organizations (NGOs) in creating pressure to implement those national plans. The NGO role includes both demonstrating the feasibility of low-cost, high impact innovations to move plans forward and also advocating for the plan at the national and local levels.

The first section below briefly reviews the rise of new international development organizations in the post-World War II era and how their work created the need for and an environment conducive to world conferences. The second section compares the Salamanca Conference with some common features of both the Health for All (Alma Ata) and the EFA conferences. The conclusions highlight some implications of the low level of participation in Salamanca of the sort of NGOs that played important roles in sustaining and advancing both a selective offshoot of Health for All (the Child Survival initiative) and a similarly selective offshoot of Education for All (Universal Primary Education).

INTERNATIONAL DEVELOPMENT AS AN ORGANIZATIONAL FIELD

In the decades following World War II, thousands of governmental and non-governmental organizations (NGOs)[3] launched activities to operationalize the right of every individual to a minimum standard of living as articulated in the Universal Declaration of Human Rights (adopted 1948, UDHR, Article 25, Para 1),[4] particularly in newly independent and lower-income countries. In the mid-1960s, the UN formalized the Universal Declaration into two binding Covenants, one for Economic, Social and Cultural Rights (CESCR) and a second for Civil and Political Rights. These Covenants, both of which came into force in 1976, gave impetus to a new wave of international activities and organization. The CESCR proposed that healthy, educated individuals would be the fuel for individual and national development, authorizing more international health and education activities to support both.

All of these organizations and activities were by no means effective at what came to be called international development and most had mixed motives. While altruism played a significant role (Lumsdaine, 1993), so did the military and economic interests of the funders. By the 1960s, the Cold War (approx. 1950–1990) had already divided the world into First (capitalist), Second (centrally planned) and Third (or Non-Aligned) World countries. Although many had expected that the United Nations would play a central role in dispensing and coordinating international development aid, the Cold War largely derailed this process (Black, 1986; Jones, 2005). Instead, the largest donor to the UN, the United States, and several other large funders lost confidence in the ability of specialized UN agencies, such as UNESCO, to manage First World funds even-handedly.

Several specialized UN agencies, including UNESCO, therefore, were not funded commensurate with their mandates. Instead at the beginning of the 1960s, mainly First World countries established a new set of organizations to advance economic, and sometimes social, development in the Third World. These included:

- Multilaterals, including UN funds such as the UN Development Programme, as well as the soft loan window of the IBRD, often referred to as the World Bank and
- Bilaterals, including country-to-country agencies such as British Overseas Development Assistance and the Norwegian Aid Agency (NORAD).

These new organizations were joined by a large contingent of international NGOs, some of which had a much longer track record of providing education and health services in the Third World, though often on a small scale. These included missionary hospitals and schools; secular humanitarian relief such as Save the Children; private philanthropies such as the Rockefeller Foundation; and, eventually, many small non-profit organizations that specialized in one or two issues, such as special needs education (Chabbott, 2003).

None of these organizations had sufficient resources or geographic reach to accomplish their mandates alone, so together, along with UN specialized agencies, they constitute a highly interdependent organizational field. Cooperation among these agencies, given their diverse origins, overlapping mandates, and even divergent notions about economic and social development, was and still is often difficult. Some framed international development as a holistic, humanistic enterprise, encompassing politics and the full range of human rights described in the CESCR. Some of the largest funding organizations, however, such as the World Bank and the various agencies of the U.S. government, framed development as a purely technical and economic enterprise, to be addressed sector-by-sector, largely by technological innovation and economic policies. Whether taking the broader or the narrower of these two positions, however, few of these organizations were direct extensions of their funders. Instead, the natural formalization of organizational activities over time produced routines, professional standards, and best practices, in short an organizational culture, somewhat independent of their funders

Critical scholars cast the narrower interpretation of development as a largely self-interested one, intended to maintain the international status quo, to preclude demands for radical political reform at the global or national level (Ferguson, 1990). Others frame it as a bargain struck between moral and realist concerns

(Lumsdaine, 1993). Defenders argue that both the international development field and many of the countries emerging from colonialism and brutal civil wars clearly had limited capacity to plan and implement complex long-term social programs. Campaigns against smallpox or the development and promotion of improved varieties of rice had indeed proven feasible; establishing universal access to an integrated system of primary health care and self-sufficiency in food in every nation-state had not. These foundational debates about comprehensive and selective approaches echo in debates about why the expanded vision of EFA or of inclusive education, writ large, have not been more vigorously pursued.

Breaking the advancement of the CESCR into sectors, each with its independent strategies and goals, started as early as 1954 with the First World Population Conference, followed by the 1963 UN Conference on the Application of Science and Technology for the Benefit of Less Developed Areas. Later UN-sponsored conferences dealt with the Human Environment, Food, Women, Water, Human Settlements, among other topics. Some of these conferences led to the formation of new UN agencies. For example the UN Environment Programme was founded after the 1972 World Conference on the Human Environment. Moreover increased funding for new organizations with no field presence may further prompt the formation of new organizations, particularly NGOs, to develop activities and expand them to underserved areas (Frank et al., 1998).

UNESCO sponsored the first education-related world[5] conference in 1965 on the Eradication of Illiteracy; the U.S. Department of State sponsored the next, in 1967, on the World Crisis[6] in Education (Coombs, 1968). At the same time, a blueprint developed for organizing and implementing world conferences somewhat independent of sector was evolving. For example, the 1990 EFA Conference in Jomtien was partly modeled on the 1978 HFA Conference in Alma Ata (Alma Ata), though in implementation it narrowed to primary education, much as HFA narrowed to Child Survival.

Despite the term "All," HFA and EFA conference organizers, trying to get as many governments on board, working under time pressures and with limited resources, did not beat the bushes to identify underserved groups and ensure their participation. For example, a few years after Jomtien, I interviewed about 50 conference participants and planners. Special needs education, or something similar, came up only once in those interviews: when the parent of a child with special needs expressed his frustration at the complete absence of the topic on the EFA conference agenda. Indeed, of the 48 thematic and illustrative roundtables held during the conference, none focused on special needs or inclusive education. In the 245 pages summarizing the outcomes of those roundtables, a paragraph discusses the disabled as one underprivileged group—"who may constitute up to 10 per cent of the population in some countries"—along with working children and girls (Haggis, 1992, p. 50). The *World Declaration on Education for All*[7] identifies five essential issues in "Universalizing Access and Promoting Equity" (Article 3), one of which constitutes removing educational barriers to underserved groups, and another demands special attention to "the learning needs of the disabled" (Inter-Agency Commission, 1990, p. 45). Disability is mentioned several times in passing in the *Jomtien Framework for Action*.[8]

WHAT DO ALMA ATA AND JOMTIEN SAY ABOUT SALAMANCA?

How does the international community make up for the oversights of a world conference? Apparently, by having another one. The 1994 Salamanca Conference shared much in common with the 1978 Alma Ata and the 1990 EFA conferences, but it also had some distinctive features.

Nation-states may rule, but organizations matter

International development organizations can and do routinely press nation-states—whether donors or recipients of development aid—to adopt programs of action and budgets to fund them that are more ambitious than their earlier actions predict. Two and four UN agencies, respectively, used their convening authority to call nation-states to world conferences at Alma Ata and Jomtien. The core funding for both conferences came from these UN agencies and other international development organizations. For example, relations between UNESCO and the U.S. Department of State office responsible for international organization affairs were so strained that the U.S. initially declined to participate in EFA. Behind the scenes, however, the U.S. Agency for International Development assembled enough discretionary funds and contributions from U.S.-based NGOs to make a contribution that qualified it, as an organization, not as the U.S. government, to be a co-sponsor. Staff members from sponsoring agencies drafted the *Declarations* and *Frameworks for Action* for both conferences. Following some hasty feedback from governments at regional conferences, staff then finalized these documents in time to be passed out at the closing ceremony. At those sessions of both conferences, delegates representing both countries and organizations were so moved that they rose and accepted the declarations by acclamation, some with tears in their eyes. Following the conference the declarations and frameworks for action, respectively, provided common scripts and templates for national plans of action.

Given the degree of resource dependence among many Third World nation-states and international development organizations, therefore, simple coercion must have played a role in a number of the ambitious national plans of actions generated in the wake of the Alma Ata and Jomtien conferences. National plans crafted independent of national budgets could be seen as an expression of good intentions, signaling nation-states' alignment with the highest international ideals, indicating their worthiness for support. However, in a world that values rationality and has enshrined high ideals such as equity and justice in multiple binding covenants and conventions, over time, both donors and recipients of development aid find it increasingly difficult not to take some action consistent with those ideals. Brunsson argues that expressions of high ideals in organizations can be useful even when they cannot be immediately attained, since over time pressure mounts to take action consistent with them (1989).

Champions play a role

Halfdan Mahler, an activist secretary-general at WHO, with strong support from UNICEF director Harry LaBouisse, championed a comprehensive approach to Health for All at Alma Ata. Shortly after succeeding LaBouisse at UNICEF, however, James P. Grant became convinced that HFA's comprehensive approach was hopelessly stalled. He used UNICEF's mandate to address all facets of children's lives to create a more selective approach to HFA focused tightly on the health of children under-five years old, what he called the Child Survival Revolution (the Child Survival initiative). To augment UNICEF's budget, he made common cause with two of the largest funders of health in Third World countries, the World Bank and USAID. In this narrower sphere, dramatic progress was possible and indeed such progress did occur, spurring Child Survival to expand from four focal interventions to seven, much less than comprehensive primary health care, but contributing to an unprecedented drop in the global child mortality rate in less than a decade.

The heads of the World Bank and UNESCO separately approached Grant in 1988, wanting to launch a major education initiative along the lines of the Child Survival initiative, though for different reasons. The World Bank wanted to invest in primary education. UNESCO wanted something to establish its effectiveness in order to bring back some major members (funders) that had left. EFA indeed helped the World Bank to focus most new education funds on primary education access for most of the 1990s. In contrast, UNESCO's modestly funded education program was left with the more amorphous, difficult to fund components of Education for All, some of which fell under the rubric of Special Needs Education. UNESCO Secretary-General Federico Mayor, one of the instigators of the EFA Conference a few years earlier, addressed the opening session of the Salamanca conference, but does not appear to have championed the issue after the conference. Since that time Grant's successor at UNICEF was a champion for girls' education for much of her tenure and former British Prime Minister Gordon Brown may play that role for the UN Secretary General's Education First Initiative. Inclusive education does not yet appear to have one or more champions.

One case study is worth a thousand words

In preparation for Alma Ata, WHO commissioned case studies of innovation at the community level, often drawing on the work of small NGOs. Conference sponsors pointed to these studies as evidence that feasible, low-cost means existed to accomplish conference goals both cheaply and without the development of new technologies.

Historically, NGOs had played a major role in the efforts to reach "all" in both primary health and education. Prior to World War II in the First and Second Worlds, and into the 1970s in the Third World, for good or for ill, private philanthropies and religious groups provided what little modern primary health care was available in remote areas. Although not formally seated at the main conference, health NGOs provided much of the labor for organizing the HFA Conference and afterwards played an important role in both HFA and Child Survival efforts.

NGOs played a similarly prominent role in primary education in the 19th and part of the 20th century. However, a shorter preparation period—less than a year—did not allow for the development of case studies prior to the Jomtien Conference. Case studies produced as much as 15 years earlier or several years later—many featuring NGOs—had to suffice. The Jomtien organizers included NGOs as full participants, at least in part in recognition of their important role in mobilizing public support for EFA in both donor and recipient countries as well as their grassroots expertise. The NGO Jomtien Committee Statement of Principles on the Involvement of NGOs in WCEFA Follow-Up Activities was published as part of the final conference report. The Statement was intended to ensure full NGO participation in follow-up activities, though this did not always occur.

To a casual observer, NGOs were a major, if not the principal provider of special needs education throughout much of the world until World War II and remain so in many countries, particularly in the Third World. Yet no case studies of community-level work appear to have been commissioned in advance of Salamanca from NGOs. Instead, a list of three recommendations emerged from five regional consultations preceding the conference included the following recommendations for developing case studies:

> Pilot projects based on inclusive education should be established and evaluated carefully in the light of local needs, resources and services. Such evaluative information can guide policy and practice in key ways and should be disseminated both within countries and to other countries that share similar circumstances. (UNESCO and Ministry of Education and Science Spain 1994, p. 18)

Furthermore, during the Salamanca Conference, the third of four themes, "Community Participation," included several reports from NGO projects and the fourth, "Partnership and Networking," included a report from Save the Children suggesting ways for NGOs, government, and grassroots organizations to collaborate. Yet few NGOs appear on the list of participants in the final conference report.

At the closing session, Victor Ordonez, speaking on behalf of the UNESCO Secretary General, noted that the conference

> ...took place at a strategic time when the approach of inclusive education has been successfully, though not uneventfully, introduced in a few countries, and when the rest of the countries were ready and eager to learn how to implement similar approaches. (UNESCO and Government of Spain, 1994, p. 24)

These statements at Salamanca suggest that many countries and some NGOs were in the process of learning how to do special needs education effectively, on a small scale. There were no low-cost, universal innovations, ready to be scaled up quickly as there had been for Child Survival. Moreover, governments in the countries with the furthest to go to meet global goals had relatively little experience delivering services in many other rural areas and small-scale NGO efforts in those areas did not seamlessly translate into government programs.

Broad goals tend to narrow

Despite the expansive HFA and EFA Declarations, the available funding focused on a much more selective set of activities. Within a few years, the main indicator for HFA was narrowed to reducing the mortality rate for children under-five (U5MR), that is, Child Survival, using a handful of low-cost health interventions. Similarly, funders narrowed EFA to universal primary school enrollment (UPE) and, later, to completion (UPC). In one sense, this was no surprise.

The Salamanca Conference represented one of several efforts to take up part of the Jomtien agenda that the international development organizations had dropped. Grossly underfunded, UNESCO did not have funds to launch major new programs in support of EFA but it could still convene international conferences and it already had a section on Special Needs Education. The Salamanca documents link its roots not simply to Jomtien, but to:

> ...the International Year of Disabled Persons (1981) and the subsequent Decade of Disabled Persons (1983–1992), the World Programme of Action in Favour of Disabled Persons (United Nations 1983), the Convention on the Rights of the Child (1989), the Asian Decade of Disabled Persons (1993–2002) and the recent adoption by the United Nations General Assembly of the Standard Rules on the Equalization of Opportunities for Disabled Persons. (UNESCO and Ministry of Education and Science Spain, 1994, p. 17)

Its origins, therefore, lay with the education of persons with special needs conventionally defined, as physical disability. In the conventional disability sphere, however, UNESCO shares mandates with both WHO (for health-related disabilities) and UNICEF (for children with disabilities, who constitute a relatively large percentage of those in emergencies).

The Salamanca Statement broadened its target group from persons with disabilities to those who, "for whatever reason, are failing to benefit from school." Salamanca thus combined into one the "underserved groups" and "disabled children" separately highlighted in the EFA Declaration. What prompted this approach? Did the broader definition of "special needs education" enable groups whose constituents represented a small percentage of all children to make common cause and thus achieve greater influence by representing a larger number of children? At the same time, in commending "regular schools with an inclusive orientation" to address "the unique characteristics, interests, abilities, and learning needs" of every child, Salamanca joined the more selective forms of HFA and EFA—Child Survival and UPE—in narrowing its focus from "all" to children.

Non-binding declarations find their way into binding conventions

Although the HFA and EFA Declarations were not binding, proponents succeeded in incorporating their main provisions into the subsequent, binding 1990 Convention on the Rights of the Child and the 2006 Convention on the Rights of Persons with Disabilities. Similarly the 1-½ pages that constitute Article 6, "Education" in the latter is informed by the Salamanca Statement. Widespread neglect of such conventions by many countries has provided professionals in international organizations an opportunity to declare "crises" and to raise funds and hold conferences to address them.

Over time, more things count and more must be counted

Neither HFA nor EFA started with a commitment to global targets, much less a mechanism to monitor them. However prominent, public statements during or following annual Child Survival Task Force meetings in the 1980s, as well as UNICEF's *State of the World's Children* report, proved an effective way to keep global attention on a selective set of HFA-relevant targets. In the 1990s, more NGOs began to monitor countries' performance in terms of world conference commitments and human rights agreements, both formal and informal: for example, the global, cross-sectoral *Social Watch* (1996) and the Bangladesh-specific *Education Watch* (Chowdhury et al., 1999). Oxfam commissioned more than two dozen papers in preparation for the end of decade conference for EFA in Dakar, and incorporated many findings into a major report, *Education Now: break the cycle of poverty* (Watkins, 2000), most documenting meager progress towards UPE. An annual *EFA Global Monitoring Report* was launched with fanfare in 2002 and in most years since.

Numbers move the funders of international development organizations. The Child Survival initiative was partially inspired by a paper that estimated that more than 10 million deaths of children under-five years old annually were "unnecessary" because a handful of low-cost, relatively universal health interventions could prevent them (Rohde, 1982). The paper, in essence, provided a price tag for saving 10 million lives that was so low UNICEF's Director argued it was morally unacceptable not to take action. Still under fire from advocates of more comprehensive, measured approaches to primary health care, the Child Survival initiative has inspired a half-dozen single disease global campaigns such as the Global Polio eradication initiative, the river blindness control campaign, and the Global Fund to Fight AIDS, Tuberculosis, and Malaria, attacking pieces of the problem, not the whole (Black et al., 2003; Rohde, 2008). In contrast, more than 10 years after Jomtien, education researchers continue to debate whether education research could ever produce low-cost interventions that might generate the same sort of enthusiasm from funders and dramatic progress towards quality UPE.

The numbers presented at Salamanca were not compelling and the cost of addressing them was not estimated, at least in part because international development agencies played a modest role in the conference. However, the 2008 International Conference on Education offered as its first recommendation under "Public Policies": "Collect and use relevant data on all categories of the excluded to better develop education policies and reforms for their inclusion." The WHO and the World Bank published the first *World Report on Disability 2011* and estimated the number of children (0–14 years old) living with physical disabilities between 93 and 150 million. However, many categories of disability/exclusion are at stigmatizing in various cultures and the discourse around disability currently rejects problematizing those categories. UNICEF's 2013 *State of the World's Children Report: Children with Disabilities* begins:

> Reports such as this typically begin with a statistic designed to highlight a problem. The girls and boys to whom this edition of The State of the World's Children is dedicated are not problems. (UNICEF, 2013, p. 1)

Without more counting, however, Alma Ata and Jomtien suggest there may be no more funding. And as counting out-of-school children becomes more established and the quality of data improves, the distinct characteristics and needs of these children should become clearer. International development organizations attempting to meet the education MDG, now focused on the last 20% of out-of-school children, of whom children with physical and cognitive disabilities represent a larger proportion than they do of the total population, are already demanding more and better demographic data on the disabled.

Rights involving physical integrity are more compelling

In all comparisons, HFA has an advantage over EFA to the extent physical life and death outcomes are more compelling than those dealing with invisible qualities, such as cognitive development. Some discussions in the special needs or inclusive education community distinguish between medical from social approaches to disability, privileging the latter. The Alma Ata and Jomtien cases, however, suggest that, to the extent that inclusive education covers many types of exclusion, those with a physical disability may find it easier to secure support than those without. In addition, Cole and Ramirez (Cole and Ramirez, 2013) found that national human rights institutions were more likely to enforce rights involving physical integrity than other types.

Information and communication technology speed the process

In 1985, UNICEF argued that Child Survival was doable in part because advances in communication technology had accelerated the diffusion of innovations, of information about "unnecessary" suffering in all parts of the world, and of social mobilization around innovations in health education. A decade later, ICT was not ready to revolutionize education, or special needs education in the first way, but was making progress on the second. More than 25 years later, advances in communication and information technology continue to accelerate and make keeping special needs education in the public eye much easier than in the past. The "hypocrisy" in the loose coupling between formal plans and real budgets and actions becomes easier to expose and reduce given the widespread use of sophisticated social networking and simple mobile telephones.

CONCLUSIONS

The 1994 World Conference on Special Needs Education in Salamanca bears many of the hallmarks of earlier and larger world conferences but it also diverges from them in several interesting ways. Like the 1978 Alma Ata conference and the 1990 Jomtien conference, Salamanca attempted to consolidate and mobilize a constituency to promote and diffuse an expanded notion of human rights derived from the elaboration of the 1948 Universal Declaration of Human Rights in the post-World War II period. In their emphasis on "all," both HFA and EFA declarations did not systematically differentiate and recognize historically disadvantaged groups. Everyone was welcome in the big tent, but special needs were muted. At Salamanca, persons with disabilities made common cause with ethnic minorities, language minorities, and others who, "for whatever reason, are failing to benefit from school."

Salamanca diverged from the Alma Ata and Jomtien conferences in significant ways. While HFA and EFA started out encompassing all age groups and only later came to focus on children, Salamanca began narrowly focused on children. The constituency of those "failing to benefit from schools" was not primarily concentrated in the Third World and as such the Salamanca conference was not dominated by development organizations. As "all" begins to be approached for UPE, however, those with special needs are likely to compose an increasing proportion of the last 10–20% of children not in school and an increasing proportion of those are likely to be found in the Third World. This should increase the involvement of international development organizations in the special needs education community. The organizational culture of these organizations demands more statistics and disaggregation of groups within the special needs education constituency and the search for more targeted responses for each of these groups.

The comparison of Salamanca with Alma Ata and Jomtien has raised several questions. Where are the numbers? Can the special needs education community recognized by Salamanca produce statistics without stigmatization? As international development organizations come to play a larger role in the special needs community, are there some constructive roles for these organizations? As these organizations look for interventions with measurable impact, are there some advantages in disaggregating into groups with more specific needs—for example, physical disabilities, language minorities, internally displaced or stateless children—or are there greater advantages to continuing to make common cause? Are there low-cost, stand-alone, high impact interventions that could render some forms of exclusion "unnecessary" in the same way some simple, low-cost interventions rendered many infant deaths "unnecessary"?

Finally, where are the NGOs? In the global North, advances in social welfare systems may have reduced the role of NGOs in the education of special needs populations. Historically, however, NGOs have played an important role in international relief and in grassroots services delivery in remote areas of the Third World. They are a major source of innovation, of mobilizing grassroots support in donor countries, and of holding governments' feet to the fire in terms of global agreements and national plans, and of sources of service. By the time of the 1990 Jomtien conference, at least 30 international associations of organizations with the words disability, special education, special needs, or inclusive education in their names and more than 100 with the word "blind" or "deaf" had been founded.[9] Yet among the 120 NGOs that participated in the EFA conference, only one clearly identifies with any of these terms, that is, the World Blind Union (f. 1984, WBU)

(Inter-Agency Commission, 1990, p. 118). Including the Kiwanis, the Lions, and a few other service organizations known for their work with specific physical disabilities, only a handful of organizations focused on special needs education appear to have participated in the EFA conference. Moreover, only a handful of special needs NGOs participated in Salamanca four years later. As concern and action around inclusive education grows in the global South, where welfare states are less common and comprehensive, inclusive education advocates in the global North will more often find themselves making common cause with small NGOs now working with learners with all manner of special needs.

NOTES

1. Except for 1940-45, when it was suspended for World War II, the ICE met annually or bi-annually from 1934 to 2008, sponsored by the International Bureau of Education in Geneva, Switzerland (f. 1920, IBE).
2. http://www.ibe.unesco.org/en/areas-of-action/international-conference-on-education-ice/archive-of-ice-sessions-and-recommendations.html, accessed 10 June 2014.
3. For the purposes of this chapter, the term NGO refers to non-profit, non-governmental organizations only.
4. https://treaties.un.org/doc/Publication/UNTS/Volume%20999/volume-999-I-14668-English.pdf
5. UNESCO had previously sponsored many regional conferences of education.
6. The word "Crisis" refers to the expected results of unchecked population growth in the Third World on education systems. The international development literature warned of similar crises in other sectors about this same time.
7. http://www.unesco.org/education/wef/en-conf/Jomtien%20Declaration%20eng.shtm
8. http://hdrnet.org/536/1/Education_for_all.pdf
9. Author calculation. *Open Yearbook*. Union of International Associations. http://www.uia.org/ybio/, accessed 10 June 2014.

CHAPTER THREE

Taking Up the Mantle of Good Hope:

A Memoir

LENA SALEH[1]

This is an account of my involvement with UNESCO before and after the Salamanca Conference. I preface this memoir with a major influence on my thinking—my brother. I go on to consider other key experiences: my education, my early professional experience in Lebanon, and the commissions I undertook from UNESCO to support activities in Iraq and Bahrain. I then reflect on the activities that I led after my appointment to UNESCO where I became Head of the Section of Special Educational Needs, up to and beyond the Salamanca Conference. I look at attempts to develop partnerships with countries to promote provision for disabled children within education and also to encourage their mainstream participation. I remark on the strengths in the position of those countries that did not have to divest themselves of a legacy of influences from the North. I give particular attention to processes to bring about change in educational policies and teacher education, with a special focus on the considerable impact of the Special Needs in the Classroom Teacher Resource Pack. I look at the preparation for the Salamanca Conference and the actions taken by UNESCO afterwards. I consider how this strengthened the voices of those pressing for the mainstream educational participation of children and young people with disabilities in an education system that was inclusive for all.

RAJA SALEH: LIVING INCLUSION

My brother has always been a point of reference for me. He was six years younger than me, an intellectual, a thinker, with his own philosophy of life. He had Down's Syndrome. He loved his name, Raja Saleh, and knew its meaning: literally translated it means 'good hope.' We were close even when he was going with us to school when I was twelve and he was six. My father's aunt used to call me 'Little Mother.' When, later, I was studying in the United States I visited Steiner schools and Camphill Homes, which were both segregated settings and I would ask myself if my brother would wish to be in such a setting and my answer was 'no he wouldn't.' When later I talked at conferences I used to say, I lived inclusion when I was growing up.

Early on we attended a Catholic primary school, St. Joseph's, in Bethlehem. There were two children with Down Syndrome in that school, my brother and a girl. We had no psychologist, or special teacher—parents and teachers had to use their common sense. After being with us at the same school for three years, Raja went to another regular school that was closer to home so he could come and go on his own, and he loved it. His schooling continued up to the age of about 16, and was interrupted when the family moved to another city. The school was very supportive, and my mother would visit regularly and my parents employed someone to coach him at home with maths and reading.

I was always intrigued about how Raja felt about himself. Yet I was apprehensive about how I could introduce this discussion with him. I never really seemed to find the right moment. While I was working in Lebanon in the early 1970s I used to come to Jordan to visit my parents and brother. On one of my visits I accepted an invitation for a television interview about 'People with Mental Retardation.' The studio was a short walk from where we lived, so I said to my brother: 'Why don't you keep me company?' So he came along. He knew the woman interviewer and liked her programmes. So he sat there in the room while I was being interviewed. When we finished, the first thing he said was: 'I could have spoken.' Imagine! It's the 1970s. I was blind to that possibility. Nobody had talked yet about self-advocacy. It was only when I was recalling this event for this chapter that it occurred to me that he might have meant something like: 'You have been talking about people like me but maybe I could have spoken from my own experience and been in a better position to contribute than you.' But I didn't see it that way at the time. We went back home and had lunch and I was washing the dishes and he was drying them and my mother was sitting in the kitchen. I told him: 'Listen, I'm so sorry we missed this opportunity for you to speak but if you want I can interview you now about the same issues.' He loved to talk and he could organize his thoughts, better than me. I asked: 'what was the topic of the discussion?' and he replied: 'mental retardation.' He said it in English. He told me: 'This is the first time I've used the term.' He knew he was talking about himself. We discussed the issues that arise for people with mental retardation in the family and in society. He understood that distinction precisely. He said: 'If the child has certain ideas the parents should allow the child to pursue them.' He gave evidence to support his ideas. He referred to a film we had once watched together called *The White Colt* about an autistic boy, who is helped in his development by his relationship with a pony. It's a classic. At the beginning, the parents could not understand that their son preferred to be with the horse rather than with them, but they came to see how the horse was able to help him.

Then he discussed the impact of society. He was a little over-protected in terms of not being allowed to use public transport on his own, but in other respects he was quite independent. He had difficulties in using money. He referred to the things he had experienced when he said: 'some of these people have difficulties in handling money so if they go to the movies the man at the counter, he should help them. If you take public transport, the driver should also help.' I went to my room to have a siesta and a little later he came to tell me: 'I thought of other things.' The discussion had got him started. He said, 'Doctors should have some psychology. Humanity is not in the degrees that doctors put on the wall. Humanity is in the minds of men (conscience des hommes).' He often would say beautiful, meaningful things that my father sometimes noted down. He had a very good vocabulary and read a lot. He used to cut out quotes and articles that he liked and filed them. He started writing about himself in Arabic under the title: 'My Life Has Been Lost and Folded.' It was bold and political. He completed two to three pages to do with leaving Palestine as well as his personal experience and his schooling. He very much regretted that he left his school when the family moved from Bethlehem to Amman.

When later I worked with an organization for parents of disabled children in Lebanon, I had suggested that he come to stay at our centre for young adults where he could make friends, instead of staying at home all day. He told me that I didn't need to worry about him but that he would 'think about it.' He always said he could occupy himself and he said it again to me then. He would put music on, he would read, he would write. But I wanted him to make some social contacts, maybe to go to the movies with others, things like that. He knew he was different, he knew he had his limitations, but he also had his gifts. To me, he had never been part of a group with special needs, so I think he wanted to think about whether he saw himself coming into this world. Eventually he came and it worked out well; he made two or three good friends. Then he would come every year and stay in Lebanon for a month or six weeks.

GAINING QUALIFICATIONS AND EXPERIENCE

I finished my Bachelor's degree in 1959 at the Lebanese American University in Beirut (previously known as Beirut College for Women) and afterwards I worked for two years in teacher education in Ramallah before going to the United States to get my Master's in Special Education. It focused on children in special schools and special classes. But by the time I left the U.S. I had developed a clear idea about promoting greater mainstream participation so that as soon as I returned (in 1963 at the age of 24 to the Teacher Education Centre in Ramallah) I put on a seminar for head teachers about coping with differences and difficulties in regular schools.

Yet early in 1964, I took a job in Lebanon to direct a new special school. The idea never crossed my mind that I would lead a new special school. It was a small residential school for 35 children mainly from the Beirut area, in Beit Mery, a lovely small resort town in the mountains overlooking the sea, fifteen kilometers from Beirut. My parents came to see where I would be working. They fully supported my interests but were surprised that I would accept a job in such uninviting premises. It turned out to be a beautiful challenge, a project that was in constant development. We worked together, children and staff, making the setting attractive and homey. We established contacts with the children's families in Beirut, as well as with the immediate community in the village. The Centre soon became a training base for student nurses, social workers, educators and doctors. For instance, there was a program at the American University for young trainee doctors to spend a week at our school. Student special educators would come for a longer internship. We had volunteers from Beirut doing ceramics with the kids. It was a very open place.

I had come back from the United States thinking I knew everything. At that time people used the terms 'educable' and 'non-educable' to distinguish between groups of 'retarded children' and this had affected my thinking. I had a group of five teachers, none of whom had any teacher qualifications. They were high school graduates with no preconceived ideas. I would say: 'we have to be careful about which kids we can send to the village market on their own,' and they said 'everybody could go!' They challenged me. The boys wanted to get their hair cut and they would tell them 'ok they could go to the hairdresser.' They said: 'we're going to do it and so we might as well tell you, we don't want to do it behind your back'; and they indeed managed well.

Eventually, in 1970, I moved from the special school to become director of the Lebanese Parents Association, an organization supporting people with intellectual disabilities. I worked with a committee of motivated parents ready to try out new ideas. One of our programs involved myself and mothers in visits to regular schools to talk to children in primary classrooms about children with differences. We would start by saying: 'we all have things in common and we all have our differences.' I would ask if any of them knew of children who seemed to be different in some ways: 'It could be your neighbor, or your cousin or brother, just raise your hand if you have.' Initially they were reluctant to speak up, but after a short while they would open up and share their stories.

We organized summer camps for young people with disabilities with the assistance of young volunteers. It went very well but a number of things happened which emphasized the work we needed to do in changing people's attitudes. We took our young people to a swimming pool up in the mountains and one of the helpers reported that people were asking if disabilities were contagious. We also had to consider our own role in stigmatizing young people. One afternoon two of the boys were wandering around and one of the families asked: 'What group are you?' And one boy said: 'We're from the Association for the Mentally Retarded.' The boy with him was very upset and asked: 'Why did you have to say that?' That same evening we had a bonfire and discussed together whether what was said meant we might have to rethink the name and approach of our association.

CONSULTING FOR UNESCO

In 1970 Iraq asked UNESCO to send a consultant for three months to develop teaching in the main special school in Baghdad. This was a time when Iraq was a major contributor to UNESCO's special education program. UNESCO sought the advice of the International League, now called Inclusion International, for an Arabic speaking specialist and I was offered the contract. That was my first contact with UNESCO. I felt hugely responsible. I was barely 30, and for me, UNESCO was a giant.

I took one week to observe classrooms. Typically, a teacher sat at her desk at the front of the class while the children copied out numbers or letters from the board, or chanted sentences in unison after their teacher. After one week I had a meeting with the whole staff to agree a plan and ask for their commitment. We brought the parents together and worked with the teachers. We rearranged the environment of the classrooms to facilitate greater interaction among the children. The teachers started to find their work more challenging and interesting and saw that the children were learning more. Nils-Ivar Sundberg, the Swedish specialist in charge of special education at UNESCO, visited me to see how the project was going. It went very well. Three years later I was asked by UNESCO to go again for another three months with the same teachers.

In 1978, I was asked to go to Bahrain. The Minister of Education had asked UNESCO for a consultant to assess the situation where primary school teachers were querying having children 'with learning difficulties' in the regular school. I was very happy to go. When I arrived at the airport, I was given a list of the primary schools and the names, ages, educational difficulties and classes attended by children with special educational needs. I selected 10 of the schools at random and went to observe classrooms. I told the Ministry: 'In including children with special educational needs in mainstream classes you accomplished already what other countries in Europe are working towards.' I suggested that they identify teachers who are interested and motivated to do some further training, who can support further developments in the schools. At the time they rejected my ideas because they had already decided to pass responsibility for children with disabilities/special needs out of education into social affairs and create a separate system. So my mission was unsuccessful. But later I got to know the Under Secretary of the Ministry of Education very well and after a few years, as they saw how other countries were taking up the UNESCO approach, responsibility for disabled children was passed back to the Ministry of Education and they created the necessary resource support in the regular schools.

Leaving Lebanon

With the outbreak of the civil war in Lebanon in the mid-seventies and the division of Beirut between East and West, we were unable to reach all our parent members as well as all the young people who were part of our programmes. The security situation also deteriorated. So I left Lebanon after thirteen years of innovation. It had been a fertile professional terrain, people were open, ready to try new ideas and new approaches. I felt we were on equal footing with others in the West and maybe at an advantage as we did not have the long history of institutionalization.

I moved to Jordan in 1976 and opted to work with the government. I contacted the Ministry of Education but I was unable to persuade the Minister of the importance of developing support to students with differences and challenges in regular schools. So I approached the Minister of Labor and Social Development, who had a plan to initiate a program in support of children with special needs. He agreed to drop the earlier plans of the Ministry for opening residential schools and opted for day schools in different towns. This entailed recruiting and training personnel, developing the program, working with parents, and mobilizing professors from the university to work on an in-service training program for teachers. This proved to be a very rich experience, opening up a new field of mainstream special needs education for the university education staff.

WORKING FOR UNESCO

At the end of 1978 I got a message from UNESCO proposing a three-month temporary post in Paris. I took the gamble of accepting a very temporary post in UNESCO on a beginner's grade. My stay was to last over twenty years up to December 1999. I caught up quickly with the history of UNESCO's engagement with special educational needs. It had begun as a result of international lobbying about the institutionalization of disabled people and their poor treatment, from academics particularly in the U.S. Gunnar Dybwad was at the forefront of such struggle. I had got to know him and his wife during my Masters course at Columbia University and we became good friends. I had attended an international seminar in Brussels organized by the International League (ILSMH). This was my first participation at an international seminar, and it was funded by the Rosemary Dybwad International Award. I found the correspondence between his group and UNESCO when I arrived. For Gunnar Dybwad's 90th birthday, I sent him a copy of the first letter he had written to UNESCO, to put in his birthday album, saying that I felt a responsibility to honor his legacy.

The programme at UNESCO seemed rather thin and very much focused on separate special education provision. Nils-Ivar Sundberg headed the programme. Besides being a specialist in the field, he had a deaf daughter and his wife was a teacher of the Deaf. Within the organization the programme was seen as separate from other programmes in the Education Sector, so we were rather isolated. This was to change gradually as I settled in. I wanted not only to get disabled children into education but also break the walls of the segregated special schools. I discussed my ideas with Nils-Ivar. He was receptive and gradually we worked closely together on a shared agenda. But at first I worked on projects that were already planned, such as a study on Early Detection and Intervention. At the same time we embarked on a new project on Terminology, a reference document in four languages, which was done in cooperation with Professor Klaus Wedell from the Institute of Education, University of London.

The International Year of Disabled Persons 1981

The International Year of the Disabled was a turning point for UNESCO in the area of special needs education and also for Member States. Federico Mayor had become Deputy Director General at UNESCO, and he led and coordinated the organization's contribution in this area. As a neurobiologist he was already sensitive to developmental difficulties. He established a Committee with representatives from all the sectors of UNESCO. Every division had to identify an activity concerned with disability that they would implement with Member States. This was one of the best working committees we ever had. Our small unit was the focal point and this is how I got to know Mayor, who became Director General of UNESCO a few years later. Halfway through our preparations, the UN office responsible for the focus on disability asked UNESCO to organize an international conference for this International Year, on behalf of the UN and the concerned specialized agencies: the World Health Organization (WHO), the International Labour Organization (ILO), the United Nations Children's Fund (UNICEF) as well as International Non-Governmental Organizations (INGOs).

Spain agreed to host the conference in November 1981 in Torremolinos. Almost a hundred countries took part. Nils-Ivar and myself were entrusted with the preparations and we worked closely with the Spanish Government. Mayor, at that time Spanish Minister of Education and Science, presided over the opening of the conference where we did our presentation. We were moved by the positive reaction of people. Then hardly out from the opening session, Nils-Ivar collapsed in the lobby and was rushed to the hospital. He had had a brain haemorrhage, and sadly he passed away on the way to the hospital. When the second session of the conference resumed, Federico Mayor made a statement to the effect that if we wanted to pay tribute to Nils-Ivar we had to work very hard to make this conference succeed. We had four intensive days, and everybody offered help in a very good spirit. It culminated with the Sundberg Declaration on Prevention, Rehabilitation and Integration.

Working internationally

After Nils-Ivar passed away, I was asked to lead the section. By that time I had built a strong resource network of people and organizations on which I was heavily dependent. They were people with whom I could talk things over, who were unstinting in their support. I could pick up the phone and ask a question of colleagues around the world. Even though I was practically on my own in the office, with only a temporary colleague to assist me, I could not have managed to address such a diversity of issues in a newly growing field with an impact on the world scene, had I not had my support system.

International work is very challenging. UNESCO had 190 Member States and its suggestions for policy and practice involved very wide consultations. At times we worked regionally but at other times our work was intended to have a global reach. We had to work on all levels, from politicians to academics, teacher educators, teachers and communities. We wanted to develop model education programmes. We would compile reports of work with countries that were derived from visits, questionnaires and locally written accounts. Then we organized regional meetings with people in regular education, special education and teacher education.

In 1982, UNESCO initiated a sub-regional project, supported by Sweden, with 13 countries in Eastern and Southern Africa. When UNESCO invited countries to join the project we insisted on working with the Ministries of Education. This initiative was instrumental in opening up Ministries of Education to take responsibility for children with special needs. Before that, special educational needs had been generally the responsibility of Ministries of Health or Social Affairs. That was an important breakthrough. We worked to create a dialogue between special and mainstream systems.

Botswana proved to be a dynamic environment, and the Ministry responded to the challenge to work with the mainstream. In Malawi, we joined forces with INGOs. There was already a well-developed project on education in integrated settings for blind children in mainstream schools. We were able to build on that and widen the scope to bring in other groups of children. I had visited Kenya at the start of this project. At the Ministry of Education, the responsible person, who happened to be the daughter of the president, Jomo Kenyata, asked me: 'What does UNESCO advise us to do in the area of education of the Deaf?' At the time there was a conflict between those who advocated oral communication in education and those who thought it was essential that deaf children be taught using sign language. Practitioners wanted a lead on which direction to take. I answered: 'I will take your question to Headquarters and you will hear from us.' In 1984, UNESCO organized a consultation of experts from the world regions. We invited the President of the World Federation of the Deaf, back then working at Gallaudet College, who came along with his own two interpreters. It was an intense five-day consultation. Kenneth Eklindh from Sweden assisted us. It was the first time that UNESCO had a meeting with sign language interpretation. We produced a substantial report, the outcome of this report made it to the international press in the USA, Germany and other countries, because it provided very clear guidelines on several issues, but primarily about the place of sign language in education. It stated that sign language was a fully-fledged language, with all the linguistic components necessary for it to be the means for educating the Deaf. This was a major breakthrough for which the Deaf community had been waiting.

In our innovation and development work we sometimes encountered a more enlightened approach in countries where there was no special provision; where they had not been infected with models from abroad involving a traditional segregating approach. We could advise newly starting countries that they could begin from where other countries are today. For example *Yemen* responded in a fantastic way. The Under Secretary of Education was an open-minded man and it was just obvious to him that inclusion in the mainstream was the way forward. He said, 'We're not going to start creating separate systems for disabled children, so let us see what we can do with our schools.' He felt they had no choice but to go in this direction. He came once to a regional Arab conference in Lebanon and made an outstanding input. He just spoke as though he were a top specialist.

We started working with *Yemen* at the end of 1989, and UNESCO sent two teacher educators to work with a cluster of schools. Prior to that, I went to the south of Yemen, visiting some schools in Aden. It was more developed than in the northern part of the country. I visited two schools, met with the teachers as well as with parents of disabled children who were invited to come to the school. The teachers of the schools would say, 'If somebody just tells us how we can work with such a child in our classroom, of course they have to be in our schools, where else would they go?' We had workshops based on a plan to develop resources in clusters of schools in the country, and this work was intensified after Salamanca.

We also had positive experiences in our work with Ghana. We were part of an interagency project with the four main UN agencies: UNESCO, WHO, ILO and UNICEF. This required inter-ministerial co-operation between Ministries of Education, Health and Labour and Social Welfare. Though Ghana had a Special Education College, there were few special schools where graduates could teach. UNESCO teamed up with people from the Ministry of Education and a teacher educator from the College. We planned to work directly with community schools, involving both community leaders and parents. UNESCO was lucky to be able to send Anupam Ahuja, from the National Council of Educational Research and Training (ICERT)-Institute in Delhi, as a key trainer. Anupam was already well versed with the Teacher Education Resource Pack, which by this time had become our lead material in working with schools. The readiness and openness of the head teachers, teachers and communities prepared the ground for the changes that ensued. After receiving training in working in mainstream schools, each special teacher from the College assumed the role of an itinerant support teacher for a cluster of mainstream schools.

Engagement with China

China was a difficult country with which to engage when I first went there in 1982, at a time when it was still under Mao's influence. They placed children with disabilities in institutions in the main big cities. With the One-Child Policy, if a child had the slightest difficulty or disability, parents would commonly put him or her into an institution and try to have another child without impairment. I saw quite a few children in institutions with a minor impairment like a mild cleft palate. I had been asked to advise on how teacher training could address challenges and difficulties that some children bring to the system. I visited the main Teacher's College in Nanjing, where John Dewey had lectured, a family of a child with disability at home, and of course the children's institutions and a couple of schools. However, it was difficult to keep my focus as it seemed that all that they wanted me to do was to finalize the list of special equipment that they intended to buy. They wanted to use a grant from UNICEF to upgrade equipment for hospitals and other institutions. This had nothing to do with the terms of reference of my mission. UNICEF had suggested to me that I might be able to talk about the plight of disabled children in China. I knew I had to say something but could not consult with colleagues back at UNESCO Headquarters in Paris. There was no internet and no telephones. Even at the risk of losing my job, I felt I had to tell them what I thought. At the end of my mission, I had a meeting with a team from the three Ministries of Education, of Health and of Social Affairs. I was the only non-Chinese among fifteen colleagues, all in navy blue uniforms. I said my conscience would not be at ease if I were to say following my observations: 'you need this or that equipment.' Instead I said: 'I think you need opportunities for people to go abroad to get training and you need to bring people here to train your teachers. UNESCO is there to support you. It's for you to decide if you want to visit places that are already supporting children with disabilities in education.'

Six months later they wrote to UNESCO requesting us to organize a study visit for a team of five people. They went to Sweden, to the UK and then they came to Paris. I organized a meeting at UNESCO with my directors and other colleagues to have a discussion with the Chinese team. The Vice Minister of Social Affairs in China, Mr. Li, was the head of the team. He said: 'Before we start the meeting, I want to apologize to Lena Saleh. When you came to China we gave you a hard time, we kept hammering on about our need for equipment and you insisted that we needed well trained teachers. You were right.' You respect people like that. I loved China, even though you're not going to tell the Chinese what they're going to do. He said that he understood that the best equipment is a good teacher. He said this in front of my colleagues – it took some humility for him to do this. The work with China then took off slowly but surely.

A decade later, in 1994, China hosted a UNESCO sub-regional conference with high-level educational officials from twelve countries from Southeast Asia. This was one of the five regional seminars that were organized throughout 1993 and in early 1994 in preparation for the World Conference in Salamanca. I felt that they were proud to host this event, and they worked very hard to make it a success. The aim was to discuss with senior education decision makers and professional practitioners how to move towards one system from separate systems of regular and special education. On that occasion we visited Den Pufang, who was back then President of the China Disabled Persons' Association. He later came to the Salamanca Conference and gave a plenary speech.

CREATING SUPPORT MATERIALS

In our projects in Africa and elsewhere from the early 1980s there was a demand for basic information about disability, support and intervention. In the early 1980s we had developed what we called Special Education Guides or Booklets, to inform people and share experiences, for teachers in both special and regular schools. We translated them into four languages but countries could also translate them freely. We sent copies to the ends of the world. We would get letters from villages and small towns stating that people are hungry for information. We also produced slide kits supported by text in several languages to share innovative experiences, from early intervention to inclusive schooling. Later we developed videos. We wanted to narrow the gap between the knowledge available in countries of the North and South. But our experience in working with many countries led us to recognize that a different kind of resource was needed in addition to materials focusing on disability.

Supporting teacher education

We realized that teacher education for mainstream public schools was of great significance for educational change. We therefore carried out a 14-country study of teacher education drawn from across all the regions. That included a sample survey of the views of primary school teachers, on their professional preparation to address the diversity of needs in the classroom. We worked with Klaus Wedell and Irene Bowman from the Institute of Education in London. We collected data on the curriculum in teacher education, the resources, the involvement of student teachers with disabilities and so on. The results were discussed with regular and special teacher educators in five regional seminars. They were invited to identify practices that could be applied in their respective countries. While there was some implementation of change at the pre-service level, teacher education institutions were resistant to new ideas; however, there was much more progress on in-service teacher education.

The Resource Pack

The 'Teacher Education Resource Pack: Special Needs in the Classroom,' developed with Mel Ainscow, combined a recognition of the significance of in-service education for teachers for changing practice with the needs of our partners for high-quality materials. I had previously read the materials for teachers that Mel had produced in Coventry, when I was working in Lebanon. I contacted him and he invited me to sit in on a teacher workshop he was running. It was an eye-opener in terms of participatory methods. This was the beginning of an intensive cooperation with Mel who in late 1987 agreed to put together a preliminary draft of materials to support mainstream teachers in 'reaching out to all learners.'

With the first draft in hand in 1989, we brought together a team of two educators, from eight countries, for a training workshop in Zimbabwe. It went very well. We had good feedback on substance and format, and the detailed positive comments from the participants gave us concrete ideas for revision. People were very positive and very enthusiastic. After this first initial training, colleagues had to go back to their countries, run their own workshop and provide a report that would further feed into the revision of the Resource Pack. It was really a very thorough process. Mel revised the Resource Pack on the basis of the reports from the field teams, and then a small group of us went through the new draft, and finally

UNESCO published it. It contained a video to demonstrate an interactive style of teacher education as a model for working with mixed groups of children. It was used at the in-service level across the regions. We promoted a cascade model of dissemination: the team in Jordan could go to Yemen, Lebanon, and Palestine and run a workshop that would create a local team there. Similarly the team in Chile worked with a number of countries in the Latin American region. At each stage people would report back to us about what they had achieved. We developed an informal newsletter where people shared their experiences and comments in using the Resource Pack, and this indeed helped to create a network amongst practitioners and a whole mass of connections with countries. It just mushroomed. It was translated into more than 40 languages. We tried to make sure that when people bought the Resource Pack we identified someone to support them in its use. It was a major success. It provided a fresh outlook for many thousands of practitioners and schools.

SALAMANCA AND BEYOND

From more than ten years before Salamanca, the development projects undertaken by UNESCO helped to prepare for the Conference. The Teacher Education Resource Pack with its influence across the world made a particular contribution to building the momentum for change. But the regional meetings on new policy orientations in support of inclusion equally helped in preparing the mindsets of our partners.

At UNESCO we were always on the lookout for new ideas. I went to Portugal, to look at the education of the visually impaired in regular schools. Anna Maria Benard da Costa was leading Education for Special Needs at the Ministry of Education in Portugal. She put a huge amount of thought and enthusiasm in bringing blind children into regular schools. I visited some schools, and then we documented the work in a video which was our first attempt to share instructive experience in mainstream education. We also learnt from the Spanish experience of Álvaro Marchesi, as Vice Minister for education, trying to change schools through an innovative 'integration project,' though this fell short of a fully-fledged program in the Ministry. This project was also well documented.

In 1992, during the General Conference of UNESCO, at a side small side meeting, Álvaro Marchesi was invited to share the Spanish experience with a group of Ministers and Directors in Ministries from fifteen countries. Over coffee I discussed with Marchesi the possibility of organizing a consultation around these ideas, and that is how the seeds for the Salamanca Conference were sown. On his return to Spain, Marchesi sent an official invitation to the Director General of UNESCO, Federico Mayor, with the offer by Spain to host the Conference. A committee of people was formed to prepare it.

Working together with my former Chief, Etienne Brunswick, we prepared a draft document outlining our suggestions for the development of policy and practice to be considered by the conference. It was sent out to about forty countries for their feedback, selected from across the regions. We then revised the document and gave it to all the conference participants upon their arrival. Victor Ordonez, UNESCO Director of Basic Education, helped to produce a power point presentation to open the conference showing the key developments in the field. He presented it at the opening session as the representative of the Director General.

More than 300 participants from 92 countries and 25 international organizations took part. The conference was organized with plenary sessions and parallel sessions, with presentation of papers and discussion groups, over three intensive days. Victor Ordonez chaired a small committee to draft a document drawing together the outputs of the conference, which was to become the Salamanca Declaration. We gave continual encouragement to all participants to share their ideas. I was very happy with the way the declaration reflected the participants' vision and desires. Perhaps some recommendations were a little conservative, but at this important crossroad you had to bring everybody with you. The conference put Salamanca on the map; people were talking about Salamanca for some time.

Hardly back at our desks from the Conference, we had to work hard and fast to finalize the report and the declaration. It gained very widespread interest and was used by campaigners and advocates around the world in order to give the weight of UNESCO to their arguments for change. Salamanca happened as South Africa was emerging into a democracy, following the release of Nelson Mandela. South Africa showed very great keenness to join this international movement. Marie Schoeman, who later joined the South African Ministry of Education, was our first contact. She was involved in a parent organization of children with Down Syndrome, vigorously campaigning for their inclusion. She made copies of the Salamanca Report and distributed it across the country.

The very positive response of people who attended the conference had an impact back at UNESCO Headquarters. Dr. Knud Mortenson, from Denmark, who was back then Chairman of the Education for All Forum at UNESCO, said that the conference was one of the best that UNESCO had ever put on. I said that the issues raised by the conference had to influence the Education for All discussions, and he made sure that our concerns were then placed on the agenda for Education for All meetings. However they met with considerable resistance from some of the representatives on the committee. They seemed to have a vested interest in maintaining their status quo, demanding proof that disabled adults and children could be part of the mainstream, although segregation was never created on the basis of such proof. I saw people's opinions as arising from personal attitudes and values that people bring to discussions with them. It was hard to get across the idea that the inclusion of people with disabilities was largely a moral position. The Committee did reach the point where they recognized that they had to say something about disabled children in the Education for All guidelines for the Education for All Forum in Dakar, Senegal, in 2000, but it was just cosmetic change, with a couple of lines about the participation of disabled children. Gender was viewed differently and seen by the committee as an important issue but 'special educational needs' was relegated to second-class status. The Director of Basic Education was very supportive of our position. However, colleagues who had their hands on the reports after the Forum did not believe that the exclusion of disabled children really mattered. They talked about statistics rather than people. We provided the figures and continued to lobby for the proper representation of concerns about disabled people to be reflected in the report.

In accordance with the recommendations put forward by the Salamanca Conference, UNESCO embarked on a project 'Inclusive Schools and Community Support Programs,' which stretched from 1996 to 2001, involving 32 countries. It covered a variety of country initiatives in different political, social and cultural contexts, all set within a common commitment to inclusive education. UNESCO was the facilitator for innovation and capacity building and national and regional networking. The reports of these country initiatives were widely disseminated to all member states and practitioners across the world.

As a complement to the Teacher Education Resource Pack, the Open File on Inclusive Education was developed to support administrators, decision-makers and people in leadership positions, guiding them with materials to move towards inclusion. The materials were the result of a collaborative effort between researchers, administrators and practitioners from across the world. The work was pulled together by Professor Alan Dyson, who worked then at the University of Newcastle, England, assisted by Sai Vayrynen, from the Inclusive Education Unit at UNESCO. This Open File assumed that a policy commitment to the principle of inclusion was already in place. It brought together experiences from a wide range of countries to be used in workshops dealing with policy, administration, working with parents and with communities.

Building up UNESCO's Regional Offices

Before I came to UNESCO Paris, there was not much activity in the regional offices in special needs education. Previously, one of the colleagues covering basic education would fill in when questions arose locally or from the central office, but they wouldn't be very focused or motivated. I discovered that there was a possibility to appoint junior specialists, 'associate experts,' for UNESCO programs that would be funded by their country for two years. We made a series of appointments to help facilitate a network of information after the World Conference in Salamanca – regional work was taken to a new level. We had particular success in Latin America with the appointment of Rosa Blanco to the regional office, with her strong links with Alvaro Marchesi and Gerardo Echeita from Spain. We worked so well together. People working at Headquarters questioned whether I was interfering in the work of the region and I said: "What do you mean, interfere, we work together."

The Bangkok office had in the early 1980s become an empire in itself. Raja Roy Singh, an Indian, was the director when I first joined. He was respected by the people working in the Headquarters; they did not touch his 'territory' because he produced effective work that had an impact. After he left, there were a number of people but the most dynamic was Sheldon Shaeffer. He had been active in the Education for All movement when he was with UNICEF. He came to UNESCO in the mid-1990s. He pushed forward the Salamanca approach and people developed their own materials, e.g. a booklet with a DVD. I first met Sheldon at the General Conference in 1999. All UNESCO Member States were represented by their Ministers of Education. A series of discussions was organized on gender and disability and ethnic minorities and so on. Sheldon Shaeffer was sitting in this group talking about inclusion and schools. I was very impressed. When he had finished I said: 'I'm really proud and delighted to hear what you are saying,' but he replied: 'No, I am here because of the ideas that UNESCO promoted throughout this last decade, and you had a role in that.'

CONCLUDING REMARKS

Working with UNESCO was an honor and a huge responsibility. You bring something with you to the organization, but then you are enriched by the dialogue and experiences you have with others. I always felt that I had the support of my superiors, in particular the Director General, Federico Mayor, but also the Assistant Director General for Education, Sema Tanguiane, as well as my immediate Directors. Their encouragement made me feel that doors were always open, and one could just take advantage of the possibilities that were out there.

UNESCO is the voice of its Members States, the politicians, its specialists around the world, as well as civil society. UNESCO isn't a person sitting at a desk. UNESCO's role was to provide support to its partners in developing new orientations in educational policy and practice. UNESCO had the role of catalyst and facilitator, creating supportive networks while recognizing that implementation of any new developments rested with the single Member States. Innovation requires clarity of principles and the necessary professional support at all levels, to ensure sustainable implementation at the grass roots level.

Although considerable importance is given by UNESCO to cooperation with developing countries, in this, as well as other shifts in policy and practice, we were equally engaged with countries from the North, as well as the South. European countries, too, looked to UNESCO for information, cooperation and leadership. This meant we developed good collaboration with OECD, and to a lesser extent with the European Commission, which had just started work in this field. Unfortunately, after 2000 it seemed that UNESCO's strong presence in the field was not maintained and a change of orientation in the organization left some countries in need of support in devising educational policies for inclusion.

The Salamanca Declaration certainly opened the door and gave an impetus for change. It had a world-wide impact – but that was twenty years ago. What is needed now is to revise the thinking of Salamanca so that it fits a new vision of Education that truly represents the rights of everyone in responding to today's challenges. Inclusive schools and inclusive education continue to be the cornerstones for moving towards a more equitable and just society for all.

NOTE

1. I am very much indebted to Tony Booth for his encouragement, guidance and help in my preparation of this chapter. Although I was very familiar with Tony's thinking and writings from the eighties, he came into our professional world after Salamanca and this was instrumental in helping us refine further our thinking and vision in working for inclusion in education.

CHAPTER FOUR

Struggling for Equity in Education

The Legacy of Salamanca

MEL AINSCOW

I was privileged to be closely involved in the process of the Salamanca conference, working alongside Lena Saleh and many other colleagues from around the world. Prior to the event, UNESCO had instigated an initiative, "Special Needs in the Classroom," that set out to develop a Teacher Education Resource Pack about inclusive practices (Ainscow, 1994).[1] At the conference we were able to present accounts of how the Resource Pack had been used in eight countries to support inclusive developments. Subsequently, the materials were translated into many languages and disseminated in more than 80 countries (Ainscow, 1999).

Over the following twenty years, the theme of inclusive education influenced thinking internationally to a level that I suspect none of us had anticipated. Particularly influential have been those sections of the Salamanca Statement which argue that regular schools with an inclusive orientation are "the most effective means of combating discriminatory attitudes, building an inclusive society and achieving education for all," and that such schools can "provide an effective education for the majority of children and improve the efficiency and ultimately the cost-effectiveness of the entire education system." These arguments led me to reposition myself within efforts to bring about educational improvement for all children and young people, focusing on the idea of equity, which I take to involve "inclusion and fairness" (OECD, 2007).

Subsequently, I have worked with many colleagues in taking forward this thinking within a series of projects, in my own country and internationally. More recently, this has led me to experience new challenges, as those guiding national policies in many countries have become preoccupied with measuring school outcomes in terms of test scores and comparing progress with that of other countries through systems such as PISA (Programme for International Student Assessment).

At the same time, a growing number of countries are using the idea of an educational "market place" that emphasizes increased school autonomy, competition between schools, parental choice and accountability as central strategies for improving schools. Many in the field argue that these policy trends represent obstacles to the creation of more inclusive education systems (e.g. Ball, 2010; Giroux and Schmidt, 2004; Kenway, 2013). Whilst sharing their concerns, I also think that it is possible to occupy the spaces that are created by the new policy contexts in order to move thinking and practice forward.

In what follows I develop this argument, using examples from projects that have attempted to adopt this approach. This leads me to formulate some suggestions that can be used to guide attempts to foster inclusive developments at the levels of schools, classrooms and education systems.

THE LEGACY OF SALAMANCA

In some parts of the world inclusive education is still largely thought of as an approach to serving children with disabilities within general education settings. As a result of Salamanca, however, it is increasingly seen more broadly as a reform that responds to diversity amongst all learners (UNESCO, 2009). The argument developed in this chapter adopts this broader formulation. It presumes that the aim of inclusive educational development is to eliminate exclusionary processes that are a consequence of attitudes and responses to diversity in relation to race, social class, ethnicity, religion, gender and attainment, as well as with regards to disabilities. As such, it starts from the belief that education is a basic human right and the foundation for a more just society.

I have long argued that the use of this way of thinking will be much more likely if it is recognized that difficulties experienced by students result from the ways in which schools are currently organized and from the forms of teaching that are provided (Ainscow, 1999). Consequently, schools have to be reformed and pedagogy improved in ways that will lead them to respond positively to learner diversity—seeing individual differences not as problems to be fixed, but as opportunities for enriching learning. Within such a conceptualization, a consideration of difficulties experienced by students provides an agenda for reform and insights as to how such reforms might be brought about.

The work referred to in this chapter has, I believe, made a contribution to the implementation of this new thinking. The fact that many of the projects I describe were developed in close collaboration with practitioners in different countries is particular relevant, leading me to argue that their findings are relevant across national borders. The processes involved emphasize forms of collaborative action research that seek to develop responses that make use of existing expertise within schools, and networking and sharing of experiences between schools, in order to move knowledge around. In so doing they seek to make use of differences—amongst students and teachers—as a means of stimulating new ways of thinking about how to make schools more inclusive.

DEVELOPING INCLUSIVE SCHOOLS

Barriers and resources

My thinking regarding ways of helping schools to become more inclusive was much influenced as a result of the development of the "Index for Inclusion" (Booth and Ainscow, 2011). Designed originally for use within the policy context of England at the turn of the century, the Index is a set of school review materials that has been refined as a result of over ten years of collaborative action research in many countries (see *The International Journal of Inclusive Education*, volume 8, number 2, for articles about some of these developments). It enables schools to draw on the resources of staff, students, parents/carers, and community representatives in order to address barriers to participation and learning that exist within their existing "cultures, policies and practices."

In connecting inclusion with the detail of policy and practice, the Index encourages those who use it to build up their own view of inclusion, related to their experience and values, as they work out what policies and practices they wish to promote or discourage. Such an approach is based upon the idea that inclusion is essentially about attempts to embody particular values within specific contexts. In other words, it is "school improvement with attitude" (Ainscow, Booth and Dyson, 2006).

The Index approach involves an emphasis on collaborative inquiry, involving coordinated and sustained efforts around the idea that changing outcomes for all students is unlikely to be achieved unless there are changes in the behaviors of adults. Consequently, the starting point for inclusive school development is with teachers: in effect, enlarging their capacity to imagine what might be achieved, and increasing their sense of accountability for bringing this about. This may also involve tackling taken-for-granted assumptions, most often relating to expectations about certain groups of students, their capabilities, behavior and patterns of attendance. At the same time, such efforts have to be linked to what is happening in other schools and in the wider community.

Using collaborative inquiry

The work on the Index for Inclusion, alongside the findings from our earlier efforts to explore the potential of inquiry-based approaches (see Ainscow et al., 2012b, for details), influenced the design of another project in England, "Understanding and Developing Inclusive Practices in Schools." The initiative, which took the form of a collaborative action research project, took place between 2000 and 2004, and involved 25 urban schools, their associated local education authorities and three universities (i.e., Canterbury Christ Church, Manchester and Newcastle). Together we explored ways of developing more inclusive practices in the schools.

We saw inclusion as a value and set of practices about which something was already known. Moreover, as established authors and researchers in the field, we had played our part in generating this prior knowledge (e.g., Ainscow, 1999; 2006; Booth, 1995; Clark et al., 1999; Dyson and Millward, 2000). We also knew—from our own work and from others in this field—that acceptance of the values and practices of inclusion were frequently resisted by practitioners who saw themselves as having other priorities and as working within constraints that made inclusive practice impossible. This was particularly the case in the then English policy context, where a "relentless focus on standards" was being imposed on schools by the Labour government (Blair, 2005).

We therefore needed a means of releasing practitioners from the constraints of national policy and enabling them to change their value positions and assumptions. We saw the use of research evidence as offering this means. Furthermore, we made the assumption that when practitioners were confronted by evidence about their practices they would—with appropriate encouragement from their critical friends—begin to recognize the non-inclusive elements of those practices and would find ways of making them more inclusive. Fortunately, this is what did most often happen.

What we noted as these developments occurred was neither the crushing of the schools' efforts to become more inclusive by the government's policies for raising standards, nor the rejection of the standards agenda in favor of a radical, inclusive alternative (Ainscow, Booth and Dyson, 2006). In most of the schools, the two agendas remained intertwined. Indeed, the focus on attainment appeared to prompt some teachers to examine issues in relation to the achievements and participation of hitherto marginalized groups that they had previously overlooked. Likewise, the concern with inclusion tended to shape the way the school responded to the imperative to raise standards.

For example, in one primary school, evidence from national tests showed that a significant proportion of children were struggling with writing, as compared to their scores in mathematics. The original emphasis had been informed by national debates on boys' underachievement, and certainly it was a group of boys who struggled most with their writing. Nevertheless, a focus on boys alone was clearly unjustified, given that boys were also some of the highest performers and that many girls were barely out-performing the lowest performing boys.

Further evidence was generated by interviewing a small number of children while they were writing, some of whom pointed to their feelings of fear of failure. Members of a teacher research group coordinating the activities were fascinated by the insights gained and wondered how widespread were these feelings about writing. With this in mind, they decided to devise a questionnaire, which was completed by all children in years five and six, with teaching assistants scribing for some children. Once again, the teachers were surprised and intrigued by the factors that children identified as barriers to good writing and began to consider how their own practices might be changed to alleviate some of these issues.

It was decided that this was a moment to engage other staff in the school. So, the group of teachers decided to use the data from interviews and the questionnaires, alongside examples from the tests, to inform the planning of a professional development day. The emphasis throughout was on interpreting the data from "their" children and how they might respond in terms of their own practice. The meeting generated a lot of debate, with many teachers giving examples of how they intended to try new ideas in relation to the insights gained. Teaching assistants were involved in these discussions, providing valuable and specific insights from their one-to-one work with pupils. The elements of 'fun' during the day—for instance, trying out a drama activity linked to writing a story—also helped to remind staff of the continuing good relationships within the school and encouraged discussion about their priorities in the face of many challenges. Even so, follow-up interviews with some teachers revealed how they struggled to see ways of changing their practice within the constraints of the school's policy. Indeed, only later, after inspectors had judged the quality of teaching in the school to be "very good," did teachers start to trust their own judgment again in determining how they might develop their practice. Significantly, two years later a number of staff were still using data from the questionnaire to inform continuing developments. "Trials" of different approaches to encouraging writing also continued to take place, with a continuing emphasis on checking things out with the children concerned.

Our analysis of examples like these revealed how social learning processes within schools influenced people's action and, indeed, the thinking that informed their actions (Ainscow et al., 2003). Often this was stimulated by various forms of evidence that created periods of turbulence in relation to existing ways of thinking and working. Particularly powerful techniques in this respect involved the use of mutual observation, sometimes through video recordings, and evidence collected from students about teaching and learning arrangements within a school. Under certain conditions, such approaches provided *interruptions* that stimulated self-questioning, creativity and action. In so doing, they sometimes led to a reframing of perceived problems that, in turn, drew attention to overlooked possibilities for addressing barriers to participation and learning.

We concluded, however, that none of this provided a straightforward mechanism for the development of more inclusive practices. We found that any space for reflection that was created as a result of engaging with evidence may sometimes be filled according to conflicting agendas. Indeed, we documented detailed examples of how deeply held beliefs within schools prevented the experimentation that is necessary in order to foster the development of more inclusive ways of working (Howes and Ainscow, 2006; Ainscow and Kaplan, 2005).

The outcomes of the inclusion project have been widely reported in the scholarly literature (Ainscow, Booth and Dyson, 2004; 2006; Ainscow, Booth, Dyson et al., 2006; Dyson et al., 2003; Howes et al., 2004; 2005). In terms of the development of a methodology for enabling research to contribute to more inclusive policy and practice, the main lesson we drew was that it is possible to infuse a critical dimension into a collaborative action research project, so that issues of social justice shape their action. We also concluded that the critical friendship of 'outsiders' (in this case, ourselves as researchers) is a way of keeping these issues on the agenda.

Organizational culture and leadership

Through this particular study it became clear that such developments are likely to involve challenges to the thinking of those within particular organizations. In particular, it requires them to develop new working relationships within their schools and with partners beyond the school gate. It follows that working in a school that is attempting to become more inclusive is not for the faint-hearted. To be a teacher in such a school means that you need to be able to accept and deal with questions being asked of your beliefs, ideas, plans and practices. In such a context, inter-professional challenge will be common. Therefore, those who provide leadership must model not only a willingness to participate in discussions and experimentation, but also a readiness to answer questions and challenges from their colleagues. Furthermore, they need to enable staff to feel sufficiently confident about their practice to cope with the challenges they will meet.

The ideas that emerged from this project are supported by a review of international literature by my colleagues that examined the effectiveness of school actions in promoting inclusion (Ainscow, Booth and Dyson, 2004). The review concludes that there is a limited, but by no means negligible, body of empirical evidence about the relationship between school action and the participation of all students in the cultures, curricula and communities of their schools. It suggests that some schools are characterized by an 'inclusive culture.' Within such schools, there is some degree of consensus amongst adults around values of respect for difference and a commitment to offering all pupils access to learning opportunities. This consensus may not be total and may not necessarily remove all tensions or contradictions in practice. On the other hand, there is likely to be a high level of staff collaboration and joint problem-solving, and similar values and commitments may extend into the student body, and to parent and other community stakeholders.

The extent to which such 'inclusive cultures' lead directly and unproblematically to enhanced student participation is not clear. Some aspects of these cultures, however, can be seen as participatory by definition. For instance, respect for diversity from teachers may itself be understood as a form of participation by children within a school community. Moreover, schools characterized by such cultures are also likely to be characterized by forms of organization (such as specialist provision being made in the ordinary classroom, rather than by withdrawal) and practices (such as constructivist approaches to teaching and learning) that could be regarded as participatory.

According to this particular literature review, schools with 'inclusive cultures' are likely to be characterized by the presence of leaders who are committed to inclusive values and to a leadership style which encourages a range of individuals to participate in leadership functions. Such schools are also likely to have good links with parents and with their communities.

Such approaches are congruent with the view that inclusion is essentially about attempts to embody particular values in particular contexts (Ainscow, Booth and Dyson, 2006). Unlike mechanistic views of school improvement, they acknowledge that decisions about how to improve schools always involve moral and political reasoning, as well as technical considerations. Moreover, they offer specific processes through which inclusive developments might be promoted. Discussions of inclusion and exclusion can therefore help to make explicit the values which underlie what, how and why changes should be made in schools. Inclusive cultures, underpinned by particular organizational conditions, may make those discussions more likely to occur and more productive when they do occur.

RESPONDING TO DIVERSITY

Teacher development

As I have indicated, efforts to develop more inclusive schools require a particular focus on providing teachers with support as they seek to develop forms of practice that reach out to all members of the class. In particular, their practices have to take account of and, indeed, make use of, the diversity that exists amongst the students. Building on lessons from the UNESCO teacher education project referred to earlier, our work with schools over the last twenty years has attempted to develop powerful forms of professional development in relation to this agenda.

This research suggests that developments of practice are unlikely to occur without some exposure to what teaching actually looks like when it is being done differently, and exposure to someone who can help teachers understand the difference between what they are doing and what they aspire to do. At the heart of the processes in schools where changes in practice do occur is the development of a common language with which colleagues can talk to one another and, indeed, to themselves, about detailed aspects of their practice (Huberman, 1993). Without such a language teachers find it very difficult to experiment with new possibilities. Much of what teachers do during the intensive encounters that occur is carried out at an automatic, intuitive level. Furthermore there is little time to stop and think. This is why having the opportunity to see colleagues at work is so crucial to the success of attempts to develop practice. It is through shared experiences that colleagues can help one another to articulate what they currently do and define what they might like to do (Hiebert et al., 2002). It is also the means whereby space is created within which taken-for-granted assumptions about particular groups of learners can be subjected to mutual critique.

This raises questions about how best to introduce such ways of working. In our own work we have made extensive use of "lesson study," a systematic procedure for the development of teaching that is well established in Japan and some other Asian countries (Hiebert et al., 2002; Lo et al., 2005; Stigler and Hiebert, 1999). The goal of lesson study is to improve the effectiveness of the experiences that teachers provide for all of their students. The core activity is collaboration on a shared area of focus that is generated through discussion. The content of this focus is the planned lesson, which is then used as the basis of gathering data on the quality of experience that students receive. These "research lessons" are used to examine the teachers' practices and the responsiveness of the students to the planned activities. Members of the group work together to design the lesson plan, which is then implemented by each teacher. Observations and post-lesson conferences are arranged to facilitate the improvement of the research lesson between each trial.

Learning from differences

Currently I am engaged with colleagues in a three-year study—"Responding to diversity by engaging with students' voices"—that is taking this thinking forward in an interesting way.[2] The project aims to support teachers in developing inclusive classroom practices by engaging with the views of students in such a way so as to ensure that personal and social circumstances—for example gender, socio-economic status, impairment or ethnic origin—are not an obstacle to participation and learning (Messiou et al., in press).

The project has involved two cycles of collaborative action research carried out by teams of teachers and researchers in eight secondary schools in three countries (i.e., England, Portugal and Spain). The schools were chosen because of the diversity of their student populations. Using an evolving framework to guide their efforts, each team experimented with ways of collecting and engaging with the views of students in order to foster the development of more inclusive classroom practices. Typically, teachers worked in trios following a lesson study approach. Meanwhile, members of the university teams monitored the process and outcomes of these activities.

So, for example, in planning their joint lesson, one trio of teachers identified students within each of their classes who they saw as being particularly vulnerable. They felt that by thinking about the lesson with these individuals in mind they might create new and different ways of facilitating the learning of all of their students. One teacher talked about a student who had an understanding of language but would not speak, even when invited. Another teacher focused on one of his students who had severe dyslexia. This led the teachers to discuss how they might plan their lessons differently; for example, they talked about getting the students to write on the whiteboard, and getting students to rehearse verbally what they wanted to say, rather than writing arguments down.

The trio decided that they needed to work with some of their students before teaching the lessons to get an idea of how they preferred to learn. They also wanted to consider how best to plan the lesson to support the many differences amongst the students. They therefore selected seven students, each from a different ethnic background, six of whom were born outside the country. The teachers got these students together at lunchtime and asked them to rank their preferences regarding different classroom activities that can be used when studying poetry. One of the teachers explained:

> Initially, they were quite reluctant to perhaps voice an opinion that they thought we wouldn't like.... We stepped back for a bit and just left the recording device on the table and let them talk about what they liked and what they didn't like, because if we're not imposing our views on them, they were more likely to be honest.

The overall aim of the lesson that was planned was to develop confidence in and awareness of a variety of dramatic techniques. Each teacher taught the lesson with their two colleagues watching, making changes in the light of the regular discussions that took place as they proceeded. It was noticeable that these became increasingly focused on matters of detail and, as a result, led to a greater emphasis on mutual challenge and personal reflection. By the end of the process the three teachers all commented that they had been challenged to rethink their lesson planning and facilitation. Through this, they realized that new approaches gave members of the class the opportunities to learn out of their "comfort zones" and, in so doing, move beyond the teachers' expectations about the capabilities of their students.

As a result of analyzing experiences such as this one, we were able to conceptualize a strategy for teacher development in respect to student diversity (Messiou et al., in press). Central to the strategy is the idea of engaging with the views of students, a process that should permeate all the processes involved and can take many forms. Our research suggests that it is this factor, more than anything else, that makes the difference as far as responding to learner diversity is concerned. In particular, it is this that brings a critical edge to the process that has the potential to challenge teachers to go beyond the sharing of existing practices in order to invent new possibilities for engaging students in their lessons, as we saw in the example. Where such changes take place, it is useful to think of them as the result of an interruption to continuing thinking and practice which brings about a transformation from "single-loop" to "double-loop" learning (Argyris and Schon, 1996)—that is, from learning which enables practice to be improved incrementally, to learning which shifts the assumptions on which practice is based.

At times, all of this proved to be challenging of the status quo within a school. Consequently, greater collaboration was needed amongst teachers in order to support the introduction of new practices. This required organizational flexibility and the active support of senior staff prepared to encourage and support processes of experimentation. In these senses, the evidence from this study supports research findings from elsewhere which suggest that classroom based research of this kind can be a powerful way of moving practice forward within a school (Talbert et al., 2010). What is distinctive in this particular project, however, is the added value that comes from engaging students themselves in the process. It is also clear that the use of the approach presents various organizational challenges that have to be addressed. In particular:

- *Finding time*—clearly time has to be found to enable staff to hold meetings and observe another's lessons. Given the potential impact of the strategy, this would seem like a sound investment. Put simply, by investing in teachers' learning there is likely to be a payoff in terms of students' learning.
- *Creating opportunities*—similarly, there is a need to make minor organizational changes in order to make it possible for these teacher development activities to occur. Links with other schools in the network added to the human resources available in this respect.
- *Facilitating trust*—the successful use of the approach demands the creation of partnerships within which colleagues and students feel able to gain mutual benefit. A helpful theoretical interpretation that can be made of what this involves is that of *social capital* (Mulford, 2007). In essence this involves

the strengthening of collaboration in order to create pathways through which expertise and lessons from innovations can spread.
- *Encouraging experimentation*—the aim must be to try out new teaching approaches in order to find more effective ways of reaching students who are being marginalized during lessons.

The implication is that senior staff within a school have to provide effective leadership by addressing these challenges in a way that helps to create a climate within which teacher professional development can take place, as recommended by Riehl (2000).

DEVELOPING EQUITABLE EDUCATION SYSTEMS

School-to-school collaboration

The approach I have outlined so far is based on the idea of those within schools collecting and engaging with various forms of evidence in order to stimulate moves to create more inclusive practices. Our research provides convincing evidence of the potential of this approach (see: Ainscow, Booth and Dyson, 2006; Miles and Ainscow, 2011). However, it has also thrown light on the difficulties in putting such an approach into practice within current policy contexts. This made us analyze the limitations of within-school strategies, leading us, in turn, to argue that these should be complemented with efforts to encourage greater cooperation between schools, and between schools and their wider communities (Ainscow et al., 2012a). And, of course, all of this points to the need for national policies that promote such activities.

In recent years, my colleagues and I have carried out a series of studies that have generated considerable evidence that school-to-school collaboration can strengthen improvement processes by adding to the range of expertise made available (see: Ainscow, 2010; Ainscow and Howes, 2007; Ainscow, Muijs and West, 2006; Ainscow et al., 2003; Ainscow and West, 2006; Ainscow et al., 2005; Muijs et al., 2010; Muijs et al., 2011). Together, these studies indicate that collaboration between schools has an enormous potential for fostering the capacity of education systems to respond to learner diversity. More specifically, they show how collaboration between schools can help to reduce the polarization of schools, to the particular benefit of those students who seem marginalized at the edges of the system, and whose performance and attitudes cause increasing concern.

It is important to realize, however, that using such partnerships is not a straightforward process. Too often they lead to meetings without any significant action. An example illustrates some of the complexities. It involves a network that used visits between schools to generate evidence regarding their shared focus on developing more inclusive practices. The aim was to look specifically at relative strengths and weaknesses within the network.

The visits were not always successful. This seemed to be particularly so when the host teachers interpreted the visits solely as opportunities for the visitors to learn. On these occasions, the hosts positioned themselves as teachers rather than learners. Typically, the visit then consisted of a demonstration or performance of various teaching strategies that had been judged to be successful, usually followed by a short question and answer session. On these occasions, those receiving the visit might merely rehearse what they already knew and respond to questions beyond the procedural as if they were challenges, rather than openings for debate.

On the other hand, successful visits were usually characterized by a sense of mutual learning amongst hosts and visitors. It was noticeable, too, that the focus for these visits often took some time to identify and clarify. Indeed, the preliminary negotiations that took place were in themselves a key aspect of the process. So, for example, during one such visit, the visitors were each invited to observe two children. A simple observation framework, designed by the teacher research team in the host school, focused on children's interactions with peers and teachers. The children to be observed were chosen by the class teacher, who, on this occasion, was the deputy head of the school. They were chosen on the basis that they were the children he knew *least* about in his class. In addition to observations, the visiting teachers were asked to interview the children. Again, a loose structure was devised but the main emphasis was on the visiting teachers following up things that they had seen during observations.

Afterwards, one of the visiting teachers said that the day had been "absolutely fascinating." He added: "There is no way in your own school you could do this." This seemed to be borne out by some of the imagery used by pupils about their teacher in interviews that day. For example, one child commented: "He's like a piranha looking round the class. He knows when I'm not listening." And, another pupil remarked: "He could be a really good teacher if he could explain but he gets too frustrated." The joking response by the class teacher to such statements was: "I want to go home! I've had enough now!"

The personal nature of these observations, and the teacher's willingness to listen to this feedback with colleagues from his own and another school present, illustrate the extent of the challenge that was sometimes involved in this sort of collaboration. Indeed, such visits were not "cosy," nor did they always result in a rosy glow. The key factor seemed to be that of mutual challenge. In the particular example, the teacher's seniority and the fact that he had volunteered for this degree of scrutiny may have been factors in creating a climate within which he felt able to enter into such a challenging dialogue with colleagues from another school.

Lessons from a city

The most convincing evidence about the power of schools working together comes from my recent involvement in the Greater Manchester Challenge. This three-year initiative, which involved over 1,100 schools in ten local authorities, had a government investment of around 50 million British pounds (see Ainscow et al., 2012a, for a detailed account of this initiative). The decision to invest this large amount reflected a concern regarding educational standards in the city region, particularly amongst children and young people from disadvantaged backgrounds. The approach adopted was influenced by an earlier initiative, the London Challenge (Brighouse, 2007).

A detailed analysis of the context led to the conclusion that plenty of good practice existed across the Greater Manchester schools. Consequently, it was decided that collaboration and networking would be the key strategies for strengthening the overall capacity of the system to reach out to vulnerable groups. More specifically this involved a series of inter-connected activities for "moving knowledge around."

Families of Schools were set up, using a data system that grouped between 12 and 20 schools on the basis of students' prior attainment and socio-economic background. This approach partnered schools that serve similar populations whilst, at the same time, encouraging partnerships amongst schools that were not in direct competition with one another because they did not serve the same neighborhoods. Led by headteachers, the Families of Schools proved to be successful in strengthening collaborative processes within the city region, although the impact was varied.

In terms of schools working in the most disadvantaged contexts, evidence from the Challenge suggests that school partnerships were the most powerful means of fostering improvements (Hutchings et al., 2012). Most notably, what we called the Keys to Success programme led to striking improvements in the performance of some 200 schools facing the most challenging circumstances. A common feature of almost all of these interventions was that progress was achieved through carefully matched pairings (or, sometimes, trios) of schools that cut across social "boundaries" of various kinds, including those that separate schools that are in different local authorities (Ainscow, 2013). In this way, expertise that was previously trapped in particular contexts was made more widely available.

Another effective strategy to facilitate the movement of expertise was provided through the creation of various types of hub schools. So, for example, some of the hubs provided support for other schools regarding ways of supporting students with English as an additional language. Similarly, so-called "teaching schools" providing professional development programmes focused on bringing about improvements in classroom practice. Other hub schools offered support in relation to particular subject areas, and in responding to groups of potentially vulnerable groups, such as those categorized as having special educational needs. In this latter context, a further significant strategy involved new roles for special schools in supporting developments in the mainstream.

The powerful impact of the collaborative strategies developed in the Greater Manchester Challenge points to ways in which improvement processes used within individual schools can be deepened and, therefore, strengthened. This requires an emphasis on mutual critique, within schools and between schools, based on an engagement with shared data. This, in turn, requires strong collective commitment from senior school staff and a willingness to share responsibility for system reform.

Beyond the school gate

Our research has led us to argue that the development of schools that are effective for all children will only happen when what happens *outside* as well as *inside* the school changes (Ainscow et al., 2012a). This means changing how families and communities work and enriching what they offer to children.

We have encouraging evidence of what can happen when what schools do is aligned in a coherent strategy with the efforts of other local players—employers, community groups, universities and public services (Ainscow, 2012). This does not necessarily mean schools doing more, but it does imply partnerships beyond the school, where partners multiply the impacts of each other's efforts. However, our experience suggests that the success of such partnerships is dependent upon a common understanding of what they are trying to achieve.

With this argument in mind, my colleagues Alan Dyson and Kirstin Kerr are currently exploring the idea of area-based initiatives modeled on the principles underpinning the highly acclaimed Harlem Children's Zone in the USA (Dyson et al., 2012). This work is attempting to improve outcomes for children and young people in areas of disadvantage through an approach that they characterize as being "doubly holistic." That is to say, they seek to develop coordinated efforts to tackle the factors that disadvantage children and enhance the factors which support them, across all aspects of their lives, and across their life spans, from conception through to adulthood.

CONCLUSION

No doubt, in another ten years we will once again stop to reflect on the continuing influence of Salamanca. My hope is that the progress that has been made in fostering more inclusive education systems over the last 20 years will have continued. For this to happen, however, those involved have to be effective in analyzing the barriers that are preventing progress in their own contexts and in mobilizing available resources in order to overcome these barriers. In this way, efforts to promote greater inclusion within education systems can, I believe, refocus national policies to "raise standards" in a way that reflects the spirit of Salamanca.

Bearing this in mind, the argument I have developed in this chapter points to a series of propositions that could be useful to those seeking to foster inclusive developments in their own contexts. These are as follows:

- In order to move policy and practice forward, there needs to be clarity regarding what is meant by inclusive education;
- The development of inclusive practices must involve mobilizing available human resources in order to overcome barriers to participation and learning;
- An engagement with various kinds of evidence can be a powerful stimulus for encouraging teachers to develop more inclusive practices;
- Inclusive schools take many forms but what is common is the existence of an organizational culture that views student diversity positively;
- Schools need to work together and with the wider community in promoting inclusion; and
- National policies have to create a framework for making all of this happen.

These ideas reinforce the idea that developing more inclusive schools is essentially a social process that has to occur within particular contexts. In this sense, inclusive development is about learning how to live with difference and, indeed, learning how to learn from difference. And, as I have argued many times, the most important factor is the collective will to make it happen.

NOTES

1. See Chapter 3.
2. This is a European Union Comenius Multilateral funded project, 2011–2014.

CHAPTER FIVE

Putting Disability on the "Education for All" Agenda

JEROME MINDES

From 1997 to 2002, a group of development professionals, educators, and disability advocates undertook an effort to get the UNESCO-led Secretariat for Education for All (EFA) to recognize disability as a part of EFA goals. They sought to erect a bridge between the 1990 EFA Commitment and the 1994 Salamanca Declaration on Special Needs Education. This review of one consortium's efforts in no way diminishes the role played by others to move this agenda forward.

A PIVOTAL MOMENT IN GENEVA

In late April of 2000, representatives of donors, ministries, international and national NGOs, experts and advocates met in Dakar, Senegal for the World Education Forum, a ten-year review of the EFA commitment.

Days after the final presentations in Dakar, a small sub-set of Forum attendees arrived in Switzerland for another meeting of development professionals who were part of the International Working Group on Disability and Development (IWGDD).

On the evening of May 3, 2000 in Geneva, about six IWGDD members met at an outdoor café and shared their frustration at the lack of attention in Dakar to disability. At that café and over the next two days, discussions about disability and EFA continued.

University educators Hannu Sovalainen of Finland and Phyllis Magrab of the United States spoke about how disability issues were again marginalized at a global conference. They were joined by Peter Evans of OECD and Don Foster-Gross of USAID, confirming that while disability was mentioned in key speeches, the final Dakar resolution was silent on the issue. Dakar was about girls' education, Peter Evans said, and nothing more.[1]

Others in attendance in Geneva included representatives of Inclusion International, the International Disability and Development Consortium, the World Bank, Danish International Development Agency (DANIDA), WHO, ILO, Rehabilitation International, UNESCO, and the UN Special Rapporteur for Disability.

These discussions set the stage for an effort by the IWGDD to put disability on the EFA map, an effort which culminated two and a half years later when Finland's foreign ministry hosted a meeting to define the terms of reference for what was to become the "Flagship on the Right to Education for Persons with Disabilities: Towards Inclusion," a formal part of the global EFA architecture at UNESCO.

From its inception in 1997 until it disbanded in 2002, I served as the IWGDD's coordinator. This chapter draws from the minutes of IWGDD meetings, especially from 1999 to 2002. In addition, in 2013, I conducted interviews with several participants, including those who at the time represented the Commonwealth Secretariat, UK-DFID, Finland, OECD, UNICEF, UNDP, UNESCO, and USAID.

THE INTERNATIONAL WORKING GROUP ON DISABILITY AND DEVELOPMENT

How the group became a venue for dialogue and action

The IWGDD was formed by individuals and organizations that planned and convened a 1997 "Global Workshop in Children with Disabilities in the Developing World." This workshop was hosted by the Academy for Educational Development (AED). Its funders and supporters included the U.S. Department of Education (Judy Heumann); the UN Department for Policy Coordination and Sustainable Development (Akiko Ito), the Dole Foundation for the Employment of People with Disabilities (Paul Hearne); DANIDA (Birgit Dysegaard); and UNICEF (Cyril Dalais).

The organizers framed the conference's purpose in a white paper which referred to this group of children as being virtually invisible to the global development community.

When the four-day conference ended, the organizers briefed World Bank officials who did not attend the conference. Participants shared what they learned and what actions donors and implementers should take to address the needs of children with disabilities. Toward the meeting's end, it was the USAID's Emily Vargas-Barón who suggested a next step.

By this time, 1997, Vargas-Barón was USAID's lead on basic education and over a career in early child development and education had nurtured action on issues that were not then in the mainstream. She did this in the 1980s on HIV and AIDS, and at this World Bank meeting she again offered solutions to ignored issues. The following is from a transcript of the World Bank meeting:

> ...we have a unique opportunity to build a collaboration across our wonderful UN system and our bilaterals, foundations, [and] many others [...] that have devoted personal efforts and financial resources to this area. I think we have many partners beyond these walls who would like to join in but they need a framework. [...] I think we could establish a quarterly meeting, perhaps more frequently at first, to get together and consider ways to inform each other what we are doing and work together on common goals.[2]

This was the genesis of the IWGDD. Vargas-Barón offered to host the first meeting of the as yet-unnamed group, held at USAID on May 13, 1997. From that time through 2002, the IWGDD met two to three times per year, bringing together disability experts and advocates with counterparts in donor and development assistance agencies.

The IWGDD was a virtual entity, existing through voluntary efforts and eventually, through modest grants from USAID, Finland, DFID and UNESCO. As member Stephen Matlin (then of the Commonwealth Secretariat) said in a recent interview, "we worked on these issues at the margins of what we were supposed to do."

Over time it's participants came from bi-lateral donors (Denmark, Finland, Japan, Sweden, the U.S., and the UK); multi-lateral organizations (the UN Secretariat, the UN Special Rapporteur on Disability, UNICEF, UNESCO, the World Bank, the ILO, WHO, and the Commonwealth Secretariat); from international organizations (OECD); international NGOs; universities; and from several global disability NGOs.

There was considerable overlap between IWGDD members and Salamanca attendees, including Lena Saleh of UNESCO (Salamanca's Coordinator); Peter Evans of OECD (Salamanca Programme Committee); and Bengt Lindqvist and Kenneth Eklindh (representing Sweden at Salamanca). Others involved in both Salamanca and the IWGDD were Finland's foreign ministry, Danida, Inclusion International, and Rehabilitation International.

This overlap positioned the IWGDD to merge what were two parallel tracks: the efforts in Jomtien in 1990 that created a global EFA commitment[3] and those that led to the 1994 Salamanca Declaration on Special Needs Education.

In the late 1990s many donor agencies did not yet have disability policies. Finland and Denmark were deploying special educators to work with ministries of education, and Finland and Sweden consulted with domestic disability advocates on foreign aid. UNESCO, largely through the efforts of Lena Saleh, its voice on Special Needs Education,[4] was the Coordinator of the Salamanca conference. In 1999, UNICEF focused on disability prevention, early identification, and early response.[5] The UN had by this time established a Voluntary Fund for Disability within the Office of Social and Economic Development.

An important force in this agenda was Bengt Lindquist, then serving as the UN-Special Rapporteur on Disability. By 1998, Lindquist had secured funds to convene disability leaders to address the issue within the context of the UN-Convention on the Rights of the Child. Another group was the International Disability and Development Consortium, an alliance established in the late 1990s by Save the Children International (UK).

USAID was one of a handful of donors that by 1997 had a disability policy. As was often the case, the pressure to do so came from the outside. On August 1, 1996, the National Council on Disability, an independent U.S. government advisory body, issued a report entitled "Foreign Policy and Disability," which concluded that "those responsible for creating and implementing U.S. overseas policies and programs generally lack awareness of disability issues, cannot articulate our national policies with respect to people with disabilities, do not incorporate the interests of people with disabilities into U.S. foreign policy objectives."[6]

Emily Vargas-Barón, then of USAID, recently identified another key outside push. This came from Eunice Kennedy Shriver and Sargent Shriver. In late 1996 Mrs. Shriver began to call on leaders of foreign aid agencies to urge them to do more for people with intellectual disability. One of those she wrote was Brian Atwood, then the head of USAID. Atwood invited the Shrivers to his office, and at that meeting made a commitment to develop a USAID policy on disability.

According to Vargas-Barón, this meeting and the ensuing policy gave her the license to advance disability issues. The USAID policy, presented on September 12, 1997, referenced that one of USAID's action steps would be to participate at the regular meetings of the nascent working group that would become the IWGDD.[7]

USAID and Finland would play key roles in giving legitimacy and resources to the IWGDD's work.

Addressing Education for All

By 1999 the IWGDD convened regular seminars. At its seventh meeting, in November 1999, the IWGDD hosted its first high-level discussion on disability and EFA.

Joining the IWGDD at this meeting were two individuals key to the discussions leading to Dakar: Mary Joy Pigozzi of UNICEF and John Lawrence, formerly of UNDP but at the time a consultant to the Dakar meeting. The session was moderated by Vargas-Barón.

In advance of the meeting, IWGDD members received the draft document being developed for Dakar. Vargas Barón noted that there were a number of references to disability in the draft, but no strong statement about disability. She noted that the Executive Summary did not mention the Salamanca Declaration, and suggested that there was a need for a clear, concise statement that EFA policies and programs need to be inclusive of children and youth with disabilities.

Lawrence noted that earlier drafts included references to the Salamanca Declaration, but most were "excised at the last moment by means and for reasons unclear" to him. Lawrence also noted that few bilateral partners expressed support for including strong statements about disability. Among those who did, he said, were USAID and Denmark.

Pigozzi noted that within Basic Primary Education, UNICEF has begun focusing on those who are excluded from education, and to identify why they are excluded. Pigozzi spoke of UNICEF's new effort to create "child friendly" schools which she defined as schools that focus on inclusion, are protective of children, and where all children can learn.

In focusing on new challenges, such as including the girl child or children with disabilities, Pigozzi noted that it is important to recognize that UNICEF often works with systems that are ill equipped to deal with even the status quo. When those systems are asked to address new needs "it is important that UNICEF addresses as well the needs of the systems in order that we don't create situations where overburdened educational systems are creating further disadvantages for the disadvantaged."[8]

The IWGDD members provided written comments on the draft to John Lawrence and waited with some hope and anticipation for Dakar.

Disability at Dakar's World Education Forum

Disability was mentioned at the April 2000 meeting in Dakar. It was the topic of a session on "Meeting Special/Diverse Educational Needs, Making Inclusive Education a Reality," which was sponsored by Finland. Disability was also referenced in a session on expanding access to early childhood care and in an "NGO Declaration on Education for All."

Where disability was completely absent was in the final Dakar Framework for Action, the document which was designed to frame the EFA agenda for the coming years. The Framework referenced children who were "disadvantaged" or "most vulnerable, especially girls."

In her keynote address at Dakar, UNICEF Director Carol Bellamy said "we must focus on the needs of those most disadvantaged and excluded from learning, ... – girls, working children, children of ethnic minorities, and children affected by violence and conflict, disabilities, and HIV/AIDS."[9] The address by Gene Sperling, then President Clinton's Senior Economic Advisor and the Head of the U.S. Delegation, went further. Sperling urged that those present "must continue to address new challenges," and mentioned three. The first was the digital divide and the second was early childhood learning. "Third, we cannot and must not leave behind those children with disabilities and special needs," he said.

> If we believe in the basic moral imperative that all children would have a chance to reach their potential, then we must include children with disabilities in our vision and our concrete plans.

Sperling was the only speaker at Dakar to frame disability as a human rights imperative.[10] The addresses by other leaders were silent on the subject of disability. To illustrate where emphasis was placed, "girls" were mentioned 34 times by UN Secretary General Kofi Annan, 13 times by UNICEF's Bellamy, 8 times by DFID's Claire Short, and 4 times by World Bank President Wolfensohn.

In the days following the Forum, IWGDD members who were present in Dakar shared their observations at its Geneva meeting. The following are excerpts from the Minutes of that meeting:[11]

"Phyllis Magrab of Georgetown University noted that the IWGDD members present in Dakar tried to keep a focus on disability issues, and noted that this was difficult." Regarding Dakar's final Framework for Action,

> Magrab mentioned that the outcome was somewhat disappointing. While earlier versions of the draft made numerous mentions of people with disabilities, the draft went through many layers of changes prior to its adoption. The final version, Magrab noted, does not mention the word disability, but does mention that education should be inclusive.

Sai Vayrynen of UNESCO pointed out "that the final Framework for Action adopted in Dakar does reference the Salamanca statement on special needs education," but agreed that "disability issues were not very visible." She noted that disability was discussed at regional meetings which led up to the World Forum, particularly those for Asia, Africa, and Latin America, but were not at all prevalent in the documents from the regional meetings for Europe and North America. The IWGDD meeting minutes note "concern about this north/south disparity, in that the major donors nations do not seem inclined to emphasize disability."

In a recent interview, Sai Vayrynen recalled how UNESCO viewed the post-Dakar discussion. Her colleague Aicha Bah Diallo, then Acting Deputy

Director General for Education, was surprised by the frustration from the disability community. UNESCO, she recalled, thought they were addressing disability equitably by using terms like inclusion, vulnerable, and marginalized.[12] They didn't understand why the word disability was important. The choice of words would become a recurring issue.

Another perspective on Dakar was given by Garren Lumpkin, who spent over 30 years with UNICEF. Historically, Lumpkin noted, UNICEF would "focus on where we have public awareness and demand, and where we can make a difference." UNICEF "wanted people to concentrate" on a clear message. A focus on girls had credence from an economic and family planning perspective, could get the world's attention, and could galvanize resources to make a difference. From this view, an intense focus on girls at Dakar was too big an opportunity to let pass, and too big an opportunity to muddy by making Dakar about anything other than girls.[13]

Dakar did provide an opening in that it strengthened UNESCO's role in creating the operational framework for EFA stakeholders, and thus made UNESCO the logical target for disability advocates.

POST-DAKAR: FRUSTRATION TO RESOLVE

The May 2000 IWGDD meeting in Geneva led to a series of steps to advance the group's role in EFA. First was news that Finland's foreign ministry was considering how to keep a focus on EFA and disability and that in this effort it may have been interested in collaborating with the IWGDD.

One cautionary note was shared by Sai Vayrynen of UNESCO, who reported that major changes were occurring at UNESCO. It is noteworthy that by this time UNESCO had completed a position paper on inclusive education and EFA; was developing training and self-study modules for teachers on disability in the classroom; and was developing training videos for the deaf.

The changes at UNESCO were worrying. By 2000 Lena Saleh had left UNESCO, and with that special education advocates lost an ally with a vast network and access to UNESCO's highest ranks. Saleh was replaced by Kenneth Eklindh, a Swedish special educator. Eklindh served as a consultant to UNESCO, which meant he did not have Saleh's status as an international civil servant nor the resources which went with her office. This also meant that the IWGDD had to find other pathways into UNESCO.

The Geneva meeting ended with the formation of an IWGDD Task Force on EFA, which by the end of 2000 included representatives of Danida; Finland's foreign ministry; Georgetown University; Inclusion International; OECD; Rehabilitation International; the Nilo Maki Institute; and UNESCO.

IWGDD: Funding for Advocacy on EFA

The frustration from Dakar had turned to a resolve to act. This took three forms: clarifying the message; getting funds to support its work; and direct outreach to engage senior UNESCO officers.

By September of 2000, the IWGDD received its first grant, from USAID. The $20,000 supported activities related to IWGDD's involvement in the World Education Forum in Dakar.[14] The grant called for the IWGDD to conduct a full meeting in the Fall of 2000 of IWGDD member organizations and others on inclusive education within the context of EFA.[15,16]

The planning session took place in Paris on October 2 and 3, 2000, and the full meeting was in London, on November 6 and 7.

Words Matter

In preparing for the fall meetings called for under the USAID grant, and in drafting letters to UNESCO's leadership, the IWGDD grappled with a key issue: what words should it use to describe what it wanted. By this time, different entities were using different terms: special needs education; inclusive education; education of children, youth and adults with disabilities.

In a memo to the IWGDD EFA Task Force in September 2000, I wrote that:

> for the purpose of this meeting [at UNESCO] … I will use the term disabilities and not the term special needs…. Special needs can refer to an array of children on the margins of mainstream basic education, including street children, HIV/AIDS orphans, children of linguistic minorities, and other categories, including children with mental and/or physical disabilities. By using the term children with disabilities I intentionally narrow the focus to reflect the goal of the IWGDD, to elevate issues of importance to people with disabilities on the broad agenda of development.[17]

There was one more issue to clarify, and that was whether to use the words "inclusive education." The following is from an email sent on October 15, 2000, to the IWGDD EFA Task Force:

> The IWGDD does not endorse specific policies, etc. It is an advocate for elevating disability issues on the donor agenda. Therefore, the IWGDD as a whole is not going to advocate for "inclusive education." Rather, it will urge that education strategies recognize and incorporate the needs and views of people with disabilities, and that people with disabilities and the organizations which serve them be represented at meetings, planning sessions, conferences, etc., at which education strategies plans, projects, etc. are developed.[18]

Not using the phrase "inclusive education" also reflected an internal reality. The IWGDD was working to enlist global disabled people's organizations and, in doing so, needed to acknowledge that these groups had a range of views. For example, the view of the World Federation of the Deaf, and to a lesser extent the World Blind Union, was that different educational approaches could co-exist. The IWGDD's interest in having a united front influenced its decision to focus on inclusive strategies rather than an outright embrace of inclusive education.

Proposing a collaboration with UNESCO on EFA

IWGDD EFA Task Force members attended the October 2000 planning session in Paris, purposely held at UNESCO so as to remind UNESCO of the IWGDD's resolve. To ensure that the goals of Dakar were achieved, UNESCO was at that time organizing an international EFA Working Group to convene twice a year to monitor and exchange information. Focusing on UNESCO's role as EFA secretariat became a key strategy of the IWGDD Task Force. During the two days at UNESCO, IWGDD members met with Jacques Hallak, Assistant Director General for Education, and with staff from several education related divisions. Over its two day meeting, the IWGDD Task Force developed a proposed action plan, with recommendations as follows:

- that the IWGDD be invited to serve as a member of the UNESCO EFA Working Group;
- that the IWGDD and the UNESCO EFA Working Group identify ways to work in concert over the coming two year period to ensure that the goals of Dakar are extended to children, youth, and adults with disabilities; and
- that IWGDD member organizations serve as a resource for UNESCO's (and other agencies') work to identify, develop, and disseminate tools, brochures, guidelines, etc., for nations and donors to use as they implement national education plans.[19]

This plan recognized two realities: that disability groups need to be represented at high level dialogues and that the broader EFA discussion was shifting to the national level.

The October 2000 planning meeting ended with the announcement that the IWGDD had been invited to submit a proposal to Finland's foreign ministry.

By November 2, 2000, UNESCO had invited the IWGDD to send an observer to the first meeting of the Working Group on Education for All, to be held at UNESCO on November 22–24, 2000, and to circulate a paper on EFA and disability to meeting participants. UNESCO also agreed to work with the IWGDD to develop materials for countries and donors.[20]

The IWGDD meeting on November 6 and 7, 2000, in London was well attended. Twenty-two organizations were represented by over 25 individuals.

DFID's David Clarke gave an overview of how UNESCO would frame its post-Dakar role. It would establish two groups: a high level political group to provide leadership to the Dakar follow-up and the Working Group on EFA, to be comprised of 30–40 representatives of donors, government ministries, and NGOs. He also reported that as part of the EFA framework "flagships" would be established on specific issues,[21] such as HIV/AIDS, early child education, literacy, gender, and emergency situations and education.[22]

Clarke's overview provided a road map for the IWGDD: to make certain that disability has a place at the EFA working group and to have a flagship on disability and EFA.

Also in November 2000, the IWGDD submitted a proposal for US$70,000 to Finland, to be used to convene IWGDD meetings coterminously with meetings of the UNESCO EFA Working Group. Funds would also be used to support travel by the IWGDD's DPO members.

Disability still not squarely on the agenda

On November 22–24, 2000, Hannu Savolainen of Finland and Nancy Breitenbach of Inclusion International represented the IWGDD as observers to the first meeting of UNESCO's EFA Working Group. Two weeks later Savolainen shared his observations. He wrote:

> persons with disabilities are not on the agenda as a priority. What was observed in Dakar continues, i.e. persons with disabilities were not mentioned in Paris presentations, only a vague reference to special needs … was made by one sub-group.

It was also learned at this meeting that UNESCO's Basic Education section was preparing papers for a possible flagship on inclusive education. Savolainen noted that the IWGDD should support this inclusive education flagship, adding:

> however, at the same time we should keep clearly in focus that this group [IWGDD] is advocating for persons with disabilities, which will be only one – although important – aspect of the proposed UNESCO flagship work.[23]

Savolainen was expressing a concern of many IWGDD members that a flagship on "inclusion" might not give adequate attention to disability.

With funding from USAID and now Finland, the IWGDD began to plan for a series of meetings with UNESCO.

The first of these was from April 18–20, 2001, where IWGDD representatives met with John Daniel, the new Deputy Director General for Education, with Aicha Bah Diallo, and with other senior staff. IWGDD attendees included Nancy Breitenbach, Judith Hollenweger of Rehabilitation International, Peter

Evans of OECD, Phyllis Magrab of Georgetown University, Birgit Dyssegaard for DANIDA, and Sai Vayrynen of UNESCO.

While the meetings were inconclusive, both Daniel and Diallo agreed that a partnership between UNESCO and the IWGDD could advance disability within the EFA effort. Diallo also spoke of UNESCO's "disappointment that the Dakar forum a year earlier did not adequately address inclusive education."[24]

Further disappointment was just a week away. On April 27, 2001, one year after Dakar, the heads of the five agencies which convened the Dakar Forum issued a statement entitled "Harness the Power of Education." The statement opened as follows:

> More than 113 million primary school-age children are denied the chance to go to school in the developing world today. Well over 60 percent are girls. The world's failure to give these children even the basic building blocks of literacy and the ability to transform their lives will have profound consequences, not only for their home countries, but for the rest of the global community for generations to come. This was the direct challenge posed by the Dakar World Education.[25]

The 1300-word statement made five references to girls and eight to gender, but no mention of disability, inclusion, or special needs.

Not everyone was silent. From March 5–7, 2001, eleven months after Dakar, Minsters of Education of Latin America and the Caribbean met in Cochabamba, Bolivia. The meeting, held at UNESCO's request, resulted in the Cochabamba Declaration. It read in part:

> Education systems should offer learning opportunities to each child, young person, and adult, cultivating a diversity of abilities, vocations, and styles, with particular emphasis on special learning needs.

The Ministers' 54 recommendations included two on special education.[26] Regional voices were again more nuanced than those at the global level in making the link between the Salamanca Declaration and EFA.

EDUCATION FOR ALL AND DISABILITY: A BREAKTHROUGH

By early 2001 the IWGDD's efforts were taking root. UNESCO was planning the second meeting of the Working Group on EFA for September 2001, and the IWGDD was invited to participate, marking the first invitation for any disability group.

In the opening remarks entitled "Education for All after Dakar–Global Overview" presented September 10, 2001, UNESCO Secretary-General Matsurra mentioned that the establishment of a flagship on disabilities would be "considered."

Heikki Kokkalla, representing Finland, and Robert Prouty of the World Bank both urged that a flagship on disability be established.

The IWGDD was represented by Nancy Breitenbach and Hannu Savolainen, who both spoke during the plenary sessions. During the last session on September 12, Breitenbach said:

> A flagship on EFA and the disability dimension would recognize growing donor interest and commitment to placing disability issues squarely on the development agenda; and would recognize as well the diversity of the disability community.... Importantly, such a flagship would also advance inclusive education as a primary approach to achieving EFA's goals for children, youth, and adults with disabilities, and insodoing recognize the leadership role which UNESCO has played.[27]

In the meeting's Final Report, John Daniel of UNESCO noted that those at the Working Group "recognized that some issues—disability and teacher/quality education to name just two—must now move higher up our list of priorities."[28]

By 2002 it was clear that would be a flagship that would have something to do with disability. What was not clear was what it would be called. UNESCO officials were calling for a flagship on "inclusive education." The IWGDD wanted the word "disability" in the title.

From recent interviews with former IWGDD members and UNESCO staff,[29] it was clear that Finland's foreign ministry helped to lock in the reference to disability. In an article written by Heikki Kokkala, published in 2006, he wrote of the "strong support and assistance of the Ministry of Foreign Affairs of Finland" to launch the Flagship. In fact, it was the Finnish foreign ministry that went to UNESCO in 2002 with an offer: Finland would provide funds to launch the Flagship, but it would have to be a flagship that used the word "disability."

By the Third Meeting of the Working Group on EFA, convened at UNESCO on July 22–23, 2002, the efforts by Finland and the IWGDD had succeeded. The Agenda for that meeting lists Carol-Lee Aquiline, Secretary-General of the World Federation of the Deaf, as a full participant representing the "EFA Flagship on the Rights of Persons with Disabilities."

The flagship was formally launched a month later at a meeting in Helsinki hosted by the Foreign Ministry. Its final name was a compromise: The EFA Flagship on "The Right to Education for Persons with Disabilities: Toward Inclusion."

What is clear in hindsight was the pivotal role Finland played. Not only did they fund much of the advocacy by the IWGDD to push for a flagship, they used their standing and resources to influence when and how the flagship was established, and what it would be named. Again, words mattered.

What the flagship was meant to be is summed up in the 2006 article by Kokkala:

> The … IWGDD, an alliance of global disability groups and experts and donors, was established in 1997 to serve as a forum for discussing strategies to make the global development agenda more inclusive. The IWGDD then assisted in establishing a framework for the above Flagship on The Right to Education for Persons with Disabilities, which was formally launched in the autumn of 2002 in Helsinki with the strong support and assistance of the Ministry for Foreign Affairs of Finland. On 1 January 2003 the Flagship was formally established with a joint Secretariat hosted by UNESCO Paris and The University of Oslo, for a period of three years…. The aims of the Disability Flagship are to act as a catalyst to ensure that the right to education, and the goals of the Dakar Framework, are realised for individuals with disabilities.[30]

In December 2004, the Flagship's launch was complete with the release of a Conceptual Paper prepared by John Lawrence under contract with the World Bank. This is the same John Lawrence who in November 1999 spoke at the IWGDD's first substantive discussion about EFA and disability. The arc of Lawrence's role is illustrative of how mainstream actors began to embrace the place that disability ought to have in EFA and in the development agenda.

The executive summary to the Paper articulates why the flagship placed emphasis on disability and not on inclusion. It reads in part:

> This paper presents a rights based case for inclusiveness for all persons with disabilities not only in access to basic educational opportunity and accomplishing the comprehensive EFA mission, but most importantly also in their engagement at all levels in the policy and processes necessary for such inclusiveness to actually work.[31]

For the Flagship and the IWGDD, it was not about a specific policy or approach, but more about the need for policies and approaches to be inclusive, and for disability to be viewed as a human rights issue.

POSTSCRIPT

The IWGDD disbanded in 2002. With financial commitments from Finland and Norway, many thought that disability would become a viable part of EFA.

It is now 25 years since Jomtien, 20 since Salamanca, 12 since the UNESCO Secretary General signaled the establishment of a Flagship on EFA and disability, and just one year from when EFA goals are to be achieved.

In the ensuing years, the EFA Flagship convened regional gatherings on EFA and inclusive education and disability, published papers, and contributed to UNESCO's work in the EFA Global Monitoring Reports and on the UN-Convention on the Rights of Persons with Disabilities. The EFA Flagship, however, never served as an effective platform to push disability higher up on the global EFA priority list.

By 2010, when the EFA Global Monitoring Report focused on "Reaching the Marginalized," disability was still addressed in aspirational terms. The report notes that "the key message to emerge is that failure to place inclusive education at the centre of the Education for All agenda is holding back progress towards the goals adopted at Dakar."[32]

By May of 2011, the bi-lateral support for the EFA Flagship came to an end. Disability issues, ostensibly, would be integrated across the spectrum of the EFA agenda.[33]

In March 2013, Qian Tang, UNESCO's Assistant Director General, gave a speech on "the vision of education in the post-2015 development agenda." There was no mention of disability.[34] Also in 2013, UNESCO and UNICEF convened the Global Thematic Consultation on Education in the Post 2015 Development Agenda. This report acknowledged the lack of disability focus in education targets and indicators, leading to their "effective exclusion from schools." The Advisory Group that helped to prepare and review this report had no disability representation.[35]

This same report cited a 2008 UNESCO estimate that children with disabilities represent perhaps 30 percent of the global out of school population at the primary school level.[36] A 2012 report by UNESCO's Institute for Statistics and the EFA Global Monitoring Report entitled "Reaching Out of School Children Is Crucial for Development," failed to once mention children with disabilities.[37]

Similarly, the Education First initiative spearheaded by UN Secretary General Ban Ki-moon lists three priorities: put every child in school, improve quality learning, and foster global citizenship. None mention disability. Education First's Steering Committee has no disability representation.

There remain active voices on these issues, including the International Disability Alliance and the International Disability and Development Consortium. More donors have disability staff expertise. There are UN sponsored events on disability and development in the post 2015 development agenda, and many donors include disability in policies and programs.

But in 2014 there is no global commitment to close the enrollment gap that leaves tens of millions of children with disabilities out of school. What children with disabilities need now is what girls' education got from Dakar in 2000: a commitment of resources and an inclusive operational architecture where donors, disability advocates, educators, and governments can share information and hold each other accountable to achieve education for all children, youth and adults with disabilities. Only then will the Salamanca Declaration be realized.

NOTES

1. The content of the discussions in Geneva are from the author's recollections as enhanced by interviews with Hannu Savolainen and Peter Evans.
2. Global Workshop on Children with Disabilities, Proceedings of Post Workshop Meeting, held at The World Bank, Washington, DC, February 7, 1997, shared on March 3, 1997 by Eluned Roberts-Schweitzer, The World Bank.
3. See Chapter 2.
4. See Chapter 3.
5. UNICEF's priorities were shared by Gulbadan Habibi of UNICEF, at an IWGDD meeting in April 1999.
6. "Foreign Policy and Disability," published on August 1, 1996 by the U.S. National Council on Disability.
7. USAID Policy Guidance on Disability, September 12, 1997.
8. Minutes of the Seventh Meeting of the IWGDD, convened at the Hotel Inter-Continental, New York City, November 18–19, 1999.
9. Plenary Address by Carol Bellamy at the World Education Forum, April 28, 2000.
10. Plenary Address by Gene Sperling at the World Education Forum, April 28, 2000.
11. Minutes of the Eighth Meeting of the International Working Group on Disability and Development, Geneva, Switzerland, May 4 and 5, 2000.
12. Skype interview with Sai Vayrynen, former UNESCO staffperson, on September 20, 2013.
13. October 30, 2013 Skype interview with Garren Lumpkin, former Regional Education Advisor for UNICEF in Latin America.
14. Award letter from USAID to David Henderson, Secretary General of Rehabilitation International, September 28 2000.
15. Ibid.
16. This was augmented by small grants from Rehabilitation International, Georgetown University, and Inclusion International.
17. Memorandum from IWGDD Coordinator Mindes to its EFA Task Force. Undated, but sent in late September 2000.
18. Email dated October 15, 2000 from IWGDD Coordinator Mindes to its EFA Task Force.
19. Memorandum dated October 20, 2000 from the IWGDD EFA Task Force (drafted by Jerome Mindes) to the full IWGDD.
20. November 2, 2000 correspondence from Jacques Hallak to Jerome Mindes.
21. See Chapter 6.
22. Minutes of the Ninth Meeting of the IWGDD, November 6–7, 2000, Marlborough House, London.
23. During an interview in September 2013, and in email exchanges, Mr. Savolainen granted permission to quote from his "confidential" memo of December 7, 2000.
24. Recollections of the April 2001 meeting at UNESCO are from a Memorandum sent on May 7, 2001, from IWGDD Coordinator Jerry Mindes to its member organizations.
25. The Statement "Harness the Power of Education" was released on April 27, 2001 by the heads of UNESCO, The World Bank, UNICEF, UNFPA, and UNDP.
26. The "Cochambaba Declaration" and the Conference's "Recommendations for Education Policies at the Beginning of the 21st Century," citing references number 11 and 26, March 6, 2001.

27. Excerpted from an article written by Jerry Mindes from "Disability World" a now defunct bi-monthly web-zine of disability news and views, Issue 10, September–October 2001.
28. Final Report of the Second Working Group on Education for All, September 10–12, 2001.
29. Inteviews with Sai Vayrynen, Hannu Savolainen, and Emily Vargas-Barón.
30. Article by Heikki Kokkala published in 2006 as part of a book entitled When All Means All: Experiences in Three African Countries with EFA and Children with Disabilities, edited by Kokkala, Hannu Savolainen, and Marja Matero.
31. Executive Summary of "Conceptual Paper, December 2004: The Right to Education for Persons with Disabilities: Towards Inclusion," an EFA Flagship.
32. Education for All Global Monitoring Report 2010: "Reaching the Marginalized."
33. A Report from Judith Hollenweger, Rehabilitation International, Chair, European Region, on a Partners' meeting on May 20, 2011 at UNESCO on "Mainstreaming Disability in EFA, Planning Future Steps."
34. Transcript of speech by Qian Tang, at the Global Consultation on Education in the Post-2015 Development Agenda, which opened on March 18, 2013 in Dakar, Senegal. Source is the UNESCO website.
35. Making Education a Priority in the Post 2015 Development Agenda, A Report by the "Global Thematic Consultation on Education," 2013
36. UNESCO (2008). Education for All Global Monitoring Report 2008: "Education for All by 2015 – Will We Make it?" Paris. Available from http://www.unesco.org/new/en/education/themes/leading-the-international-agenda/efareport/reports/2008-mid-term-review/
37. Policy Paper 04, June 2012, "Reaching Out of School Children Is Crucial for Development," a joint publication of the EFA Global Monitoring Group and the UNESCO Institute for Statistics.

CHAPTER SIX

The UNESCO Flagship:

The Right to Education for Persons with Disabilities: Towards Inclusion

SIRI WORMNÆS

Following a meeting of the UNESCO Education for All Working Group in September 2001, Director General Koichiro Matsuura announced that UNESCO would form a flagship programme on education for all and disabilities.

> An EFA flagship initiative is a structured set of activities carried out by voluntary partners, under the leadership of one or more United Nations specialized agencies and NGOs, that seeks to address specific challenges in achieving the EFA goals.
>
> (UNESCO, 2004a, p. 7)

The Flagship entitled "The Right to Education for Persons with Disabilities: Towards Inclusion" was established January 1, 2003. This chapter describes and discusses objectives and selected activities from the initial three-year period of this Flagship, as experienced by the author, who was a member of the Secretariat.

The Flagship's main objective was to be an actor in the move towards ensuring that persons with disabilities are included in national and international education plans, and that they receive a qualitatively well-adapted education, just as other citizens do. Another objective was to contribute to the development of inclusive education. The Flagship was just one of a multitude of individuals, organizations, agencies, and projects that were working towards this end.

The development from the Jomtien World Conference on Education for All via the Salamanca Conference to the Dakar Conference illustrates the change in perspectives regarding education for persons with disabilities. A previous commonly held belief was that persons with disabilities and learning difficulties required segregated special education and rehabilitation programs. The delegates at the Jomtien Conference agreed that "steps need to be taken to provide equal access to education to every category of disabled persons as an integral part of the education system" (UNESCO, 1990, p. 5). A central point in the Salamanca declaration was that excluded or marginalized groups should be included in the regular school system, preferably in "the neighbourhood school that is, the school that would be attended if the child did not have a disability" (UNESCO, 1994, p. 17). In Point 6, the declaration referred to experience demonstrating that it is within inclusive schools that children and youth with special educational needs "can achieve the fullest educational progress and social integration" (ibid.: p. 11). At the same time, the document expressed a worry that necessary attention on persons with disabilities might disappear when they are not a particular focus. Based on experience following the Salamanca Conference, this worry was still of concern in the year 2000. UNESCO was the global overarching player that had a focus, in the UN member countries, on the implementation of the intentions that had been stated in the Jomtien, Salamanca and Dakar Declarations. At the World Conference on Education in Dakar, the international community confirmed its commitment towards the goal Education for All (EFA). In order to reach that goal, UNESCO established a number of so-called EFA Flagship programmes, each focusing on "specific EFA-related areas and problems requiring special attention" (UNESCO, 2004a: p. 7). One area was education for persons with disabilities.

The International Working Group on Disability and Development (IWGDD), an alliance of global disability groups, experts and donors had since 1997 discussed strategies and initiatives towards ensuring the continued focus on disability issues on the international EFA agenda. In cooperation with the National Commission of UNESCO in Norway, the other Nordic countries, and the World Bank, the IWGDD played an active role in the creation of the Flagship for disability and inclusive education.

UNESCO was the lead agency for the Flagship. UNESCO's Office of Inclusive Education (which later became part of the Office of Early Childhood and Inclusive Education) in its headquarters in Paris, France, cooperated with the Department of Special Needs Education at University of Oslo in Norway in hosting a joint Secretariat. The Department of Special Needs Education at University of Oslo had a three-year commitment for this effort.

Although activities varied between the EFA Flagships, all were carried out by voluntary partners, under the leadership of UNESCO and non-governmental organizations (NGOs). The other EFA Flagships focused on the Impact of HIV/AIDS on Education; Early Childhood Care and Education; Education for Rural People; Education in Situations of Emergency and Crisis; Resources on Effective

School Health (FRESH); Teachers and Quality of Education; Girls' Education; and Literacy.[1]

EFA Flagships did not have specific budgets within UNESCO, but the UNESCO Office contributed financially to some of the Secretariat's activities and travels. The University of Oslo granted me the opportunity to spend 45% of my working time as Associate Professor on Secretariat activities during the Flagship's first three years (2003–2005). The Norwegian Ministry of Education and Research financed a part-time (25%) secretary position and covered the Norwegian share of the Secretariat's running costs during this period. The Flagship had no additional financial resources. It used UNESCO's network and offices around the world to request input and to reach out with its messages.

The Norwegian Education Trust Fund of the World Bank financed a consultancy for a background concept paper for the Flagship. Terms of reference for the consultancy were developed in cooperation with the Secretariat. The consultant requested input about priorities and activities from a great number of persons and organizations. The document was completed in December 2004 (UNESCO, 2004b). It was considered a significant document that would set the agenda for the Flagship in the time that followed. Based on the concept paper, the Flagship started the process of working out an action plan and a strategic plan for activities. This work was in progress when the University of Oslo finished its three-year-long service on the Secretariat.

"NOTHING ABOUT US WITHOUT US"

The Secretariat's first task was to establish a Steering Committee, appointed according to guidelines from preparatory network meetings in Helsinki and Oslo. The slogan "Nothing about us without us" expresses the idea that no policy should be decided by any representative without the full and direct participation of members of the affected group(s). This slogan served as a guide during the establishment of the Steering Committee, as well as for the Flagship's work. The Steering Committee was established with 20 members, representing most organizations of the International Disability Alliance,[2] in addition to UNICEF, a few national UNESCO commissions, the World Bank, OECD, and two public officials in national ministries of education. The members were appointed for a period that expired at the end of 2005.

The Flagship attempted to ensure that many voices were listened to, and that perspectives presented by global, regional, and country representatives, as well as by persons with disabilities and their family members, and professionals in the field of education were considered. To underscore the global commitment and strengthen networks, Flagship-initiated arrangements took place in different countries. The

Annual Steering Committee meetings were held in Norway, in Uganda in conjunction with a conference, and in Thailand, following a regional workshop there. Working group meetings were held in Egypt, France, and Thailand.

THE FLAGSHIP'S DUAL MANDATE

The Flagship's title reflects a mandate to promote two main, interrelated issues: 1) the right to education for persons with disabilities and 2) a move towards inclusive education. The mandate was the result of a compromise between diverse opinions about the main focus.

The right to education requires more than legislative rights to be enrolled in school. It also requires that transportation, architecture, and physical environments are accessible and safe. It requires protection against discrimination, including freedom from abuse, neglect, and violations in schools. It also requires teachers who are qualified to teach learners with a diversity of abilities and needs.

> Inclusion in education is seen as a process of addressing and responding to the diversity of needs of all learners through increasing participation in learning, cultures and communities, and reducing exclusion within and from education.
>
> —(Booth, 1996, in UNESCO, 2003b, p. 7)

While *The Right to Education* was an uncontroversial issue, the move towards *Inclusive Education* was a theme of continued discussions among persons, organizations, and other stakeholders. A challenge related to the Flagship's dual mandate was illustrated during preparations for a regional UNESCO workshop in Bangkok, for South and South-East Asia in 2004, organized jointly by the Flagship and the UNESCO Office in Bangkok. The workshop's title was "Getting All Children into School and Helping Them Learn." The regional UNESCO Office in Bangkok was worried that the Flagship's focus on education for persons with disabilities would limit the participants' understanding that the phrase "all children" also refers to persons from ethnic minorities, diverse language groups, street children, orphans, children with HIV, etc.

Another challenge was that inclusion was sometimes misinterpreted as a placement issue. "By including, you are excluding" was once said by someone who had experienced the lack of educational differentiation and adaptation in settings where pupils with disabilities were seated among pupils without disabilities. Some argued that one should *in principle* be in favor of inclusive schools, but be open for different opinions and alternative approaches. Others claimed that there would always be a need also for special schools for persons with disabilities who do not receive qualitatively good education in mainstream schools. There were arguments in favor of promoting "model schools" with inclusive practice. However, there were no objections to the need for education, or about the intention to move *towards* inclusion.

The Flagship's initiatives were aimed at contributing towards the understanding that ensuring the right to education for *all* is necessarily linked to a development *towards* inclusive education, as well as to the understanding that inclusive education is more than a placement issue. The Flagship also argued that the right to education means the right to *quality* education, not just the right to a chair and a desk in a classroom, or to be registered as a pupil in a school (Wormnæs, 2004).

ADVOCACY AND RAISING AWARENESS

The Flagship had no power to enforce changes in the UN-member countries. One strategy was to identify arenas where discussions and/or presentations about education and/or disability issues were in focus. Sometimes, the Flagship would influence agendas and content at relevant conferences and meetings by recruiting speakers, giving presentations, and participating in discussions. People were encouraged to participate and give presentations, to raise questions, and to raise awareness about the right to education and/or about the move towards inclusion. It was considered important to help place disability on the agenda in settings where education was the main focus, and to place education on the agenda in settings where rights for persons with disabilities were the main focus.

One event that was organized by the Secretariat was a conference and meeting in Uganda, for initiators and Steering Committee members, as well as stakeholders in the country. This proved to be valuable in forthcoming discussions about the way forward, because the participants had shared some reflections and examples from Uganda.

Another example happened in 2005. There was a conference in the United Arab Emirates, "Urban Children and Youth in the MENA (Middle East and North Africa) Region: Addressing Priorities in Education." The networking that the Flagship participated in when preparing for the conference and at the conference itself was considered to be successful. In cooperation with the World Bank, the Flagship mobilized, encouraged, and supported a number of young persons with disabilities to participate, to take the floor and be active during discussions, and to ask questions. Through their qualified contributions, they focused on and illustrated the potential among persons with disabilities. Their participation put the right to education also for persons with disabilities on the agenda, and illustrated the added value.

One example of awareness-raising was the Flagship event at UNESCO's General Conference in Paris in October 2003. In conjunction with the conference, the UNESCO Commissions of the Nordic countries hosted a luncheon as support for the Flagship initiative. More than 40 countries were represented, many through their Ministers of Education, Heads of national delegations, or Ambassadors. The importance of addressing the needs of children with disabilities was emphasized. UNESCO members were requested to focus especially on them. In addition, topics included the need for reliable and valid data and statistics for monitoring progress of EFA, the need for external funding for implementing EFA, the value added by NGOs on the policy, advocacy, and service levels, a presentation of findings from an interim report on Millennium Development Goals for Universal Primary Education, and finally an argument in favor of partnership with the private sector about EFA.

At the 8th International Congress on Including Children with Disabilities in the Community, which took place in Norway in June 2004, the Secretariat arranged a pre-conference about the international perspective on children's rights and the implementation of EFA and children with disabilities.

In October 2004, the four collaborators, Asian Pacific Partners for Empowerment, Advocacy and Leadership (APPEAL), UNESCO Bangkok, the Section for Early Childhood and Inclusive Education of UNESCO in Paris, and the Flagship Secretariat, jointly arranged a regional workshop in Bangkok, primarily for South and South-East Asia. The overall purpose was to share experiences of inclusive education practices in the region and to explore future strategies and actions within the framework of EFA. Among the issues discussed were national plans and their implementation in relation to getting all children into school.

The Flagship was represented in committee work in New York City, where Article 17 (about Education) and Article 19 (about Accessibility) of the Convention on the Rights of Persons with Disabilities (UN, 2006) were discussed and negotiated.

In 2005, UNESCO Paris and UNESCO Bangkok were joint hosts for a round table conference with the title "Putting the Convention into Practice: Ensuring Education for All."

The Secretariat had dialogues with the Norwegian Education Trust Fund of the World Bank and the Norwegian Ministry of Foreign Affairs about the need to have a focus on persons with disabilities in poverty reduction and education strategies.

The Flagship's focus area cut across several of the other eight Flagships. There are persons with disabilities who have HIV/AIDS. Early childhood is important for persons with disabilities. There are persons with disabilities who live in rural areas. Persons with disabilities are vulnerable in emergency and crisis situations. Effective school health is important for persons with disabilities. Teachers' competences and skills are important for persons with disabilities. In certain regions, girls with disabilities are especially vulnerable. Literacy is one of the main focus areas in education. That is why the Flagship *The Right to Education for Persons with*

Disabilities: Towards Inclusion approached the other Flagships to argue for placing disability and education on their agendas, even if their main issues were girls' education, education in emergency situations, etc.

The Flagship's Secretariat identified and utilized opportunities at conferences, seminars, and workshops to disseminate information about existing resource material (such as books, booklets, videos, and web sites) and to remind planners, administrators, teacher educators, and other stakeholders about the right to education for persons with disabilities and about the international agreement to move towards inclusive education.

NATIONAL EFA PLANS AND DEVELOPMENT FRAMEWORKS

The Dakar Framework for Action (UNESCO, 2000) placed the main responsibility for achieving EFA on countries, and requested all countries to develop or strengthen existing national plans of action by 2002 at the latest. Nevertheless, when the EFA Flagship started its work in 2003, several countries were still in the process of developing their plans. The Flagship Secretariat advocated for participation of DPOs and persons with disabilities in that work. They discussed with stakeholders how to help ensure that issues related to persons with disabilities were included in EFA plans, as well as in poverty reduction plans and other developmental frameworks.

The Secretariat had received information that illustrated shortcomings. One country had developed two sets of national educational plans, worked out by two different sections of their Ministry of Education. One was for education in general, while the other addressed education for learners with disabilities and special needs. The two plans were neither integrated nor referring to each other. Through a dialogue with officers in the Ministry, we argued that this was a misinterpretation at best; by no means was it a successful step towards inclusive education.

National EFA plans are still considered crucial for developing coherent policies and plans that will "bring about real and sustainable change in education systems throughout the world and achieve the goal of Education for All" (UNESCO, 2013).

EFA GLOBAL MONITORING REPORTS

The EFA Global Monitoring reports have since 2002 been important EFA instruments. They show how the world develops towards the EFA goals. The 2002 report has the title "Is the World on Track?" In the summary, it states:

> This report is about opportunities to learn. Its primary purpose is to assess the extent to which the benefits associated with education are being extended to all children, youths and

> adults around the world and whether the commitments made two years ago in April 2000 at the World Education Forum in Dakar are being met.
>
> —(UNESCO, 2002, p. 12)

In order to monitor the implementation of the right to education and the development towards inclusion for persons with disabilities, reliable data must make their situation evident. The Flagship commented to editors of the EFA Global Monitoring report that the situation for persons with disabilities was not sufficiently documented in the 2002 report, for example regarding school enrolment, grade repetition, completion of education, and adaptation of the educational environment. As a result, the Flagship was invited to submit a short background paper, about EFA, gender and disability in Norway, to the editor of the EFA Global Monitoring Report for 2003/04. The report had the title "Gender and Education for All. The Leap to Equality." The paper emphasizes that girls with disabilities in education are mainstreamed in plans and implementation strategies in Norway (Dalen and Wormnæs, 2003). It describes a strategy along the three separate dimensions: education, disability and gender.

The following is a quote from the 2003/2004 report:

> Girls with disabilities are a large and diverse group whose educational needs have gone largely unnoticed by those committed to promoting either gender equity or disability equity. Evidence is scarce, but it seems clear that these girls are not faring well.
>
> —(UNESCO, 2003a, p. 131)

When this report was presented at an EFA Forum meeting in Oslo in 2004, the Secretariat was invited to give a prepared comment. The opportunity was used to emphasize the need for more data about the educational situation for persons with disabilities worldwide.

Through an internet consultation about the content for the 2005 report "EFA: The Quality Imperative," the Flagship Secretariat also contributed its comments.

The Flagship informed network members and professionals that literacy would be the main issue for the 2006 report, encouraging submission of information and points of view to the editors. This may have contributed to the increased attention on education for persons with disabilities in the report.

According to the World Blind Union, the report's web site for consultation was inaccessible for persons who are blind. The Flagship raised the issue of reading accessibility with the Editor of the EFA Global Monitoring Report.

STATISTICS, INDICATORS AND DOCUMENTATION

Through the establishment of an international ad hoc working group about educational statistics and indicators, the Flagship aimed at raising awareness and contributing to reflection about validity and usefulness of existing data, and about the need for more data. The thirteen participants in the ad hoc working group were key persons from different fields and interests: educational statistics, indicator development, special needs education and disability organizations, UNICEF, UNESCO Asia Pacific, and the UN Special Rapporteur on Disability.

At meetings and conferences, the Flagship informed relevant persons, organizations, and institutions about the need for quantitative and qualitative documentation about a range of phenomena of great importance not only for promoting the right to education towards inclusion, but also about the need to study the present situation and to monitor development towards education for all. Attention was drawn to the fact that in some countries the educational situation for children with disabilities was well documented if they attended special schools, but not if they were in inclusive settings.

One issue that was raised and discussed in the ad hoc group was the use of the International Classification of Functioning, Disability and Health, called ICF (WHO, 2001), in studies about education for persons with disabilities. The Flagship attempted to reach out beyond the disability community with the understanding that disability is not an inherent personal and individual characteristic. A person's functioning also depends on the context, including expectations, tasks, and environmental factors. In the ICF framework, a learner's special educational needs may be described as depending not mainly on his or her body structure or body function, but also on demands regarding participation and activity, on contextual factors in school, including teacher factors, and on personal characteristics. The Flagship was responsible for a session about this at the 20th Rehabilitation International World Congress in Oslo, Norway in 2004.

In 2001, the Washington Group on Disability Statistics was established. It focused on disability measures and accepted the ICF as the basic framework for their development of small sets of general disability measures suitable for use in censuses and surveys, as well as for the purpose of informing policy about equalization of opportunities.

The International Disability Rights Monitor (IDRM) documented and assessed the rights and conditions experienced by persons with disabilities internationally. In its 2004 report of 24 countries in the Americas, it commented that a limitation to its research was the lack of international consensus on how to define disability. The report referred to ICF as an interesting international standard, giving examples of activity-based items in a census from Brazil that were compatible with ICF (IDRM, 2004, p. 86).

The statistics group discussed the need to gather and categorize data based on the type of school or class that children with disabilities attend, rather than on the nature of their disabilities. There seemed to be a tendency that data were less reliable at secondary level than at primary level. According to the office representative, the development of new indicators for monitoring the EFA process in UNESCO's regional office for Asia and the Pacific was influenced by the exchange of information and discussions in the Flagship's working group.

Upon invitation, the working group members provided input regarding UNICEF's module for household surveys (Ten Questions). The participating disability organizations gained new insight into the reality of data collection in large-scale surveys. Their representatives claimed that participation in the meetings contributed to their possibilities for influencing the field in a more qualified manner than was previously done.

The Flagship identified other areas in need of examination and documentation (through quantitative or qualitative studies), including the complex relations between functional limitations, economy, and education; education as a vehicle for economic and social integration of people with disabilities in low-income countries; the links between begging, disability, and education; family members' opinions about the needs for education for their child with disabilities. The working group discussed and advocated for constructive and critical interpretation of school data. Among the issues that were brought up in Flagship presentations were: Reasons for non-enrolment; exclusion; non-attendance; and drop-out from school. Parental attitudes and families' fear of discrimination related to cultural factors and teacher competence are also critical, as discussed in articles from selected Pakistani and Ugandan contexts (Wormnæs and Olsen, 2009; Ojok and Wormnæs, 2012).

TEACHER EDUCATION

The discrepancy between 1) formally adopted national policies that guarantee persons with disability the right to quality education in the regular school system, while taking into account the learners' diverse needs, and 2) practice on the ground was a concern for the Flagship and a reason for establishing an ad hoc working group also about teacher education.

> What goes on in the classroom, and the impact of the teacher and teaching, has been identified in numerous studies as the crucial variable for improving learning outcomes. The way teachers teach is of critical concern in any reform designed to improve quality.
>
> —(UNESCO, 2005, p. 152)

The Flagship held discussions about how to contribute to a development where teachers are trained according to the EFA commitment. Its point of departure was that most children can benefit from ordinary education in mainstream schools if they are allowed to attend, are welcomed, are met with good environments and with appropriate teaching approaches. It was assumed that the resistance to accepting children with disabilities in schools was partly due to attitudes and/or partly to the teachers' insufficient knowledge and ideas about how to include all pupils in the learning process.

There are several reasons for difficulties in qualifying school teachers for inclusive schools. One reason is that student teachers start pre-service training with beliefs about teaching, learning, and the curriculum. Their own childhood experiences in school may predispose them to consider classroom practice in particular ways. The so-called "apprenticeship of observation," which took place when they first attended school and observed their own teachers, was first described in a seminal work by Lortie (1975). This phenomenon has been confirmed in numerous studies, serving as an inspiration to emphasize the need for good teaching and good role models (e.g., by Mewborn and Tyminski, 2006) and the need to examine the various influences that earlier experience has on prospective teachers (Hawley, Crowe and Brooks, 2012).

The Flagship's working group attempted to 1) highlight aspects of teacher competence that are required in order to move towards quality education for persons with disabilities, 2) report on successful rather than less successful experiences in previous attempts to address this issue, 3) discuss approaches for improving teacher competence.

The working group claimed that there was a need to examine, challenge, and develop contents of regular and special teachers' education in colleges and universities, with the intention of giving student teachers a good understanding of how to make inclusive classrooms and how to enhance learning for children with learning difficulties and disabilities.

Although all teachers are supposed to master a range of teaching approaches, the working group claimed that there is a need for specialist training for some professionals that can provide support to teachers in regular classrooms.

The Flagship advocated for the exploration of diverse modes of teacher education, including distance and flexible education. The use of available technologies (such as photos, videos, and internet sources) are means that may expand access to training material and training opportunities in rural areas. According to the Flagship's working group, education and training courses for awareness and implementation of effective inclusive education should also be provided to educational administrators, school management personnel, head teachers, supervisors, inspectors, and others.

CONCLUDING REMARKS

The main issues that occupied the Flagship during its three first years, from the beginning of 2003 to the end of 2005, were embedded in its title. Although apparently non-controversial, the right to education was in need of being reiterated and interpreted, in order to be enforced. It was necessary to show that it applied to *all*, with no exception. While primary education had been prioritized in many countries, the Flagship attempted to emphasize that the right to education should also include pre-school, secondary, and tertiary education. The Flagship emphasized that the legal right to education is worthless if school environment, educational approaches, and content are not adapted to the needs of the learners.

The phrase "towards inclusion" in the Flagship's title expressed an intention. The Flagship attempted to illustrate and provide ideas about how educational institutions and practice could move in the direction of inclusive education. Many stakeholders had experienced resistance and scepticism. Sometimes this was grounded in prejudice; sometimes it was grounded in realistic fear of, or inability to, create practical, emotionally safe and constructive learning environments for persons with disabilities. The Flagship attempted to contribute to dissemination of ideas, experiences, and approaches, and to emphasize the importance of documentation.

The Flagship's tools were spoken and written information, arguments, documentation, photos, videos, and the facilitation of personal encounters and accounts.

In 2005, at the end of its three years in office, the Norwegian part of the Flagship Secretariat handed the baton over to Finland. The *Right to Education for Persons with Disabilities: Towards Inclusion* had gained momentum, but it was still far from being a reality for *all*.

NOTES

1. http://www.unesco.org/education/efa/know_sharing/flagship_initiatives/
2. http://www.internationaldisabilityalliance.org/en

SECTION TWO

Implementing the Salamanca Statement and Framework for Action: National Differences

CHAPTER SEVEN

Inclusive Education, Education for All, and the Policy Cycle

XAVIER RAMBLA

Inclusive education is becoming a popular theme in debates on policy-making. Although initially presented as a method to trigger change toward social justice at the level of single schools, both the academic literature and international recommendations are more and more interested in applying this concept to the whole policy cycle. Concern with inequalities and injustice both within and around schools provides arguments to broaden up the reach of the term. Thus, about twenty years after the Salamanca Statement launched inclusive education in 1994, and a few years before the evaluation of Education for All will be conducted in 2015, a growing number of scholars and policy-makers think that both notions should be explicitly aligned.

The first section of this chapter will sketch a method of policy evaluation that may be quite helpful so that governments, civil societies and international organizations learn from a variety of applications of "inclusive education." The second section will ponder to what extent education policies become more sensitive to issues of inclusion by drawing on a "theory of change" inspired on inclusive education. Since researchers and policy-makers necessarily collaborate in education policy-making, the third section will scan specialized bibliographical databases in order to find out in which way the views of international agencies on inclusive education are discussed. The final section will overview the relationships between the international organizations that are currently working in accordance with this philosophy.

UNESCO (2009) has emphasized the synergies between inclusive education, Education for All and a holistic approach that takes into account the whole policy cycle. However, so far while a "theory of change" and some academic interest can be identified, effective implementation in a significant number of education systems remains unclear.

LEARNING FROM A VARIETY OF POLICIES AIMING AT INCLUSIVE EDUCATION

If inclusive education is to respond to the diverse needs of students endowed with disparate physical and psychological conditions, raised in both stable and vulnerable social environments, and socialized in different cultural contexts, it will inevitably be conveyed by a great variety of policies. While particular approaches to organization and pedagogy will be at stake in single schools, similar approaches to curriculum design, students' distribution into educational institutions, and teacher training, as well as ideas on inter-sectoral collaboration, will be specially important too.

Coherently, an appraisal of inclusive education will get the most out of a method of policy evaluation that makes sense of this heterogeneous set of interventions. This method can suggest significant preliminary observations that may lead further assessment later on. "Realist evaluation" promises these necessary advantages not least because it stresses "theories of change" (Pawson and Tilley, 2004; Pawson, 2006).

Realist evaluation draws on epistemological realism so as to distinguish the conception of reality assumed by social and educational policies, on the one hand, and the empirical evidence coming out from both basic research and evaluation studies that deal with that external reality, on the other hand. Policy designers are defined as social subjects whose agency is situated within the opportunities and constraints posited by the social structure. In these circumstances the knowledge that underpins their conception of reality, altogether with their interests, guide their agency. Therefore, the same general ideas may be translated into quite different policies, and these policies may be implemented in quite different ways, depending on these varied conceptions and interests. According to realist evaluation, an independent investigation of the validity of the assumptions underlying the stakeholders' views of reality may provide evidence on the likely outcomes of heterogeneous interventions. Such a perspective of evaluation is particularly helpful to explore whether some types of measures inspired on inclusive education, which will inevitably be translated into a set of heterogeneous interventions, are likely to work.

Realist evaluation understands that (public, social, educational) policies are theories of change insomuch as they entail some hypotheses about the mechanisms that may provoke an expected outcome in a given context. In line with current developments in public management, many interventions are publicly presented with an explicit formulation of this theory (Pawson and Tilley, 2004: pp. 2–6)—in fact, inclusive education is featured in this way.

However, these theories are embedded in social systems where many factors other than their validity are influential. By inquiring whether the hypothesis that links context, mechanism and outcome is confirmed by evidence, evaluators may establish families of policies with analogous assumptions, but have also to focus on each case study to find out what works for whom. Research on the political interests of the involved parties may spell out other clues of success and failure, and sometimes may raise new normative questions about the side-effects of policies. Some practitioners or some group of beneficiaries may be able to adapt the policy to their particular needs; at the same time, some beneficiaries may become excluded in new and unexpected ways. Eventually, since the final outcome depends on the influence of the policy on the reasoning of the target group, this outcome is exposed to the many uncertainties of social interaction. Therefore, many writers often conclude that evaluation can only report on the contribution of some factors to the expected outcome (Mayne, 2008; White and Phillips, 2012), because policies cannot be isolated and kept constant. These writers attempt to highlight what factors are essential, both in expected and unexpected ways, and in which aspects this intervention has produced a partial but positive effect (Klugman, 2011; Ligero, 2011).

Realist evaluation, thus, highlights the importance of knowledge by taking account of the assumptions embedded in the official design and the reasoning of the people who are exposed to the intervention on the ground. It distinguishes families of policies according to the commonalities and discrepancies between their theories, and observes who reacts in which way to these interventions. It does not provide a one-size-fits-all conclusion on whether a policy works or doesn't, but a thick description of varied circumstances where it may contribute to certain goals. In this vein, it also delivers a powerful input for the managers of knowledge who want to transfer some policies from one country to another one, as some international agencies seem to do with inclusive education. Needless to say, if evaluation is respectful with case studies and becomes aware of power relations in the implementation of policies, it can also become an empowering instrument, which can build on the capacities of the governments and the civil societies of the countries where these transfers are aimed.

In this chapter I argue that the current formulation of inclusive education, mostly conveyed by Booth and Ainscow (2002) and UNESCO (2009), entails an explicit "theory of change" that could be appraised in the terms of realist evaluation. Thus, I highlight the coherence of the assumptions presented in this theory, the contribution of some scholars to defining them, the reception of these ideas in a variety of journals, and the interest of some international agencies in this proposal. These points attempt at contributing to future case studies where realist evaluations of policies inspired on inclusive education are conducted in diverse countries. Let me also clarify that the concept "theory of change" is borrowed from the literature specialized in policy analysis, which neither deals with the epistemological and methodological discussion of what a "theory" ought to be nor attempts to assess to what extent a given "theory of change" fits with a normative definition.

IS INCLUSIVE EDUCATION UNDERPINNED BY A "THEORY OF CHANGE"?

The UNESCO (2009) *Policy Guidelines on Inclusion in Education* have been a watershed between two phases in the definition and the potential of inclusive education as a policy approach. Since this document presents a "theory of change," currently inclusive education entails an approach to the whole cycle of education policy. Moreover, the Guidelines underscore its centrality by stressing the connection between its tenets and Education for All, the main framework of educational planning and international educational development of the last decades.

The UNESCO (2009) Guidelines claim that inclusive education depends on attitudinal change, curriculum development, reform in the teaching profession and comprehensive support for the whole policy cycle. So, it relies on a set of factual, and causal, statements about what happens in reality beyond the official discourse. Right now this point requires theoretical clarification and academic discussion, and in the middle term it will have to be submitted to rigorous evaluation.

Attitudinal change is particularly relevant because inclusive education aims at changing former professional beliefs on special education. The key assumption is that children with special education needs will only be properly catered for if schools learn to deal with diverse students, whatever the reason of their diversity, either physical, psychological, social or cultural. A new culture of organization is necessary so that schools undergo experiences of collaborative work and institutional learning. And the emergence of this culture depends on the awareness of a varied set of stakeholders such as teachers, parents, the local community, the private sector and special institutions. In fact, it is noticeable that governments are not directly mentioned in the former list, as stated by the very Guidelines, although they are present somehow to the extent that they run schools, promote the policy and launch awareness programs.

Box 5: Checklist on attitudinal change
Is the concept of inclusive education well known and accepted?
Do parents take an active role in education?
Have awareness programs been launched to support inclusive education?

Are the local community and the private sector encouraged to support inclusive education?
Is inclusive education seen as an important factor for economic and social development?
Are competencies available at special schools or institutions well used to support inclusion?
—(UNESCO, 2009, p. 18)

Then, entails the following step. This curriculum is fostered by principled beliefs, sensitivity to diverse social groups and feedback mechanisms. Success in transforming the curriculum in an inclusive direction relies on a professional and social adherence to the philosophy of human rights. Professional intervention must also be concerned with the social conditions of children, youth, adults, workers, people with a different health status and ethnic minorities. Finally, the curriculum is likely to contribute to inclusion if its definition and development keep in mind a wide vision of challenges to justice, democracy and sustainable development, and teachers and schools are able to receive these wider ideas. Feedback between general visions and classroom practices is crucial at this point.

Box 6: Checklist for inclusive curricula
Are principles of non-discrimination, appreciation of diversity and tolerance being fostered through the curriculum?
Are human rights and children's rights part of the curriculum?
Does the curriculum address the coexistence of rights with responsibilities?
Is the curriculum inclusive of all children?
Is the content of the curriculum relevant to the needs and future of children and youth?
Are the programs, learning materials and teaching methods well adapted and relevant to the lives of youth and adults?
Does the curriculum allow for variation in working methods?
Does the curriculum promote education on health and nutrition?
Does the curriculum incorporate HIV/AIDS prevention education?
Is the curriculum sensitive to gender, cultural identity and language background?
Does the curriculum discuss education for sustainable development?
Does the curriculum reflect visions and goals of wider development in your country?
Is feedback gathered and integrated for regular revision of the curriculum to take new visions and circumstances into consideration?
—(UNESCO, 2009, pp. 19f.)

In addition, UNESCO makes principled and technical claims on teachers' work. In correspondence with the general mission, these professionals can only contribute to inclusion if they address their activity to all children, promote multiculturalism, and cooperate with parents and civil society. But the Guidelines also hypothesize that particular techniques are appropriate for this task, namely reminding of in-service training, recognition of mother-tongue instruction, safety, interactive methods, intergenerational issues, project-oriented work properly coordinated with theoretical teaching, and the importance of materials to respond to special needs. This is really a wholesome array of hypotheses about educational change in schools.

> Are there enough trained teachers deployed appropriately throughout the country?
> Is the teaching inclusive of all children, protective, gender responsive and encouraging of the participation of the learners themselves?
> Is the professional development and motivation of teachers enhanced by providing incentives and ongoing professional development?
> Is multilingualism embraced, particularly the recognition of the importance of mother-tongue instruction in the first years of school?
> Are the learning environments safe and healthy?
> Are teaching methods interactive?
> Are teaching methods adapted to different age groups (children, youth and adults)?
> Are teachers encouraged to work in teams?
> Is the work project-oriented?
> Is teaching predominantly theoretical?
> Do materials cater to the needs of all learners with learning difficulties (visually impaired, hearing impaired, etc.)?
> Are teachers encouraged to cooperate with parents and civil society?
>
> —(UNESCO, 2009, p. 21)

Finally, three main guidelines deal with the policy process. Mostly, their wording emphasizes a holistic understanding of the education system, embracing all types of learners, all approaches and all social sectors. Here, the underlying mechanisms appear to be the strategic value of the views embedded in the official policies and the contribution of the other sectors. If this policy network shares a sound view of the big picture, the argument suggests that the desired transformation is likely to succeed.

Policy concerns	Policy questions
Inclusive education is mainly presented as a set of separate interventions for different groups of learners	Holistic approach 1. Do policies in your country view inclusive education as a way to change the entire education system so that each learner is included in better quality education? 2. Do policies present a vision of a system unifying formal, non-formal, mainstream and segregated provision? 3. Do other sectors contribute to education (cooperation between sectors such as ministries and also with the private sector)?

—(UNESCO, 2009, p. 24)

In sum, the UNESCO (2009) *Policy Guidelines on Inclusion in Education* portray four levels of social reality where inclusive education must impinge. Their main point is that aligned changes in attitudes, curriculum, teachers' work and policy-making are enough for education systems to deal with the needs of each student whatever her origin, culture and physical or psychological condition. A logical corollary entails that change at one level is coherent with changes at the other levels. Similarly, the argument expects that bottlenecks may be formed if change is blocked at any level. This detailed account of the expected outcomes of inclusion in education, doubtless, is an exhaustive "theory of change." On these grounds, the achievement of any singular government can not only be appraised with regard to statistical indicators but also with regard to the validity of these hypotheses in varied initiatives and settings. It is a consistent tool for policy evaluation.

SOME RECENT TRENDS IN ACADEMIC WORK ON INCLUSIVE EDUCATION AND SOCIAL JUSTICE

The rationale of an official approach to a policy area is normally based on parallel debates in academia. In fact, our previous overview of inclusive education and inequalities already noticed that some scholars were working in the field, mostly at the level of single schools, and realized a general difficulty in scaling up the Index for Inclusion from schools to entire educational systems (Rambla, Ferrer, Tarabini and Verger, 2008). However, the publication of the UNESCO Guidelines has transformed the landscape by precisely proposing an index adapted to a general view of policy-making. Since that overview was written in 2008 in the immediate months after the International Conference of Education, convened by the UNESCO International Bureau of Education, right now it is quite relevant to inquire to what extent later scholarly publications have considered the scales of inclusive education located above schools. Three main topics seem to emerge from this new reading of the literature, namely social justice, educational change and teacher education.

A heterogeneous set of papers has discussed whether inclusive education fosters social justice. Their diversity is derived from their very theoretical foundations, since some of them draw on critical sociology (Slee, 2008; Kamp and Mansouri, 2010; Curcic et al., 2011), others follow the school effectiveness movement (Marchesi, 2009; Murillo and Duk, 2010), and finally, a third group applies Martha Nussbaum's theory of basic human capabilities (Polat, 2011). The main academic supporters of the UNESCO (2009) Guidelines also retrieve notions of social justice, albeit in a more general and indirect way (Acedo et al., 2009; Acedo and Opertti, 2012). While critical sociologists are suspicious of the ideological implications of inclusive education in a context of aggravating inequalities in many countries, the authors who posit the alternative views are much more confident on its potential. It is not easy to produce a short summary of this discussion because of the contrasting epistemological assumptions of the involved perspectives. Notably, critical sociology aims at unveiling the deep power relations that are not visible in many official policies with a democratic intention, whereas school effectiveness and human capabilities aim at relating empirical observations with normative reasoning. However, at first sight it is plausible to notice that inclusive education might legitimate the social order at the same time as it counteracts some consequences of social inequalities. But this is not the place to debate the contrasting epistemological assumptions; actually, it is advisable to wait for a sound base of empirical evaluations to be published.

For more than a decade, the main academic work related to inclusive education has been authored by Ainscow Mel and Booth Tony (2002), who published their *Index for Inclusion* twelve years ago. That was a practical handbook summarizing evidence on changes favoring inclusion in school-based case studies. It was an 'index' because the book provided a checklist of detailed questions that both synthesized former research and attempted to educate the gaze of professionals so that they found out new ways of promoting inclusion. The main goal was spelling out the barriers to learning, thus stimulating ideas on how to overcome them. So, a circular process of diagnosis, intervention and evaluation was shown to trigger significant changes in school settings.

This was the main available theoretical framework in 2008, when the state of the art reflected somehow a mismatch between factual claims at the micro and the macro level. Certainly, educational change had been documented in a number of specific schools where teachers' attitudes had been transformed, the curriculum had been widened and organization had become more collaborative. But although these micro-changes were not informative of the broader processes that produce and reproduce social inequality (Rambla et al., 2008), later on the same authors have shown awareness of this problem, as they have argued that power relations are also at stake (Ainscow and César, 2006). Their point on the rationality of educational organizations is particularly salient. In their view, inclusive education can neither take for granted that organizations have been designed as the best means to attain given ends nor that the original design steers their functioning indefinitely. On the contrary, schools must be contextualized in their particular situation, where other social processes have often altered or at least qualified their formal structure.

Ainscow has also written about his work with schools located in the Manchester urban area. For ten years he has led a team of teachers and researchers who have implemented and evaluated the Index for Inclusion in a network of schools with an intake composed by working-class students, some of them coming from ethnic minorities, and many of them facing conditions of social vulnerability. The latter improvement of these institutions in the standard tests of performance has become a proof of success that accredits the effectiveness of the method (Ainscow, 2005; 2010; 2012). Further analysis has observed that a "common sense of purpose" shared by teachers, parents and the community had been a crucial factor of progress. This finding underpins the sociological theory of social capital to the extent that this type of dense and close social network also explained the relative advantage of Catholic schools in the US as observed by James Coleman in the eighties. This pattern of wide, multi-lateral collaboration is the best milieu to build new capacities—consisting of teaching strategies, leisure education, career guidance and community engagement—that eventually yield an improvement in academic performance (Ainscow and Miles, 2008; Ainscow, Dyson, Goldrick and West, 2012). Remarkably, this point also underpins several hypotheses included in the "theory of change" as expressed by the UNESCO (2009) Guidelines.

Some authors have also focused on the role of leadership in inclusive education. Their conclusions highlight that head teachers may become strategic actors if they lead their schools with a system-wide view. That is, their role depends on their concern with the interests and the potential of the varied stakeholders as well as on inducing teachers to collaborate with one another (Mullick, 2013).

The proponents of the Index for Inclusion have also engaged with international cooperation. They have collaborated with the Enabling Education Network (EENET) to train teachers in many Southern, mostly Asian, countries so that they transform their own schools. According to their scholarly account of this experience, these teachers are not only learning how to improve their work but also producing relevant lessons that professionals from the North should learn (Ainscow and Sandill, 2010).

The third leading topic in the academic discussion of inclusive education has to do with teacher education. In accordance with their reliance on a general change rather than a specific response to each special education need, the proponents of this approach aim at raising sensitiveness to inclusion among future teachers rather than multiplying more specialized courses about each of the impairments that may hinder learning (Booth, 2011). Therefore, they stand for teacher education programs that stress values that are associated with solidarity; respect and sustainability; use a cross-disciplinary curriculum that makes student teachers aware of the diversity of learning environments and challenges, and propose activities that put students in contact with the local and the regional environment of universities and teacher training institutions (Booth, 2011; Florian et al., 2010). Such education must also be aware of the power relations that impinge on the education of different social groups (Purdue et al., 2009). In their view, teacher education should instill into students the necessary competences to challenge biased notions of education, sometimes of inclusion itself, that eventually legitimate segregation and discrimination (Florian and Black-Hawkins, 2011; Lalvani, 2013).

In contrast with the discussion of educational change, the controversy on teacher education cannot be understood as a direct contribution to the "theory of change." The rationale for vindicating a reform draws on normative statements about both basic and higher education that are not easy to translate into the factual terms of this theory. However, it contains a complementary reasoning on the point about teachers' work that the UNESCO (2009) Guidelines mention.

Table 1 has been elaborated in order to estimate the presence of these debates in the literature. The data map out the journals where the sample of articles on which the former review is based have been published for the recent years. Then the bibliographical indexes attributed to them by the Institute for Scientific Information (ISI) and SCOPUS are also listed. This information reveals that the *International Journal of Inclusive Education* is a relatively prestigious journal to the extent that it has been accepted by the two registers. However, it is also visible that many pieces on inclusive education are published in journals with a more feeble professional recognition, and that a better-positioned journal such as *School Effectiveness and School Improvement* pays little attention to the topic.

Table 1. Presence of inclusive education in specialized journals.

	ISI JCR (2011)	*SCOPUS SJR (2011)*
Prospects	Not indexed	391
Journal of Educational Change	Not indexed	828
International Journal of Inclusive Education	350	474
School Leadership and Management	Not indexed	762
School Effectiveness and School Improvement	800	1,139
Disability and Society	Not indexed	465
Revista Latinoamericana de Educación Inclusiva	Not indexed	Not indexed
Asian Journal of Inclusive Education	Not indexed	Not indexed

(ISI Web of Science and SCOPUS)

In brief, some correlations are quite noticeable between the rationale posited by the UNESCO (2009) Guidelines and the views of academic writers. Mostly, Ainscow's work is not only prominent in journals but has also been adopted by the international organization as the main source for consultancy. However, the attempt to extend inclusive education to the whole policy cycle has also resonated in scholarly debates about social justice and teacher education, even though these pieces of research have not been so influential as Ainscow's work on educational change.

INCLUSIVE EDUCATION AND POLICY TRANSFER

This section is a tentative appraisal of policy borrowing and transfer affecting inclusive education, which in the end is an international recommendation addressed to governments. Bilateral policy transfer has been common for more than a century since educators began undertaking pedagogic trips to learn from other countries, and governments demanded information from other countries in the nineteenth century. At that time, the German Humboldt model of higher education, the French Republican school, or the U.S. concept of differentiated education for Afro-Americans traveled from country to country in this way. Moreover, policy transfer was one of the main links between the nations engaged with each of the two blocks that engaged in the Cold War.

But nowadays the links and pace of policy transfer have undergone a dramatic transformation. No longer is a minister satisfied with bilateral exchanges, nor do governments discuss necessary reforms over long periods. The emergence of a global educational agenda, led by UNESCO and the World Bank in both consensual and conflictive ways, has also implied a proliferation of contacts between ministers and experts enrolled in international organizations. Time is also at stake since these policy innovations are diffused throughout continents very quickly. In fact, five years after the 2008 International Conference of Education we clearly witness the diffusion of policy guidelines about inclusive education in Asia and Latin America; this is a quick pace compared to the old rate of policy transfer.

International organizations are the hubs of these exchanges affecting education policies (Jakobi, 2012). Somehow, they have become banks of knowledge that accumulate information about evidence-based recommendations and policy evaluations. But some of them have also become the reference to establish new social norms about what a desirable education should be. The major role of UNESCO normally consists of this legitimation of norms.

In the same way as the list of academic journals indicates a growing interest in inclusive education in Asia and Latin America, regional supra-national organizations have promoted the idea in these two world regions. They are the Organization of Ibero-American States (OEI, in Spanish and Portuguese) and the Asian Development Bank (ADB). The ADB lends money to governments so that they carry out certain projects; its recent publication about inclusive education announces a significant diffusion by means of its operations. The OEI shares UNESCO's focus on education and culture. It could be defined as a type of commonwealth supported by Spanish and Portuguese official aid for development, but the role of Latin American governments is relatively independent and assertive in this (and many others forum). Actually, it is one among many Latin American competitive regionalisms such as the Free Trade Area of the Americas, the Venezuela-led ALBA and others. So far, it has equipped influential countries like Brazil or Chile with new opportunities to present their policies internationally, keeping a strategic distance from the US and the World Bank lines of action, which were imposed on them during the financial crisis in the eighties.

The Asian Development Bank has adhered to the tenets of inclusive education in a similar vein as UNESCO. The following quotation clearly reflects the breadth of its engagement. In the view of the Bank, inclusive education has to do with all learners regardless of their condition and age, entails concern with enrolment and quality in all educational initiatives, must start with a diagnosis, implies a cultural change, and is a continuous process. This definition is likely to summarize the conditions that future loans will require of borrowers, and the terms of the following evaluation. Notably, if this is to be done, inclusive education may escalate significantly in the region where the ADB delivers its loans.

> In summary, an inclusive approach to education
> * insists on getting all children and youth into regular public schools and mainstream systems or private systems of (at least) equal quality, and of illiterate adults in literacy programs;
> * is concerned with not only initial enrollment, regular participation, and grade promotion but also longer-term achievement through the quality of education; access to education of poor quality is not access;
> * requires both an analysis of the causes or drivers of exclusion and the proactive searching for, and targeted support to, those excluded;
> * implies the restructuring of school cultures, policies, and practices to meet the diversity of students; and
> * above all, is not an outcome, ever perfectly achieved, but rather a process, always "in process."
>
> —(ADB, 2010, p. 6)

Nonetheless, scholars warn of a rhetorical gap between official discourses and effective policies in Asia (Sharma, Forlin, Deppeler and Guang-Xue, 2013). Although these concerns are quite relevant in that, governments declare their interest and universities are debating what to do with teacher education, researchers do not find signs of actual implementation of inclusive education in many countries. Certainly, the quick pace of policy paradigms may account for this bias, but some cultural reasons are also salient. In fact, some religions transmit their own view of special education needs, which may be translated into both supportive or contrary attitudes. For this reason, if it is hard to craft a consensus on the integration of students with SEN into regular schools; in Asia, it is even harder to propose a general overhaul of the system on the grounds of catering for these and other vulnerable students by means of mainstream educational practices.

Between 2008 and 2010 the Organization of Ibero-American States (OEI) became a significant player in Latin American politics because it enacted its Educational Goals 2021. This educational strategic plan requires governments to commit to common goals, which are concretized in different benchmarks and tracks of progress depending on the countries. Thus, in this open method of coordination (quite analogous to the system adopted by the European Union) intellectual affinity is as important as effective achievement. Since the first draft of the plan went through a long process of open consultation with governments and civil societies until it was finally approved in 2010, it is plausible to interpret that such affinity was at least partially constructed in these years.

The white book of the Educational Goals 2021 devotes a whole sub-section to inclusive education. Notably, it is related to the second general goal, which is the common basis of four other specific goals. Unsurprisingly, the same labels as the ones used by the ADB are explicit in the wording of these objectives. The OEI requires governments to do their best in order to improve access and survival in the system, support ethnic minorities, foster intercultural bilingual education and respond to special education needs. Intercultural and bilingual education may be a particularity since multilingualism is much more widespread in Asia than it is in Latin America. In this continent the label refers to the commitment to teach their own language as well as Spanish or Portuguese to the children of the communities who peopled America before Columbus arrived, many of whom keep a large number of languages. Although these communities only amount to a significant share of the population in Bolivia, Ecuador, Guatemala, Mexico, Paraguay and Peru, certainly they are present everywhere.

The relevance of the concept in the white book and the timing of publication suggest that OEI is simply taking UNESCO (2009) Guidelines for granted. On the one hand, the plan simply translates UNESCO's view into Spanish and Portuguese. In several meetings and seminars the main officials have repeatedly insisted on their closeness to UNESCO. On the other hand, it was elaborated at the same time as the International Conference of Education took place, and the white book was published a year after the Guidelines.

> GENERAL SECOND GOAL
> ACHIEVING EDUCATIONAL EQUALITY AND OVERCOMING ANY KIND OF DISCRIMINATION IN EDUCATION
>
> SPECIFIC GOAL 2. Guaranteeing that all children have access to the educational system and prevent them from dropping out by means of support schemes and family involvement
> (…)
> SPECIFIC GOAL 3. Providing special support to ethnic minorities, aboriginal people, African-American population, students living in urban slums and rural areas in order to achieve educational equality
> (…)
> SPECIFIC GOAL 4. Quality intercultural bilingual education must cater to all children belonging to ethnic minorities and aboriginal peoples.
> (…)
> SPECIFIC GOAL 5. Support to the educational inclusion of students with special education needs by means of the necessary adaptations and support.
>
> —(OEI, 2010, pp. 148f.)[1]

So far, it is very difficult to assess the effects of the Educational Goals. Not only were they adopted just a few years ago, but also their budget has been severely affected by the financial and fiscal crises in Portugal and Spain. At most, a partial piece of research informs of the relationship between this plan and national politics in Brazil. In this country the Federal government has managed to build a large coalition that supports its own national plan for education, which shares the objectives and the timing of the OEI Educational Goals. The Brazilian plan has become a powerful instrument of consensus-building because it sets the standards for sub-national plans. It has also attracted the support of the civil society and transnational networks and agencies involved in educational planning, such as OEI (Rambla, 2012).

Besides the role of international organizations, the diffusion of inclusive education in Asia and Latin America is also indicative of the growing importance of social networks in the global politics of education policy borrowing and transfer (Steiner-Khamsi, 2004). Thus, Mel Ainscow has actively collaborated with EENET, Enabling Education Network, whose Asian regional branch is the most active in the world. In this context he has led several courses for teachers that have inspired his ideas on inclusive education and North-South cooperation in this field. Significantly, in Asia an international agency has get involved in the topic too, and a journal on inclusive education has just been published.

As to Latin America, Alvaro Marchesi is a prestigious Spanish professor of education who has been in charge of OEI for some years. His influence in endorsing inclusive education is noticeable in his very publications and some pieces of news widely disseminated in websites that focus on the topic. Marchesi has been the main intellectual and policy-maker who has worked to design, disseminate and promote the OEI Educational Goals. He has been the General Secretary of the Ibero American States Organization for some years, and has publicly voiced his support for the proposal of revising the whole policy cycle according to the guidelines of inclusive education.

DISCUSSION AND FINAL REMARKS

After the International Conference of Education launched a broad understanding of inclusive education in 2008 (ICE 2008), the consequences of the Salamanca Statement have become more visible. While at that time the approach that aligns inclusive education with more ambitious goals in terms of educational development had remained a matter of experimental attempts in a few schools, nowadays UNESCO has already published a "theory of change" that governments may use if they are to guide their educational policy on these tenets.

Experts are currently debating on some components of this "theory of change" in the journals. But this interest is only restricted to some groups of writers. Similarly, a couple of international agencies have adopted a similar view of inclusive education. But they are regional agencies whose action is limited to Asia and Latin America.

So far, the academic and official reception of the ideas expressed by UNESCO on a wide notion of inclusive education yields a mixed balance. Even though the ICE-2008 and the Guidelines (2009) have pushed for it, the academic and the official interest in this topic are not general. This proposal may be compared to the issues included in a recent collective book (Verger et al., 2012) on global education policy and international development, namely participation, Education for All, decentralization, lifelong learning, conditional cash transfers, school-based management, child-centered pedagogies, educational interventions in zones of conflict, and public-private partnerships. At first sight, in abstract terms, it would have not been surprising to find many connections between inclusive education and most of these issues. But a second reading of the former sections simply highlights a small interest in relating our topic with EFA, and a reiterative association of inclusive education and child-centered pedagogy. Booth and Ainscow's (2002) focus on the need to overcome the barriers to learning, in fact, expresses this connection.

To conclude, this particular meaning of inclusive education—concern with inclusive education policies, has been conveyed in a sound enough "theory of change" to enter the political and the scholarly discussion. However, so far this approach has only convinced some groups of scholars and policy-makers, mostly based in Asia and Latin America. Triggering the interest of other key prestigious journals and mainstream policy debates remains an open challenge.

NOTE

1. Original in Spanish, translation: the author.

CHAPTER EIGHT

Ongoing Exclusion Within Universal Education:

Why Education for All Is Not Inclusive

JONATHAN RIX AND JOHN PARRY

> Why is there any need for special education in a school system which is intended to educate the entire population (the so-called compulsory education system), and why has this need been continually growing?
>
> —(KIVIRAUMA AND KIVINEN, 1998, p. 153)

The issue that Kivirauma and Kivinen raised when considering the relationship between special education and the general school system anticipated a tension underpinning the original 'Education for all' agenda. The Jomtien Declaration and Framework for Action represented a comprehensive international commitment to develop access to high quality basic education for every child. The availability of such provision was regarded as a pivotal human right, essential to well being at a personal and societal level (Miles and Singal, 2010) and as aspirations appear beyond critique. However whereas the 'all' may be less contested (it encompasses all children regardless of ethnicity, gender, ability) the notion of 'education,' in terms of content, context and setting, may be more contentious. The direction set by the declarations at Jomtien steered the signatories on a course towards universal primary education but not necessarily universal inclusive education. There was no clear statement that inherent within such universality was the principle that all children should learn together within inclusive schools (Peters, 2007; Kiuppis, 2014). Consequently when participants reconvened in Salamanca four years later, those allied to furthering the rights of disabled children and those labeled with special educational needs were motivated to provide greater clarity on this dimension of the 'Education for all' agenda.

The statements that emerged from the Salamanca conference re-emphasized that disabled children and other marginalized young people should be positioned within the 'all.' No child could be considered ineducable or cast outside the domain of universal schooling (Miles and Singal, 2010). Additionally the Salamanca vision clearly framed 'education for all' children within an inclusive system:

> schools should accommodate all children regardless of their physical, intellectual, social, linguistic or other conditions. This should include disabled and gifted children, street and working children, children from remote or nomadic populations, children from linguistic, ethnic, or cultural minorities and children from other disadvantaged or marginalized areas and groups.
>
> —(UNESCO, 1994, p. 6)

In doing so Salamanca served as a reminder that: *A commitment to providing education for all children is not about 'bums on seats,' but about revisiting our conceptions about schooling and the purpose of education* (Miles and Singal, 2010, p. 12). Its Framework for Action not only affirmed that all schools should serve all children but that this inclusive approach raised the quality and experience of education for everyone (Ainscow, 1999; Rustemier, 2002).

However in the two decades post-Salamanca there has been increasing pressure on the delivery of *inclusive education for all* within school systems that are entrenched in a competitive market environment and a regime of standards, benchmarks and accountability (Armstrong, Armstrong and Spandagou, 2011). Tomlinson suggests that as governments have pursued the development of knowledge economies through education more young people have been seen as surplus to the mainstream (Tomlinson, 2012). Even in countries like Sweden that have historically engaged with inclusion, the 'turn toward neo-liberalism and educational consumerism' has relegated some groups of young people to receiving 'schooling for surviving the social and economic consequences of curtailed citizenship' rather than 'schooling for full citizenship or social transformation' (Beach and Sernhede, 2011, p. 257). Consequently in a climate of subservience to ever narrowing definitions of success and achievement, student diversity can become something to be managed and controlled whilst the principles of Salamanca inform tokenistic inclusion policies rather than educational practice.

In this chapter we acknowledge that the marketization of education has impacted on both the *Education for all* and *Inclusive education for all* agendas but we also recognize that the specific cultural context within different nations and localities will also shape how universal education is interpreted and developed

(Miles and Singal, 2010). We will therefore look at three countries in order to consider not only the wider constraints imposed by neo-liberal educational ideology but also the particular legacy of previous policies, practices and provision within each state. In doing so we hope to explore recurrent trends, contradictions and tensions in their development of inclusion within an *Education for All* agenda and discuss how widening participation in established education systems often simply reconstitutes the exclusion of those who are perpetually marginalized. Our discussions will underline why, despite the declaration at Jomtien, meeting at Salamanca was a necessity to provide a blueprint to reconstitute traditional education systems and how following that blueprint encounters frequent obstructions and diversions.

A UK EXPERIENCE

Looking firstly at the UK we find that, over the two decades since Jomtien and Salamanca there has been no significant shift towards universal inclusive education. Figures from each of the four nations show that their mainstream systems continue to struggle to include a consistent proportion of the pupil population who are consequently accommodated within the special school sector. It seems that although the education policy of the four UK nations has become increasingly devolved, this is one area where there is a great deal of parity.

In Scotland the numbers being placed outside the mainstream in units and special schools has remained relatively constant: 7140 pupils in 2005 and 6976 in 2012 (The Scottish Government, 2012a). Significantly this consistency of placements has occurred against a backdrop of a steadily declining total school population, from over 700,000 in 2005 to 671,000 in 2011 (The Scottish Government, 2012b). The data from Northern Ireland indicate similar stability over a five year period with 4598 pupils placed in special schools in the province in 2008/9, rising slightly to 4653 in 2012/13 and the total school population during the same period fluctuating between 324,000 and 325,000 (Northern Ireland Statistics and Research Agency, 2012). In Wales, (see Figure 1) there has been a 1 per cent drop in attendance of special schools in a 17-year period, though the numbers attending have gone up slightly, reflecting a slight increase in pupil numbers overall during this time. Figures from England (see Figure 2), showing a drop in special school attendance of about 3 per cent between 1995 and 2011, indicate that more pupils are being included in mainstream schools. However this needs to be balanced against the increase in pupils attending pupil referral and special units which remain largely separate from regular schools.

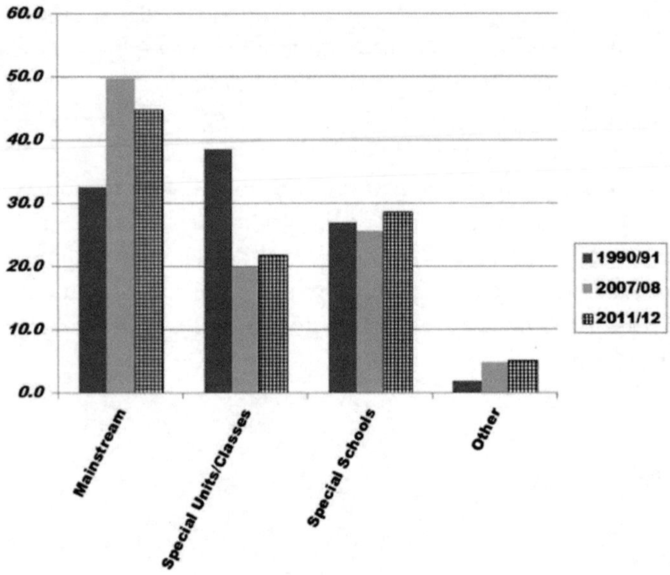

Figure 1. Destination of pupils with statements in Wales (Source: Welsh Government, 2012).

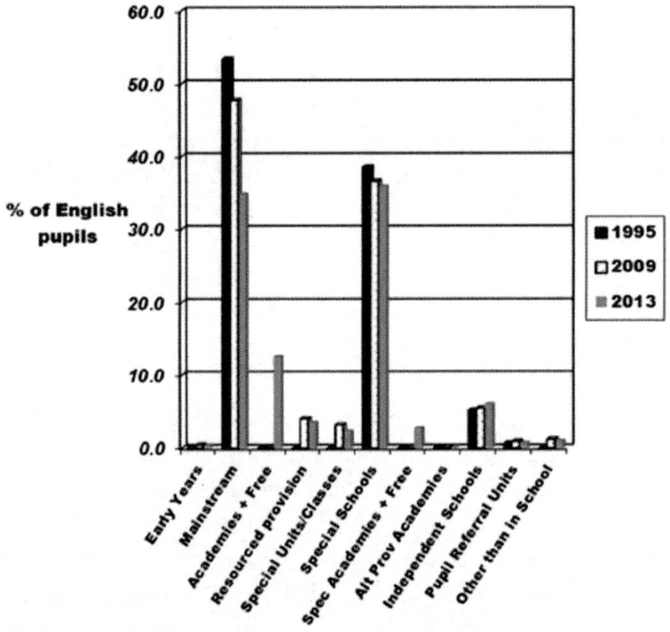

Figure 2. Destination of pupils with statements in England (DfEE, 1998; DCSF, 2009; DfE, 2011a).

The data suggests that far from any 'bias towards inclusion' (DfE, 2011b, p. 5), a situation of stasis remains and that the pursuit of *education for all* in the UK has meant making sufficient provision for pupils divided along the established lines of mainstream and special. This is not the full picture however. Many mainstream schools have engaged with the process of providing quality education for all children (Dyson and Gallanaugh, 2007; Laluvein, 2010). For example, in their focused research in Scottish primary schools Florian and Black-Hawkins were able to identify clear examples of inclusive pedagogy where teachers were:

> shifting the focus from one that is concerned with only those individuals who have been identified as having 'additional needs' to the learning of all children in the community of the classroom.
>
> —(Florian and Black-Hawkins, 2011, p. 818)

However what also became clear from this research was that those teachers who wished to develop such inclusive pedagogy were faced with 'a number of challenges and dilemmas in practice' (p. 819) which were created by school policy rather than the classroom situation. For example setting pupils by 'ability' limited the teacher's opportunities to group children more flexibly and the required approach to differentiation, matching activities to perceived individual ability, marginalised children and fragmented the opportunities of interactive learning.

Florian and Black-Hawkins's research highlights that 'the determinist beliefs that pervade education policy make it difficult for teachers to take alternative decisions and actions that reject such beliefs' (p. 820). Wayne Veck found that learning support assistants (LSA) were similarly constrained in their role not so much by specific policies but by entrenched attitudes and practices revolving around their one-to-one support role with students (Veck, 2009). With this restricted remit the LSAs were devalued as practitioners and their educational contribution overlooked within the college in which they worked. The one-to-one support allowed the students access to rather significant participation in the classroom and 'became part of the "rituals and cultural practices" that fortified borders between who is valued and who is not, between who is judged to fit and who must be excluded' (Veck, 2009, p. 47). Veck suggests that this fixed approach to providing support denies the LSA 'the opportunity to enhance educational spaces for all students' and will consequently 'block inclusive imagination' (p. 49).

In longitudinal research carried out by the authors in two UK secondary schools there was similar evidence of established processes and practice undermining intentions to develop inclusion (Parry et al., 2013). Drawing upon two research visits ten years apart to each school, this study showed in both cases there was a shift away from practices which were previously seen as being central to the development of inclusion. In one school the focal point of the provision was a resourced unit for a group of pupils identified with 'complex special educational needs,' located in a separate building on the campus. Initially students from this base were included in a wide range of lessons in the main part of the school and within-year group activities along with the rest of their peers. A decade later, despite an extensive construction programme which saw the facility relocated to the heart of the school building, it was evident that the unit had become more of a separate school within a school. Students only attended certain 'non academic' lessons in the main school and their opportunities to socialize with peers in the communal areas during break times were restricted by the availability of staff to 'supervise.'

Inclusion and participation in the second school was promoted through its focus on engaging with the local community, vibrant pupil councils and supporting all children to learn in ordinary classrooms. On the return visit ten years later the pupil councils had become inactive and the location of community services on campus had failed to materialise. A wide range of pupils were still accommodated within the school but the LSAs reflected that they spent more time in a new Additional Support Department teaching groups and individuals than in the main school. As with the first school major rebuilding had also taken place resulting in a brand new fully accessible school. However the Additional Support Department was now situated in the basement as part of the modernisation or as the LSAs observed 'stuck away in the corner,' 'less integrated' and 'out of sight, out of mind.'

Both schools attributed their increased use of separate provision for specific groups of pupils as a necessary response to a national standards agenda which required a focus on pupil performance, league tables, a specified curriculum and successful inspections. The connection between children's perceived level of difficulty, amount of support available and time spent in the mainstream classrooms increasingly framed decisions about the placement of pupils. Decisions were being made in response to widening participation for what the two settings perceived to be a changing pupil demographic, children labelled with 'complex and profound learning difficulties' and 'challenging behaviours.' Consequently this meant a fragile compromise between managing students who might disrupt long standing classroom routines and addressing these same pupils' potential failure in the established educational structure (Armstrong et al., 2011). Increasing stratification of provision around specific individuals or groups of pupils became the framework which both schools believed was necessary to continue to respond to the educational needs of the children, a framework embedded in 'the institutional separation of "regular" and "special" schooling' (Slee, 2008, p. 99). The resilience of such compartmentalization and its underlying influence on education systems is a theme that resonates when examining the developments in the United States.

A U.S. EXPERIENCE

As is evident from the building projects at the heart of the UK experience above, many countries have been increasing expenditure on education for all and in particular upon special education. In the United States (U.S.), for example, between 1996 and 2005 41% of all increased expenditure was on special education, to a point where it was estimated at 21% of all education spending for 13.8 % of the school population. Since 2005 this growth stabilized with some slight drops for some types of impairment (e.g.: 'specific learning disabilities' and 'mental retardation') and rises for others (e.g.: 'Autism' and 'other health impairment') but still represented 13.1 percent of all students in 2009–10 (Scull and Winkler, 2011). Despite this expenditure however, familiar problems seem to remain. In summarizing their study of the recent trends Scull and Winkler conclude:

> America needs to approach special education with greater creativity and flexibility in the future than it has shown in the past. Instead of engaging in polarizing discussions around whether to mainstream students versus serve them in pull-out settings—or around the disproportionate identification of students by race—let's focus on how to differentiate learning for all students. In other words, how can we make education "special" for every one of our students, reserving unique services for the small percentage of severely disabled children who need them?
>
> —(Scull and Winkler, 2011, p. 16)

These challenges exist within a system which has undertaken sustained policy development focused upon marketization and standardization and produced a legislative framework entitled No Child Left Behind. This marketization policy agenda would appear to have had little positive impact. In their reports on the impact of Charter Schools (U.S. schools freed from centralized control) the Center for Research on Education Outcomes at Stanford University (CREDO, 2009; 2013), found that in 2009 there was a slightly negative picture of average charter school performance, with academic development being slightly lower than traditional state schools, whilst in 2013 results were a slight improvement on the 2009 study (see Figure 3). However any slight gains had to be set against Charters having over 35% fewer Special Education Students (8%) compared to the overall National Average of all schools (13%) and having more focus upon the teaching of English and Math.

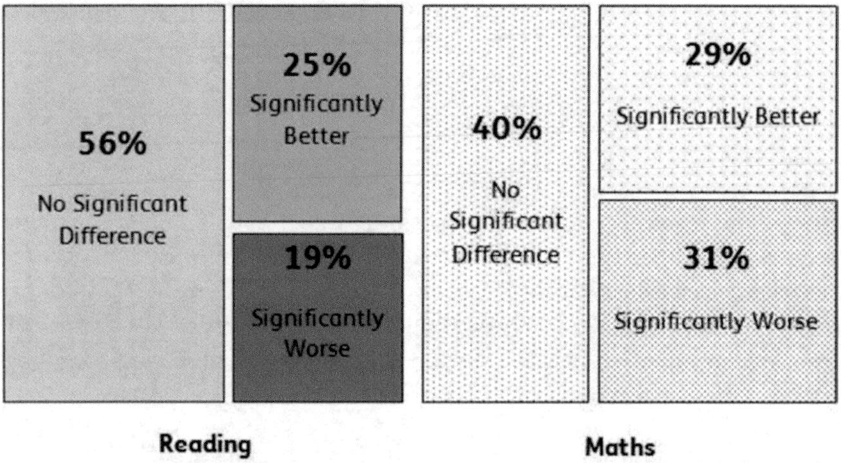

Figure 3. Academic growth of charter schools for all students in reading and math compared to their local markets. (There were small identified learning gains in these two subjects in Charters that were in the 2009 study but not new Charters.)

Standardization approaches similarly seemed to recreate marginalization in the name of Learning for All and Inclusion. Waitoller and Kozleski (under review) report upon a professional learning school relationship between a university and three elementary urban schools in the U.S. aiming to transform schools for inclusive education. They identify the pervasive notion of *quality for all students,* and how this is used to drive change, in particular through team curriculum-design, classroom observation, and performativity—a standardization technology using public displays of data to judge, compare and supposedly control quality. These displays of data (i.e.: data walls) were seen as objective and neutral and served as a rationale for correcting teaching practices. The intention is that teachers can inspect, correct and appraise themselves. The data walls presented all the students scores on standardized tests and served as a point of discussion at weekly meetings. It became evident to the university partners that the dominant professional vision of an inclusive teacher had been a need to identify which students were falling behind their peers:

> In the professional vision of the school, inclusion for all students meant auditing and inspection for all.
>
> —(Waitoller and Kozleski, in press)

The students were reduced to single scores representing performance on a narrow skill. The authors concluded that as a result of these work practices:

> Inclusive education has resulted in the continuation of labeling and segregation of those students considered different from the dominant culture of the school.
>
> —(Waitoller and Kozleski, in press)

These were not the old labels of special education though:

> We demonstrated that though teachers and administrators aimed to erase special education disability categories from their discourse and practice during Friday meetings, new labels and sorting mechanisms emerged according to the assessments dictated by the school district.
> —(Waitoller and Kozleski, in press)

Another cornerstone of the standards agenda, evidence-based practice would also seem to be problematic. In noting the minimal impact of evidence-based practice in the context of the U.S., Scull and Winkler (2011), speculate that approaches such as Response to Intervention (RTI) may be partly responsible for a drop in numbers identified with specific learning disabilities but they cannot call on research comparing different parts of the country or which can demonstrate the wider impact of RTI. Similarly, where some researchers feel there has been clear research evidence the impact has been shown to be negligible. For example, McLesky and Waldron (2011) examined a range of different study types in segregated settings to identify components of High-Quality, Intensive Instruction for Elementary Students with Learning Disabilities and then considered the extent to which these could be delivered in mainstream settings. They identified a range of very practical and manageable practices, but somewhat ironically, even though all these findings come from research conducted within segregated provision McLesky and Waldron had to recognize that these approaches were used rarely if at all in either separate provision or the mainstream.

The U.S. experience suggests that the policies aiming to use the values of markets and standards do not create a new space, but perpetuate the old divides between schools and within schools. As the findings of McLesky and Waldron seem to demonstrate these seemingly dramatic shifts in policy do not bring into question the old ways of working. The unreconstructed aim to achieve education for all means that quite a few children are still being left behind. In the next section we will consider one countries experience to explore what some of the old ways of working may be.

A NORWEGIAN EXPERIENCE[1]

A number of countries have taken what might be seen as a more dramatic step in their aims to deliver inclusive education. They have closed their special schools and by implication required the mainstream to adapt. Norwegian Special Schools closed in 1993 to become advisory centers alongside the Pedagogical Psychological Service (PPS) which oversaw the assessment and funding of school provision for children with special educational needs. However, the closure of special schools has by no means meant the end of segregation and separate provision. The national data for 2010 recorded the ongoing presence of official 'strengthened schools' providing segregated provision for about 0.3% of pupils, and full-time special education in the mainstream for 0.8% and part-time for 7.6 per cent. However there is also an unknown amount of provision which falls outside of the official statistics and considerable separation within everyday classrooms.

The Norwegian Education Act 1998 gave all pupils the right to adapted education[2] whilst maintaining that pupils had the right to special education if they did not, or were unable, to benefit satisfactorily from ordinary tuition. Despite many people seeing these two clauses as being in conflict subsequent policies embedded the dichotomy. For example, Equity in Education for All (Utdanningsdirektoratet, 2008) required positive discrimination, at a national systemic level and at an individual level, with Inclusive education, Adapted education and Special education all having a key role.

Interviewees suggested that the concepts and tensions between 'adaptive' and 'special' were formed from the 'legacy' of the previous policy context. This resulted in the belief that a young person with learning difficulties needed to be with his/her peers but, nevertheless, needed to learn something different from the rest of the class group. The consequence was not only withdrawal from the classroom but also internal exclusion within the classroom. For example pupils were taught at the back of classrooms by a special teacher while their peers worked on something completely different. There was a belief that different practices could be inserted into various spaces, which meant the spaces themselves were not being modified.

The lack of a nationally organized system of training and provision was seen as leading to practices varying from school to school. Locally, all kinds of provision could emerge. For example a parent talked effusively of a school she had worked at where they had a shed to accommodate a child with Down syndrome; this meant the child could work on her own but at the same time still see the other children. It was noted by all interviewees that children experienced segregation in both mainstream and strengthened schools, often spending most of their day in separate rooms. For example, at a strengthened school pupils had separate rooms to work uninterrupted with a special teacher, despite attempts by management to move to small group work. Staff described this as an old habit, arising from a wish not to be interrupted or distracted, as something 'into our veins' and hard to eradicate, even after the PPS criticized the practice.

The type and amount of support pupils received depended upon what was considered to be 'benefiting' from 'normal' (adaptive) education. This 'normal' education seemed to emerge from a long tradition with a focus upon literacy and numeracy and 'some basic things from daily life.' Teachers questioned why pupils could not do what their peers were doing rather than whether they needed to be doing an activity at all. This deviation from the normal curriculum was regarded as 'special education.' Special education became norm-referenced in relation to the pupil, focused upon them rather than the learning environment and determined by individual practitioners in PPS.

Interviewees found it hard to delineate the practical difference between ordinary adaptive and special adaptive education but they believed that there was a difference and that some pupils needed the latter. The following diagram was drawn for us:

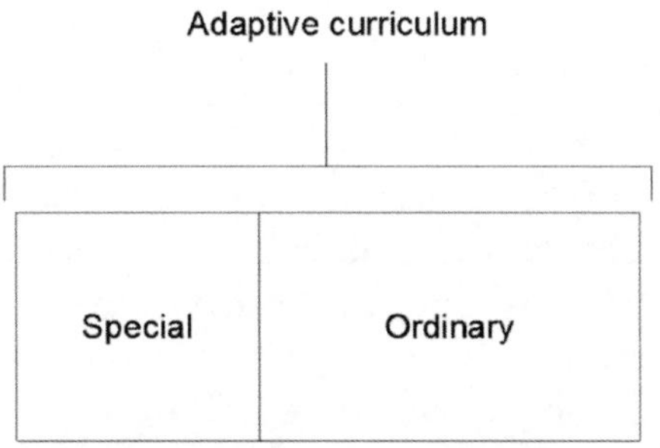

The research team was not able to form a clear picture of the difference. It appeared that all these concepts defined each other. However, it was equally evident that practitioners were well aware of their professional responsibilities and of the moral force of national legislation. Interviewees explained that no teachers would question the policy or the theoretical concept of inclusion; but they seemed willing to live with the contradictions. For example, the official goal of policy was to identify children with special needs as early as possible, but the steady increase of special teaching from grade 1–10 resulted in a Norwegian saying that 'we practise late intervention rather than early intervention' (see Figure 4)

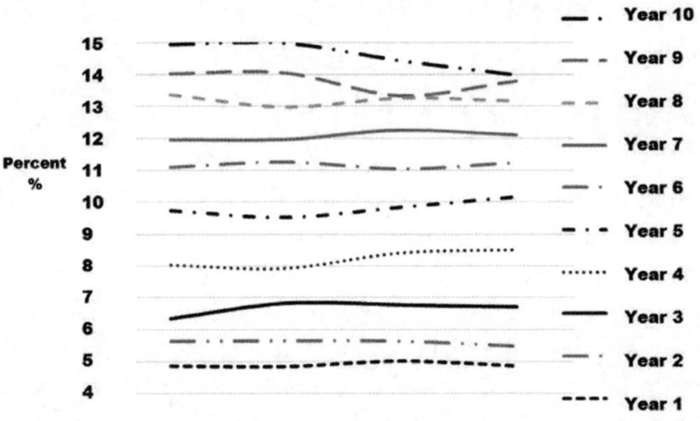

Figure 4. Graph representing incremental support needs across years in Norway. Each shaded line represents the percentage in special education from year 2 at the bottom to year 10 at the top. (Source: Hausstätter, 2011, in Rix et al., 2013, p. 121).

This pattern of changing support reflected the attitudes of managers and staff. They described how inclusion was 'very easy' when the children were young, but problems emerged as schools got closer to and entered the secondary phase. This was described partly as a consequence of an increasing academic focus and partly because of a developmental view of children's relationships:

> … because the older they got, the tougher the curriculum got, the more theoretical, the less they were part of their group of peers in the school. So the difference between them and their peers grew as they grew older, so they had little to do, or less and less to do in the mainstream school.

The managers and staff did neither raise the issue of 'pupil voice' nor the capacity of young people to have diverse relationships outside schools. By implication, their view of an inherent teenage disinterest in those on the social margins was counter-balanced by policy clearly related to social awareness and acceptance of 'difference'; however these policies were in turn set against the top-down pressure for schools to demonstrate higher grades in academic outcomes, as well as the previous policy contexts. Inclusion, it was suggested, had been initiated within a 'conservative' education system. Practice within this system had not changed or had only appeared to change before it reverted to previous practice. As a support teacher who had been working for two decades asked:

> Why haven't we come further than this? […] What is going on in the ordinary education is still the same.

Many interviewees suggested that teaching in Norway 'used to be more or less a private thing for the teacher' that is, the teacher operated in isolation and without interference. There was a strong sense of teachers focused on good exam results rather than integrating children into their class. The longstanding response of teachers was that

> In general, teachers, when they face students with special needs or problems … don't really know how to look at the problem.

Teachers wanted further resources to address problems. Teachers and schools became 'clever' at producing an administrative decision which resulted in special education provision and parents become very protective of their children's allocated hours of support. There seemed to be some awareness of the risks of focusing upon diagnoses and functional assessment but interviewees noted a deep respect for, and desire to listen to, 'expertise.' Despite a lack of definition of the nature of this expertise there was considerable respect for colleagues further up the hierarchy or within certain elevated professions, and there was little evidence of distributed leadership. Similarly, attitudes to children, colleagues and matters of education were directly linked by interviewees to issues of training and the implied expertise which it provided. However, the focus of this training (for example emerging from a different subject-base or the different theoretical allegiances of different universities or a different field of education, health and care) varied enormously, and as a result there were many examples of different 'cultures meeting,' not only between professional groupings but within them too. For instance, teachers were aware of, and extremely loyal to, their initial training institution and could identify where their training differed from their colleagues. Several interviewees, from a range of backgrounds, described the importance of 'speaking the language' of other groups. Despite the reliance upon expertise therefore the range of professionals involved undermined the roles the expertise could play, since the communication served as a barrier to professionals working together, compounding the traditional differences generated by training.

This reliance upon expertise also meant that it was seen in place where it might not be expected to exist. Ordinary teachers therefore were dependent on special teachers and assessors to determine programs for pupils in their class; they frequently had an unease about who had responsibility for the pupil. However, support assistants working with children with special educational needs did not require any formal training and qualified teachers did not require additional training. They had the expertise of experience.

CONCLUSION

The issues identified above are representative of many countries (if not all) which have an established education system. The challenge of delivering inclusion in a system aiming at education for all is about 'a web of ideological positions, entrenched interests, and education and social policies' (Richardson and Powell, 2011, p. 280), but also about the organizational location of its services and the everyday reality of mainstream provision:

> The main source of special education clients remains the "regular" classroom and "regular" educators, especially those who even if well meaning suffer from a lack of resources and training and thus neglect to serve all students regardless of the students' individual characteristics. Conversely, general education is dependent on special education when it supplies additional and specialized pedagogies and services, offers an alternative educational environment when general education is challenged, and accepts those students removed from general education.
>
> —(Richardson and Powell, 2011, p. 281)

It would seem that special needs education and universal education's need for 'special needs' are both reinforced and broadened by the widening of participation within schools. An unreconstituted education system, attempting to deliver education for more young people, inevitably pushes greater numbers to the margins.

The call for Education for All within an unreconstructed education system can only be answered by the expansion of special education. As a consequence any call for Inclusive Education for All, as at Salamanca, has to be a call for the reevaluation of our ideas about education and the systematic ways in which we deliver on those ideas. If it is not then Inclusion becomes inherently associated with Special Educational Needs. This creates a self-perpetuating cycle. As Slee (2008) recognizes the association with SEN undermines the chance of inclusive education achieving its educational and social reform agenda. It accepts the prevailing medical and psychological understandings of disability, targeting the 'defects' within an individual and ignoring the contribution of wider political, economic and social factors in the construction of disablement. It also limits our thinking, reinforcing 'an unwillingness to engage with the cultural and institutional grammar of schooling to identify the social nature of disablement' (p. 108).

The wealth of literature which has emerged in recent years demonstrates that change needs to be system wide, at all levels of education. It provides plentiful scope for reflection too. For example, schools could engage in a fluid process of 'continuous struggle' (Allan, 2008, p. 101), involving a change in the 'behaviour' of adults (Ainscow and Sandill, 2010), adopting a pedagogy which is underpinned by a principle of transformability (Hart, 2010), drawing flexibly upon a class-community and cooperative learning structures (Naraian, 2011), and using a curriculum based upon values and rights (Booth, 2011). They can do so too with increasing numbers of specific pedagogic approaches which have been shown to be effective and which are accessible for all practitioners, building on skills they already have available to them (Rix and Sheehy, 2013). Despite these opportunities, however, as we have attempted to show within this chapter, separate and segregatory provision continues.

There has been minimal impact from a range of different policy processes, be that a call for inclusion, special school closure, a choice agenda or a drive for higher standards for all. The wider legacy of education seems to be the barrier. It is our reliance upon traditional ways of teaching using traditional subjects and assessment, focusing upon numeracy and literacy, within primary and secondary structures which underline an academic-vocational divide. It is about the bureaucratic need for funding streams, professionals' processes of training, their established ways of working and their models of thinking. And of course anybody who has an interest in the subject knows that this is why inclusion is so hard to realize. As one Norwegian practitioner so succinctly explained:

> I guess it is a little of many things. It's got to do with workload. It's got to do with money. It has got to do with curriculum. And it also has got to do with attitudes, because people's attitudes are different. [....] We are locked in and we don't have time to do this [share our competence] so, I have chosen to say it is a system problem.
>
> —(Rix et al., 2013, p. 145)

NOTES

1. This section is based upon research conducted in 2011 in 50 countries by the first author with colleagues from the Open University. As part of this research they conducted interviews, visited settings and explored the policy processes in Norway, Italy, Ireland and Japan (Rix et al., 2013). The underlying challenges to inclusion raised here in relation to Norway could equally be applied to these other countries.
2. Education that was 'adapted to the abilities and aptitudes of individual pupils.'

CHAPTER NINE

From Integration to Inclusion and the Role of Special Education

RUNE SARROMAA HAUSSTÄTTER AND MARKKU JAHNUKAINEN

The Salamanca Statement was presented in a period where most Western countries were working on integrating children who were excluded from the ordinary educational system. The process of integration started as part of the general social critique in the late 1960s (Simons and Masschelein, 2005), and integration was far from being fulfilled when the Salamanca Statement was ratified in 1994. In spite of the lack of fulfillment with integration, the concept of integration was quickly abandoned in favor of the new popular concept of inclusion. This transition of concepts has lead to confusion both at a political and an academic level—a bewilderment that relieves itself when we look into how inclusion is transformed into actual education. One reason for this confusion might be the lack of fulfillment of integration. Hence, the lack of accomplishment with integration meant that transition from integration to inclusion had to relate to the goals of the previous concept of integration, making the distinction between integration and inclusion even more blurred.

The realization of inclusion into educational practice was left to the national or local level—in most cases the same people who at the time were faced with the challenge of integrating students with special needs into ordinary education. In other words, the new concept of inclusion was not supported by a global strategy on how to create inclusive education. And perhaps even more challenging, at the same time the realization of inclusion inherited the previous challenges faced by integration. This mix of the old goal of integration and the newcomer inclusion might very well be one central reason why Kiuppis (2011) found that the concept of inclusion did not present itself as a common fixed, global goal of education, but on the contrary, the goal of inclusion was nationally altered to fit already existing educational strategies.

The fact that the realization of inclusive education differs enormously between countries is central in this chapter. We claim that the relationship between integration and inclusion is a central reason for the difference experienced today when nations develop their inclusive strategy. Drawing from the development of inclusive education in two different countries, Norway and Finland, this chapter will try to highlight the relation between integration and inclusion, and will subsequently discuss challenges facing the goal of creating inclusive schools when it is operationalized into strategies of education.

INTEGRATION AND INCLUSION

In order to understand the transformation of inclusive goals into educational practice it is necessary to point to the development of inclusion as an alternative to the goal of integration. Before the Salamanca Statement, from the 1960s, integration was the dominant way to describe the policy development within this field in most Western countries. As a Western concept, integration was established as a goal for educational systems that had already developed a segregated school system for people with different disabilities. This was a segregated school system supported by the special educational profession. The goal for integration was to restructure the educational system so that all children had the right to education, the education should be offered in local schools, and that there would be a reorganization of the special education system (Vislie, 2003). The goal of integration highlighted the role of special education as part of the general educational system and it emphasized the right all children had to receive sufficient educational support for further life. Integration according to Vislie was demanding (2003, p. 19):

- *rights to schooling and education* for disabled children. Although 'all children' at that time were said to have a right to education, there were groups of children in most countries who did not have this right. Due to their disability, they were either provided for in other institutions (social, medical, etc.) or not in any institution at all (by category, excluded as 'not educable').
- *right to education in local schools* for disabled children, originally formulated as an attack on the centralized institutions normally established as special schools for designated categories of disabled pupils (e.g. the separate special school system).

- *total reorganization of the special education system,* focusing on aspects of it, from the identification of its clients to the financial issues followed by integration, the internal local school organizational structure, and the handling of teaching and learning, including special education, in integrated classes.

According to Vislie (1995) two strategies of integration were developed during the 1970s and 1980s. The first strategy was related to the development of the special educational area to meet the new demands of integration. The second strategy was to reformulate the regular school system to meet an increased diversity of students. Norway and Finland will, as discussed later, function as examples of how these two approaches were adapted into educational practice. To sum up, the concept integration developed as part of the general social critique in the 1960s, and it dominated the policy rhetoric in several Western countries in the 1970s and 1980s. Integration developed as a response to the segregated school system that developed extensively in the 1950s and in the 1960s. In other words, it seems fair to say that integration is a process established as a response to a segregated school system. The focus was on children with special needs and the goal was to integrate these groups of children into the ordinary school system. According to Tetler (2000) integration is about making us whole human beings. In this respect the point of integration is to re-establish the student after segregated processes.

Turning to the concept of inclusive education, Tetler (2000) points to the difference between these two concepts and argues that inclusion has to do with the integrity of all children. In other words the point is not to re-establish us as humans, as we are all complete humans and the goal of inclusive education is to foster this wholeness. As pointed out by Haug (2003a) the concept is highly ideological and political—and closely linked to general goals of mutual acceptance and participation in society. The concept can be defined in several different ways but most aspects seem to be covered by Haug's (2003b) definition which states that inclusion is:

- to increase fellowship. All children should be members of a school class and take part in social life at school together.
- to increase participation. Genuine participation, as distinct from being an onlooker, involves two processes: the creation of opportunities for everyone to be involved socially with others and active encouragement to be involved.
- to increase democratization. All voices should be heard. All students shall have the opportunity to comment upon and to influence matters concerning their own education.
- to increase benefit. All students should have an education that enables them to learn and participate (p. 97).

This definition underlines that inclusion is not about focusing on an individual or a small group of pupils and adapts the curriculum according to their specific needs. Inclusion is not about integrating groups of students with special needs into an already pre-defined school structure. An inclusive school is an institution that changes and adapts to the needs of all students according to the general goals of inclusion. As pointed out by Sebba and Ainscow (1996) inclusion is more about the process, and not the state of being inclusive. In other words, an inclusive school is a school that works towards becoming inclusive and according to Haug (2003b), this implies a kind of fellowship and participation that is fostered through a school organization that welcomes and can deal with diversity. This is a process of changing the school to facilitate all students. However, this implies a process that will continually change according to the tasks faced in education. Inclusion is therefore essentially about how we define good education (Biesta, 2010) and the process of developing the educational system further. Hence, according to Hausstätter (2013) inclusion as a goal for education needs to stay unfinished as a continuous reminder of the difficulties faced by the educational system when developing a school for all.

To sum up, inclusion is presented as a general principle of education. It is a contribution to the discussion on what we mean by good education for all. In addition, it is clear that strategies of integration are not in conflict with inclusion; on the contrary, success with inclusion is dependent on integration. Educational systems that have developed a segregated alternative for groups of children need to carry through the process of integration before or at the same time as they develop strategies of inclusive education. This might be the reason for the previous strategies found in the framework of integration; the development of the special educational area to meet the new demands and the strategy to reformulate the regular school system were not abandoned when the goal of inclusive education was presented through the Salamanca Statement. On the contrary, the two strategies seem to be adapted as strategies for inclusion and how inclusion is brought into the educational context.

THE ROLE OF SPECIAL EDUCATION

As pointed out, one of the strategies for integration is the development of special education to support the integration of students with special needs. The role of special education in relation to integration is therefore not very problematic. However, if we turn to the framework of inclusive education the relationship to special education becomes more complicated (Hausstätter, 2011).

Special education was first developed as an alternative to support the education of people with disabilities (Richardson and Powell, 2011; Thuen, 2013), and then incorporated into institutions that in some form or other took care of disabled people (Danforth, 2009; Kirkebæk, 1993). The historical heritage of the special educational profession has been presented as not compatible with inclusive education, and that an inclusive school must be established on new grounds without the need for special education (Gallagher, Heshusius, Iano, and Skrtic, 2004). However, in spite of the challenging historical heritage of special education, the Salamanca Statement is not categorically against special educational support, but on the contrary the statement emphasizes the necessity to support all children and does not reject the fact that some of those children have special educational needs. However, this help should be offered as part of the ordinary educational system and not as a segregated support system. Thus, before students are offered special education, it is necessary to clarify why there is a need for special education and if this need for support can be reduced through changing the school structure or the standard education offered:

> The expectation to the inclusive school is that it must master the variety, inequality and differences well and better than the school has done before. This will reduce the need for special measures. This means that one should change from teaching classes and groups towards cooperation in order to provide individual assignments, supervision and challenges to all pupils. A so radical and difficult reform requires a broad effort from all to succeed, because it is necessary to break the fundamental and deeply established pattern both in normal education and special education. (Haug, 2003b: p. 92)

In other words, the relationship between integration, inclusion, and the role of special education as presented is not clear-cut. Challenges experienced with integration are influencing the way inclusion is handled, and the role of special education as a support to ordinary education is not yet clear. As stated in the introduction, this unclear relationship will lead to national differences in the practice of inclusive education. These differences will further lead to differences in the use of special education. In the second part of this chapter, Norway and Finland are presented as examples of how different historical traditions have led to different approaches to inclusive education.

EXAMPLE

Norway and Finland are chosen due to both their similarities and their differences. As pointed out by Takala and Hausstätter (2012), the Norwegian and the Finnish school systems do have a lot in common, but there is also a historical difference between these two countries that seems to cause different approaches to inclusion. The countries are similar in size and population. They are both rich countries that have developed within the Nordic welfare state model. Both countries are dominated by a public school system with only a small percentage of pupils in private schools. However, there are some intriguing differences. Most of the special schools were closed down in Norway as part of the integration reform, whereas Finland still has a substantial amount of children in special schools or in special classes. Secondly, Finland is rated as one of the best school systems in the world by OECD (PISA), whereas Norway's results are about average. One reason for the success of the Finnish school system might be the special educational support system (Hausstätter and Takala, 2011; Itkonen and Jahnukainen, 2010; Kivirauma and Ruoho, 2007).

Although there are some differences in the historic roots of the educational systems in Finland and Norway, both countries had the same school structure after the Second World War. Until the 1970s, the system was based on a six/seven year primary education followed by a two-track parallel school system divided between a vocational or an academic alternative. In addition, the school systems had an extensive development of a segregated special school system both with special schools and special support classes in this period. However, the school system changed a lot in the 1970s as part of the huge social awareness that dominated this time period. Both Finland and Norway changed their basic education into a nine-year compulsory system. The dominant argument for this change was that research had shown that students' choice between the vocational or academic route was defined by social and economic factors and not by their academic skills (Hernes, 1974). A nine-year compulsory system should give more equal opportunities for all to develop their abilities. However, this change in the school structure increased a central challenge of the ordinary school system. More students meant an increase in the diversity of the student population. Norway and Finland reacted differently to the challenge of diversity, and these differences experienced 40 years ago might give an explanation for the differences experienced today. These differences will also have implications on how the goal of inclusion is faced.

1970s reform

Both countries had developed an extensive special school system before the school reform in the 1970s. However, Finland and Norway reacted differently to the challenges of diversity that were part of this reform. The Finnish strategy was to focus on the special educational support system and to develop systems that could meet the diversity challenge. In practice this meant that Finland started to train special teachers that could be part of the support system in ordinary schools. However, the special school system was not abandoned; it was developed as part of the compulsory schooling. The number of special schools as well as the number of students placed in these schools did not start to decrease until the early 1990s (Jahnukainen, 2011).

The Norwegian strategy was quite different. Norwegian policy development was highly influenced by the normalization and integration debate (Tøssebro, 2010). The first sign of this is the integration of the special educational school law into the ordinary educational act. In 1975 Norway had one school law for all children. Throughout the 1970s and the 1980s more and more children with learning disabilities where integrated into the ordinary school system. The process ended in 1993 when almost all special schools and all central institutions were closed down. It is necessary to point out that the Norwegian special educational system did not have a central position in these changes. One reason for this was the growing idea that special education was a central reason for the problems defined by the theories of normalization and integration.

Norway and adapted teaching

The goal of integrating students physically into the ordinary school system was more or less fulfilled in 1993—one year before Norway ratified the Salamanca Statement. The close down of special schools and the strong drive toward integrating students with special needs in the 1980s and the early 1990s meant that the ratification of the Salamanca Statement did not lead to any new national strategy when meeting children with special needs. The process of integration had already fulfilled most of the organizational strategies of the Salamanca Statement. However, for the concept of inclusion to mean more than just integration, the academic field of education presented definitions of this concept that emphasized the change that inclusion meant. In the Norwegian framework the definition presented by Peder Haug covers the Norwegian understanding of inclusion. An inclusive educational environment shall according to Haug (2003b) focus on increasing *fellowship* among students, giving all students the possibility of *participation* as part of a process of *democratization*, and on top of this giving all students the necessary support so that they *benefit* from the education offered. The Norwegian understanding of inclusive education is as seen, not about integrating students in ordinary education, but about the transformation of teaching so that it supports all learners. In other words, it was the second aim of integration presented by Vislie (1995) that became the dominant focus for the Norwegian inclusion debate: to reformulate the regular school system to meet an increased diversity of students.

The choice of this strategy meant that the approach of special education was reduced and Norwegian educational policy was highly influenced by the criticism raised by advocates for inclusive education. One result of this is that even though almost all of the Norwegian students are integrated in ordinary education, a lot of national research points to the fact that many students are still not included in education. One established way of measuring the degree of inclusion in Norwegian schools is to relate inclusion to the amount of special education used.

The tension between ordinary education and special education is highlighted by §5 in the Norwegian education law. The Norwegian legislation emphasizes that students that do not benefit from ordinary education have the right to special education. Special education is thus used as a measurement of how well ordinary education is able to educate all students, hence also a measurement of inclusion.

The amount of special education in Norway was therefore reduced to about 5% in the late 1990s and early 2000s. However, the focus on international test results and a new school reform in 2006—the Knowledge Promotion Reform—lead directly or indirectly to an increase in the amount of special education. Today about 8.5% of the student population receive special education (Figure 1).

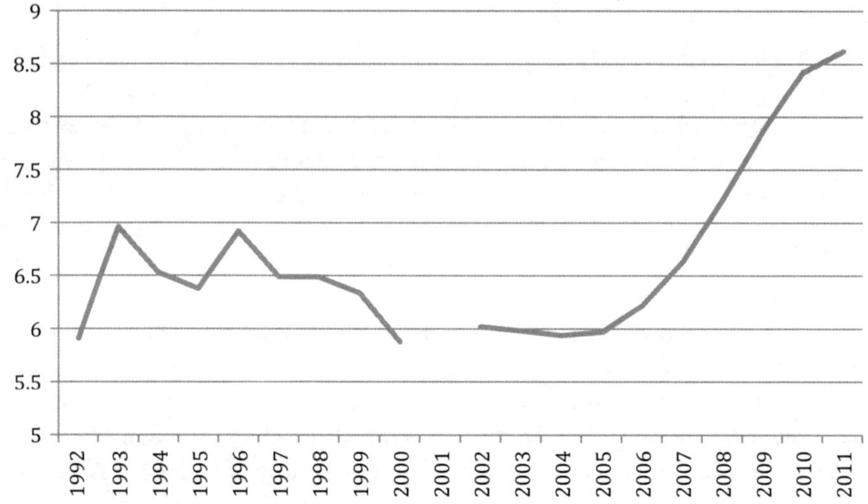

Figure 1. Amount of special education in Norway, grade 1–10 (GSI, https://gsi.udir.no).

Over the last decade, the strategy presented, to reduce the need for special education and to foster inclusion, is within the Norwegian context presented as *adapted teaching*. According to the school legislation, all Norwegian students have the right to adapted teaching.

As part of the Knowledge Promotion Reform a lot of resources were used in the school system to develop the school and the ordinary teachers' ability to support students with adapted teaching. The theoretical framework for this approach is presented by Bachman and Haug (2006). According to them, two solutions are outlined to meet the goal of adapted teaching: a student centered approach (narrow approach) and a classroom approach (wide approach) as can be seen in Table 1.

The student-centered approach is the dominant way of meeting the goal of giving adapted teaching to all students among Norwegian teachers. This approach focuses on the abilities and possibilities of each student. The academic level of each student is evaluated and necessary teaching is then planned accordingly. The problem with this approach according to Bachman and Haug (2006) is that it supports an individualistic learning environment and not necessarily an inclusive learning environment. It also reduces the teacher's responsibility for the students' learning progress (Biesta, 2004) and the ability for the teacher to create an environment for learning where students learn to relate to each other to become good citizens. The alternative to this student-centered approach is the classroom approach. The entity of teaching within this framework is the whole group of students. The idea is that the teacher should give students the possibility to work together and to share their different knowledge. As part of this teaching the student also has to relate to others and through this develop social skills. The point of this approach is to emphasize that learning is something that goes on in a social environment and in this case it is the classroom that is the environment for teaching. The teacher is in this approach a facilitator of the communication between students in relation to the goal of the teaching. Classroom management is therefore emphasized as a crucial competence for the teacher in relation to adapted teaching.

Table 1. Adapted teaching.

Student-centered approach	*Classroom approach*
Individualization of teaching through individual plans, work schedules and learning styles	Focus on collective approaches in teaching as well as individual approaches
Focus on intrinsic motivation	Focus on both internal and external motivation
Portfolio assessment of individual work	Development of a collaborative school culture
Emphasis on the individual instead of the community	Emphasis on structure and clarity in teaching
The focus is on the individual student when students have problems in school	The students' problems in school are put into a contextual relationship where the focus is on the learning environment and teaching
Differentiation and possible segregation of students	Emphasis on social participation for all students

However, it is important to emphasize that the distinction between the student-centered approach and the classroom approach mainly has been through an academic way of dealing with the concept of adapted teaching. In general, the practical field of education has practiced adapted teaching within the framework of the student-centered understanding. The focus on the classroom approach is however increasing. A reason for this change in perspective is that the amount of children receiving special education has risen extensively over the last seven years and this is linked to the fact that special education is clearly related to the student-centered approach of adapted teaching in Norway (Nordahl and Hausstätter, 2009). The main problem with this increase is the lack of professional knowledge within the special educational area to deal with special educational needs as part of ordinary education support. This type of knowledge became the Finnish strategy toward integration and inclusive education.

Finland and part time special education

The gradual change from a two-track parallel school system to a one-track comprehensive school system following the *Comprehensive School Act* of 1970 created the basic structure for the current school system in Finland. This change to a truly heterogeneous 'school for all' was speeded up by the development of the student welfare services as well as the special education services which are referred to as 'part-time special education' in the Finnish context (Jauhiainen and Kivirauma, 1997). In other words, Finland chose the first strategy regarding integration and a school for all in order to develop the special educational area to meet the new demands (Vislie, 1995). The influences for this form of organizing additional services for students with milder learning difficulties originally came from Germany and Sweden. However, the scope and the brevity of this activity have continued developing during the years more intensively in Finland than in other countries. At the same time the special schools still exists, although the majority of the services are offered elsewhere than in traditional special education environments (Jahnukainen, Pösö, Kivirauma and Heinonen, 2012).

The part time special educational support was introduced in the 1960s and has gradually been developed since the 1970s. The key player in this low threshold system of meeting the diverse population is the specialized teacher, whose work load is not dedicated to a small group of students only. Instead, s/he deals with the whole school population doing assessment, co-teaching, teaching small groups, and consulting the classroom teachers (e.g. Rytivaara, Pulkkinen and Takala, 2012). Basically, there is at least one such teacher available for around every 300 students in every school. During the 2010–2011 school year about 120,000 (or 21.7%) comprehensive school students (age group 6 to 16) took part in this service. In addition to this 'everyman' additional need service, there is also more traditional 'full time' special education available in the Finnish system for students with more severe special needs. It covers around 44,000 students (school year 2010–11), which is around 8.1% of the comprehensive school population (Figure 2).

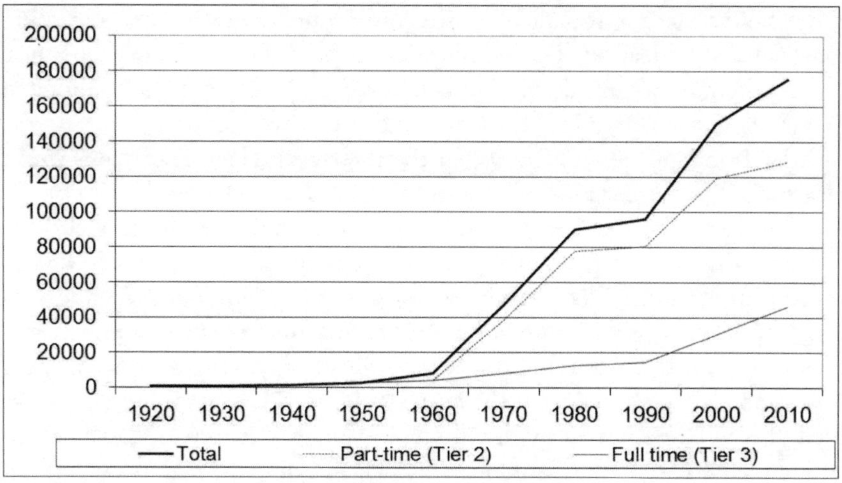

Figure 2. The number of students in special education in Finland, 1920–2010 (Sources: Kivirauma, 2002; Jahnukainen, 2011; OSF, 2010a; OSF, 2010b).

To meet the challenge of inclusive education in Finland, the above-mentioned system with two main service options has recently been modified into a three-tiered system defined under the title of Learning and Schooling Support (*The Act on the Amendment 2010*). The *first* tier consists of all actions made by the regular classroom teacher in terms of differentiation as well as in terms of school-wide efforts to meet the diversity of students. This basically transfers more responsibility to classroom teachers as well as to the school community. The *second* tier consists of remedial support by the class teacher, co-teaching with the special educator and temporal individual or small group learning with the part-time special educator. In practice, this is highly equivalent to the former definition of 'part-time special education.' The *third* tier consists of the whole continuum of special education services from fulltime general education to a special school placement and is mostly equivalent with the previous 'full time special education.' Every student in the special support tier must have a Personalized Education Plan (Finnish acronym HOJKS). However, the personalization does not necessarily mean adaptation/individualization of the curriculum, but instead it often means personalized ways of learning and showing progress. In 2010, around one of four students with a Personal Education Plan was following the adapted curriculum (e.g. Kirjavainen, Pulkkinen and Jahnukainen, 2014).

When comparing the Finnish special education system with some other school systems, it is evident that the broad use of the Tier 2 level service is a very distinctive feature in Finnish compulsory school. Using this kind of additional service has been the tool for creating a truly comprehensive public school system for 98.6% of the age group (primary education; OECD, 2011). The broad use of this low threshold service is also a key for the lower number of students placed in 'traditional' special education. The number of Finnish students in special education in K–12 systems has been defined to be around 6.4% (Graham and Jahnukainen, 2011), while in the U.S. it is almost two-fold (e.g. Powell, 2011).

Official statistics demonstrate that the pressure in Tier 2 service is in different learning difficulties (Figure 3). Further analysis (e.g. Kirjavainen et al., 2014) shows that there is heavy pressure on the early years in this service model. This has at the same time both a preventive as well as a rehabilitative function. The effectiveness of the Finnish Tier 2 service is based on the premise of early intervention without 'waiting to fail.' In practice, this means that as soon as the classroom teacher or the parents notice that some additional support is needed, the possible intervention can be started with the special educator. If more intensive support is needed, this will be decided by the Student Welfare Group (e.g. Sabel, Saxenian, Miettinen, Kristensen and Hautamäki, 2011), and more formal assessment needs to be made.

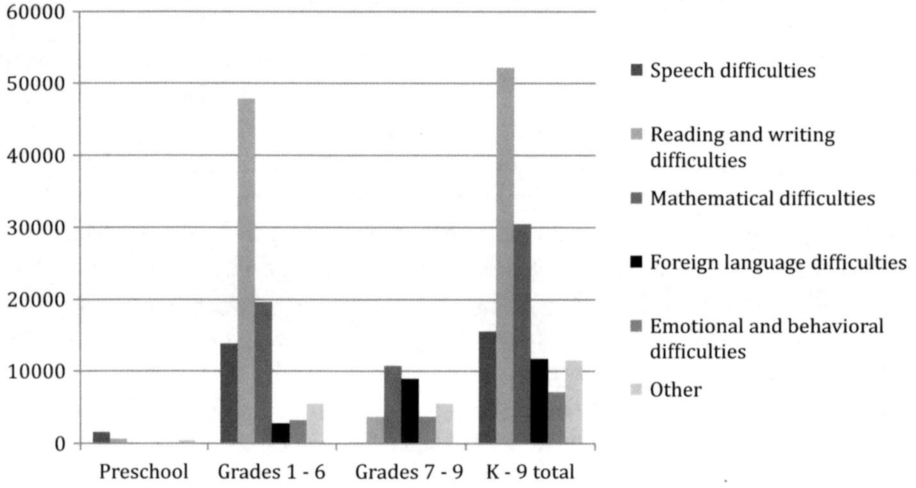

Figure 3. Primary reason for part time special education (Tier 2/ intensified support) in Finland by the level of schooling in school year 2009 – 2010 (Source: OSF, 2010b).

DIFFERENT ROUTES TO INCLUSIVE EDUCATION

Twenty years after the Salamanca Statement there is a diversity of different models and approaches to develop an inclusive school. Our point in this chapter has been to point to the fact that the development of inclusive strategies has to be related to the historical context of the educational system. In our example, we have linked this development of inclusive strategies to the general development of the educational system in Norway and Finland in the 1970s and the aim to integrate all students into a common educational system. The Nordic model of education is often handled as one, united entity. Although it is clear that there are strong similarities, it is also evident that there has been a political shift in more diverse directions. Our analysis of the Norwegian and Finnish models for developing inclusive education is a good example of that diversification as it shows how these models function as good examples of the two strategies presented by Vislie (1995).

Although both countries have carried through strong reformulations of the regular school system toward inclusive education, the differences are striking. The Norwegian strategy is the implementation of inclusive education using the reformulation of the regular education as its media. In Finland, the reformulation has been made inside the special education system and expanding the service options to cover one third of the school age population. Both strategies have their weaknesses and strengths. The Finnish strategy seems to be an essential contributor to the high international results attained by Finnish students. In the light of the inclusion movement, the backside of this strategy is a substantial use of segregated special education support; although new kinds of more inclusive strategies have been implemented, they have not necessarily cut the use of more traditional settings. The Norwegian strategy has reduced the use of segregated support to a minimum. However, the reduction of the special educational support system seems to cause problems in schools today because they are not able to give the necessary support to students with special needs. In other words, in spite of these clear differences between Norway and Finland, the question of which of the two countries has the most inclusive model and the best strategy toward inclusion will stay unanswered—simply because there is no definitive description of how inclusion should present itself in education.

CHAPTER TEN

Salamanca and beyond:

Inclusive Education Still Up for Debate

DÓRA S. BJARNASON AND GRETAR L. MARINÓSSON

VIGNETTE 1

Peter, aged 9, and Sif, aged 11, were siblings. The year was 1952. They lived on a farm in Iceland with their parents and their older brother, Jón, who was 15. Theirs was a traditional farmhouse with turf walls but their father and big brother were building a new house from concrete that would have electricity from a homemade power station in the brook above the farm and running water inside. Peter and Sif walked to school every day. It took them an hour each way in fair weather. Peter was a "halfwit" and the other children teased him sometimes. Nobody expected him to learn at school, least of all his parents. The teacher was kind to take Peter in. He seemed to like school, sat and doodled and did not disturb the other children so he was tolerated. Sif was tired of dragging him along. She had a secret: Her dream was to stop school after her confirmation and get a job as a home help in the nearest town and maybe later move to Reykjavík (interview with Peter's sister, 1983).

VIGNETTE 2

Benedikt is the son of Dóra, a university lecturer in Reykjavík. Benedikt has multiple impairments. In the early 1980s they had just arrived from the USA, where Benedikt attended a regular school. His enrolment in his local school in Reykjavík was an experiment, with a special permission from the Minister of Education and the Reykjavík School Board. Benedikt's schooling went well for the first three years. Despite his impairments, he had adequate support, became a fully-fledged part of his class and had friends. Gradually, things became more difficult. Against Dóra's will, a new special teacher began to pull Benedikt out of his class for instruction. Dóra interfered, not very diplomatically. Additional hurdles were erected: one year Benedikt could not get help to go to the restroom, another year he could not attend school on Wednesday afternoons because of staff meetings and so forth. Still the friendship between the classmates grew, and some of the teachers identified and worked with Benedikt's talent for music and his interest in art and physics. From the perspective of the children, he was part of their class, but from the perspective of some of the staff he was a square peg in a round hole. However, he graduated with his class and still retains many of his friendships from school (from Dóra S. Bjarnason´s diaries from the 1980s and early 1990s).

VIGNETTE 3

Gunnar, aged 10, was in grade 5 at a school in a fishing village. He had Down Syndrome and serious health problems. There were 16 children in his class. He was happy, joined almost every lesson, liked the music lessons most of all, and got extra training from a developmental therapist. Three other children in the class needed extra support for a variety of reasons. Sometimes Gunnar forgot his things, such as his sports bag or his school bag on his way to the classroom. Mostly somebody helped him or reminded him. Often, when he met other students, younger or older, he gave them a hug. Everybody in the school seemed to know and like Gunnar. Life was good; he was simply one of the group. The family moved to Reykjavík when Gunnar was 11 years old. He joined a big school where he was well received and where he continued to learn and participate in an ordinary class with his age peers (interviews with Gunnar's principal and his mother, 2014).

INTRODUCTION

The vignettes above are indicative of changes during the last few decades of the 20th century in reaction of Icelandic regular schools to children with disabilities when they apply for entry. Some schools accepted and did their best for the children before Salamanca, and some schools resisted even after inclusive education was adopted as an official policy in the country.

The Icelandic educational policy and practice are similar to that of other Nordic countries, and many others on both sides of the North Atlantic and in

Australia and New Zealand. Yet, the timespan for changes in the field of special education was shorter and until the last decade of the 20th century lagging behind similar developments elsewhere (cf. Thomas and Loxley, 2001; Richardson and Powell, 2011). Iceland adopted the vision of the Salamanca Statement and Framework for Action on Special Educational Needs (UNESCO, 1994) soon after the publication of the report in Icelandic, in 1995. Along with other international and national education policy documents the statement provided a foundation for national and local education policy in the country. Iceland went a step further than most of its neighbors in including every learner except 1.3% (0.5% in special schools and 0.8% in special classes) of its compulsory education students in ordinary schools and regular classes in 2013 (Statistics Iceland, 2013). Some of the consequences of this development are discussed in the chapter.

The focus of the chapter is to map out and reflect on whether, how and with what results the Salamanca Declaration and Plan of Action has affected the Icelandic education policy and practice in the past twenty years. We start by exploring some milestones in the emergence and development of special education in Iceland, then move on to highlighting aspects of the inclusive education development before and after the Salamanca declaration, and finish by discussing the challenges that still remain to be overcome.

Background

Iceland was one of Europe's poorest countries at the beginning of the 20th century, but that was about to change fast. The first compulsory education legislation was passed in 1907 (Lög um fræðslu barna, nr. 59/1907). In the early 20th century, alongside industrialization and urbanization, "the problem of delinquent and immoral children" (largely children of the poor working class) became a public issue. Certain children could be excluded or excused from compulsory schooling under the law. They were, on the one hand, children who according to their teachers or headmaster were unable to be with other children because of their moral deficiency or disobedience, and on the other hand, children whom a doctor deemed lacking in mental or physical abilities and unable to learn with other children. Children with tuberculosis or other prevailing infectious diseases were also excused from compulsory schools, but tuberculosis was the biggest killer of children and youth in the 1920s and 1930s (Garðarsdóttir, 2008, p. 258).

The 1946 law on the education of children (Lög um fræðslu barna 34/1946), paved the way for the establishment of a few small pedagogic institutions for delinquent and disabled children, but it is not clear to what extent education was made available to the children (Jónasson, 2008b, p. 272). Regular schools were expected to deal with children with learning difficulties. A special class was established at a lower secondary school (age 13–15) in 1951 for non-disabled youth who were not interested in academic learning and needed to work. The first school psychologist was hired by Kópavogur town in 1956. The first IQ test was adapted from the Stanford-Binet and standardized in the 1950s and later used to place children in special schools. School maturation tests were adapted from abroad and used to place children at the appropriate ability levels in regular schools, for example in classes ranking from A to E, with class A having students scoring highest on the test and E students ranking lowest. From the 1950s some children seen as disabled or immoral were placed in institutions. Some of these children received some formal education (Garðarsdóttir, 2008, pp. 247–262; Jónasson, 2008b, p. 280). Children living in institutions for imbeciles were entitled to special education from 1972 (Reglugerð um kennslu á fávitastofnunum, 1972), and by 1977 they were in accordance with the Special Education Ordinance (Reglugerð um sérkennslu, 1977) placed in special schools or special classes.

A School Psychological Service was established for the Reykjavík schools in 1960 and after the passing of the 1974 Compulsory School Act also in other urban areas (Marinósson, 1979; Björnsson, 1991). In 1961, a small special school, Höfðaskóli, opened in Reykjavík for children with IQs 50 to 70 who had been living at home. Soon other special schools and units were on the agenda at the same time as the normalization principle and the concept of integration, based on equity and human rights, were beginning to impact social and educational policy and practice overseas (Bjarnason, 1995). In 1971, a small group of parents of young children with multiple impairments established a Day School for their children in a neighboring town to Reykjavík. These children had no educational options and their parents argued for their human rights to education and for their place in society (Þjóðviljinn, 1975). In 1975, this school became the assessment and diagnostic section of a new special school, called "The school at Crater Hill" (Öskjuhlíðarskóli). The Day School was thus the forerunner to the State Diagnostic and Counselling Center that opened in 1986.

Integration in the air

In 1974, a new compulsory school legislation was passed. It emphasized social equity and equality of opportunities. The law prescribed one school for all children aged 7 to 15, which would strive to meet the diversity of children's needs, talents and interests. Following that legislation the National Curriculum advised against ability groupings and advocated individualized learning and choice between subjects (Jónasson, 2008a, p. 116). That law also defined segregated settings as an alternative for disabled children and home/hospital schooling for chronically sick children. Two types of special schools were established: a special school for children with IQ below 50, and another for those with IQ 50 to 70. Special classes were also established for children with sensory, motor and emotional problems, as well as "support classes for slow learners," mostly grafted on to unchanged regular schools. Thus, despite the integrative thrust of the Act the Special Education Ordinance from 1977 based on the Act framed and legitimated several segregated educational services that were both new and had developed since the early 1950s. The Law on Support for the Intellectually Disabled from 1979 and the legislations on the Affairs of the Disabled from 1983 were located within the same ideology of integration in schools and society (Margeirsdóttir, 2001; Bjarnason, 1995, 1996). At the same time, "integration" became a mantra of radical parents and professionals, particularly those attached to the new umbrella association of parents of disabled children and some professionals called Þroskahjálp [literally "Support for development"], established in 1976. The claim was founded on the human rights perspective that disabled people should have access to civil society like other citizens.

Teacher training on the move

The training of special education teachers has been part of teacher training in Iceland for over 40 years. The first special educators were trained abroad, mostly in Norway. Since 1968, the Icelandic Teacher Training College (from 1971 the Iceland University of Education that amalgamated with the University of Iceland in 2008 as a School of Education) has offered a special education program increasingly emphasizing inclusive education (Marinósson and Bjarnason, 2011).

Students could, until 1985, take their first year in special education in Iceland but complete their studies in Norway where the studies were offered at Statens Special Lærerhøjskole. In 1985, the special education program at the Iceland University of Education was revised and changed with the help of a visiting professor from Britain. The new two-year program was influenced by the Warnock Report from 1978 (D.E.S., 1978). Its emphasis became pedagogy in place of psychology, and practice at the cost of theory (Marinósson and Bjarnason, 2011). Thereafter special education was offered as in-service and postgraduate training on top of a teacher's certificate for a ten-year period, 1985 to 1995, also since 1991 as professional skills training by local authorities in cooperation with the University. In the early 1990s, an American Fulbright professor, together with the program's Icelandic director, shaped the program towards the policy and practice of inclusive education reforms. The focus was shifting away from the medical model perspective towards a social relational model perspective. Still, the master's program in special needs/inclusive education has retained both approaches (Bjarnason, 2010; Marinósson and Bjarnason, 2011).

Salamanca Statement and Framework for Action

In a world where millions of children are deprived of education altogether, not the least poor girls and girls with disabilities, the inclusion mission by UNESCO sounded utopic in the beginning. Nevertheless, most governments in the world have since the World Conference in Salamanca (UNESCO, 1994) chosen inclusion as their central education policy. To what extent or how they manage to make it a reality is another matter. The policy also gained support in Iceland based on developments in Italy, Denmark and the U.S. in the 1960s (Bjarnason, 1995) and later on conventions declared by the UN in the 1990s.

Slee (2011, p. 117) suggests that "The Salamanca Statement has become a linguistic and policy touchstone enlisted to support both those who argue for what is spuriously referred to as 'full inclusion' and also those who frame conditions around the location and duration of inclusion." To cloud the water even more, our research findings (Marinósson and Bjarnason, 2007; Gunnþórsdóttir and Bjarnason, 2014), as well as similar findings by colleagues elsewhere (Kozleski, Artiles and Waitoller, 2011; Allan, 2012) highlight that there is little agreement on the meaning of the term inclusion. Further, it is sometimes taken to refer primarily to a goal of inclusive education policy and practice, and sometimes to a process (cf. Kiuppis, 2011, p. 95). In the Icelandic media and research literature, the term inclusion is sometimes used as synonymous with integration or situational integration, individualized teaching and learning. Finally both in Iceland and abroad the term inclusive education is often used in the press and by some teachers and academics as a synonym for special education (see Gunnþórsdóttir, in press) rather than an educational policy aimed at improving schools for all learners.

Post-Salamanca: Heading for inclusion in school and society?

A useful way of thinking about inclusive education is captured by Dianne L. Ferguson as:

> a process meshing together general and special education reform initiatives and strategies in order to achieve a unified system of public education that incorporates all children and youth as active, fully participating members of the school community; that views diversity as the norm; and that maintains a high quality education for each student by assuring meaningful curricular, effective teaching, and necessary support.
>
> —(Ferguson, 1995, p. 48)

Inclusion is seen as a democratic approach to quality and equity education for all children and where active participation of diverse students in the learning community of the school is at the forefront (Armstrong et al., 2011; Kozleski et al., 2011). We, the authors, have changed our understanding of the term inclusive education with time. For a pedagogical discussion of the term we use Ferguson's definition above. However when discussing the term in the context of educational policy and systemic structures we lean towards the understanding of inclusive education as an intersectional construct that exists on multiple axes that encompass sociocultural, historical, psychological and institutional factors for individuals, groups and social organizations.

We have demonstrated, by drawing on the example of Iceland, that integration existed before 1970 and inclusion before Salamanca. The term inclusion came to Iceland with the Salamanca Declaration. The Ministry of Education had the Statement and Framework for Action translated and sent to every school in 1995. This suggested that the Minister at the time took the declaration seriously and hoped to implement it at the level of policy and practice. The translation of the term was however somewhat unfortunate. Icelandic does not have one word for "inclusion," so the term *skóli án aðgreiningar* was used in the translation, literally "school without segregation." This sounds negative, stiff and bureaucratic. Because of the references in point five of the Salamanca Statement to children with special educational needs, the fact that the Statement refers to every child was largely lost in the Icelandic discourse, both in academia and in general use. The term was—and still is in some cases—used to focus on the placement of children diagnosed with impairments or taxing learning or behavioral problems. A new and broader definition is taking over from *skóli án aðgreiningar*. It is in Icelandic *skóli margbreytileikans* that literally translates into "school of diversity," as a synonym for inclusive education. Accordingly, students' learning is organized around student diversity as a norm where the teacher has the role of a facilitator, creating knowledge with students.

Two years after Salamanca, the compulsory education schools were turned over from the state to the municipalities (Lög um grunnskóla, nr. 64, 1995). This opened up new possibilities for systemic changes and diversification of schools. Soon some schools began to experiment and change the learning, teaching, school cultures and communities in harmony with versions of inclusive ideas of that time. In 2002, the Reykjavík Education Authorities published the School Board's policy on special education. It was shaped in consultation with both public and private stakeholders in the fields of education and care of children, and designed within the remit of Icelandic compulsory school legal framework, including the national curriculum, and the Salamanca Declaration (Reykjavíkurborg, 2002). This new special education policy prescribed inclusive education for both non-disabled and disabled children and proposed the closure of some, but not all, special classes in favor of resource rooms and added support inside the classrooms. Yet, about 1% of all compulsory school students were expected to attend special classes (autism units, classes for blind students and for students with mobility problems) and special schools. The policy created a stir in many school staffrooms in Reykjavík. It was seen to be too radical, to come from above, and as if rammed down the throats of both teachers and principals. Teachers went on strike over pay in 2004 and felt that their strike action brought little improvement. Many teachers felt disempowered, swamped with work, underpaid, unprepared and unable to teach disabled children. The greatest complaints from teachers, in the late 20th and early 21st century concerned having to include children with behavior problems, children who have always been part and parcel of schools. According to a study from 2007, the teachers wanted more support from their principals and more resources from the local education authorities (Reykjavíkurborg, 2007).

Quo vadis?

Teachers were—and still are—trying to include a broad variety of children in relatively unchanged schools using more or less traditional teaching methods (Marinósson, 2011; Bjarnason, 2004; Gunnþórsdóttir and Bjarnason, 2014). Furthermore, a small group of vocal parents of disabled children began to argue for more, better and bigger special schools (Ólafsdóttir, 2013). These arguments have reappeared with singular regularity year after year, when schools, PISA results or teachers' pay are discussed in the media (Fréttablaðið, 2014). What little research we have in the field of education shows clearly that teachers tend to be caring and sensible people who want to impact the lives of children and their learning (Mýrdal et al., 2001; Axelsdóttir, 2012; Gunnþórsdóttir and Bjarnason, 2014). Key elements of the education policy of inclusive education often resonate with teachers' values and perspectives on equity, social justice, quality education for each and every learner and their active participation in the school culture. Many teachers do not appear to see how their values and hopes are reflected in the inclusive educational policy (Axelsdóttir, 2012; Gunnþórsdóttir and Bjarnason, 2014).

Since 1995 inclusive education has been at the center of Icelandic educational policy. However, the concept of inclusive education appeared for the first time in the legal text in 2008—when new education laws were passed for all school levels—(Lög um grunnskóla, 2008; Lög um leikskóla, 2008; Lög um framhaldsskóla, 2008). Earlier regulations had included the idea to a certain extent (e.g. Lög um grunnskóla, 1974) but in the 2008 Act it is stated for the first time that the compulsory school is an inclusive school (article 17). As a whole the Act emphasizes equity, equal opportunities and an appropriate education for all children, irrespective of their physical, mental or sensory capacities, their socio-economic situation, national/ethnic origin or linguistic competences. But in the article on specialized services and support system for schools the emphasis is on diagnostic psychological services in place of pedagogic or therapeutic work. Students should be evaluated from the first year of schooling to secure them appropriate teaching and support. Further, students who may have psychological or social problems affecting their learning are entitled to diagnostic services, if the parents agree. There is a real probability that diagnostic reports to schools will cost more than the pedagogic work the children are provided with following the diagnosis. Furthermore, the Act of 2008, article 42, has opened wider the possibility of schools establishing special classes "*when ordinary teaching and learning do not fit the needs or situation of learners.*" The Reykjavík School and Leisure Board built on this legislation in its latest review of its policy from 2002. In their policy document entitled "Inclusive Education and Special Support for students in Compulsory Schools" (Reykjavíkurborg, 2012) the possibility is opened up for eight special classes, so called "participation classes," placed in ordinary schools but administered from one of the two special schools that remain in Reykjavík. Currently there are two such participatory classes in Reykjavík schools, one administered by a special school for children with serious behavior problems, the other by a special school for children with intellectual or multiple impairments. Two more such classes are currently on the drawing board. In all, the Reykjavík schools have 1.3% of its compulsory school population in special schools and special classes. The Icelandic regular compulsory schools support between 23% (in 2002) and 27% (in 2013) of students seen to have special needs and/or Icelandic as a second language. Most are pulled out of class for support; others are supported in regular classes. So there is an inbuilt contradiction in the law: on one hand the school is inclusive and on the other a mechanism of identification, evaluation and categorization of individuals with special needs functions in parallel.

If we have managed to give a glimpse of the social mood since the second half of the 20th century to the present, it is clear that in Iceland like in most other western countries education has been a political battleground. The rights of individuals were for the longest time tied to their social standing and those with less than perfect cultural capital were therefore ignored, marginalized and even ostracized. The transformation to the attitudes of today must therefore seem extraordinary. A common sight in our compulsory schools is children playing together who before would not all be allowed into school. Their presence is accepted unequivocally and the social and educational needs of these children are met in a regular class. The policy of educational inclusion is nevertheless still a perplexity in Iceland, not the least among teachers who complain of lack of knowledge, incomplete training for the job and scarcity of expert support. We still do not know for certain how to make it work; at present, therefore, the policy is an aim to be reached for, a process to work on, an ideology to be realized in practice. For that we need to get teacher education right, we need to follow this up with continuing education programmes for teachers in the classroom, we need to change the funding rules and the support system in line with the policy, we need to reach a tipping point where a critical mass of teachers say that this is an exciting challenge that can be overcome for others to follow suit. Then we shall hear less of the "normal" and the deviations from the normal and more of the diverse talents and characters of our students who need to be helped to develop each in their own way.

CONCLUSIONS

The vignettes at the beginning of the chapter highlight changes in perspectives, values and supports of children with disabilities in Icelandic schools. The chapter has shown that the Salamanca Declaration was important for Icelandic education policy and practice in the last decade of the 20th and the first decade of the 21st century. It legitimated the inclusion of learners with significant additional needs in all regular schools and classrooms, it speeded up closure of some special schools and some special classes in the country, and it helped shape the national education policy on equity, equal opportunities and schooling for all. Yet, amongst Icelandic teachers there still is an underlying dominant construction of a medical nature of students with special educational needs and disabilities: The regular school should be for "normal" students and those who do not fit the bill are either subjected to a system of "correction" or, if that does not work, a system of exclusion kicks in. The Model of the Diverse School does not have favor with all teachers. One of the reasons is that their professional purpose is to improve (educate) individuals. It is therefore reasonable to expect that the individuals are measured and if found wanting that something is done to ameliorate the situation (Gunnþórsdóttir and Bjarnason, 2014; Marinósson, 2011). A related explanation is that education is at its core a normative activity where perfection is striven for. It is too much to expect of teachers to accept the alternative which is to take everyone as they come and practice unconditional acceptance.

The change in educational ideology and practice that accompanied integration of students with disabilities into the education system in the 1960s and 1970s and later inclusive education that affected the whole system was perhaps more drastic than was recognized by education authorities at the time. In light of later knowledge of the processes of school change we should perhaps all have made a greater effort to support teachers in their effort. Had the Ministry, the University of Education and the municipalities joined together in a concerted effort of continuing professional development programmes this might have taken a shorter time and met with less resistance. And it is not too late to take this route.

We cannot carry on with a policy that is out of favor with many of those who work in the system. We need to resolve the impasse with a new solution, a model that is transparent and easily understood in place of one that raises the hackles of those who are supposed to carry it out. In this model individual needs are catered for as part of daily school work (Slee, 2011). There is no 'regular' and 'deviation from the norm' in this school but variegated tasks to meet a diversity of interests, types of talent, culture, character and needs. For this to work all available knowledge is utilized: pedagogic, medical, sociological, psychological and managerial.

Thus expert knowledge is part of school work but geared towards the aims of education.

The Salamanca Declaration can be thought of on the one hand as a dead or historical document that captured and defined ideological and practical concerns about western and global education policies and practices in the 1990s. If that is so the document was instrumental at the time: It shaped and legitimated the educational policy and practices already at work within the field of special needs education in the West and the resistance against social and educational exclusion globally. The declaration and plan of action can also be thought of as a living manifesto that each generation concerned with education, schooling, human rights and social justice in a democratic society needs to analyze, redefine and make their own in the light of 'current broad social and economic changes, affecting an increasingly fragmented social and economic landscape' (Knight, in Slee, 2011, p. viii).

CHAPTER ELEVEN

Technocracy and Inclusive Education in the United States

SCOT DANFORTH

Since the 1997 revision of the Individuals with Disabilities Education Act (IDEA) and the 2001 No Child Left Behind (NCLB) law, the instructional agenda of the public schools in the United States has been dictated chiefly by national accountability reform. The federal and state governments have identified the year-to-year improvement of standardized test scores as the highest priority of public schooling, thereby placing enormous pressure on school districts, building administrators, and teachers to produce rising levels of assessment outcomes. Educational historian Diane Ravitch has described this movement as the "technocratic approach to school reform" (Ravitch, 2010, p. 29), a format for school change that attempts to "fix education…by developing a good data-collection system that provides the information necessary to incentivize the workforce—principals, teachers, and students—with appropriate rewards and sanctions" (Ravitch, 2010, p. 11).

In my own work as the leader of a large, urban teacher education program, I frequently visit public schools to meet with building principals and school district administrators. I have often observed the symbolic artifacts of the technocratic approach to school management.

- A local school district requires that all schools have a "data wall" in the front office, a public display of standardized test scores for the past five years. Typically, these walls are adorned with a series of paper visual displays such as bar graphs or line graphs represent changes in reading, mathematics, and science test scores for different grade levels and student populations.

- One school principal, in an act of mocking resistance to the policy, showed me her "real data wall"—a large bulletin board filled with photographs of students in her school engaging in a variety of interesting and enjoyable activities in the local community.
- Many school principals greet me with an obligatory presentation demonstrating standardized test score growth in recent years. In some cases, I am handed a neatly prepared packet of graphs and tables. More than once, I have been treated to a PowerPoint slide show projected onto the wall of the principal's office. There seems to be an assumption that I want or need this information.
- The otherwise blank walls of one school district leader displayed just two messages.

"In God we trust. All others bring data!"
"Without data, all anyone has is an opinion."

The sum total of my experiences talking to public school leaders have left me convinced that the "technocratic approach" to school improvement enacted in the current accountability reform measures is a highly influential, even dominant administrative apparatus with profound effects on public schooling. Standardized test scores are undoubtedly the coin of the realm. Tallying, representing, worrying about, and somehow raising those scores constitutes the central work of school professionals. The managerial climate surrounding and impacting the work of educators with students is flush with technocracy.

The purpose of this chapter is to examine this technocratic orientation to the management of American public education, specifically in regard to the inclusion of students with disabilities. I will explore three questions. How did American government policies create a technocratic system of public school governance? What are the primary conceptual and practical features of a technocracy? What implications does this administrative system have for inclusive education in the United States?

An analysis at the intersection of technocratic administration and inclusive education sheds light to both sides, allowing for a greater understanding of how technocracy impacts instruction in the public schools and how the democratic mission of inclusive education is faring under accountability reform. The specific case of inclusive education, while certainly not facilitating a comprehensive analysis of the administrative and instructional priorities of public schools under an accountability reform regime, allows for a deep and insightful probe into the inner workings of the current administrative machinery of American public schooling.

Before embarking on an analysis of these three questions in the United States, I must offer two preliminary instructions for readers not familiar with special education and inclusive education in the United States. First, it has become common among many European educators to distinguish between "integration" and "inclusion" (Ainscow, Booth and Dyson, 2006; Ballard, 1999; Vislie, 2003). For example, the Alliance for Inclusive Education in London describes integration as the placement of disabled students in general classrooms with some modifications and supports. This arrangement does little to alter the curriculum, instructional practices, or ideological underpinnings of the general education system. In contrast, inclusion is described as a more thorough reform of general classrooms and schools in order to create learning communities that support and value a pluralistic diversity of students (Alliance for Inclusive Education, 2014). By these standards, most of what Americans call inclusion is more aptly termed integration.

Secondly, readers should note that numerous international agreements and documents such as the Salamanca Statement and the United Nations Convention on the Rights of Persons with Disabilities play virtually no role in American education. School leaders and teachers, for the most part, have never heard of these policy statements. The American educational context is overwhelmingly ethnocentric, oblivious of research and policy developments in other countries, and, as this chapter will explore, intensely focused on the authoritative requirements of federal educational accountability laws.

THE END(S) OF SOCIAL JUSTICE?

In the United States, ever since the passage of comprehensive special education legislation (PL 94–142) in 1975, inclusive education has been favored but optional. Schools and educators have been allowed considerable leeway in regard to the classroom placement of each disabled student. The placement of students with disabilities has been guided by a principle called Least Restrictive Environment (LRE). This legal concept states:

> To the maximum extent appropriate, children with disabilities, including children in public or private institutions or other care facilities, are educated with children who are not disabled, and special classes, separate schooling, or other removal of children with disabilities from the regular educational environment occurs only when the nature or severity of the disability of a child is such that education in regular classes with the use of supplementary aids and services cannot be achieved satisfactorily.
>
> —(IDEA, 2004, TITLE I, B, 612, 5a)

This legal principle undoubtedly encourages public schools to educate disabled students in general classrooms. But one need not have a complete legal education to quickly wonder how the phrase "to the maximum extent appropriate" is interpreted by different public schools, school districts, and states.

Taylor (1988; also see Nisbet, 2004) has argued convincingly that the LRE principle actually operates as a deterrent to inclusion. By defining inclusion as the priority while admitting that segregation may be a suitable choice for some students in some situations, it grants practical legitimacy to segregation. Inclusion is offered as a best case scenario alternative. Segregated special education placements are reified as necessary and rational, especially for students understood as having "severe" disabilities. Generally speaking, the greater the functional limitation, as interpreted by the school professionals, the more reasonable a segregated classroom or school seems.

Educators, parents, and students working to create more and better inclusive education opportunities have needed arguments sturdier and more persuasive than LRE. Beginning with the Regular Education Initiative of the 1980s (Osgood, 2005), a social justice argument steeped in the concepts of liberal democracy has served as the chief rhetoric in favor of inclusive education in the United States. This argument portrays disabled students as an excluded, oppressed class of children seeking the justice of integration and equality in the school community (Artiles, Harris-Murri, and Rosenberg, 2006; Lipsky and Gartner, 1996; Sapon-Shevin, 1999). The goal of inclusion is a specific version of the broader American civil rights narrative whereby African Americans, women, gays and lesbians, and other political minority groups have sought legal and civil equality. The story of disabled Americans fighting for the accessibility of those same valued social spaces has greatly mirrored the more well-known narrative of African Americans achieving the right to access public restrooms, lunch counters, and ultimately public schools and universities (Fleischer and Zames, 2011; Pelka, 1997; Shapiro, 1994; Stroman, 2003).

Sapon-Shevin (1999, p. 26) has expressed the social justice rationale as a mode of moral persuasion that asks educators circumspect questions about the ultimate purposes of education and the kind of world we hope to live in.

> (I)nclusion is not about disability, nor is it only about schools. Inclusion is about social justice. What kind of world do we want to create and how should we educate children for that world? What kinds of skills and commitments do people need to thrive in a diverse society?

At the heart of the social justice argument is a moral case, a call to teachers and school leaders to scrutinize beliefs and values in order to better align the practices of schooling with the ethical commitments of a liberal, multicultural society.

Prior to the enactment of the 2001 No Child Left Behind (NCLB) law, the legislative centerpiece of accountability reform, the social justice argument was the primary mover of the inclusive education movement. It was a political rationale that leveraged some degree of success in convincing American educators to teach more disabled students in general classrooms. For example, in 1992, 39.82

percent of all disabled students were highly included, spending at least 4/5 of their school day in classrooms with nondisabled peers. By 2001, 48.44 percent of disabled students were highly included (Individuals with Disabilities Act Data, 2012; U.S. Department of Education, 2004).

One might argue that the administrative and policy context of the schools prior to the accountability reform movement propelled by NCLB allowed teachers and administrators sufficient flexibility to consider and respond to the social justice argument. Seeking the values of liberal democracy within the public schools, while not simple or easy, was a viable option for educators who found the social justice logic morally compelling. School-based educators had adequate freedom under administrative policies to attempt to embrace an inclusive education agenda driven by the social justice rationale.

But the administrative and policy context of American schooling changed dramatically with the implementation of federal accountability reforms in the late 1990s and early 2000s. NCLB, combined with the 1997 and 2004 modifications to the Individuals with Disabilities Education Act (IDEA), recast the inclusive education movement within a complex set of administrative prerogatives designed to systematically produce higher academic test scores among children. The US Department of Education began interacting with state and local educational authorities in a hierarchy of administrative pressure, the higher levels compelling and corralling the lower levels on a playing field of public school test score data. The goal was to produce efficiencies of human action, in school organization, classroom instruction, and student learning, as evidenced in continuous rises in standardized reading and mathematics (and more recently, science) test scores (Dudley-Marling and Baker, 2012; Ravitch, 2010).

ACCOUNTABILITY REFORM POLICIES AND STUDENTS WITH DISABILITIES

The history of how accountability reforms in American education developed in relation to the schooling of disabled students is a tale of the expansion of standardized testing to populations of students previously exempted and ignored by state assessment. Prior to the 1997 reauthorization of the Individuals with Disabilities Education Act (IDEA), the federal policy on the education of students with disabilities emphasized access to public schooling without placing a high priority on the quality of educational provision. The main victory of the 1975 Education for Handicapped Children Act (EHA) was the federal mandate that all states provide a public education for students with disabilities without an exclusion option. Public school systems across the nation were required to educate all disabled students. The federal policy focused more on getting students with disabilities into schools and classrooms than on achieving positive academic outcomes (Hardman and Dawson, 2008; Hehir, 2005; Kleinert, Kearns and Kennedy, 1997).

Before the passage of IDEA 1997, students with disabilities were frequently ignored by state systems of standardized academic assessment. Federal policymakers and educational leaders did not expect students receiving special education services to make significant academic gains. School districts did not pay close attention to their educational progress. In 1991, the majority of the states did not even know how many or if their students with disabilities were taking state-mandated tests. Over half of states did not keep track of participation rates for students with disabilities on state assessments (Ysseldyke, Dennison and Nelson, 2004). Kleinert, Kearns, and Kennedy (1997) estimated that only 50% and 60% of all students with disabilities in the United States were participating in mandatory systems of state educational assessment before the policy changes adopted by the 1997 IDEA.

Operating in a climate of minimal accountability for academic achievement, many educators viewed the special education system as a powerful purveyor of low expectations for student learning. Kleinert, Kearns, and Kennedy (1997, p. 95) observed, "Unfortunately, one effect of excluding specific groups of students from state and district educational performance measures can be a decreased concern for what those students are learning." Former federal director of special education Thomas Hehir (2005, p. 111) lamented, "The education of students with disabilities has been plagued by low expectations, which is why many in the disability community have sought to have students included in state and national accountability systems. The hope is that by including students in statewide assessments, more attention will be paid to assuring that these students receive quality programs."

The authors of the 1997 reauthorization of IDEA focused on a pair of related concerns. First, they were convinced that expectations for the academic success of students with disabilities must be raised. Second, the problem of low expectations was conceptualized as closely linked to the fact that students with disabilities often did not take the states' standardized achievement tests. States did not test students with disabilities because they expected little from them. But this logic was also true in reverse. The failure to track the academic performance of disabled students in districts and schools allowed educators to undervalue the achievement of those students (Hardman and Dawson, 2008; Hehir, 2005).

The 1997 IDEA pressured states to include students with disabilities in all state academic assessments. States were required to develop suitable adaptations and modifications of tests to meet the performance needs of these students. Also, for students for whom the adaptations did not provide reasonable access to the standard examinations, states were required to develop and utilize alternative assessments. IEP teams were entrusted with the decision of selecting the most reasonable testing accommodations or assessment alternatives for individual students. Further, the federal government mandated that states report the performance of students with disabilities on all state assessments (Ysseldyke, Dennison and Nelson, 2004; Kleinert, Kearns and Kennedy, 1997). This sent "a clear message to everyone—teachers, administrators, and, perhaps most important, families and students themselves—that the learning of all children fundamentally matters" (Kleinert, Kearns and Kennedy, 1997, p. 207).

The 1997 reauthorization initiated a dramatic policy shift toward greater accountability for teachers, schools, and school districts for the academic achievement of students with disabilities. This shift was fortified seven years later by the 2004 IDEA (Hardman and Dawson, 2008; Hehir, 2005; Ysseldyke, Dennison and Nelson, 2004). The 2004 reauthorization linked explicitly with the 2001 No Child Left Behind legislation to hold schools accountable for the measured progress of students with disabilities on standardized tests of reading and math. It ensured disabled students' access to and progress on the general curriculum.

> Federal policy evolved into implementation of the view that the only way students with disabilities can be viewed as successful as their peers without disabilities is to ensure that they have an opportunity to learn the same instructional content. To ensure compliance with this provision, federal policy required that a student's individualized education program (IEP) have a statement of measurable annual goals that enable the child to access, participate in, and progress in the general curriculum. Further, the school district must ensure that the IEP team reviews each child's IEP periodically to address any lack of expected progress in the general curriculum
>
> —(Hardman and Dawson, 2008, p. 7)

Although the revised versions of IDEA did not create a specific mandate for students with disabilities to be included in general education classrooms, they made it increasingly difficult for school districts to adhere to the law through practices of segregation. Historically, and practically, the location of the general curriculum in American schools was the general classroom.

NO CHILD LEFT BEHIND

The 2001 reauthorization of the Elementary and Secondary Education Act, often called No Child Left Behind, is the cornerstone of the federal educational reform. The legislation mandated that all states develop a complex regime of standardized tests in reading and mathematics to be utilized in an aggressive system of top-down accountability. States were required to create their own standardized tests with three levels of performance, often termed *basic*, *proficient*, and *advanced*. Each state is allowed to define a proficient level of academic performance. Public schools must test all students in mathematics and reading in grades 3 thru 8 and once during the high school years. Based on each state's definitions of proficient mathematics and reading skill levels for each of the assessed grades, the federal government required that all students perform at proficiency level by 2014.

States, districts, and schools were ordered to disaggregate achievement data by race, ethnicity, low income status, disability, and English learners. In order to ensure that all of these sub-groups were progressing steadily toward the goal of full proficiency, states were required to create timelines detailing the standards of Adequate Yearly Progress (AYP). Each sub-group must gradually rise toward 100% proficiency during the years leading up to 2014.

Districts and schools who fail to meet the performance standards are subject to punishments. For example, schools not reaching AYP for every subgroup are designated as School In Need of Improvement (SINI) and face a progressive series of administrative sanctions. Each successive year of failure turns up the scope and power of the administrative intervention.

Five years of failure to meet AYP for any sub-group prompts the most dramatic action. Schools are forced to completely restructure, essentially wiping out the ineffective school and starting over from scratch. The five restructuring options include becoming a charter school, replacing principal and staff, handing control over to a private educational management company, and falling under state control. The final option is "any other major restructuring of the school's governance" (Ravitch, 2010, p. 98), an ambiguous reform option chosen by most schools and districts (Elledge et al., 2009; Nagle et al., 2006; Ravitch, 2010; Wong, 2008).

In totality, NCLB created a system of administrative compulsion armed with the weight of bureaucratic sanctions designed to force public schools in the United States to prioritize standardized test scores. The provisions related to the disaggregation of scores for specific minority group populations, including students with disabilities, allowed state and federal level educational leaders to apply that pressure with tremendous specificity. Measures of academic achievement for disabled students, by fiat, must increase.

This effectively positioned the inclusion movement in the United States under a technocratic regime of governmental administration. At this point, in order to further understand how this system of governance construes and influences inclusive education, I will examine the unique conceptual and practical features of technocratic management. What is technocracy? What does it offer as a form of governance? What does it provide to the leadership and administration of educational programs?

TECHNOCRACY AS IDEOLOGY

In order to provide a clear theoretical investigation of the multiple dimensions of technocracy, I will present technocratic governance as a Weberian ideal type, an analytical portrait drawn in essential and immoderate form. In real life application, technocratic governance is highly variable and often tempered by contrary administrative traditions and structures (Putnam, 1977; Kimura, 2010).

Technocracy has often been defined in terms of the specific expertise of a growing class of upper level government workers. Meynaud (1969, p. 29) defined technocracy as "the political situation in which effective power belongs to technologists termed technocrats." Similarly, Ridley (1966, p. 36) described technocracy as "government by technicians. A technocrat is a technician with power." More recently, Fischer (1990, p. 17) wrote that technocracy is "a system of governance in which technically trained experts rule by virtue of their specialized knowledge and position in dominant political and economic institutions."

An expansive research literature has theorized technocracy as far more than the academic or vocational expertise of specific government workers called technocrats. This literature has examined technocracy as a complex conceptual and practical apparatus for decision-making. Scholars theorizing technocracy as an active philosophy of governmental activity have offered a list of surprisingly similar terms; "technocratic outlook" (Ridley, 1966, p. 42), "technocratic mentality" (Putnam, 1977, p. 385), "technocratic ideology" (Centeno, 1993, p. 311), "technocratic mind-view" (Bell, 1973, p. 349), and "technocratic consciousness" (Fischer, 1990, p. 41). These theorists have explored technocracy as a complex ideology of governance, an "ethos and decision-making style" (Centeno, 1993, p. 311), a discourse of management involving a series of identifiable theoretical and practical features. In this light, technocracy involves a systematic way for government bodies to think about, organize, interpret, and take action upon society. It explains "how the world works, a conception of how it should work, and a set of tactics for changing it" (Fischer, 1990, p. 41), a full and deliberate approach to policy conceptualization, implementation, and management.

The primary feature of this ideological complex is the claim to a rational methodological foundation, a value-free, scientific approach to decision-making. Daniel Bell (1973, p. 350) describes technocracy as a systemic worldview that translates "the vital to the rational," rendering human social issues as logical puzzles to be defeated by instrumental reasoning.

"Problems must be resolved in a rational, scientific manner" (Ridley, 1966, p. 42). Social and economic problems are stripped of political and subjective content in order to make decisions based on rationality (Putnam, 1977). Common understandings of social meaning derived from experience or cultural practices are set aside in favor of mathematical algorithms.

> In its emphasis on the logical, practical, problem-solving, instrumental, orderly, and disciplined approach to objectives, in its reliance on a calculus, on precision and measurement and a concept of a system, it is a world-view quite opposed to the traditional and customary religious, esthetic, and intuitive modes.
>
> —(BELL, 1973, P. 350)

The complexities, vagaries, and inconsistencies of everyday life are distilled into fields of metric regularity and schemes of statistical determination.

Central to technocracy's claim to administrative superiority is the act of positioning technocratic decision-making outside the messy realm of political activity. "A technocrat's task is to assure that the higher rationality… is protected from the undue influence of political interests" (Centeno, 1993, p. 313). Technocratic governance is championed as apolitical, above the impure tug-of-war of interest group political argumentation. The "technocrat is skeptical and even hostile toward politicians and political institutions" (Putnam, 1977, p. 386). She is "hostile to political ideologies or, indeed, to any theoretical systems" (Ridley, 1966, p. 42). The goal is to avoid the corrupting influence of political discourse, avoiding the clash of differing opinions, perspectives, and goals (Gunnell, 1982). From a self-described apolitical position, the technocratic belief holds that social "progress can be achieved only by the 'depoliticization' of problems" (Ridley, 1966, p. 42). The technocrat is the right person with the right method to achieve that scientific, value-free stance.

TECHNOCRACY AS SCIENCE

Arguably, the science that technocracy positions at the heart of its practices lacks much of the quality and character of modern social science. Scholars have described the technocratic version of scientific practice as "broad but shallow" (Centeno, 1993, p. 310), a rather bare, simplified form of positivism (Clarence, 2002). It is mathematical, espousing quantification while eschewing the theoretical complexity and analytic rigor of contemporary social science research.

This positivist epistemology reflects the attempt to apply the philosophy and methods of physical science to human social activities. Positivism is often defined as an orientation toward knowledge that seeks precision through the measurement of observable phenomena. Descriptions of teaching and learning are valued only when articulated as measurement and mathematics (Phillips, 1983; Phillips and Burbules, 2000).

Depression-era American proponent of technocracy, engineer Howard Scott, wrote, "Technocracy makes one basic postulate: that the phenomena involved in the functional operation of the social mechanism are metrical" (Scott, 1933, p. 39). The solitary requirement is that human activity be represented as precise measurements. Applied to educational management, technocracy prioritizes mathematical representations of human behavior in schools, the charts, graphs, and trends lines of measured activities.

The conventional social practices of social science that provide conceptual depth, such as framing pertinent research questions, carefully designed data collection methods, and rigorous modes of data analysis, are less important than the primitive priority of simple quantification.

For example, public policy scholar Clarence has critiqued technocracy as ignoring the purposive centrality of "scientific controversy" (Clarence, 2002, p. 4) in the real work of researchers. Technocracy disregards the value of disagreement and debate to the process of scientific research within a vibrant community of investigators. Scientific progress depends on periods of debate and uncertainty among researchers. Theoretical positions, causal explanations, and substantive arguments collide on the path toward scientific consensus. Periods of discord are necessary for innovation and advancement. Technocracy deploys a singular fetish with one prominent feature of scientific research—quantitative data—while ignoring how scientific disciplines actually operate.

Further, technocratic understandings of science elide "the basic idea that evidence must be interpreted. How it is interpreted is subject to the way in which an individual understands the social world and what they consider to be important" (Clarence, 2002, pp. 4f.). The technocratic ideology of scientific method sidesteps the lessons learned in the intense social science debates of earlier decades—the "paradigm dialog" (Guba, 1990)—concerning issues of epistemology and methodology (Smith and Heshusius, 1986). Thoughtful conversations among social scientists and philosophers of science that generally resulted in widespread acceptance of a range of quantitative, qualitative, and mixed methodologies have not informed the isolated cloister of technocracy (Clarence, 2002).

TECHNOCRACY AS POLITICS

Social progress tends to be understood by technocracies in specific, constrained ways. Economic expansion through the improved efficiency of market capitalism, a common feature of growing neo-liberal forms of governance, is often an assumed goal of technocratic regimes (Ridley, 1966; Centeno, 1993). This requires the state to take authoritative control, providing a rational system of organization (Putnam, 1977; Ridley, 1966) that improves the "systemic efficiency" of economy and society (Centeno, 1993, p. 311). Technological progress and growth in material productivity are often viewed as interdependent goals rightly pursued by the state.

By contrast, questions of economic, social, and political equity typically do not register as priorities within the technocratic mentality. Technocracies are often "less concerned about distributive questions of social justice" (Putnam, 1977, p. 385), such as civil rights, the distribution of wealth, and equality of educational or employment opportunities. This is likely due to the technocratic disdain for the political theories and practices embraced by advocates for social justice for excluded or devalued cultural groups. If social progress can only occur when problems are purified of the stain of politics (Ridley, 1966; Putnam, 1977), then the strategies and goals of civil rights groups appear irrational and unseemly.

The human values and social purposes sought by civil rights campaigns do not appear on the ideological radar screen of technocracy due to the inability of technocratic governance to provide a substantive analysis of policy ends or goals. Frequently, policy researchers examine the value of a given policy in light of ends and means, the ultimate goal sought by the policy and the strategic operation designed for reaching the goal. "Technocratic policymaking focuses on instrumental action that is purposive and not conducive to debates regarding values or ends." (Centeno, 1993, p. 327). It provides a rational method for delivering ends, for reaching a given goal, but no systematic process for the analysis of the ends themselves (Putnam, 1977). It "gives little guidance, except in broad terms, where there is a choice between different ends" (Ridley, 1966, p. 44). Technocracy "rejects ideological or moralistic criteria," the very language of social value and ethical discernment that policymakers, politicians and citizens employ in debating whether specific social ends are worth pursuing (Putnam, 1977, p. 387).

Certainly, this does not mean that technocracies do not make value judgments. Many scholars point to the ideological nature of technocracy that hides behind the value-free mask. Centeno has observed that "technocrats cannot escape the constraints of their value orientation" (Centeno, 1993, p. 312). The claim of epistemic and practical superiority due an agnostic purity is a false front contradicted by the technocrat's "faith in the applicability and superiority of professional and technological methodologies and paradigms" (Ridley, 1966, p. 44). Technocracy is devoted to a modern version of efficiency expert F.W. Taylor's famous "one best way" (Kanigel, 1997), a single approach to framing and solving problems. Centeno (1993, p. 312) describes this as an "ideology of method…a belief in the ability to arrive at the optimal answer to any discussion through the application of particular practices."

In fact, what is frightening to scholars about technocracy is its incognizant "great confidence" (Ridley, 1966, p. 44). Technocrats ordained with what they understand as a powerful practical methodology for knowing the truth tend to lack the intellectual skills of self-examination and self-awareness. As a method of governance, it marches forward with unhesitating bravado and unflinching purpose. Fortified by the "assumption that rationalism is beyond dogmatism, and that scientific analysis knows no ideology" (Centeno, 1993, p. 313), technocracy views itself as immune from error. It is untempered by capacities of self-correction, insight, and reconsideration that might exist within a more flexible and humble framework.

The educational policies of NCLB and IDEA assume that government can improve society through the application of technocratic practices to social communities called schools. The regularity, order, and rationality of machines can be injected into the otherwise disorderly and intemperate public schools through technocratic governance. Appealing to "the commonly held fiction that education is non-political" (Cremin, 1961, p. 13), technocratic management supplies the steady hand of rationality to the public schools. The subjectivities of interest group politics and inconsistencies of teaching and learning are removed by administrative intervention, through what Daniel Bell (1973, p. 350) called the "perfection of administration."

Overall, despite the assertion that technocracy lacks political content or bias, it has a distinctly authoritarian, "anti-democratic" (Ridley, 1966, p. 44) bent. It is "fundamentally unsympathetic to the openness and equality of political democracy" (Putnam, 1977, p. 386). Democratic governance involves an open dialog among many perspectives and a diversity of interests. Technocracy considers such a conversation to be an inefficient carnival of unreasoned, selfish opinions. "Only the state can provide the leadership that is necessary, because only the state stands above interests" (Ridley, 1966, p. 44).

TECHNOCRACY AS EDUCATIONAL MANAGEMENT

In American public education, under accountability reform, dictates are issued down the ladder, seeking compliance at each level; from federal government to state departments of education to local districts and, finally, to schools and teachers. Apple (2004, p. 23) has described this development as "the increasing power of the 'evaluative state,'" the rise of federal and state bureaucracy in an intense regulatory regime. Local perspectives on problems and solutions are ignored in favor of statistical models held at upper administrative levels. Administrators at the upper ladder rungs employ a variety of rewards and punishments—"the carrot and the stick" (Fischer, 1990, p. 191)—to achieve compliance down through the multiple levels of the management system.

When educators or citizens critique the policy demands issued from the top of the system, the technocratic state limits the intrusion of democratic dialog in governance through the closed fist of expert discourse. Technocracies "define policy agenda in such a manner that all challenges must be made on their own terms" (Centeno, 1993, p. 322). Within the high stakes testing regime of accountability reform, this means that a person must be armed with "data" or "evidence" as defined by the technocratic ideology—quantitative, standardized measures of student academic achievement—in order to participate in debates around the management of the public schools. Critics of the accountability reform movement in American education are easily dismissed because they do not operate within the technocratic discourse of quantification.

> (T)he mystique of expert knowledge can also serve as a powerful obstacle to those who wish to challenge the system….Those who wish to challenge the policies of such experts must engage them using the same professional discourse.
>
> —(CENTENO, 1993, P. 318)

What constitutes a legitimate argument is defined by technocracy in terms that severely limit the participation of non-experts in the policy discussion. In the case of American public education, even parents, teachers, and many researchers do not utilize the technical discourse required.

A veteran educator would find that the greater proportion of her thoughts and insights about students, learning, and teaching had no legitimacy under these discourse rules. An experienced educational researcher would discover that "data," as defined by the technocrat, only includes a small subset of what the field of educational research considers to be "data" (e.g. Green et al., 2006). Any educational policy proposals lacking this brand of "data," not fulfilling the technocratic ideology, are simply words spoken in a suspect tongue. "The claimed methodological objectivity of technocratic governance makes its proposals self-evident and its opponents appear irrational (at best) or self-interested (at worst)" (Centeno, 1993, p. 327).

INCLUSION UNDER TECHNOCRACY

What are the implications of technocratic educational governance to inclusive education in the United States?

I recently conducted a small study of the opinions of seven public school administrators, a group consisting of elementary and secondary school principals as well as district level personnel. I asked all seven to explain why public schools are shifting more students with disabilities—in most cases, students described as having mild to moderate levels of impairment—into general education classes. All seven cited top-down pressures from school district and the state department of education administrations on schools to produce higher test scores (Danforth, in press).

Subsequently, as I have shared these findings with many school leaders and public school teachers, they have nodded in agreement. But they have also raised a number of serious concerns about the shape and content of inclusive education under technocracy. I will conclude this essay by exploring two specific concerns that educators working under the technocratic regime have articulated repeatedly to me in recent days. I will name these (1) the problem of *hollow inclusion* and (2) the problem of the *new segregation*.

What if educators, at least nominally, do the right thing for the wrong reasons? If technocratic systems of educational management coerce school principals and classroom teachers into placing more disabled students into general classrooms, regardless of their beliefs about disability, equality, and community, what outcomes might we expect?

I use the term *hollow inclusion* to describe inclusive practice carried out by educators whose professional actions are not supported by (1) a sufficient understanding of the political and ethical rationales supporting inclusive education, (2) a strong personal commitment to teaching for social justice, and (3) adequate professional knowledge and skills in the practices developed by educators and parents working for decades in the living tradition of inclusive education.

Hollow inclusion is a result of the bifurcation of means from ends that is endemic in technocratic educational governance. While the top-down push for teaching more disabled students enacts the technical pursuit of increased standardized test scores, it lacks the depth of philosophical, political, and pedagogical resources and expertise that are characteristic of the social justice approach to inclusion. Educators who are strong-armed into participating in inclusion often lack a deep understanding of the moral and political rationale that social justice advocates have articulated and expounded for decades.

Further, teachers and school principals who participate quite reluctantly in inclusion often ignore or are unaware of the living tradition of inclusive practice, the accumulated craft wisdom that educators and parents have developed over decades of intensive experimentation (e.g. Florian, 2006; Florian and Black-Hawkins, 2011; Black-Hawkins and Florian, 2012). That tradition has created a variety of specific professional practices framed within a social justice orientation to the cultural diversity and the progressive role of public education in the lives of undervalued children and families. It is a tradition of pedagogical action that unites means and ends, teaching strategies and democratic purposes. When principals and teachers reluctantly pursue inclusion under a technocratic orientation that divorces means from ends, isolating the actual work of teaching from the larger ethical and democratic goals of inclusive education, they often fail to avail themselves of the rich living tradition of inclusive schooling that educators have developed over the past thirty years.

Under the system of technocratic governance, the line of demarcation, the political division, is drawn on the basis of professional judgment about which disabled students are likely to produce higher standardized test scores. Those expected to utilize the general education instruction in a way that yields higher assessment outcomes are placed in general classrooms. Those viewed as unlikely candidates for score increases are segregated into special education classrooms and schools. I use the term *new segregation* to describe this technocratic rationing of humanity, a micro-economy of social value, because it signifies a redistribution of student identities and classroom locations on the basis of technical criteria. In an era of increasing inclusion, students excluded under new segregation experience a reallocation and reification of stigma. The newly segregated students are understood as unable to improve on standardized tests when presented conventional forms of general classroom instruction.

Apple (2004) warns that the competitive system of high stakes testing creates a schism whereby so-called "'motivated' parents with 'able' children" become attractive to educators and funding for traditional special education—that is, less attractive, noncompetitive students—is in jeopardy.

Working class children and students of color are uniquely vulnerable to exclusion in this scheme of competition and identity economics. Students are caught in the strategic maneuvers of educators who, like it or not, pursue higher scores for schools and sub-populations.

> (S)pecific students are seen as moveable. Other students' abilities are seen as increasingly fixed and less worthy of attention. The class and race characteristics of these latter students are striking. Poor and working-class students, students of African descent, and other ethnically "different" children are not valued commodities on this kind of market.
>
> —(Apple, 2004, p. 37)

Resources and general classroom seats are reserved for students viewed as embodying opportunities for rising score trajectories. In the United States, disability segregation inevitably plays out in a fierce game of social class and race (Fierros and Conroy, 2002).

The less movable students set aside as unworthy to compete have a new educational disorder that necessitates the new segregation. It is individual deficit in test-taking talent, a psychological or educational defect involving an impairment of what technocratic schools most value, the individual aptitude for scoring higher with each successive performance on standardized measures of academic knowledge and skill. It is an inability to compete in standardized assessment, pencil and paper gymnastics.

The combination of a deterministic version of science, an authoritarian orientation to governance, and an amoral approach to the pursuit of policy goals should make educators quiver. Researchers and practitioners alike should quake with trepidation. Even as the technocratic state shifts increasing numbers of disabled students into general education classrooms, ostensibly bringing a new jolt of energy to inclusive education reform, we should be frightened. When democratic ends are achieved by anti-democratic schemes of management and activity, we should be prepared to discover that the democratic character of those achievements is not deeper than a shiny surface coat of paint. Beneath the veneer, if we are willing to scrutinize, lie ways of operating schools and classrooms that violate our basic ethical sensibilities.

CHAPTER TWELVE

The Politics of Inclusive Education in South Africa

SIGAMONEY M. NAICKER

Many South Africans, particularly those who operated in the margins of society in the 350 years of colonial rule, embraced inclusive education and saw it as a panacea to the brutal alienation they suffered. Education White Paper 6 on *Special Needs Education: Building an Inclusive Education and Training System* was launched in 2001. White Paper 6 was one of 7 white papers on education that was introduced by the new South African government after the democratic elections in 1994. The 7 White Papers created a national framework for policy implementation in the democratic South Africa.

A substantial number of educationists, parents, and children welcomed the concept of inclusive education in South Africa. Activists in policy debates and in other policy forums that led to the publication of the White Paper 6 viewed inclusive education with a great deal of optimism and enthusiasm. The hurt and pain of exclusion in their personal lives under apartheid led to a celebration of inclusion as a policy which was one of the seven White Papers on education that heralded in a new education policy framework. Inclusive education in South Africa was not viewed as a theory of education but rather a social theory for South African society.

Sudden radical change in policy is always accompanied by a reconstructed body of knowledge with associated practices. Radical education change of a paradigmatic nature ruptures theories, assumptions, models, practices and tools. The euphoria that accompanied the change in the South African education system in 2001 was met with a more sober reality as the challenge of Inclusive Education began to strike home during the next two decades of implementation. Inclusive education had to compete with and overhaul a special education system that had deeply entrenched structures, knowledge, practices and extraordinary levels of inequality concerning race. Associated with this challenge was South Africa's colonial past and the dominant perceptions created by racist thinking and practices. The status quo in South Africa prior to the implementation of White Paper 6 reflected a society where world class facilities in special education were enjoyed by the white sector of the population and to a lesser extent some minority groups at the expense of the majority Africans. The structures, facilities, human resource expertise, knowledge, and practices amongst the different race groups were disparate and the White Paper had to contend with these challenges over the next two decades. The biggest challenge that faced South African educationists was concerned with the development of new theories, assumptions, models, practices and tools. It is against this background that this paper discusses the development of inclusive education in South Africa in relation to politics of: (i) race, (ii) knowledge, (iii) practices and, (iv) the challenges of implementation.

THE POLITICS OF RACE

Social activists regarded the Education White Paper 6 as a framework for social transformation given South Africa's racist and classist history. It is virtually impossible not to talk about race and class in South Africa when raising the issue of education. Education is a deeply political issue and one's views on education can never be neutral. Racial domination lends itself to a number of influences on any population or group of people. Within the South Africa context, 350 years of colonial rule and the subjugation of the masses of black people to second class citizens impacted on almost every aspect of life in South Africa. This phenomenon has been well documented but the focus of this analysis relates to inclusive education. The influence and authority of race has been influential in shaping the minds of educationists in South Africa. Whilst there was a significant shift in mind-sets during the resistance to apartheid, the influence of apartheid on educational thinking and practices remain. It will continue to influence practices since shedding the yoke of apartheid thinking and practices requires a paradigmatic shift that is proving to be a huge challenge. The influence of the mind on the sub-conscious and the unconscious is very difficult to fathom. The point is that the influence on thinking has been a result of a socialization process. In forums convened to reconstruct knowledge that shifted towards inclusive education, there was a great deal of scepticism and heated exchanges about generating new theories based on new assumptions about teaching and learning. South Africa did not transplant a western concept of inclusive education but the White Paper crafted a model that was based on realities in South Africa.

In the period immediately after the launch of the White Paper, inclusive education thinking and practices had to contend with a white supremacist ideology which was accompanied by bodies of knowledge that emerged from traditional psychology (medical model). South Africa's teachers were trained in apartheid style institutions which promoted this type of thinking. Of course there were some radical and more liberal institutions that called into question the canonical text. Some excellent alternative psychological positions were generated by intellectuals who were progressive. The pocket of progressive thinking was restricted to a few when it came to knowledge construction. Introducing a new theory, assumptions and practices is always a difficult task. What this illustrates is that change in a country with South Africa's history is a complex one (Naicker, 1999).

From an educational perspective, the oppressed during the apartheid era were trained to think that they were inferior. This has intellectual, social and psychological implications. The oppressors created the knowledge and implemented knowledge as canonical texts. Both the knowledge and practice were embedded in the minds of people since a large majority of current educationists were trained during the apartheid era.

The class privilege of the oppressor allowed them to gain access to resources, knowledge and culture which was reproduced over generations. This was the dominant culture which everybody aspired, to including some of the oppressed. The use of the military to subjugate and use their economic power to advance themselves over 350 years meant that the "so called" second class citizens also were reproduced in a second class environment under harsh intellectual, economic and social conditions. With the development of the political consciousness, thinking changed. Human agency on the part of the oppressed ensured a resistance that created different mind-sets often accompanied by violence that was perpetrated against the oppressor. However, deep psychological and sociological barriers persist since the scars are deeply embedded in the psyche of many people.

How does this affect the transformation from special education to inclusive education? Besides the development of knowledge which will be explained in the next section, the legacy of racial privilege left behind large scale inequality in terms of special education provision. In attempting to level the playing fields as was the intention of the Education White Paper 6, the development of inclusion had to contend with large scale inequality based on race.

Table 1. Census data: Distribution of disabled persons per category per province (Department of Education, 2001).

Prov.	*Sight*	*Hearing*	*Physical*	*Mental*	*Multiple*	*Not specified*	*Total*	*% per prov.*	*% of population*
EC	161898	68531	115717	41432	35997	38604	462179	17.39	1.14
FS	133614	33045	41960	13947	16461	18127	257154	9.68	0.63
Gaut.	211769	59868	69936	24033	26030	63906	455542	17.14	1.12
KZN	183758	76034	129894	42646	24895	44863	502090	18.89	1.24
MP	98322	31895	41381	12211	9019	19085	211913	7.97	0.52
NC	18529	6083	9052	3791	2403	7137	46995	1.77	0.12
NP	113088	51416	60078	22578	16019	33690	296869	11.17	0.73
NW	129442	37571	54706	17768	16913	23134	279534	10.52	0.69
WC	40603	18965	35051	14146	6499	30174	145438	5.47	0.36
TOT.	1091023	383408	557775	192552	154236	278720	2657714	100.0	6.55
% per disability	41.05	14.43	20.99	7.25	5.80	10.49	100.00		
% per population	2.69	0.94	1.37	0.47	0.38	0.69	6.55		

According to the White Paper, the provision of resources for learners who experienced any form of barrier was skewed to certain provinces of the 9 provinces. The geographical and racially skewed provision benefitted white learners mainly.

- The incidence of disabilities in the Eastern Cape constitutes 17.39% of the disabled population yet the province has only 10.79% of the total number of special schools.
- Gauteng has 17.14% of the disabled population but has 25.26% of the schools.
- The Western Cape has 5.47% of the disabled population but has 21.58% of the schools.

The White Paper argues that this mismatch between needs and provision is a direct result of previous apartheid policies that allocated facilities on a racial basis. These policies also centralized provision within the Western Cape and Gauteng so that the vast majority of learners today attend residential special schools in a province other than their own, since no facilities were available in their province of residence (Department of Education, 2001).

A comparison between the overall incidence of disabilities and the number of learners accommodated in school also reveals stark disparities, for example:

- 0.28% of learners in the Eastern Cape are enrolled in special schools yet the overall incidence figure for the population of disabled persons (of all ages) is 17.39%.
- This pattern is repeated across provinces indicating that significant numbers of learners who—based on the traditional model—should be receiving educational support in special schools are not getting any.
- While the national total incidence figure for disabilities (of all ages) is 6.55%, the total numbers of learners in special schools is 0.52%.

What this means is that within the special education system in South Africa, provision was made for white children. In view of this backlog, the White Paper suggests that an inclusive education and training system and a wider spread of educational support services will be created in line with what learners with disabilities require. This means that learners who require low-intensive support would receive this in ordinary schools and those requiring moderate support would receive this in full service schools. Learners who require high-intensive educational support would continue to receive such support in special schools.

Table 2. Estimating the number of disabled learners who are out of school (Department of Education, 2001).

Population selected:	*Total*	*Using WHO min. of 2.2%*	*Using WHO max. of 2.6%*
A: Total population age 7–15 using Census '96 shows learners in compulsory age	8,291,000	182,000	216,000
B: Total population age 6–15 using Census '96 shows inclusion of Grade R	9,225,000	203,000	240,000
C: Total school population age 6–18 using Census '96	11,734,000	258,000	305,000
D: Total population in public + independent ordinary + special schools, 1999, DoE figures	12,378,000	272,000	322,000
E: D + Grade R cohort from B	13,312,000	293,000	346,000

According to White Paper 6, the estimate relating to disabled learners out of school is 260,000. In view of these challenges, the White Paper proposed a model that included three key pillars for the building of an inclusive education system (Department of Education, 2001). This included special schools as resource centers, full-service schools and district based support teams. This model will be described in greater detail later on.

Education, as one of the pillars of separate development, was used as an instrument to ensure that all four groups accepted the idea of that policy. The disparities in special education and education support provision were clearly racial. Table 3 illustrates these disparities (Behr, 1980).

Table 3. Provision and schools for the different types of disability (Behr, 1980).

Disability	*White*	*African*	*Colored*	*Indian*
Aural	5 schools	7	2	1
Visual	2 schools	4	1	1
Cerebral Palsy	4 schools	3	1	1
Physically Disabled	4 schools	None		
Epilepsy	3 schools	None	1	None
Autism	2 schools	None	None	None
Mental Retardation	41 centers	None	None	3
Industry/Reform	3	None	5	1
Remedial	Provision exists	None	None	Provision exists
Educable Mental Retardation	Provision exists	None	Provision exists	Provision exists

Behr (1980) reported that 'Whites' made up 17.5%, 'Africans' 70.2%, 'Coloured' 9.4% and 'Indians' 2.9% of the population. Table 3 shows clearly that special education provision favored 'whites.'

Given the low levels historically of education provision for African learners, it becomes clear that serious gaps will exist in terms of teacher provision for future, as well as for the management and leadership capacity. The implementers and the various provinces in South Africa, besides other challenges, will have to address these limitations.

THE POLITICS OF KNOWLEDGE

How is it possible for people in dominant structures and in senior positions in a country to accept the knowledge construction of people they regarded as second-class citizens? The majority of them went to schools, lived in areas and were socialized with a group of people who alienated and marginalized the majority of black people. How is it possible for people who have been socialized into believing that they are superior to listen to a discourse that is contrary to everything they, their ancestors and their children have been socialized into? Special education had racist and medical roots. Of course, medical knowledge was important, but in the case of special education in South Africa it was associated with the 1948 Special Schools Act (Naicker, 2005).

Although it mainly concerned white learners, the Act provided the first signal of the model of special education in South Africa based on the medical model. The Special Education Act worked on the assumption that learners were deficient and their deficiencies were pathological, a viewpoint that was strongly influenced by medical thinking (Naicker, 2005). The pathological perspective associates disability with impairment and loss and does not take systemic deficiencies into consideration.

The 1948 Special Schools Act in white education introduced into special education a medical and mental diagnosis and treatment model (Naicker, 2005). This model, which focuses on the individual deficit theory and views the person as a helpless being, is firmly entrenched in the medical, charity and lay discourses (Fulcher, 1989). Incidentally, 1948 was the year that Apartheid was first introduced in the statute books of South Africa.

For the period 1948 until 1994, the knowledge has not been called into question at a systemic level. The contestation of special education knowledge and practices only emerged formally when President Nelson Mandela appointed a National Commission of Education Support Services in 1996. The National Commission included members of the traditional special education establishment, as well as a very representative group of progressive organizations including the disability sector. The disability sector and the progressive organizations were advancing an inclusive agenda arguing that special education did not serve the best interests of disabled people and children who experience barriers to learning. The recommendations of the National Commission shaped the development of Education White Paper 6.

One of the major outcomes of the National Commission Report on Education Support Services (Department of Education, 1997) was the development of the discourse on barriers to learning. The Commission crafted a response to the medical model by viewing the learner within a context, ensuring that both the learner and the systemic issues are considered when identifying challenges learners experience.

The definition in the White Paper (Department of Education, 2001) is clear: barriers to learning can be located within the learner, within the centre of learning, within the education system and within the broader social, economic and political context. These barriers manifest themselves in different ways and only become obvious when learning breakdown occurs, when learners 'drop out' of the system or when the excluded become visible. Breakdown refers to children experiencing difficulty with learning as is so often the case in South Africa. More than 50% of learners do not make the grade norm for reading and numeracy and the attrition rate in the schooling system is about 50%. Sometimes it is possible to identify permanent barriers in the learner or in the system which can be addressed through enabling mechanisms and processes. However, barriers may also arise during the learning process and are seen as transitory in nature. These may require different interventions or strategies to prevent them from causing learning breakdown or excluding learners from the system. The key to preventing barriers from occurring is the effective monitoring and meeting of the different needs among the learner population and within the system as a whole.

The White Paper identified a number of barriers which include the following:

- Socio-Economic Barriers
- Lack of Access to Basic Services
- Poverty and Underdevelopment
- Factors Which Place Learners at Risk
- Attitudes
- Language and Communication
- Disability
- Inflexible Curriculum
- Inappropriate and Inadequate Provision of Support Services
- Lack of Enabling and Protective Legislation and Policy
- Lack of Parental Recognition and Involvement
- Lack of Human Resource Development Strategies
- Inaccessible safe environment

—(Department of Education, 2001, p. 18)

In a country such as South Africa with its history steeped in the medical model, the discourse on barriers to learning was critical to change the gaze of teachers in working with challenges learners faced in the classroom. It also becomes obvious that looking for individual deficits and not examining the above factors will lead to very reductionist and unsound pedagogy. The White Paper argued that the relationship between education provision and the socio-economic conditions in any society must be recognized. Effective learning is fundamentally influenced by the availability of educational resources to meet the needs of any society. In many countries, especially our own country, there are inadequate numbers of centers of learning and other facilities to meet the educational needs of the population. In most cases, inadequacies in provision are linked to other inequalities in the society such as urban/rural disparities, as well as inequalities arising from discrimination on grounds such as gender, race and disability. Barriers result not only from the inadequacy of provision, but also from policies and practices which are designed to perpetuate these inequalities.

The White Paper 6 provided very useful insights to teachers in teasing out each barrier. For example, concerning socio-economic factors, one of the most significant barriers to learning remains the inability of learners to access the educational provision that does exist and their inability to access other services which contribute to the learning process. In most instances the inability to access education provision results from inadequate or non-existent services and facilities which are key to participation in the learning process. For example, in many poor communities, particularly in our own country in rural areas, learners are unable to reach centers of learning because there are no transport facilities available to learners or the roads are so poorly developed and maintained that centers cannot be reached. While such barriers affect all learners in poorly serviced communities, it is important to recognize that particular groups of learners are more severely affected by these barriers. In general transport systems which do exist are inaccessible to learners with disabilities, particularly learners who use wheelchairs. So, for example, learners with disabilities who should be attending school or who wish to go to adult education classes are unable to even reach the school or class because the public transport system which is available is either physically inaccessible or unwilling to transport them. (Department of Education, 2007) At the same time they are unable to walk to school or classes and in this way they are totally excluded from the education system.

According to White Paper 6 the lack of access to basic services is the effect which sustained poverty has on learners, the learning process and the education system. For learners, the most obvious result of poverty, often caused by unemployment and other economic inequalities, is the inability of families to meet basic needs such as nutrition and shelter. Learners living under such conditions are subject to increased emotional stress which adversely affects learning and development. Additionally, under-nourishment leads to a lack of concentration and a range of other symptoms which affect the ability of the learner to engage effectively in the learning process. Poverty-stricken communities are also poorly resourced communities which are frequently characterized by limited educational facilities, large classes with high pupil/teacher ratios, inadequately trained staff and inadequate teaching and learning materials. Such factors raise the likelihood of learning breakdown and the inability of the system to sustain effective teaching and learning. Learners from families where one or more of the breadwinners are unemployed or poorly paid are also more likely to leave school as soon as possible to go out to work to supplement the family income. This perpetuates the cycle of limited skills with fewer work opportunities, increased likelihood of unemployment or poorly paid work and, thus, on-going poverty and exclusion from education and later mainstream economic and social life (Department of Education, 2001).

Curriculum and assessment has been identified by White Paper 6 as a barrier to learning. Assessment processes are often inflexible and designed to only assess particular kinds of knowledge and aspects of learning, such as the amount of information that can be memorized rather than the learner's understanding of the concepts involved. The seriousness of such barriers is most obvious where there are large numbers of learners who are forced to repeat aspects of the curriculum, even if this means remaining in levels where the age gap between the learner and the other learners is significant. A further area of barriers arising from the curriculum is that which results from the medium of teaching and learning. Teaching and learning for many learners takes place through a language which is not their first language. This not only places these learners at a disadvantage, but it also leads to linguistic difficulties which contribute to learning breakdown. Second language learners are often subjected to low expectations, discrimination and lack of cultural peers. Educators furthermore often experience difficulties in developing appropriate support mechanisms for learners who do not use their primary language in school (Department of Education, 2001).

This oppositional discourse to the medical model presented a new body of knowledge for teachers and education in terms of understanding barriers to learning in South Africa. The White Paper provided a narrative to all the barriers mentioned and ensured that an emerging discourse for inclusive education was on the educational roadmap. Besides this body of knowledge, other significant interventions included the model of inclusion that was proposed with its associated practices.

Based on its historical legacy of white privilege, knowledge production in South Africa, particularly in the field of psychology, educational psychology and special education, had its roots in traditional white universities that were highly resourced and could be compared to some of the best institutions in Europe and America. The historically disadvantaged universities differed in terms of their intellectual output but were assisted and supported by overseas based universities. Progressive academics and universities visited and funded many of the historically disadvantaged universities in South Africa. It followed that the knowledge production and type of intellectual tradition differed markedly in both sets of universities. These universities shaped the ideological agenda of practices in schools based on the intellectual tradition. It also follows that inclusive education theory and practice was influenced by a more sociological tradition rather than traditional psychology (Naicker, 1999). The barriers to learning concept was entrenched in the sociological tradition and offered a more comprehensive account of why children do not succeed in school.

As mentioned, South Africa did not transplant a western model regarding inclusive education. Based on the data mentioned in Tables 1, 2, and 3, the South African model of Inclusive Education was based on three pillars. These included Full-Service Schools, District Based Support Teams and Special Schools as Resource Centers.

Full-Service Schools are the first pillar and will be transformed from an ordinary school and would be equipped and supported to provide for a greater range of learning needs. As learning needs and barriers to learning arise within a specific context and vary from time to time, it is obvious that full-service schools should be supported to develop their capacity and potential for addressing and reducing barriers to learning, as well as seeing their educational provision in a flexible manner.

District-based support teams refer to integrated professional support services at district level. Support providers employed by the Department of Education will draw on the expertise from local education institutions and various community resources. Their key function is to assist education institutions (including early childhood centers and schools) to identify and address barriers to learning and promote effective teaching and learning. This includes both classroom and organizational support, providing specialized learner and educator support, as well as curricular and institutional development (including management and governance), and administrative support.

Special Schools as resource centers imply the qualitative improvement of special schools for the learners that they serve and their phased conversion to special school resource centers that provide professional support to neighboring schools and are integrated into district-based support teams (Department of Education, 2007).

The above model is intended to be implemented with a different approach to assessment and support to address the backlogs inherited from the previous dispensation. The implementation of this model has had to contend with the existing structures of special schools and remedial support for learners in mainstream schools. The implementation of this model involved an initial field test which was to be completed in three years and later moving to scale throughout South Africa. The initial three year field test took a decade since there were many challenges relating to understandings and the demands of practical implementation. The challenges posed to the National Department and the 9 provinces related to employing suitable and skilled staff, motivating staff who were in senior positions to buy into the new policy, developing new frameworks of thinking and practice and ensuring that all stakeholders support government in advancing inclusive education. The real challenge was to move from the policy to practice.

THE POLITICS OF PRACTICE

South Africa has made some progress in the area of education. The development of a single education from 19 different departments based on race and ethnicity is indeed a major achievement. The development of 7 policy papers was also an excellent achievement. In the area of Inclusive Education, one has to assess the power dynamics in relation to transformation from a special education system to inclusive education. Whilst the factors that South Africa had to contend with were discussed above, the last 13 years has included some very positive signs for the future.

Changing personnel in senior positions and developing practical tools that are consistent with the ideology of inclusion is indeed a great challenge. Other established democracies that span centuries have their own struggles with inclusion.

South Africans have learnt that policy at a theoretical level that has to be translated into practice requires a massive effort, but more especially, if one has to implement seven White Papers in an environment where financial resources and human resources are limited. At the ideological level, all stakeholders, including those who made up the new progressive breed of progressive activists and those who were required to depart from their most fundamental assumptions on education, struggled with the praxis, that is. linking the theory to a new practice.

The practice of inclusive education in South Africa must be viewed against the background of the competing priorities in a developing economy. Further, and as articulated earlier on, the implementation has had to deal with a diverse audience of people, many of whom were schooled in South Africa's conservative education system.

The implementation of the Inclusive Education Model in terms of its three tiers had to be supplemented by an adapted curriculum as well as an assessment model that was consistent with the notion of barriers to learning. Further the following steps were set out as key levers for changing the system:

- Criteria for the revision of existing policies and legislation for all bands of education and training, and frameworks for governance and organization;
- A strengthened district-based education support service;
- The expansion of access and provision;
- Support for curriculum development and assessment, institutional development and quality improvement and assurance;
- A national information, advocacy and mobilization campaign; and
- A revised funding strategy (Department of Education, 2001, p. 20).

Substantial set up work had to be done regarding legislation that governs full-service schools, district based support teams and special schools as resource centers. One of the levers for change was to employ senior personnel in the national department as well as the nine provincial departments. A change in theory, assumptions, model, practice and tools requires skilled personnel with adequate levels of knowledge to deal with the transformation. Whilst progress was achieved and the language of inclusion became visible in documentation and speeches, it was not sufficiently supported by people who were skilled to accomplish the task. The personnel with specialized education knowledge were both relevant and irrelevant from the old system. Whilst their specialized training was important, it acted as a stumbling block in terms of advancing inclusive education. They were unable to see the possibilities of an inclusive education system as their point of departure was a dual system of education.

The lack of skilled personnel meant that the country had to utilize enthusiastic people who were willing to learn and develop expertise through trial and error. It was like fixing a plane while flying it. There was no shortage of such people but the system of inclusive education in South Africa could best be described as a process of trial and error and critical role players learn on the job in view of the dearth of skilled personnel. Progress has been limited but there is a sense of optimism which resulted in the National Ministry declaring the year 2013 as the year of inclusion.

One of the most successful features of inclusive education in South Africa over the last thirteen years has been advocacy. There has been a limited resistance to inclusive education and the concept is widely discussed and embraced by thousands of teachers.

South Africa has witnessed three substantial revisions of the initial outcomes based curriculum. One of the main reasons cited for these revisions relate to lack of progress of the education system. In each of the three revisions training of teachers took place. Inclusive Education was an important feature of all the training sessions. Training was done by officials appointed by the Department of Education. The link with higher education is sorely missing and their involvement has been limited. Much of this has to do with the lack of trust between higher education and the Department of Education.

Whilst their enthusiasm and commitment was evident during this process of training teachers, there was a lack of understanding in terms of the conceptual and operational implications of an inclusive education system. For example, the concept of barriers to learning never took hold in the training sessions and this powerful body of knowledge did not surface sufficiently in the training documents after a period of 12 years. Further, there was a lack of understanding amongst personnel in the mainstream of education about the possibilities of inclusive education. It must be noted that all of them or the large majority were socialized in mainstream education within the framework of the medical model.

South Africa performs very poorly in literacy and numeracy. An analysis of grade 3 literacy and numeracy results suggest that South Africa is one of the poorest performers internationally. The tables suggests that in both literacy and numeracy more than half the schooling population are not reaching the grade norm of 50% in the 9 South African provinces in Grade 3.

Table 4. Performance in Grade 3 Numeracy.

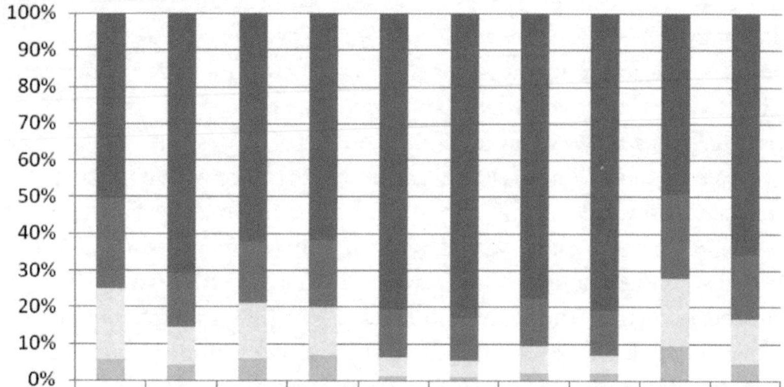

	EC	FS	GP	KN	LP	MP	NC	NW	WC	SA
Not achieved	51	71	62	62	81	83	78	81	49	66
Patially achieved	24	15	17	18	13	11	13	12	23	17
Achieved	19	10	15	13	5	5	7	5	18	12
Outstanding	6	4	6	7	1	1	2	2	9	5

Table 5. Performance in Grade 3 Literacy (Department of Education, 2011a).

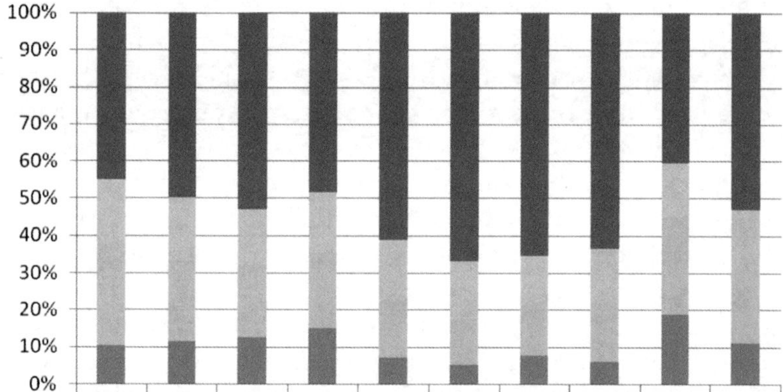

	EC	FS	GP	KN	LP	MP	NC	NW	WC	SA
Not achieved	45	50	53	48	61	67	66	63	41	53
Partially achieved	17	17	15	16	16	15	14	15	14	16
Achieved	27	22	20	21	16	13	13	15	27	20
Outstanding	10	11	13	15	7	5	8	6	19	11

This performance has resulted in South Africa being one of the most underperforming countries in terms of its education system. Whilst there could be a number of other variables that point to poor performance, it is quite clear that thinking and knowledge underpinning inclusive education can play an important role in South Africa given the number of social factors that impinge on education performance. There is a clear relationship between poverty and the literacy and numeracy data. However, the Department of Basic Education has introduced Action Plan 2014 which for the first time uses Annual National Assessments in each school to establish strengths and weaknesses of the system (Department of Basic Education, 2011a). The idea is to develop pedagogical responses to weaknesses in performance. This has been accompanied by the third revision of the curriculum which focuses on school functionality and curriculum coverage (Department of Basic Education, 2011b). Each learner is provided with a textbook and workbook and there is a major focus on supervising curriculum coverage. Therefore, there is both support and pressure on the school system. There is also a renewed teacher education emphasis. All these interventions are accompanied by the Year of Inclusion emphasis. It can be argued that the South African education system is making a considerable effort. Recent results suggest marginal improvement in performance which is a sign of a turnaround.

Another major intervention in the system related to assessment. In order to shift away from the practices of the medical model relating to assessment, the Screening, Identification, Assessment and Support (SIAS) (Department of Basic Education, 2010) strategy aims to facilitate the shift from the individual learner as the driving organizer for support provision to that of the range, nature and level of support programs, services, personnel and resources that will be made available for special and ordinary schools. Consequently the range, nature and level of support programs, services, personnel and resources rather than the individual learner will be the focus of budgets, norms and standards for support provision (Department of Basic Education 2012c). This instrument will assist in placing learners in special schools as resource centers, ordinary neighborhood schools and full-service schools. It took several years to produce this document, which is consistent with the White Paper.

According to the SIAS strategy, the availability of the range, nature and level of support programs, services, personnel and resources can be at site level or at nodal sites to be accessed by a cluster of schools. This will be one of the main mechanisms to ensure that learners can access support without the need to move to another than their ordinary neighborhood school. Highly specialized support resources, personnel, programs and facilities for a group of learners with high support needs requiring access to the same support program or resources can be provided at site level such as in special schools or specialized settings attached to ordinary schools. Specialized support resources, personnel, programs and facilities that are more portable and require less operational and organizational planning will be provided at circuit or district level to be accessed by learners at mainstream schools (e.g. learning support/remedial education, assistive devices, counseling and therapeutic services). The Full-Service School will be the point within a circuit or district from which services will be made available to a cluster of mainstream schools.

Several teacher education initiatives have been planned to ensure that special schools as resource centers become hubs of learning based on the category of disability. This is a result of a dearth of training that has taken place in various special schools, particularly those in the disadvantaged sector and in mainly non-white areas. For example, regarding visual impairment, in 2009 the Department of Basic Education conducted a survey in all schools for learners with visual impairment. The overall findings revealed that the quality of management and of teaching and learning in the majority of schools was not up to standard; that the majority of the teachers lacked the necessary specialization to teach at such schools, such that a total of 124 teachers had no knowledge of Braille (Grade 1) and 510 of contracted Braille (Grade 2); and that there was a serious lack of IT equipment for both the production of Braille as well as of large print LTSM as well as knowledge to produce Braille. Specifically learners with low vision are not accommodated through effective use of latest screen reading and enlargement technology. The new framework for the development of teachers in inclusive education for visual impairment has begun (Department of Basic Education, 2012a).

Another intervention relating to Deaf and hard of hearing is also in progress. According to the framework for teacher development in the area of Deaf and hard of hearing the Department of Basic Education in 2009 conducted a survey of all schools for learners who are Deaf and hard of hearing. It was found that the qualifications of teachers and standards of curriculum delivery were unsatisfactory. Of the 903 teachers in the 43 schools, only 249 are trained in South African Sign Language, leaving 654 teachers without any training in this area of specialization. In view of the fact that the DBE is currently in the process of writing a curriculum for South African Sign Language for Grades R–12, the training of teachers will be a critical requirement for its successful implementation (Department of Education, 2012b).

These training initiatives and investigations suggest that the Department of Basic Education is taking responsibility for the backlogs through research and intervention programs that address the considerable backlogs of the apartheid era. Two decades of democracy are indeed a short time for a democracy but the challenges being experienced suggest that there is a long way to go for Education White Paper 6 to be implemented successfully.

CHALLENGES OF THE INCLUSIVE EDUCATION SYSTEM IN SOUTH AFRICA

The discussion thus far has provided the context to the challenge of inclusive education in South Africa. Whilst there is overwhelming support for the policy, the number of out of school disabled youth, poor provision regarding teacher training for black teachers and the need to implement inclusive education within a conservative context captures the real challenges South Africans face.

The Department of Basic Education (DBE) in South Africa has committed 2013 to the entrenchment of Inclusive Education, thus calling 2013 the year of inclusion. This is a very bold approach by the education authorities. As mentioned earlier, there is much more to do for inclusive education to be successful in South Africa. Whilst progress in the area of inclusive education at a theoretical, planning level and the beginning steps of White Paper Six have been achieved, more work has to be done in the area of teacher education, human resource development in general, building and developing full-service schools, support and creating special schools as resource centers and empowering district based support teams. The following presentation to the education standing committee (Department of Basic Education, 2012c) reveals the limitations of the implementation:

- Analysis found glaring disparities in the provision of access to specialist services to schools across provinces and within each in terms of types of professionals.
- There is a huge lack of specialist professionals and in three of South Africa's provinces the availability of specialists is below 0.5%. These provinces are yet to budget for inclusive education. There is a lack of therapists, psychologists, social workers and professional nurses.
- The ratio for teachers without knowledge of South African Sign Language (21.8%) is higher than that for teachers without knowledge of visual impairment (10.9%). Areas of deafness and visual impairment appear to experience major challenges. Although South African Sign Language development has begun, this is one of the most neglected sectors.

The lack of quality and trained staff is a major problem that hinders the further development of Inclusive Education/Special Education in South Africa. Specialists are central to the assessment and identification process. Availability of therapists is also critical for assessment of learners for provision of assistive devices and technology particularly for students with physical disabilities. If the three provinces yet to be budgeted for the expansion of Inclusive Education do not occur, White Paper Six will ultimately fail in these provinces. According to the report made by the Department of Basic Education to the standing committee, visual impairment and deafness are isolated because they are highly specialized compared to other disabilities that largely depend on Curriculum Differentiation. The report also cautioned about appropriate and relevant conversion of ordinary schools to full-service schools. Specifically, the report stressed that a conversion is more than making schools environmentally accessible for learners with physical disabilities as there is a need for an inclusive education ethos. Ultimately, the report calls for provinces to get more involved in the inclusive education process through budgeting and more advocacy and training.

It is encouraging to note that the Department of Basic Education has prioritized teacher training that will enjoy the following foci:

- Training all teachers on Screening, Identification, Assessment and Support (SIAS) and Curriculum Differentiation including CAPS training for one per school (2012–2014).
- Improving specialized skills—visual impairment, Deaf and hard of hearing, autism, intellectual disability, communication disorders, cerebral palsy—short courses and bursaries for HEI accredited courses.
- District support teams—effective management of special schools, full-service schools and supporting implementation of inclusion at all levels (guidelines training).

At a general level, it seems that the envisaged White Paper Six educational shift in paradigm has been largely underestimated. Paradigm shifts are complex and ambitious projects and poor results in the South African education system suggest that deeper training of teachers should take place to address the challenge of poverty and education. If poor learners and poor achievers are to be advanced in the system, teachers need effective special education knowledge based instructional tools that will create a different consciousness within the school culture so that inclusive education can flourish.

SECTION THREE

Conceptual Confusions as Roots for Conceptual Innovations

CHAPTER THIRTEEN

Waiting for Inclusive Education? An Exploration of Conceptual Confusions and Political Struggles

JULIE ALLAN

The field of inclusive education is marked by a number of conceptual confusions and contestations. The confusions have arisen through a series of practices that have been concerned with creating certainty and clarity about inclusive education, but which have produced rather different effects. This chapter examines the efforts at conceptualizing and operationalizing inclusive education and some of the confusions that have arisen as a consequence. It considers the lack of reflection and debate on the purposes of inclusive education and its consequences, then examines elements of politics and policy that have shaped the development of inclusive education, limited its emergence and added further layers of confusion and illustrates this with particular reference to three countries—England, Sweden and the United States. The purpose of exploring these layers of confusion and of the limitations of the debate about inclusive education is to try to identify what is lacking in our understanding. This is not merely to demonstrate that which is in deficit, but to help establish what might be possible and what might be better avoided. A comparison of the three countries is of particular significance because of their rather different political contexts and contrasting educational histories that appear currently to be both converging and diverging. The English education system has had recent experience of the effects of neo-liberal ideas such as competitiveness, freedom of choice and performativity in a context of devolved responsibility for education; Sweden's traditions of comprehensive schooling, resting upon national independence and with democratic values and social welfare as cornerstones, are increasingly being challenged by these ideas; and the United States' system of early and high stakes testing threatens to undermine its own promise of No Child Left Behind by precipitating the segregation of particular groups. The governments of these countries, whilst appearing to offer continued support for inclusive education, at least at a rhetorical level, are also contributing, through their legislation and policies, to the "irresistible rise of the SEN industry" (Tomlinson, 2012, p. 267). The chapter concludes with some reflections on the possibilities for better—rather than clearer—thinking about inclusive education.

PRACTICES OF CONFUSION

The confusion that surrounds inclusive education is a product of a series of practices that were intended to clarify and specify but which have instead muddled and obfuscated, making it one of the "most highly charged areas in education and social policy" (Apple, 2008, p. vii). These practices have involved seeking to define inclusive education; identifying the precise population upon whom inclusive education should be practiced; establishing aspirations in respect of inclusive education and celebration of those deemed to be pursuing these "effectively"; and training the teachers considered responsible for inclusive education. Each of these practices has been undertaken with great benevolence and zeal—by policymakers, researchers, teacher educators and teachers—but with, perhaps, little awareness of the uncertain effects they have produced. These practices may well have arisen from different realities and may pose no such confusion for the individuals behind them. Nevertheless, together they appear to amount to what Alisdair Macintyre (1998, p. 31) has called a "moral wilderness," which produces "limitations and mistakes" (p. 31) in our thinking and which is generated, in part, by a "culture that knows how to speak but not to listen" (Riedel, 1990, p. 1).

Defining

The Salamanca Statement, whilst underlining the principles of an inclusive school, specifying some of the features of an inclusive school and asserting that "inclusion and participation are central to human dignity and to the enjoyment and exercise of human rights," does not provide a definition of inclusive education. The act of not specifying what inclusive education *is* and attending instead to what it *does* might have been prescient, were it not for the subsequent conflation of schooling and education. Furthermore, the turn, in Salamanca, to a declaration that "inclusive schools must recognize and respond to the diverse needs of their students..." introduces a level of reification—in asserting that the school, rather than the teachers working within it, should display the recognition and response—that is unclear and allows for a deferral of responsibility. This obfuscation may not, however, have had much significance to those in the field, many of whom may have been influenced more by the idea of Salamanca than by the precise detail of the text.

The failure to define inclusive education—to identify what it *is*—has been a source of much lamentation and frustration, with accusations being leveled in different directions. The House of Commons Select Committee on Education and Skills (2006) fiercely criticized the government of the time, whose "changing definition of inclusion is causing confusion," while researchers have been accused of a lack of clarity and of a failure in the "transformation from ideal into practice" (Haug, 2006; B. Persson, 2006). Such efforts to define inclusive education, however, take it firmly into an essentialist trap from which there is little prospect of escape.

Assigning

Salamanca is unequivocal about inclusive education being about "all children regardless of individual differences or difficulties." In spite of this, inclusive education continues to be directed at discrete groups of children whose differences or difficulties prove problematic for mainstream schools. Furthermore, the constitution of this group may vary at different times and as Tomlinson (2012, p. 267) notes there is an increasing tendency for more middle class parents to "claim classification." Thomas (2013) describes inclusive education as "like an island, considered as a separate territory from mainstream education, with its own discourses, policies and practices." He attributes this status to its emergence from, and continued association with, special education and with its "deficit-related beliefs" (2013) that continue to dominate explanations of school failure. A dangerous cycle emerges, whereby children's failure, which may have its roots in school-generated factors such as alienation, hostility and mistrust (Thomas, 2013), allows difference to emerge and to subsequently be validated and exaggerated through existing school structures (Allan, 2008; Slee, 2011).

Aspiring

There is no shortage of guidance to help us "find" inclusion and an abundance of metaphors that involve either journeys or roads, for example the European Union's *Pathways to Inclusion*, with its training course promising a "moving towards an inclusive education," or exercises in building, such as the Training and Development Agency's (2012) "Pillars of inclusion." Even the *Index for Inclusion* (Booth and Ainscow, 2011), translated into 39 languages and in widespread use by schools (P2i, 2012) suggests, in its name, that it is pointing or guiding towards something. The abundance of "what works" materials that exist in relation to inclusive education convey a promise of a destination that can be reached providing certain simple measures are followed. These measures, however, represent inclusive education as a technical problem, provide "clarity bordering on stupidity" (Maclure, 2005, p. 393) and ensure sight is lost of "what matters" (Ferri, Gallagher and Connor, 2011, p. 222).

Training

The preparation of teachers for inclusive education centers on the recognition and management of difference. Intensively packed teacher training programs contain discrete slots into which are squeezed a quick rehearsal of inclusive education mantras followed by the most prevalent "conditions" the students might be expected to encounter. This is supported by textbooks—the "big glossies" (Brantlinger, 2006, p. 45)—which pathologize and typologize children's difficulties and project a level of confidence and certainty that they can be managed effectively in the classroom. However, as Brantlinger (2006) argues, the realities, as presented in the textbooks, bear little resemblance to what beginning teachers confront in their own classroom and consequently add to their confusion and anxiety about how to respond to individual children. Texts which address inclusive education offer little reflection and theorizing about it, providing instead what Thomas (2007, p. 1) refers to as "theory junk sculpture," a "cacophony of incompatible explanations," and a series of empty platitudes about being inclusive.

Sleeter (2008, p. 1947) suggests that teacher education is currently "under siege" from neoliberalist policies, and although she acknowledges that these have traditionally tended to undermine equity and democracy, they are currently bringing into sharp focus needs that have been inadequately met. Sleeter argues that as curricula become increasingly prescribed, controlled and scripted, together with the expectation that teachers will deliver this faithfully, teacher education has degenerated into a form of technical support geared towards raising student test scores. This, together with the shortening or complete avoidance of university based teacher education, occurring in both the U.S. and England, further removes beginning teachers from exposure to equity-oriented training.

MISSING THE POINT—OR THE PURPOSE

At the same time as there have been strenuous efforts to clarify and specify the nature of inclusive education, demarcate its intended population, guide towards some ultimate destination and deliver training to those designated as responsible, there has been an absence of important debate and discussion about key aspects of inclusive education. Fundamentally, there is a lack of sustained debate about the purpose of inclusive education, in spite of pleas for this from some quarters (Slee, 2011; Thomas, 2013). This is perhaps not surprising, given the absence of such a debate in respect of education in general, but it is nevertheless a glaring omission. There has also been little discussion about the consequences of inclusive education for children and their families. In its place, much attention has been devoted to "outcomes," but these are rather different in nature, focus on the short rather than long term and are more concerned with the teachers' actions than with the students' experiences. Finally, there has been scant regard for the ethical responsibilities that come with inclusive education and which involve whole schools, communities and societies.

SEN expansion through policy and legislation

Sally Tomlinson (2012, p. 267, original emphasis) notes the simultaneous expansion in special educational services and personnel, with the increasing expansion of the inclusion of children with special educational needs in mainstream schools and concludes that there is now an "expanded and expensive *SEN industry*." She suggests that such an expansion has been "irresistible" to governments who have struggled to balance educational provision for those who may not contribute to the knowledge economy with the need for social control of such individuals. Tomlinson identifies a number of factors associated with this expansion which include the continued need for resourcing on the basis of a diagnosis; an increasing number and range of parents seeking such a diagnosis for their child; teachers, under pressure to raise standards, seeking to remove troublesome students from their classrooms; and an expanding number of professionals and practitioners needing to increase their client base. In the three examples discussed below—England, Sweden and the U.S.—while the nature of the temptations and the particular pressures these have arisen from have varied, each of the countries has been unable to resist making a contribution to the SEN industry through its policy and legislation, whilst continuing to advocate inclusive education.

England: Inclusion free schools

Recent educational reforms in England have established new types of schools which introduce some new freedoms, for example from local education authority control; some new types of schools, notably academy schools and free schools; and some new forms of control, for instance routes out of "special measures," a status given to underperforming schools following inspection, which involve adopting academy school status but which come with certain obligations. These reforms may be contributing to the rise of the "SEN industry" by introducing new possibilities for selectivity and segregation that are apparently driven by parental and community choice and by encouraging schools to exclude more troublesome students (House of Commons Select Committee on Education and Skills, 2011). Evidence available on Swedish free schools, on which the English model is based, suggests that free schools are benefiting children from families that are highly educated and has found no advantage for low educated families and immigrants (Böhlmark and Lindahl, 2008; Allen, 2010).

The call by Mary Warnock, the chief "architect of inclusion" (CSIE, 2005), to bring an end to this "ideology" (Warnock, 2010, p. 13) because of what she saw as its "disastrous consequences" (p. 37) for individual children, has had a significant influence on the direction of policy in England in recent years and has precipitated a declared government intention to expand the "SEN industry." Warnock proposed a new concept of inclusion that maintained special schools, but set out what she claimed was evidence of the harm done to individuals, particularly those with communication disorders. The impact of Warnock's radical change of mind can be seen in the government's Green Paper on special needs and disability and subsequent proposed legislation which promises to "remove the bias towards inclusion" (DfE, 2011, p. 5) and draws attention to the "disproportionately poor" (p. 4) life chances of a large number of children, Inclusive education is implicated (but this is implied rather than directly asserted) as a partial cause of the reduction of life chances for children with special needs because it may be perceived as the only option available. The new legislation will enable parents to choose either a special or mainstream school or alternatively a newly established academy or free school and will allow special schools under threat to be rescued. "We will also prevent the unnecessary closure of special schools by giving parents and community groups the power to take them over" (DfE, 2012, pp. 7f.). The usual caveats, that choice is available unless the child's needs are not met, is incompatible with the efficient education of other children or is an inefficient use of resources, remain, but nevertheless the government has provided significant scope for the expansion of special school provision.

Sweden: A school for all?

Sweden, which operates a highly decentralized education system, has been a leader among the Nordic countries of "calculative practices" of national testing, with recognition by OECD that the centralization of these practices of evaluation and assessment have been crucial to the effectiveness of the system as a whole (Nusche et al., 2011). The new Swedish Education Act, in effect from July 1, 2011, further enhances the supervisory power of the Swedish Schools Inspectorate by allowing it to impose fines and other sanctions on those running schools (Rönnberg, 2011). The Swedish government, like many others, is currently concerned with quality in education and this is played out in public through the favorite expressions of the current Education Minister in Sweden, Jan Björklund, which are "flumpedagogik" and "flumskola," "woolly pseudo didactics" and "a degenerated school system fostering woolly thinking and imprecise knowledge" (Täljedal, 2011, p. 319). As Bergh (2011) has argued, a linguistic struggle for control has led to educational quality becoming less linguistically powerful than results-based quality, market quality and system quality. The increasing emphasis, within the compulsory school system, on early testing and basic skills, together with the growth in parents and children selecting schools could, according to Göransson et al. (2011, p. 551), "challenge the inclusion concept in Sweden." Furthermore, they argue, schooling appears to have become more individualized, which is undermining inclusive values such as fellowship and equal opportunity.

Sweden does not have a word for either inclusion or inclusive education, but instead refers to "a school for all" (B. Persson, 2012). The concept of inclusive education has tended to be assumed as self-evident or rarely a subject of debate, but this means that it is not subjected to critique or questioning, which could be an important aspect in determining its credibility and value (E. Persson, 2012). Furthermore, B. Persson (2003) notes that research within special and inclusive education has tended to be dominated by the categorical perspective, existing separately alongside research done from a relational perspective, with insufficient debate between the two. Göransson et al. (2011, p. 550) point out that the existence of a separate government agency, the National Agency of Special Needs Education and Schools, "suggests ambivalence towards inclusive education." While policy seeks to orient schools away from pursuing medically based categorizations, these are necessary for accessing support from the national agency and thus validate a special needs expansion.

U.S.: No child's left behind

The high stakes testing generated by the No Child Left Behind Act has been described as a form of "educational eugenics" because of its system of sorting children after testing at the age of eight in spite of the claim that its purpose is to ensure children have better options when schools are not performing (Barack Obama, referred to in Palast, 2009). The purpose of eugenics is clearly about expanding the SEN industry:

> Identify the nation's loser class early on. Trap them, then train them cheap. Someone has to care for the privileged. No society can have winners without lots and lots of losers.
>
> —(Palast, 2009)

According to the social capital theorist Robert Putnam (2007, p. 143), diversity produces distance between people, discomfort and anomie, forcing them to "hunker down—that is, pull in like a turtle." This uneasiness about diversity that

Putnam notes as prevalent in parts of American society surfaces within educational policy and practice in the form of "naysayers [who] point out that inclusion does not work" (Connor, 2012, p. 118).

Beth Ferri (2012) has drawn attention to a particular U.S. reform, *Response to Intervention* (RTI), which is explicitly maintaining segregated provision and "reinvigorating" many of the foundational assumptions of special education practices. RTI is an intensive intervention approach to students identified as being at risk of failure as a result of learning or behavioral difficulties. It also involves a process of systematic monitoring of performance and, most controversially, provides an alternative basis for the eligibility for a diagnosis of learning disability to the pre-existing IQ/achievement discrepancy model. A key feature of RTI is its early and intensive screening, aimed at discovering students "at risk" even before the teacher notices them having problems in the classroom (Ferri, 2012). Claims have been made that RTI will reduce the overrepresentation of minority ethnic students in special education (Gresham, 2007), although this is not supported with research evidence. As Ferri and others have noted (e.g., Gallagher, 2010), there is a fuzziness behind RTI which arises from a discourse that "speaks of fidelity, universal protocols and standardization on the one hand and [has] a glaring lack of consensus or research behind the model on the other" (Ferri, 2012, p. 867). Yet this discourse is so powerful, and has such strong backing from the educational textbook publishers that individual directors have ties to (Paley, 2007) that, as Ferri (2012, p. 877) notes, trying to interrupt its contribution to the expansion of the "SEN industry" would be "like stopping a moving train."

CONCLUSION: STILL WAITING?

> Let us do something, while we have the chance! … What are we doing here, *that* is the question. And we are blessed in this, that we happen to know the answer. Yes, in the immense confusion one thing alone is clear. We are waiting for Godot to come …
>
> —(Samuel Beckett, referred to in Knowlson and MacMillan, 1993, p. 73)

The conceptual confusion that surrounds inclusive education seems to have stemmed from a series of practices, intended to be helpful, but which have created the opposite effects. Attempts to pin down inclusive education have generated frustration at the ontological hokey pokey that has resulted; assurances that inclusive education is for all children have been beset by efforts to ensure those most in need of support receive it and these have in turn encouraged more people to seek diagnostic validation. Inclusive education guidance is aspirational, taking teachers towards some destination which also appears to be unreachable, while the training of new teachers merely fuels their anxieties about children who appear challenging.

Governments have contributed both to the conceptual confusion and to the rise of the "SEN industry." Their actions could be seen as willful efforts to control increasing numbers of children not expected to contribute to the economy; alternatively, they could be interpreted as mindless, a failure to apprehend the likely consequences for particular children and their families. The latter reading suggests possibilities for them to be helped to envisage alternative and better—rather than clearer—ways of thinking about inclusive education.

Rather than seeking to pin down inclusive education and instead of taking the teacher on a journey towards inclusive education, notions of the inclusive educator as a gardener could be more helpful. Such an idea has been projected by Buber (1997); by Pestalozzi (1951, p. 32): "the gardener wisely tends the rarest plants, from their first sprouting to the maturing of their fruit"; by Veck (2012); and earlier by Rousseau (2000 [1762]). It is also an image produced by an Estonian teacher during a Council of Europe project (2010) on policies and practices for sociocultural diversity and which depicted the gardener teacher as open and ready to respond to whatever diversity she encountered in her garden/classroom. Such an image appears to both step out of the essentialist trap and remove any sense of a destination to be travelled to.

CHAPTER FOURTEEN

Heterogeneity, Radical Otherness and the Discourse on Inclusive Education—A Philosophical Reflection

MARKUS DEDERICH

Since the Declaration of Salamanca, the idea of inclusion has become an essential topic of education. Its main points and intentions were underscored and anchored in Human Rights by the UN-Convention on the Rights of Persons with Disabilities. Accordingly, the discourse about inclusion, which for a long time was led almost exclusively by special education and was centered around its pros and cons, has given way to how it can be implemented politically and educationally. Inclusion in schools stands at the center of attention. As shown by Gottfried Biewer's definition, the underlying conception of inclusion is complex and comprehensive:

> Inclusive education designates theories of cultivation, education and development that reject labeling and classifications, take their starting-points from the rights of vulnerable and marginalized people, pleading for their participation in all areas of life and aiming at structural changes to standard institutions to cater to the diversity in requirements and needs of all users.
>
> (Biewer, 2009, p. 193)

One of the key concepts in this definition is "diversity." Together with the concepts of "plurality" and "heterogeneity" it stands at the centre of the discourse on the theoretical foundations of inclusion. With problems in mind such as the broad spectrum of talents, socio-economic and cultural backgrounds of pupils, the search for just ways of compensation of disadvantages and a fair distribution of resources, or the struggle for recognition of disadvantaged persons or those with disabilities, it is obvious that there is probably no central aspect of inclusive education that is not affected by these key-concepts. The idea of inclusion and the efforts to implement it in the field of education raise a whole bundle of difficult and far-reaching questions. These are not only of theoretical interest, but also of considerable practical relevance. Which dimensions of diversity are relevant for education? Do physically or mentally impaired, socio-economically disadvantaged children and youths, and those coming from another culture, form distinct groups that have to be identified and named as such in order to ensure proper educational responses to their specific needs? Or do such identifications have to be overcome, for instance, because of their stigmatizing or discriminating effects? Does the successful implementation of inclusion require the overcoming of the presumably universal tendency to assess differences among people in hierarchically structured ranking orders?

Such questions show that determining the relationship between equality and diversity has a normative dimension. This is closely associated with problems of equality of education and opportunity and the question of what enables people to lead good and successful lives. In the German discourse on inclusion it is a broadly shared consensus that on an ethical level the relation between equality and diversity is to be conceptualized as "egalitarian difference." Accordingly, the most important precondition for successful inclusion is overcoming the construction of hierarchies of differences in favor of recognizing and valuing diversity and heterogeneity. How this is to be precisely understood will be discussed below.

However, this position has a fundamental theoretical blind spot that is ethically relevant, namely, the omission of what has been called "radical otherness" or "radical difference" in various philosophical contexts. The following considerations try to clarify that it makes a difference to reflect basic questions of inclusion not only from the viewpoint of diversity and heterogeneity, but to reconsider them within the theoretical framework of "radical otherness." This shift makes it necessary to rethink the assumption that inclusion is a substantial contribution to realizing equality of all people, whilst simultaneously being able to recognize their diversity.

The following considerations are philosophically oriented and thus do not claim to provide solutions to practical problems. Their aim is to expose a "pre-empirical" ethical foundation of education as such, from which the educational and political implementation of inclusion and the norms guiding it have to be thought through. This is to take place in three steps: First of all there are some explanatory remarks about the idea of equality. After that, basic outlines of the German discourse on diversity will be sketched. It will become clear that inclusive education is linked to the aim of appraising diversity and heterogeneity. In a further step, this program associated with high pretensions to individual and social ethics will be contrasted with Emmanuel Levinas's radical thinking on diversity or otherness.

Finally, consequences of the thinking on radical otherness for the theoretical and ethical foundations of inclusive education will be discussed.

EQUALITY AND RELATIVE DIFFERENCES

We shall start with a brief exposition of the term "equality." As already has been stated, the principle of "egalitarian difference" – the recognition of empirically different people as of equal value – is the normative core element of inclusive education. In accordance with political thinking since the Age of Enlightenment, the pedagogy of diversity stands under the sign of equality. Within the theoretical frame of "egalitarian difference," inclusion is held to be the sole ethically legitimate form for implementing or realizing this principle.

According to Liesen (2006), equality is an indispensable prescriptive concept for the ethical legitimation of special education. The normative significance of equality is made plausible above all by the reference to ethically illegitimate relations of inequality. It implies "a critique of inequality that is associated with the demand to ameliorate the consequences of anthropologically-based natural inequality and doing away with socially conditioned inequality in the area of participation" (Ganslandt, 2004, p. 778).

As Gosepath (2010) states, there are various meanings and ways of employing the concept of equality that have to be differentiated. Firstly, equality can mean numerical identity (i.e. the identity of an object with itself in all its features) or qualitative sameness (i.e. the sameness of several objects with regard to at least one property). Secondly, equality is not a two-place relation, but at least a three-place one, comprising the compared objects or states of affairs as well as the criterion of comparison, the *tertium comparationis*. Accordingly, only what is unequal can be equal in the sense of qualitative sameness. The feature drawn upon decides whether something has to be classified as equal or unequal. This means, however, that equality is not a property of objects, but a relation. Thirdly, equality can be used descriptively or prescriptively. With descriptive equality, the standard of comparison is itself descriptive (such as the sameness of persons with regard to their body weight). Prescriptive assertions of equality, by contrast, have both a descriptive and a normative component. The descriptive component serves to identify the objects, states of affairs or persons that are to be compared. The normative component specifies how these objects, states of affairs or persons are to be treated (cf. Gosepath, 2010, p. 920).

The use of the concept of diversity has to be analyzed in analogy to the concept of equality because differences between people, too, can only be established on the basis of criteria or measures, i.e. by comparison. I will call this understanding of difference "relative" or "empirical difference." It is relative because it relates the differences of individuals to an overall structural order (such as origins, language or culture) providing the features and measures for comparison and differentiation.

BASIC OUTLINES OF GERMAN DISCOURSE ON DIVERSITY

The German discourse on heterogeneity and diversity in education is almost exclusively focused on relative or empirical differences. As shown by Lutz and Wenning (2001), two different orientations can be distinguished within this discourse: a vertical orientation focused on social situations of inequality and a horizontal orientation that investigates the conditions for constituting binary, complementarily arranged or diametrically opposed oppositions. The two authors sketch a series of bipolar and simultaneously hierarchically ordered differences producing inequalities (e.g., opportunities for education and participation, for acquiring economic capital or social standing) and underlying asymmetrical social relations, i.e. those characterized by significant power differences. Lutz and Wenning distinguish between body-oriented differences (gender, sexuality, "race," skin color, ethnicity, health, physical capacity, etc.) and socio-spatial differences (class, nation, state, North-South, East-West, stage of development of the society, etc.) (cf. Lutz and Wenning, 2001, pp. 20f.).

Hinz (1993) and Prengel (1995), two widely known authors in the German academic discourse on inclusion in education, spotlight heterogeneity and diversity. Both utilize heterogeneity and diversity not only in a descriptive-analytical sense, but try to demonstrate them to be normatively essential concepts for educational, policy-making and socio-ethical tasks. Despite all differences between their conceptions, Hinz and Prengel agree on several important points: firstly, they criticize the highly selective educational system existing in Germany. Secondly, with their respective core concepts, they mark relative differences, i.e. those differences tied to criteria or features. Thirdly, they analyze the consequences of hierarchic diversity within the educational system. Fourthly and finally, they postulate that the normative principle of "egalitarian difference" makes it compulsory to overcome a selective educational system and establish an inclusive one.

The concept developed by Hinz (1993) is based, on the one hand, on a dialectic of equality and difference and, on the other, on the idea of equality of the diverse. Diversity and heterogeneity signify certain educationally relevant, empirical differences among children and youths such as gender, socio-cultural origins and certain preconditions for learning. These "particular special features" (Hinz, 1993, p. 46) are to be regarded as of equal rank on a normative level and must not be valued hierarchically. Equality, by contrast, refers to the ethical value of the individual and his or her rights. In this sense, appreciating diversity and renouncing all attempts to level it in order to produce homogeneity is a demand of equality. The demand not to hierarchize empirical differences and to value them as such ends up in a conception of justice that holds egalitarian and differentiating justice in balance (cf. Hinz, 1993, p. 45). In this way it is legitimized that equals are treated as equals and unequals as unequals, namely, according to their (educationally relevant) needs. The equality of all consists in being respected and treated as different. This shows that Hinz couples a descriptive understanding of heterogeneity with a normative conception of equality. Simultaneously, however, equality and difference are treated as symmetric or complementary concepts. According to Hinz, in human development there is, on the one hand,

> the tendency toward being equal, of approaching others and sharing with them, and on the other, the tendency toward being different, of demarcation from others and personal autonomy. These tendencies do not form any mutually exclusive or mutually restricting poles, but are reliant on each other in a dialectical tension.
>
> —(Hinz, 1993, p. 42)

In a philosophical regard, the model of heterogeneity just described can be reconstructed as a specific relation between the universal and the particular. Within the framework of this model, the particular can only be perceived and thought of in distinction to the universal. The ethical implication of this account, which is not unproblematic, will be taken up again below.

Beforehand, however, some remarks on Prengel's *Pädagogik der Vielfalt* (Pedagogy of Diversity, 1995) shall be added. This theory, too, stands under the sign of equality. It conceives equality and difference as a relation based on criteria of comparison. Accordingly, equality and difference are markers of a partial relation on the basis of criteria of comparison. Therefore it is necessary "to determine a criterion of comparison, in regard to which something is equal or different. "There must be a 'tertium comparationis' that is clearly defined." (Prengel, 1995, p. 33). Such formulations show that Prengel focuses on relative differences; this focus is embedded in the scheme of universal and particular. This becomes apparent in the following passage, in which the normative aspect of the relationship between equality and difference is explained in a particular way:

> Ideas of equality without exclusion imply accepting that what differs as of equal value and thus qualitatively go beyond ideas of equality valid only for what is of the same kind, thus excluding anything that deviates. Equality as the equal value of what differs thus represents the fulfilment of promises associated with the universally formulated concept of equality.
>
> —(Prengel, 1995, p. 47)

According to Prengel, diversity is given the normative function of correcting deformations in the idea of equality. She writes,

> radical plurality is formed from the irreducible specificity of different ways of living and forms of knowing and thinking; each of these enjoys a high valuation of its unique specificity. However, by virtue of each of these models receiving the same right to unique specificity, the postulate of equality is fulfilled by recognizing diversity.
>
> —(PRENGEL, 1995, P. 49)

Prengel develops her theory referring to post-modern philosophers such as Lyotard. By doing so, she attracts the accusation of arbitrariness, with which philosophers of post-modernity are often confronted. Responding to this critique she states that the pedagogy of diversity is not concerned with a "stance of indifference" (Prengel, 1995, p. 49), but with the "valuing of difference" (ibid.), which implies a criticism of power and domination.

Although, in comparison to Hinz, Prengel presses on further with the thinking of diversity, ultimately, she, too, remains on the level of relative differences and cannot overcome the schematism of universal and particular. The reason for this must have become evident before: her thinking of diversity, too, stands under the normative primacy of equality. Despite her recourse to philosophers who have given voice to radical otherness, Prengel therefore does not succeed in consistently integrating diversity in the sense of radical otherness, the non-identical or singularity.

Why, however, is radical difference significant with regard to the relationship between equality and difference, and the discourse on inclusion? Why should the idea of egalitarian difference be complemented by the idea of an ethically significant radical otherness? An answer to these questions is to be prepared in the following subsection.

RADICAL OTHERNESS

In German special education, the strand of discourse starting with radical difference or radical otherness, has been developed above all in special education for pupils with severe learning difficulties (cf. Stinkes, 1993; Fornefeld, 1995). These works share the critiques by Hinz and Prengel of the negative effects of categorizing specific educational "problem groups" such as the "cognitively disabled." They, too, try to redefine the relationship between equality and difference. In doing so they pursue the aim of overcoming a medical model of disability oriented toward defects, deficits and deviations from the norm. However, this happens within a slightly different philosophical framework.

With their approaches toward determining the relationship between equality and difference, philosophical theories of radical otherness go against the tide of the mainstream of philosophy. This determining feature demands another point of access to the relationship between universal and particular. Theorists of radical otherness show that the universal forms an overarching ordering framework which enables the particular to be distinguished. Thus, the particular can only be conceived in relation to the universal. Such a comprehensive universal order Levinas calls a "totality." With this term he refers to all-encompassing political, social, religious or theoretical systems that leave nothing other, no outside or exteriority. The core of Levinas's critique says that the precedence of the universal leads to a negation or an exclusion of all that is not absorbed into the relevant all-encompassing order, which does not fit itself into the logic and structure of a totality, and therefore cannot be identified as something particular at all. This critique pertains also to relative difference. This can only be established on the basis of criteria of comparison that are valid within given orders such as a medical or educational system. Within such a framework, phenomena such as significant retardation in development, long-term learning difficulties or behavioral disorders can only be conceived as a negation of order, as a deviation or pathology. In this sense, difference is that which is not expected, which does not fit, which disturbs the given order or puts it into question. Apart from people with disabilities, Jews and homosexuals are historical figures symbolizing such deviations from the given universal, all-encompassing order.

Historical experiences of violence, of persecution, expulsion, exclusion and annihilation make it plausible why authors such as Theodor W. Adorno have subjected structures of thinking anchored in Western philosophy to a fundamental critique and have tried to give voice to radical otherness, singularity or, as Adorno says, to the non-identical (Adorno, 1997). The central motive for this type of philosophical thought is to protect the individual human being – whoever, or whatever, he or she is – against the violence of comparison and of creating hierarchies of human value. This is based on the insight that deriving the particular from the universal and thus extinguishing the singular and non-identical is the expression of a fundamental blindness to diversity (cf. Schnell, 2008).

Radical thinking of otherness becomes vital when phenomena of figure and ground lose their non-ambiguity, when totalities show cracks or become brittle. When that which has been sorted out and excluded before, the "other of order," calls attention to itself, a plurality of views of the world, of meaning and of paradigms is expressed and a polyphony of speech becomes audible. This process has been worked out especially by philosophical conceptions attributed to so-called post-modernity (cf. Welsch, 1991), but also phenomenological investigations have engaged extensively with it (cf. Waldenfels, 1987). The thinking of differences in the sense of radical otherness turns against any kind of obsession with unity, totality or universality and tries to appraise a diversity of irreducible forms of living, speaking and thinking. As Welsch emphasizes, this thinking has an anti-totalitarian and emancipatory impulse because it uncovers "that final unity cannot be achieved other than repressively and totalitarianly" (1991, p. 36).

EMMANUEL LEVINAS

Probably the most consistent thinker of radical otherness in the twentieth century was Emmanuel Levinas (1906–1995). His critique of a thinking of universality and unity is based on a specific ethical approach. He questions the predominant tendency within the philosophical tradition toward building up ethics on the basis of abstract and universally conceived norms. This approach is countered with the immediate encounter between the self and the other. According to Levinas, the other expresses a resistance against being completely drawn into systems of knowing, but nevertheless affects the subject with its presence, laying upon it a responsibility that cannot be dismissed.

Before this basic thought can be explained further and the relevance of Levinas's philosophy for the discourse of inclusion in education can be shown, however, a few basic remarks are required. Levinas's ethics of radical otherness is to be understood as a pre-positive founding, not as a normative grounding and orientation. Nevertheless, as will be shown, such a pre-positive founding does not remain without consequences for normative questions in the narrower sense. This implies, however, that an ethics of inclusion requires clearer normative principles that meet the requirements of justice as well as the protection of human dignity.

What is Levinas basically concerned with in regard to the relationship between equality and difference? In his writings he was able to show that most of philosophy has thought the other not as itself, but always as conceptually subordinated or derived from a universal concept. The German philosopher Thomas Bedorf names some examples of this:

> If the other is understood as a category of being (Plato), being is the central concept; if I encounter humanity in the other (Kant), the other disappears into the concept of a reason-endowed universal; if the other is inserted in a dialectic of reflective self-consciousness (Hegel), the law of movement of consciousness stands in the foreground; if, finally, the other is conceived as a "disclosive" moment of being (Heidegger), otherness is again degraded to an object of ontology (doctrine of being).
>
> —(Bedorf, 2012, p. 68)

In contrast to this, Levinas determines the other as singular, "infinite" or as "exteriority." This means that the radical other stands outside any totality (cf. Levinas, 1988, p. 111). But it also means—and this is a crucial point—that the other stands "outside any proportionality to power and the freedom of the self" (ibid.). As already mentioned, the other in its radical otherness withdraws from the grasp of conceptual knowledge and insertion into a system of knowing that is built upon universal principles to which all sensuous singular phenomena can be related. Precisely in this way, the schematism of universal and particulars is evaded.

But Levinas goes even one step further, shifting the relationship between self and other (in other words, the problem of intersubjectivity) toward an ethical horizon. As he shows, the other becomes ethically significant by directing a claim or a demand toward an individual, even before this individual actively turns toward the other, recognizes and acknowledges him or her, feels a resonance of sympathy or antipathy, etc. The presence of the other does not impact an individual as a freely chosen affection. Since we do not have a choice about being addressed by the other, making a response to the other's presence is inescapable, no matter how it may turn out. This constitutes the core of the ethical relationship between me and the other; I find myself inserted into a responsibility I cannot shirk.

Levinas distinguishes the factual *that* of affection and the consequent having-to-respond from the actual response, that is, the *what* or *how* of my responding to the other. He is concerned above all with this *that* of the claim and the ethical relationship between self and other resulting from it. His main interest lies in the *phenomenological* question as to how it comes to an inescapable ethical obligation toward the other.

Difference understood in the sense of the radical otherness of the other, and its simultaneous closeness that affects me, undermines and makes impossible a stance of indifference and found in asymmetric relatedness of non-indifference.

> In the otherness of the other lies not merely its relative differences but, beyond that, the ethical significance of its existence that has been brought to the concept of non-indifference. By virtue of this non-indifference, the other in its difference is precisely not 'indifferent.' In non-indifference lies precisely that which has the effect that the other ineluctably 'impacts' us...
>
> —(Liebsch, 2000, p. 413)

This is signified when Levinas speaks of "ethics": *that* I am intended and addressed in such a way that makes it impossible to elude the claim as such, because the claim is always prior, whereas the response—even if it amounts to rejecting the claim as unjustified—follows subsequently.

Now the question arises as to whether or not the idea of an asymmetrical ethical responsibility can be linked to the idea of justice and thus that of equality. According to Levinas this is clearly the case. Despite the asymmetry in the relationship of responsibility, the idea of the equal value of what is different and thus the possibility of justice is indispensable for truly human societies. However, Levinas's philosophy compellingly opens up the insight that the idea of equality cannot shake off the excess of radical otherness. Rather, the idea of justice based on equality has to be tied back to the asymmetrical ethical relation between self and other. But that does not mean that justice is derived from responsibility. Rather, responsibility and justice are two principles, each in their own right, which necessarily complement each other, but also remain in an indissoluble tension with one another.

How is this to be understood? According to Levinas, the dyadic situation of face-to-face is fictitious, because sociality is determined by a multitude of others. Our social lives always comprise more than one single other. Regarding these other others, Levinas speaks abstractly of the "third person" or, in brief, of the 'third' (Levinas, 2011, pp. 343ff.). So there is me, the other and the other others. The figure of the "third" does not necessary refer to people alone. It also refers to the specific institutional or social context in which a relation is embedded. Thus, for instance, the context of school that defines one individual as a teacher and another as a pupil assigns, among other things, roles and rights to them. It is the context of school that, on the one hand, imposes the demand on the teacher to appraise different pupils in their individuality. On the other hand, the teacher has to treat his pupils justly, i.e. according to the measure of norms that apply to all. This is apparent, for instance, when resolving conflicts or assessing performance comparatively. The way in which a teacher encounters an individual pupil is therefore also always mediated by the factual or virtual presence of other pupils (the "third persons") and is embedded in a situational, social, political or structural context, i.e. an order with its legitimate expectations, rules, norms and laws. It is the presence of other pupils and their legitimate concerns that demand justice. In the case of simultaneously occurring or conflicting claims, the necessity of comparing arises, drawing on and weighing criteria related to or conditioned by the context. Such criteria play a central and indispensable role, especially in law and conceptions of justice.

Therefore, the appearance of the third person is "the moment of justice" (Levinas, 1995, p. 237). The presence of the third person makes it necessary to compare people with each other despite their singularity, i.e. to treat them as if they were equal in some respects. The price of comparison, however, is that the individual is "reduced to the particularity of a specimen of a genus" (p. 237).

This brings up the question as to how the other and the third person are related to each other. Both coincide (without becoming identical with one another) where unequal entities are compared, where rules, norms and criteria of value claim binding force and can be asserted powerfully. In this way, despite his/her radical otherness, the other becomes an equal among equals who has a claim to justice. Nevertheless, Levinas insists—precisely also with regard to experiences of power, violence and political totalitarianism that can befall an individual human being—on the origin of justice and of right residing in the uniqueness of the other human being. Therefore, according to Levinas, even in the light of justice, "attention must be drawn to the hidden human face beneath the identities of citizens of state" (Levinas, 1995, p. 327). The word "face" has various layers of meaning in Levinas. It is the expression of closeness; it is an ethical appeal; its stands for the vulnerability and finitude of human life; it embodies the singularity of the individual human being and eludes any fixating upon a "thus-and-not-otherwise".

In view of the radical otherness of the other that is embodied in the other's face, the ideas of equality and justice are fractured and infected by a moment of violence. In this sense the German philosopher Bernhard Waldenfels writes,

> making equal is a part of any achievement of order that brings something into an order that does not already belong to this order from the start. In this sense, any justice, which always has consisted in treating equals equally and unequals unequally, is infected by a moment of injustice. This is part of the constitutive features of any contingent order that proceeds selectively and exclusively.
>
> —(Waldenfels, 2006, pp. 127f.)

Jacques Derrida, the French philosopher, has incisively worked out the tensions inherent in the constellation of the radical other and the third person, and has uncovered its paradoxical structure. This becomes comprehensible in the attempt to capture radical otherness in language.

> On the one hand, any attempt to speak of the other fails due to the limits of language because the radical withdrawnness of the other resists its re-presentation in the symbolic order. On the other hand, however, the means of language have to be used if the other is to be helped to gain expression at all.
>
> —(Bedorf, 2011, p. 181)

Symbolic comprehension means fixing something *as* something and insofar is to be conceived as a process conforming with power. This paradox is continued in social situations.

> On the one hand, the contextually identified social other…is the necessary reduction of absolute otherness; the absolute other, in turn, can only appear as an excess in embodiments of social otherness.
>
> —(Bedorf, 2011, p. 183)

And finally, the paradox becomes even more apparent where the realization of responsibility toward the other proves to be impossible in view of the demand for justice by the other others, as does the realization of comprehensive justice in view of the absolute claim of the radical other.

To underscore it once more: these considerations are not associated with the political pretension to omit or even weaken the viewpoint of justice (as contained, say, in the idea of human dignity). What is intended is no more, but also no less, than a correction to the point of access to the ethical and political problems of inclusion. Nevertheless, reference must be made to a problematic aspect of the ethical point of access to the other demonstrated by Levinas that aims to avoid identification and categorization, because, with his insistence on the radically conceived otherness of the other, Levinas skips over social and political phenomena such as factually local relationships and affiliations. The "real mediations of invariably restricted, selective and exclusive affiliations and non-affiliations" (Liebsch, 1999, p. 67) accordingly find little consideration. In this way the danger arises of overlooking the concrete (family, social, cultural) identities of people in favour of protecting radical otherness. The idea of "egalitarian difference" is also exposed to this danger because, with its emphasis on equality, it all too easily passes over real experiences of alienness and assumes that these could be overcome easily through appropriate measures of inclusive education.

Like the "missionary of the universal" who knows only "human beings" without regard to skin color, descent and gender, the prophet of the alien who resists the universal runs the danger of no longer making any differences where it is precisely their difference that is vital for human beings as alien (p. 68).

CONCLUDING REMARKS

Under the sign of inclusion, determining the relationship between equality and difference, and coping, in a way compatible to heterogeneity, with ethically unacceptable inequality become central problems for education as a whole. Viewed from Levinas's ethical perspective, it becomes apparent that even an inclusive education runs the danger of becoming totalizing by omitting radical otherness. Therefore, according to the basic thesis of this chapter, an ethics of responsibility for the other in view of his/her radical otherness is an indispensable foundation for the idea of inclusion. Present-day discourse on inclusion in education proceeds almost exclusively on the level of structure, focusing on problems of resources, universal principles of justice, framework conditions of educational policy, questions of pedagogical conceptions, etc. By contrast, the interpersonal level—i.e. the level of the encounter between self and radical other on which teachers are confronted with inescapable claims—is left largely out of account. Proceeding from Levinas it proves to be imperative to again appraise more strongly this level of a "lived ethos."

It follows from the preceding considerations that pedagogy which has as its aim a comprehensively conceived education and a maximum degree of human autonomy requires a normatively ordering framework based on reason and built upon an ethos of responsibility. This framework must be shaped in such a way that it serves to protect human dignity, corresponds to principles of human rights and contributes to realizing educational justice (cf. on this in more detail Dederich, 2013, pp. 233ff.).

Despite the very fundamental orientation of the preceding reflections, the question concerning their practical educational relevance is nevertheless posed. With regard to relative differences, their relevance is obvious. The aspect of heterogeneity in the sense of relative otherness is a central topic of recent discussions in educational theory, especially in inclusive education. Switching from homogeneity to heterogeneity, from unity to diversity, really does have the quality of a paradigm shift in a highly differentiated educational system such as the German one, and demands a far-reaching rethinking of questions concerning didactics, method, school organization and vocational training.

But what about the practical relevance of radical otherness? Despite the abstractness of the problem of radical otherness it, too, does not remain without practical consequences. On the one hand, a radical thinking of otherness in education necessitates an appraisal of the singularity of the other human being that cannot be cognitively captured, even with diagnostic instruments, because this thinking makes it apparent that the other is more than is perceived, understood, evaluated, recognized and given a status in social contexts. This applies also in view of the ethical necessity of comparing human beings with one another under the sign of justice and treating them as equals. On the other hand, the thinking of radical otherness changes the point of access to questions of ethics. Socio-ethical problems of recognition and justice that are important for education are conceived from the viewpoint of responsibility, so that the discourse about universal principles and norms is always tied back to the ethically relevant needs of the concrete other.

In addition, the thinking of radical otherness touches upon a series of further problems that have not been discussed in this chapter, but are of great significance for education. First of all, it shifts the discourse on autonomy and self-determination into another light and forces a rethinking of the (politically and socio-historically thoroughly understandable) tendency to overemphasize autonomy and self-determination, so as to conceive human beings also as interdependent, dependent and needy. Secondly, it makes it necessary to reformulate the concept of subject as a central figure in educational theory. Thirdly, it opens up the possibility of thinking disability in a strictly relational sense as alienness (cf. on this Stinkes, 1993), rendering it fruitful in a pedagogical sense. Fourthly and finally, it necessitates the untimely question as to whether inclusion is the only legitimate response to non-indifference and the demands of a non-excluding ethics that have been brought into view by Levinas.

CHAPTER FIFTEEN

Education and Inclusivity

Imagining and Building Education for All (Both Within and Without Schooling)

SUSAN BAGLIERI AND ALICIA A. BRODERICK

The Salamanca Statement and Framework for Action offers guidelines to be considered for "integrating children with special educational needs[1] into inclusive schools," calling upon all governments "to adopt as a matter of law or policy the principle of inclusive education." In the Preface of the Statement, it is also made clear that "Special needs education…cannot advance in isolation. It has to form part of an overall educational strategy and, indeed, of new social and economic policies. It calls for major reform of the ordinary school." The United States participated in the 1994 World Conference on Special Needs Education in Salamanca, Spain, thus affirming the Salamanca Statement and Framework for Action on Special Needs Education. Despite the explicit positioning of the scope of developing inclusive policies that call for major educational reforms of ordinary schools, U.S. practice creates a policy environment in which special education and the needs of students with disabilities are characterized as separate from general education. Thus, reform toward inclusive education is positioned to disappoint at the policy level.

The Individuals with Disabilities Education Improvement Act (IDEIA) from 2004 is the U.S. policy that structures education for children with disabilities. Although it specifies that children served under its authority be placed "to the maximum extent appropriate" (IDEIA, 20 USC § 612 [a][5]A]) in the Least Restrictive Environment (LRE)—widely interpreted as the general education setting—the endorsement for a continuum of special educational placements protects the provision of exclusionary schools and curriculum (Taylor, 1988). Another feature of IDEIA is the hallmark practice of creating an individualized educational plan for each child to ensure that provided instruction is appropriate to the individual's strengths and needs. When the first versions of IDEIA were developed in 1975, providing access and appropriate education to students with disabilities remedied a history of their exclusion from schooling. However, largely unchanged since its first iteration, the IDEIA provisions, which create a continuum of placements and emphasize the individual as the locus around which special education circulates, now divert attention from inclusivity as *whole system* reform, as suggested by the Salamanca Statement. Rather than focus educational reform efforts on the development of inclusive schools in which all children belong, participate, and benefit from a child-centered educational approach, U.S. [special] education policy has focused more narrowly on the integration of students with labeled disabilities into existing, and increasingly non-inclusive, schools, calling the achievement or approximation of that partial and often contingent integration, ironically, "inclusive" education.

While a comprehensive analysis and critique of U.S. policy on either inclusive education generally or the education of students with labeled disabilities specifically is beyond the scope of this chapter, we draw upon scholarship in Disability Studies in Education to offer a partial critique of U.S. policy failings in regard to both of these issues. We then discuss policy related to Universal Design for Learning (UDL) and pose questions generated through unschooling movements to propose two useful and purposefully dissimilar avenues through which inclusive education may be pursued. Exploring ideas found within U.S. policy, as well as those that are explicitly outside of policy, can shape schooling toward better approximations of Education for All (UNESCO, 1994).

CONTOURS OF "INCLUSION"

Within dominant U.S. discourse the two most central facets of the concept of "inclusive education" or "inclusion" seem to be "(a) that it is fundamentally about students with identified and labeled disabilities, and (b) that it is fundamentally about issues of place; that is, where are students so labeled to be educated?" (Baglieri, Bejoian, Broderick, Connor, and Valle, 2011, p. 2125). Baglieri et al. further note, "the now banal term *inclusion* has been so frequently associated with children labeled disabled that its usage reifies taken-for-granted assumptions that the 'natural' position of this group is one of dis-belonging" (p. 2123). To contemplate multiple meanings of inclusive education and reflect on the Salamanca Statement's call for large-scale movement toward disability rights in education, we are compelled to examine and trouble the discourses in which inclusive education has become primarily about disability and place or, more analytically stated, disablement and schooling.

Disablement

Disability Studies in Education (DSE) scholarship centers on studying what Campbell refers to as *disablism:* "a set of assumptions (conscious or unconscious) and practices that promote the differential or unequal treatment of people because of actual or presumed disabilities" (2009, p. 4). Due to a focus on understanding *disablism* and documenting the workings of *disablement*, Campbell argues that efforts to strategically facilitate a progressive response to societal inequities are effectively reactionary ones, designed to reform, redress, or compensate for injustices, and in some cases even to "assimilat[e] people with disabilities into normative civil society" (ibid.). Though originally conceptualized in the Regular Education Initiative (1986) as a progressive policy response to the systematic exclusion of many disabled students in public schools, inclusive education may nevertheless be regarded as an example of just such an initiative emerging in reaction to, yet not having been terribly disruptive of, the deep cultural foundations of normative schooling practices.

Inclusion, as it is practiced in most public schools today, is an active and central instrument in constituting what Campbell refers to as the two core elements of ableism's regime: "the notion of the normative (and normate individual) and the enforcement of a constitutional divide" (2009, p. 6) between abled and disabled identities. Because inclusion in the U.S. is predominantly approached as fundamentally an issue of place in relation specifically to the education of students with identified and labeled disabilities, therein lies the failure of its realization as an integrative initiative. In order "to include" students under IDEIA, we must first evaluate and label them as disabled, the irony of which is generally lost in many discussions seeking to improve inclusive educational practice. Reflecting upon such ironies, Davis asks, "Would it be such a miscarriage of justice if all of us were protected from discrimination and the denial of access, just as all of us are protected from voter fraud and unwarranted search and seizure?" (2002, p. 5). Davis argues that,

> Disability studies can provide a critique of and a politics to discuss how all groups, based on physical traits or markings, are selected for disablement by a larger system of regulation and signification [e.g., schooling]. So it is paradoxically the most marginalized group—people with disabilities—who can provide the broadest way of understanding contemporary systems of oppression.
>
> —(ibid., p. 29)

Deploying disablement as a framework to animate the workings of various oppressive systems is, in other words, useful to articulate the structures of many inequities in education. Oriented differently, we can imagine how the many inequities in schooling emerge from a single mechanism in service to policing boundaries that delineate the norm according to which race, gender, sexuality, language, ability, and their varying intersections and complexities become judged, generalized, labeled and subsequently marginalized (Baker, 2002).

DSE illuminates the significant extent to which schooling has relied upon disablement as a central organizing mechanism. The "inclusion" movement has, oxymoronically, maintained Campbell's constitutional divide between normal and abnormal, nondisabled and disabled, general and special. As we use the theoretical tools of disability and disablement to consider how varied diversities are positioned in schools, a vast complex of systemic oppression is exposed. In our efforts to seek belonging for some, perhaps we have been distracted from and failed to ask the larger question that flows from its premise: Is "being included" into designated "inclusive" spaces in contemporary, compulsive, public education necessarily positive or desirable?

Schooling

In contemplating several decades of work toward inclusive education, Graham and Slee (2008) pose the cogent query: "Into what do we seek to include?" (p. 277). It is difficult to describe the context of public education in the U.S. without drawing upon or encountering the pervasive narrative of "broken" or "failing" schools. However, there is some dispute as to whether current reform efforts (e.g., "accountability" measures largely manifest through the proliferation of standardized testing and the "threat" of publication of those scores; "merit pay" for teachers on the basis of their students' performance on said testing; charter schools, voucher systems, and school "choice"; etc.) are fixing what ails our schools, or are actually instrumental in precipitating their ongoing demise in order to pave the way for the increasing privatization of American public education. Diane Ravitch, as a professional historian of American education, has recently (2010; 2013) become a strong voice in support of the latter position, calling what is currently happening in American schools "astonishing":

> It is not meant to reform public education but is a deliberate effort to replace public education with a privately managed, free-market system of schooling. Public education, established in America's towns and villages in the mid-nineteenth century, born of advocacy and struggle, is now in jeopardy. This essential institution, responsible for producing a democratic citizenry and tasked with providing equality of educational

> opportunity, is at risk. Under the cover of "choice" and "freedom," we may lose one of our society's greatest resources, our public school system—a system whose doors are open to all.
>
> —(Ravitch, 2013, pp. 4–5)

We concur with Ravitch's assessment of the state of the schools we are attempting to "include" disabled children "into," and have previously written about the extent to which neoliberal ideologies underlie the increasing privatization of American public schools, thereby simultaneously and actively undermining the central values of pursuing equitable and inclusive schooling experiences for all (Valle et al., 2011).

However, while Ravitch's critiques and indeed our own have largely centered upon the more recent political context of the neoliberal Bush-Obama educational policies embodied in the No Child Left Behind statute (2001) and the competitive Race to the Top initiative (2009), cogent critiques of the context of contemporary schooling have been longstanding and consistent, if politically marginalized, within the U.S. For example, according to Illich, pupils are "'schooled' to confuse teaching with learning, grade advancement with education, a diploma with competence, and fluency with the ability to say something new" (1970, p. 1). Similarly, according to Charlton, schooling plays a particularly notable and efficient role in the cultural process Gramsci referred to as hegemony: "Schooling has two principal 'political' functions. Its narrow purpose is to teach acquiescence to power structures operating in the educational arena. Its broad purpose is to teach acquiescence to the status quo, especially the discipline of its workforce" (1998, p. 31). Aronowitz similarly argues that a central measure of students' "success" in schooling is the degree to which they are compliant with and consent to the power structures that control them, and cogently excavates the "gulf between schooling and education" (2008, p. 10), and aptly refers to the advent of the "standards movement" as "a euphemism for the subordination of pedagogy to tests" (p. xviii).

Each of these writers critiques the central disciplinary role of schooling practices. The almost exclusive conceptual focus within the U.S. that inclusive education is somehow (a) about students with identified and labeled disabilities and (b) about matters of place has been a distraction that has diverted our collective attention from the sobering realization that schooling in general (largely through misguided efforts at "educational reform") is failing to educate our children and that many, if not most, of our students experience some form of disenfranchisement, alienation, marginalization, and exclusion in their schooling experiences. Therefore, when we critically examine the context of contemporary public education in the U.S. in consideration of Graham and Slee's (2008) "included into what?" we must of necessity acknowledge the degree to which our focus on inserting/"including" disabled students into noninclusive schools has actually prevented us from achieving the Salamanca Statement's call for "major reform of the ordinary school" as "part of an overall educational strategy and, indeed, of new social and economic policies."

INCLUSIVE EDUCATION: WITHIN AND WITHOUT SCHOOLING

Schooling, we have described, is an exclusionary enterprise by its very nature. Contemporary schooling practices disable most students in some way; some are merely better protected from its effects than others by their positionality vis-à-vis ableist, white, class, and other forms of cultural privilege. With Ravitch, however, we agree the desire to educate a diverse citizenry is a worthy enterprise. It is one that necessitates expansive and critical, rather than regressive and reactionary, thought to imagine what Education for All can be. Interrupting the inertia of inclusion and the apparatus of schooling to seek education for all must be a strategic endeavor. We propose two strategies to help rethink policy and curriculum toward inclusivity. The first imagines growth within the current contours of schooling and outlines the possibility and potential of developing the concept of Universal Design for Learning (UDL), which has been recommended as an instructional design strategy in U.S. educational policies. The second strategy puts forth what can be learned from Flexible Learning Strategies (FLS; UNESCO, 2013) in practice with out-of-school-children and youth, as well as from children who are increasingly electing to become educated outside of schools (unschoolers). We believe that there is much to be learned from education outside of school and contend that schooling may well become more inclusive by being responsive to lessons learned from education within and without schooling.

UNIVERSAL DESIGN FOR LEARNING: INCLUSIVITY IN EDUCATION WITHIN SCHOOLING

Universal Design for Learning is a multi-faceted approach to instructional design that seeks to reduce barriers to learning by offering flexibility and variety in a) presentation of information, b) activities in which learners engage, and c) performance on which students are assessed. In other words, a UDL environment should provide multiple means of accessing information, flexible strategies and methods to support learners to engage with information, and multi-modal possibilities for learners to demonstrate learning. Rose and Meyer (2002), through their work at the Center for Applied Special Technology (CAST), are most frequently credited with transforming universal design from an architectural concept to an instructional theory and practice. UDL's principles seem highly congruent with UNESCO's assertion that:

> a child-centred pedagogy is beneficial to all students and, as a consequence, to society as a whole....A child-centred pedagogy can help to avoid the waste of resources and the shattering of hopes that is all too frequently a consequence of poor quality instruction and a "one size fits all" mentality toward education. (UNESCO, 1994, p. 7)

Now in its second decade of use, the concept is currently promoted among the top instructional prospects for improving school outcomes for children and adults. As a policy initiative, UDL has the potential to actively disrupt the still-dominant "one size fits all" mentality toward curriculum and instruction in U.S. education, thus better aligning policy with the goals of child-centered pedagogy and EFA.

UDL IN POLICY

UDL is positioned prominently in the U.S. educational policy landscape. It is specified as a recommended instructional approach in the Technology-Related Assistance for Individuals with Disabilities Act of 1988, the Individuals with Disabilities Education Improvement Act of 2004 (IDEIA), and in the Higher Education Opportunity Act (HEOA, 2008). The most recent policy definition appears in the HEOA:

> (24) UNIVERSAL DESIGN FOR LEARNING. – The term universal design for learning means a scientifically valid framework for guiding educational practice that –
>
> (A) provides flexibility in the ways information is presented, in the ways students respond or demonstrate knowledge and skills, and in the ways students are engaged; and
>
> (B) reduces barriers in instruction, provides appropriate accommodations, supports, and challenges, and maintains high achievement expectations for all students, including students with disabilities and students who are limited English proficient.

The policy definition of UDL largely reflects the originating work of Rose and Meyer (2002) and is inclusive of students with disabilities, rather than indicated specifically for students so identified. Of no small importance, the body of these authors' frequently cited work asserts, as well, that UDL is meant to be a total model of instructional design and is not specific to special education (Hall et al., 2012).

UDL thus occupies a different position and status than the idea and practice of inclusion. Although definitions and discussion surrounding inclusion of students with disabilities are present in the U.S. lexicon in force, the term and concept has not been taken up in U.S. educational policy, nor has it been widely claimed as a general education initiative. Rather, inclusion has emerged as one of many possible placement options for disabled students, and is consequently claimed by (or relegated to) special education theory and practice. While the possibility for inclusion to affect change in general education practices is sometimes noted as a benefit-to-all, there is no urgency to conceptualize inclusion primarily in this capacity. In comparison to inclusion, UDL is more clearly defined as an educational policy initiative and better positioned to have an impact on general education instructional design.

UDL AND DISABLEMENT

A foundational principle of UDL is that "individual qualities or abilities are not static and fixed; rather they are continually shifting, and they exist in relationship to the environment" (Hall et al., 2012, p. 2). Its practice derives from the understanding that "variability [among people] is systemic rather than random" (p. 3). If educational practice flows from these two prongs, UDL can interrupt disablement in schools. By focusing on the situated nature of ability and personal qualities—that is, the manner in which the physical and social context of an activity structures the possibilities for participation, personality, and identity—the practice of designating a child or adult as "disabled" is permeated. If we anticipate and invite opportunities for learners to shift identity and participation we interrupt the idea that disability resides "in" the learner and obviate the stigma on which disablement is built. Viewed through Davis's (2002) "dismodernist" lens of Disability Studies, there is potential for the development of a language and politics to articulate UDL as a tool to destabilize the pull of normative school practice.

UDL allows an interpretation of the school and classroom as complex environments in which instructional design is viewed as necessarily changeable and readily flexible. The appearance of UDL in various U.S. policy statements presents an opportunity for inclusive-oriented fields of study to ally around a shared concept for reform. As Edyburn (2010) points out, UDL is in its second decade of implementation and the field is ripe for new directions in theory and practice. We acknowledge that UDL is positioned in policy as a "best practice" with promise to increase student achievement as measured by standardized assessments, and not for its liberatory potential. We propose, however, that further work to develop the conceptual underpinnings of UDL can be undertaken to outline its potential to interrupt normative school practice and position it as a device able to address exclusions deriving from perceptions and experiences of race, class, language, gender, sexuality, and their intersecting positionalities and influences. We further advocate that researchers exploring UDL as it is in practice consider its impact on identity and disablement to examine whether it can de-center normative thinking. Actively expanding that which has been proffered in policy can be a way to transgress disablement within schooling toward inclusivity in education.

UNSCHOOLING: INCLUSIVITY IN EDUCATION WITHOUT SCHOOLING

According to UNESCO:

> In 2012, 61 million children of primary school age and 71 million of lower-secondary-school-aged children were out of school over the world. Without bold and sustained action, global commitments to universal primary education will not be realized if current trends continue, leaving millions of children out of school and denied their right to education
>
> —(UNESCO, 2013, p. 2)

UNESCO also acknowledges that "typically, it is the marginalized, poor and remote rural populations, and those affected by conflict and discrimination, who are denied access to school" (p. 3), but also that barriers to education for some children "are partly a question of…the inappropriate and inflexible nature of the formal school model itself" (ibid.). In response to previous EFA initiatives, UNESCO's development of Flexible Learning Strategies (FLS) "represents a shift away from a piecemeal approach to provision for the educationally excluded towards more systematic, flexible and rights-based/inclusive interventions, appropriately designed to match their needs and circumstances" (p. 2). FLS aims to provide high-quality and flexible educational experiences aimed at students who have been out of school, recognizing those experiences as legitimate and equivalent to formal educational experiences, and aimed to facilitate lifelong learning and global citizenship (UNESCO, 2013).

EDUCATION AS COLONIZING

Prakash and Esteva, in their text *Escaping Education*, challenge the dominant presumption underlying EFA and other global initiatives: that education is a human right because it is a universal good. These authors present the framing of education as a "human right," rather, as a modern "Trojan horse" (2008, p. 1) of recolonization:

> In the epic now evolving at the grassroots, the social majorities are taking steps to liberate themselves from the social minorities. Those classified and categorized as uneducated, underdeveloped, poor or undeveloped are struggling for their freedom from those who

> consider themselves to be educated or developed. Step by step, the former are dismantling all the institutions and projects of the latter which discriminate against them—including the educational enterprise.
>
> —(ibid., p. 2)

Prakash and Esteva clearly position this educational enterprise and its political economy as the "elementary doorkeepers of the Neoliberal Global Economy" (p. 6). There is undoubtedly much to be learned about *inclusivity in education* from the example of FLS aimed at historically excluded groups of students. Nevertheless, such efforts necessarily involve "interventions" ("flexible" and "inclusive" though they may be) and, as such, are, at the very least, potentially, if not actually colonizing.

In their discussion of Illich's (1970) radical critique of education, *Deschooling Society,* Prakash and Esteva argue that "*consumption,* the *fundamental* function of a *schooled society*, is exquisitely learned through the ritual of schooling" (2008, p. 92), and even more incisively pose the question, "Why should the ritual of schooling be a precondition, a compulsory ticket for other forms of social participation?" (p. 93). Why indeed? We argue that there is much to be learned about inclusivity in learning from those communities and individuals that exist and grow and thrive largely outside of schooling and other forms of formal education. This includes both learning from those communities often regarded as "underdeveloped" and targeted for colonization, as well as those relatively privileged few within the "developed" world who have (or whose parents have) purposefully and electively sought to get themselves or their children out of schooling, to avoid the mechanisms of hegemony already in place.

UNSCHOOLING IN THE U.S.

Contemporary performances of the unschooling counter-cultural movement are far from ideologically unified or pure, and run the gamut from the traditions of deschooling (Ilich, 1970), to unschooling (Holt, 1976/2004), to more conservative homeschooling. In his groundbreaking text, *Instead of Education*, John Holt (1976/2004) traces his response to Illich's challenge to "deschool society" by developing meaningful and radical alternatives to formal education. Holt argues that:

> Education, with its supporting system of compulsory and competitive schooling, all its carrots and sticks, its grades, diplomas, and credentials, now seems to me perhaps the most authoritarian and dangerous of all the social inventions of mankind.... My concern is not to improve "education" but to do away with it, to end the ugly and antihuman business of people-shaping and let people shape themselves.
>
> —(Holt, 1970, p. 4)

It is from these radical political and intellectual roots, exemplified by the works of Illich and Holt, from which the modern unschooling movement in the U.S. has emerged. Gray and Riley point specifically to the paradox present in our current age of accountability as reason families seek unschooling:

> Teachers and educators commonly claim that the goal of school is preparation for the "real world." What if the child's classroom were the "real world"? Unschooling is a growing counter-cultural movement. At a time when the culture as a whole is moving toward more narrowly defined curricula, more standardized testing, and more hours, days, and years in school, an increasing number of families are choosing to keep their children out of school and not do anything like schooling at home.
>
> —(Gray and Riley, 2013, p. 2)

Wheatley, for example, describes unschooling as a "wonderful oasis for children's development and for democratic living" (2009, p. 28). He describes unschooling in his experience as oases of "learning from life and play," "individualization" (p. 28), "time" (p. 29), "loving learning" (ibid.), "initiative, creativity, and better boredom" (ibid., p. 30), "the whole child" (ibid.), and "democracy" (ibid., p. 31), among others. Wheatley's oases are in contrast to the barren conditions, noted by Gray and Riley (2013), offered as the conceptualization of education in school continues to narrow.

Choosing to unschool in the U.S. is increasingly less radical and a decision of last resort. Wheatley positions himself and his spouse as living a "dual life" in which they are "teacher educators who 'unschool' [their] two children" (2009, p. 27). One of us (second author) is similarly positioned, although perhaps in an even more fragmented way, as being an inclusive teacher educator who unschools her elder child, while continuing to send her younger child to a public school. The apparent contradiction in seeking those oases for my (second author's) own child(ren) even while attempting to build more inclusive systems of education for all is not lost on us. Thus, in seeking experiences of inclusivity for our own and other people's children, we are compelled to ask a set of questions that must include consideration of how the educational enterprise is exclusionary by its very nature, and what can be learned from the pursuit of inclusivity outside of schooling.

As long as we continue to labor under a parochial conceptualization of "inclusivity" that limits our thinking to concerns of place and primarily in regard to disabled students, rather than thinking expansively about the qualitative nature of the experience of learning, we are unlikely to achieve inclusivity of that experience. We argue that experiencing autonomy, freedom, child-centeredness, and democracy in one's learning are crucial facets of inclusivity necessary to educate a diverse citizenry and to prepare them for active participation in democratic and global citizenship. Such experiences cannot remain the privilege of those in positions to opt out of public schooling; we have a duty to learn from those experiences and to provide similar learning experiences for all.

POSSIBILITY IN THE WROXHAM SCHOOL

The reform of the Wroxham school in Hertfordshire, England (Swann et al., 2012) provides an example of a school that embodies most of the tenets we discuss here in this manuscript: inclusivity in education for all, with flexible and relevant and responsive curricula, and with meaningful and authentic democratic learning, freedom, and autonomy experienced by children and adults alike. The book offers a hopeful narrative of how a single school (once regarded as "failing" or in "special measures") emerged as an inclusive, flexible, and responsive school community that nurtured the needs of each of its members/learners without succumbing to the damaging narratives and pedagogies of "fixed ability" thinking. As a counter-balance to the dominant "reform" models in education already discussed in the U.S. context, which are largely similar in the UK, the authors of this pivotal study argue that there is another way:

> While it is true that there is no one right way, however, there is a strong measure of agreement, among the Wroxham staff, about what *not* to do.... People at Wroxham do not assume that differences in attainment can be explained by the limited potential of some children. They do not sort pupils into ability groups and differentiate their teaching on the basis of predicting what each group will achieve. They do not see a child's struggle with a particular concept as evidence of a lack of ability, but as evidence that this is an important site of learning for the child and for themselves.... Linked to this set of practices is the finding that Wroxham teachers increasingly avoided the language of "special educational needs" to talk about children.
>
> —(Swann et al., 2012, p. 116)

In a sense, it could be argued that the Wroxham school adopted a dismodernist (Davis, 2002) lens for thinking about learners and learning. That is, rather than working "to include" students "with special educational needs," they abandoned the necessity to so constitute and categorize their children before simply teaching them (and learning alongside them). By asking questions of themselves such as, "Do all the children feel emotionally safe, comfortable and positive about their participation in learning activities?" "Are classroom activities experienced by all children as interesting, enjoyable and purposeful?" and "Do all the children experience sustained success and achievement in their learning, and recognition of that achievement?" (p. 111), the faculty of Wroxham school circumvented the discursive necessity of disabling some of their students in order to educate any of them.

We believe that schools like Wroxham are what the framers of the Salamanca Statement had in mind when they argued for "special needs education" to proceed in the context of the ongoing development of "inclusive schools" involving "major reform of the ordinary school." Indeed, the framework offers guidance for schools to proceed with inclusive school development:

> Local administrators and school heads can play a major role in making schools more responsive to children with special educational needs if they are given necessary authority and adequate training to do so. They should be invited to develop more flexible management procedures, to redeploy instructional resources, to diversify learning options, to mobilize child-to-child help, to offer support to pupils experiencing difficulties and to develop close relations with parents and the community. Successful school management depends upon the active and creative involvement of teachers and staff, and the development of effective cooperation and team work to meet the needs of students.
>
> —(UNESCO, 1994, pp. 23f.)

At Wroxham, it was the local administrator who extended flexibility and authority to the community to make decisions and act in ways that were responsive to individual students and to design curriculum that reflects principles of UDL. The result was a community in which students, staff, faculty and families enjoyed autonomy through which they were empowered to act democratically.

Seeking to create learning and educational experiences that enliven, enrich and engage our children in democratic vivacity is a goal of education espoused by constituents who draw from a range of perspectives on schooling. Disability studies allows us to characterize the challenge of inclusivity in education as one that must seek to configure anew and seek reform that transgresses the disablement that has come to characterize education and schooling. We have proposed the appearance of UDL in U.S. policy for its potential to shape a policy climate that nurtures inclusivity, rather than stymies it, as has unfolded under the IDEIA. We propose that directions in how to enact curriculum, teaching and participation that actively "includes" can be found in the foundations of deschooling, the experiences of unschoolers, and the ethics that underlie the argument to escape education. The story of the Wroxham school, though achieved within the confines of a regressive and increasingly neoliberal educational policy climate, paints a portrait of what can be possible when we focus on inclusivity for all. Inclusivity cannot consist in an ever-increasing desire and ability to hunt down (Baker, 2002), evaluate, label, and identify; and fix, remediate, or ameliorate disability. It must lie, rather, in our recognition that "'them' is actually 'us'" (Davis, 2002, p. 4), that "we are all disabled by injustice and oppression of various kinds" (pp. 31f.), and that inclusivity is an educational project that can seek education and learning for all.

NOTE

1. We draw upon a range of syntactic usage to refer to students identified with disabilities in this paper, ranging from "children [or students] with special educational needs" to "children [or students] with labeled disabilities" to "disabled children [or students]." The first example is drawn directly from the language of the Salamanca Statement, and relies upon both "person first" syntax ("child with") and the euphemism "special educational needs" as the object of that

prepositional phrase. Except when drawing directly upon the language of the Statement itself, we prefer either "identity first" syntax ("disabled student") or the slightly more cumbersome "child with labeled disabilities," which still draws upon person first syntax, but also highlights the socially constructed nature of disability by explicitly referring to the labeling process. For a more detailed discussion of these complex and nuanced issues, please see Baglieri and Shapiro (2012), Broderick and Ne'eman (2008), and Brown (n.d.).

CHAPTER SIXTEEN

Inclusive Pedagogy

An Alternative Approach to Difference and Inclusion

LANI FLORIAN

As the idea of providing basic education for *all* the world's children, youth and adults has gained global currency, the policy statement of the World Conference on Special Needs Education in Salamanca, Spain, calling for students with disabilities to be educated within an inclusive education system has generated a great deal of interest and multiple interpretations of what it means to provide an inclusive education. A few years prior to the Salamanca conference, the "Education for All" (EFA) movement was launched at the World Conference on Education for All, 1990, in Jomtien. This conference introduced a global initiative in support of the idea of education as a human right and called upon all countries to provide for the basic learning needs of *all* people. The Salamanca conference aligned the education of students with disabilities to the EFA agenda by recognizing that all children should be educated within an inclusive education system. It stipulated: "a child with a disability should attend the neighborhood school that would be attended if the child did not have a disability" (UNESCO, 1994, p. 17). Subsequently, the idea of *all* children being educated together in an inclusive educational system was adopted as a strategy to achieve EFA (Peters, 2003), and over time, the conceptualization of inclusive education was broadened beyond the education of students with disabilities to encompass Roma children, street children, child workers, child soldiers and children from indigenous and nomadic groups—in other words, anyone who might be excluded from or have limited access to the general educational system within a country. As a result, inclusive education is defined and enacted in different ways in different areas depending on how schooling is organized and who has access to it (Ainscow and Miles, 2008).

Multiple definitions and interpretations of inclusive education not only reflect the differences in context in which it is implemented but the contested nature of the concept, in part because of its origins in special education. Although special education is often traced to 18th century Enlightenment ideas of equality when

> ...Enlightenment philosophers directed attention to those in society denied equality by social status and simultaneously studied persons with disabilities in attempts to solve the vexing problems of those denied equality by nature.... Reform movements to improve the conditions of disadvantaged and marginalized groups and rapid educational advances were achieved within the new set of social boundaries. Intervention for disabled persons was no longer merely a subject of philosophic curiosity: permanent facilities and pedagogical models emerged in a number of national contexts.
>
> —(Winzer, 2014, p. 24)

These facilities and models, forms of which are still with us today, represent the historical legacy of special education. But over time separate systems of special education for "some" learners operating in parallel to mainstream education for "most" others have come to represent injustice on the grounds that separate forms of provision for different kinds of learners are inherently unequal. As a result,

> By the early-1970s, the educational integration of students with disabilities was the central theme of special education. Notions about segregation that had appeared so connected and obvious a decade earlier were quite rapidly replaced with a movement toward new delivery models designed to bring marginalized students into mainstream classrooms.
>
> —(ibid.)

The problems associated with policies of integration soon became apparent. If students in special education were those thought to need something different from that which was available to others of similar age, then how could a policy of integration work? Many efforts to integrate students with disabilities focused on preparing them to fit into an unchanged mainstream. But other efforts sought to change the mainstream following sociological critiques that showed how the structure of schools as organizations rather than differences between individual pupils could create special educational needs (Tomlinson, 1982; Skrtic, 1986; 1991). In this way focus was shifted from the problem of the child to the problem of the school. Research on individual differences continued but new strands of research began to emerge. Scholars in the UK began to argue for a re-conceptualization of what they termed the "special needs task" as part of the process of school improvement (Ainscow, 1991).

By recognizing that children with disabilities should be educated within an improved inclusive education system, the Salamanca Statement linked the education of students with disabilities to a broader rights-based international education agenda that opened up new possibilities for practice, but the idea of inclusive education as a response to exclusion has challenged traditional systems of special education. This has prompted a long period of debate involving "methodological, practical, ethical, and socio-political considerations" (Gallagher, 2014) about the nature and purpose of special education.

However, the discourse of special education, like the legacy of separate forms of provision, has remained firmly fixed in policy and practice. Today, most national and supranational education policies promote the idea of educational inclusion while retaining a traditional special needs orientation to inclusion that relies on individualized approaches such as the identification and assessment of individual need, and specialist provision. Article 24 of the UN-Convention on the Rights of Persons with Disabilities specifies that States shall ensure "an inclusive education system at all levels," that "persons with disabilities receive the support required, within the general education system, to facilitate their effective education," and that essential staff training "shall incorporate disability awareness and the use of appropriate augmentative and alternative modes, means and formats of communication, educational techniques and materials to support persons with disabilities."[1]

How can students with disabilities receive the support they need without perpetuating the problem of marginalization that can occur by treating them differently from others? This chapter introduces the concept of inclusive pedagogy as an alternative approach to individual differences that is distinguished from notions of inclusive education and inclusive practice that are based on the process of providing for all by differentiating for some. As will be shown, the inclusive pedagogical approach actively avoids the problems associated with marking some learners as different and in so doing offers new opportunities to develop practice.

The inclusive pedagogical approach has been developed in response to concerns about variability in the quality of provision that is available within and across educational jurisdictions. While almost every country can point to examples of inclusive schools where students with disabilities and others encountering or identified as having difficulties in learning have access to good quality provision, every country has too many others who do not have such access. This chapter argues that such variability is fundamentally unfair but can be addressed by focusing on two key areas of educational development: the lessons that are being learned from the study of good quality practices and how these lessons can be shared in ways that lead to improvements in situations where the provision is less well developed.

THE PROBLEM AND THE CHALLENGE

As specified in Article 24 of the UN-Convention on the Rights of Persons with Disabilities, the availability of specialized support is an important aspect of inclusive education. However, the professionalized and bureaucratic nature of such support can be problematic. Of concern is when the pursuit of inclusive education via practices that are structurally similar to special education reproduces rather than resolves practices that exclude or marginalize some students. A key problem for inclusive education is to avoid the repetition of exclusion within the classroom (Allan, 2006; Slee, 2010).

Twenty-five years ago, Fulcher (1989) showed how national policies on what was then called "integration" could be counterproductive. Following Abberley (1987), she noted:

> The themes of difference, loss and marginal identity, combined with the political logic of extra resources, exclude the more appropriate themes of pedagogy and teaching practices.... To move away from exclusion, different themes and different questions must replace this discourse. The relevant themes are those of teaching styles and the relevant questions should focus on solving the problems which lead to exclusion.
>
> —(Fulcher, 1989, p. 21)

There have been many analyses that document the problems which lead to exclusion as well as studies that record the attempts that schools have made to become more inclusive. This work has shown that inclusive education is a complex endeavor, characterized by tensions between competing policy demands. In the main, efforts to mediate these tensions have involved individualized approaches to inclusion at both the school and student level. What Fulcher points out is the antithetical nature of combining rights based discourses with the discourse of professionalization. This can be illustrated by examining the limitations of individualized approaches to inclusive education. While these approaches have been useful to some extent, they also limit the development of more inclusive practice. Elsewhere (Florian, 2010) I have suggested five interrelated reasons why individualized approaches may be limiting the development of more inclusive practice. These are because:

1. Different teaching strategies are not differentially effective with different types of learners (Ysseldyke, 2001).
2. Studies of specialist teaching suggest that the salient distinction in teaching students with special educational needs is what Vaughn and Linan-Thompson (2003) have called the "delivery of instruction" (p. 145). Here the emphasis is on how teaching strategies are modified or adapted rather than on the use of different strategies from those that are effective with others.
3. Including *all* students by differentiating for *some* still marks some students as different and can reproduce exclusion rather than facilitate inclusion in classroom learning activities.
4. When students who encounter difficulties in learning are identified as having "special educational needs" an intractable cycle is formed—they are

assumed to possess difficulties in learning, and judgments are often made based on assumptions that they possess *all* of the characteristics associated with the particular difficulty in learning. In other words, despite known variation between individuals within any given group, the tendency is to assume the group members have the same learning needs.

5. Identification of "special educational needs" often results in lowered expectations about what it is possible for a student to achieve.

These problems do not mean that there are no educationally relevant differences between learners. Indeed it is important to acknowledge, understand and respond to difference, but important questions about which differences matter and how one should respond must also be addressed. The many sources of variation within and between any identified groups of learners make educationally relevant distinctions between them difficult because the variations between members of a given group make it hard to predict or evaluate provision for individuals in it. As Fulcher (1989) argued, the "logic of extra resources, exclude[s] the more appropriate themes of pedagogy and teaching practices" (p. 21).

To move away from exclusion, a change of focus is needed. The key challenge lies in determining how teachers might respond to differences between individual students without perpetuating the marginalization that can occur when some are treated differently from others. Specialist teaching related to particular impairments is, of course, an important "use of appropriate augmentative and alternative modes, means and formats of communication" as stipulated in the UN-Convention quoted above; for example, the teaching of sign language to students who are deaf. As such, it is an essential aspect of inclusive education. However, it is important to note that sign language has also been shown to improve the language skills of hearing children (Daniels, 2001). As in the case of adaptations to the physical environment undertaken to improve accessibility for people with physical disabilities, there are benefits for everybody. Just as curb cuts improve accessibility for those who push prams as well as use wheelchairs, specialized supports can be mobilized to improve learning opportunities for everyone. As will be discussed below, a shift in focus away from traditional approaches to individualization that provide for all by differentiating for some can help to open up new possibilities for inclusive education that respond to human difference but avoid the "repetition of exclusion" problem.

THE INCLUSIVE PEDAGOGICAL APPROACH

In recent years, a group of colleagues in England and Scotland have been developing the concept of inclusive pedagogy (Florian and Kershner, 2009; Florian and Black-Hawkins, 2011) as an approach that is distinguished from earlier concepts of special and inclusive education, which are based on the process of providing for all by differentiating for some. The approach rejects the idea that it is educationally helpful to base teaching approaches on categories of learners, particularly when the categories are described in terms of attributes about people. It has been developed in response to the concern that an emphasis on studying human differences perpetuates the belief that they are predictive of difficulties in learning and potential achievement.

Over time, it has become increasingly clear that teaching strategies are more appropriately aligned with what is being taught than who is learning, and the strategies used by teachers of students with special educational needs are not different to the strategies used by classroom teachers (and vice versa), although the application may be different. This is an important insight that challenges the argument that classroom teachers do not have the skills to teach students who have been identified as having special educational needs, a frequently cited reason for excluding these students from mainstream schools in many situations. This is not to suggest that classroom teachers can teach all learners without support. Rather, it requires attending to the idea that teachers are already responding to individual differences between learners within the context of classroom teaching. Every classroom contains diversity and teachers expect there to be differences between learners. Teachers take account of all kinds of difference in their daily practice because learners vary across many dimensions. Teachers know that what works for most does not work for some, depending on the circumstances. It is only at the point when the difficulties students experience in learning come to be defined as disabilities or special educational needs, that the historic traditional systemic response of separating begins. When the magnitude of the difficulty exceeds the teacher's capacity to respond with confidence, the student is often assumed to need specialist teaching or special provision. The act of obtaining support requires that the student is identified as having a difficulty and the distinction of being marked as different from other learners is complete.

As an alternative way of working, the inclusive pedagogical approach begins with a shift in pedagogical thinking from an approach that works for *most* learners existing alongside something additional or different for those (*some*) who experience difficulties, towards one that involves providing rich learning opportunities that are sufficiently made available for *everyone*, so that all learners are able to participate in classroom life. By focusing on how achievements in learning are realized through participation in the community of a classroom, the inclusive pedagogical approach acknowledges individual differences between learners but avoids the problems and stigma associated with marking some learners as different. The approach has emerged from our studies of the craft knowledge of teachers committed to developing more inclusive practice, which are providing a rich evidence base of practical strategies that can be used widely in support of inclusive education (Black-Hawkins and Florian, 2012; Florian and Black-Hawkins, 2011).

The inclusive pedagogical approach sets out to replace traditional approaches to teaching children, identified as having special educational needs, that are based upon the argument that such children necessarily require something "different from" or "additional to" that which is "ordinarily available to others of similar age" as many definitions of special needs education specify. The approach is located within Alexander's (2004) socio-cultural framework on pedagogy where the complexities inherent in providing for differences among students are subsumed within a set of interrelated ideas about children, learning, teaching and curriculum, as well as the school and policy contexts by which they are legitimized (for a discussion see Florian and Kershner, 2009). A socio-cultural perspective is important because it permits a consideration of individual differences as something to be expected and understood in terms of the interactions between many different variables rather than fixed states within individuals. Difference is not the problem, rather understanding that learners differ and how the different aspects of human development interact with experience to produce individual differences is the theoretical starting point for inclusive pedagogy. This stance focuses on how the teacher thinks about everybody in the class and how they will work together, as opposed to differentiating for some on the basis of judgments about what some cannot do compared to most others of similar age.

Importantly, the stance does not deny the importance of responding to individual differences. Indeed students may appear to be experiencing similar difficulties in learning but differences between them (i.e., one is a learner with English as a second language and the other a learner on the autism spectrum) means that the nature of the misunderstanding is different in each case, necessitating different responses to the difficulty in learning. While some argue that an inclusive pedagogical approach might lead to "an over-reliance on generalist teacher practices" at the expense of attention to individual differences (Ravet, 2011, p. 667), the inclusive pedagogical approach does not ignore individual differences between students. Rather it encourages the teacher to *extend the range of options that are available to everyone in the community of the classroom*. This is a subtle but important shift in thinking about individual differences between learners that focuses on learning as a shared activity and thereby avoids the potentially negative effects of treating some students as different.

EXTENDING WHAT IS GENERALLY AVAILABLE

The approach to inclusive pedagogy detailed below sets out to replace traditional approaches which rely on individualized teaching because of the unintended negative effects of individualization. It builds on previous research (Black-Hawkins, Florian and Rouse, 2007), which examined how some schools have developed strategies to raise the achievement of all their children, whilst safeguarding the inclusion of those who are more vulnerable to exclusion and other forms of marginalization. While this study explored schools as institutions and considered how values and beliefs within a school's culture shape the teaching and learning that takes place, subsequent studies focused on teacher craft knowledge about how they extend what is generally available to all (Florian and Black-Hawkins, 2011; Black-Hawkins and Florian, 2012).

The studies were informed by the view that learners vary across many dimensions and teachers are constantly making multiple decisions about how to respond to all kinds of differences, and it is only when the magnitude of difficulty experienced by a learner exceeds the teacher's capacity to know how to respond that the learner is considered to have special or additional needs. Findings from these projects suggest that teachers engaged in inclusive pedagogical practice work out what they can do to support the learner while maintaining a commitment to everybody (Hart et al., 2004), while avoiding situations that mark some students as different. This does not rule out the use of specialists or specialist knowledge but it is the way that support is provided that is distinctive. While the identification of special educational need may happen as a result of seeking support, this is because of how the professional discourse and bureaucracy operate. That is, administrative rules require identification of a problem. However, when teachers are using an inclusive pedagogical approach, they consult specialists for support of their efforts to ensure that the learner is meaningfully engaged in the community of the classroom. It is in the *ways* that teachers respond to individual differences, the pedagogical *choices* they make and *how* they utilize specialist knowledge that differentiates inclusive practice from other pedagogical approaches. This is illustrated below in Table 1 where the inclusive pedagogical approach is contrasted with an additional needs approach to inclusive practice.

Table 1. Contrast of "additional needs" and inclusive pedagogical approaches (Florian, 2010, p. 69).

Additional needs approach to Inclusion	*Manifest in terms of inclusion*	*Manifest in terms of exclusion*	*Inclusive pedagogical approach*
	Most and Some		*Everybody*
A student with autism uses Voice4Me on an iPod Touch to communicate with his teacher and peers during a field trip to an historic airfield. The tool is selected specifically because a visual approach will reduce the "processing burden" for the student and enhance both his learning and enjoyment of the trip. He selects a sequence of symbols/icons/pictures, which represent words and/or phrases to tell stories about the trip. The student uses an iPhone to collect photos and videos of the site, assign meta-tags and upload the content to a website of the group's field trip.	Student participates in the trip. Student works alongside peers. Student participates in learning activities by contributing photographs to a webpage, which is created by all the class illustrating selected idioms.	Peers of the student complain it is unfair that they are not allowed to use their digital phones. Student with autism is marked as different because he is getting special treatment.	Focus is on everybody in planning for the school trip and the building of a webpage to document the trip. While a visual approach is likely to be supportive for some students, immersion in the social context of the site will be more relevant for others. All students are involved in planning how to document the trip—types of information (such as narrative accounts, photographs, audio recordings, maps to illustrate where students went, statistical information such as distance travelled). Students then plan how this data could be collected and negotiate who would be responsible for the different tasks. Returning from the trip the class collate their different forms of data to generate stories about the event and develop the website page.

As is shown, the inclusive pedagogical approach is defined not in the *choice* of strategy but in its *use*. While the additional needs approach to inclusion focuses only on the student who has been identified as in need of additional support, the inclusive pedagogical approach focuses on the students' *relationships* in the community of the classroom. In this way learning opportunities are made sufficiently available for *everyone*, so that all learners are able to participate in the community of the classroom (for additional examples of this approach see Florian and Black-Hawkins, 2011; Florian and Spratt, 2013).

The inclusive pedagogical approach, with its focus on extending what is generally available to all, while taking account there will be differences between learners, offers an alternative strategy to inclusion that relies on addressing individual differences in isolation. By accepting the notion of individual differences among learners without relying predominately on individualized approaches to responding to them, classroom teachers, with the support of specialists, can help to ensure that the promise of inclusive education to provide good quality educational opportunities and experiences for *all* is less variable and less difficult to secure for those students who experience difficulties in learning and have not had positive experiences of mainstream education. The challenge now is working out how to share this lesson in ways that lead to improvements in provision that are less well developed.

TEACHER EDUCATION FOR INCLUSIVE EDUCATION

A growing network of scholars is beginning to consider how inclusive education can be improved by focusing on teacher education and teacher professional development. Debates about how to best prepare teachers to work with diverse groups of students are raising awareness of the role that teacher education plays in achieving inclusive education at national (e.g. Blanton et al., 2011), regional (e.g. European Agency for Development in Special Needs Education, 2011) and international levels (Opertti and Brady, 2011). As this awareness becomes linked to Education for All, fundamental questions about what teachers need to know and be able to do in order to implement a policy of inclusion are being raised and the importance of preparing primary and secondary class teachers to teach students with disabilities is increasingly recognized.

While there are debates about how best to prepare teachers for inclusion, many years of experience in offering additional courses or infusing specialist knowledge into teacher education courses suggests that these approaches are insufficient to improve practice in schools. A growing awareness that the consequence of these approaches has been to reinforce the idea of specialist knowledge rather than develop appropriate pedagogical approaches for teaching diverse groups of learners is leading to proposals for new models of teacher education (see for example, EADSNE, 2011).

CONCLUSION

It has become axiomatic that inclusive education requires differentiated approaches to whole class teaching so that individual differences between learners are accommodated. However, as this chapter has argued, these practices are limited insofar as the discourse of individual differences relies on the logic of exclusion whereby differentiated teaching for some is the process by which all are "included." The resulting repetition of exclusion (Allan, 2006; Slee, 2010) has been thoroughly discussed in the literature, as has the dilemma of difference (Norwich, 2008). This chapter has described the inclusive pedagogical approach, a key lesson learned from the study of classroom teachers' successful practice, as a strategy to overcome the barriers to inclusion that are embedded in this individual needs approach. Studies of teachers' craft knowledge of inclusive practice have enabled an articulation of inclusive pedagogy as a way of working together with all members of a classroom community *(everybody)*, as opposed to individualizing for each student. This is an important insight from a promising line of research that can help to provide concrete examples of practice and ways of working that aim to support those who aspire to be more inclusive to develop the capacity to do so.

Ensuring that all students have access to good quality provision in mainstream schools has been an elusive goal of inclusive education. Yet the continuing challenges of Education for All are reliant on the development of inclusive practice. Today, the Global Partnership for Education, a network of countries dedicated to improving access and quality to education, supported by multilateral agencies including UNESCO and UNICEF as well as donors, civil society organizations, private sector foundations and regional banks, has identified inclusive education as a key priority for action. However, such actions must address the problem of variability in the quality of current provision. While there are many examples of inclusive schools where all students have access to good quality provision, far too many others do not have such access. The inclusive pedagogical approach has been developed to help address this problem.

NOTE

1. See Appendix B.

CHAPTER SEVENTEEN

Tanzanian Girls and Women with [Dis]abilities Claim Their Right to Education

ELINA LEHTOMÄKI AND SANNA HUKKANEN[1]

In this chapter, three globally agreed and interconnected components of the Salamanca Framework are explored from the viewpoints of girls and women with disabilities in Tanzania. While some of these girls and women have accessed school, others remain illiterate. Their experiences and views represent a common situation in sub-Saharan Africa and elsewhere in the global South.

The preamble of the Salamanca Framework for Action states that "every person with a disability has a right to express their wishes with regard to their education." Action 13 recommends special efforts to encourage the participation of girls and women with disabilities while Action 48 speaks to the necessity of training and education for empowerment. In this inquiry, we enquire about what girls and women with disabilities desire in terms of their education, what special efforts they deem necessary and how they can be empowered.

There are several justifications for a focus on girls and women with disabilities. In Tanzania and elsewhere in sub-Saharan Africa, education is defined as a basic human right. However, distance to schools, experiences of discrimination, inadequate toilet facilities and poor safety in schools or on the way to school limit girls' educational opportunities, reduce families' willingness to send their daughters to school and increase the risk of dropouts (Burke and Beegle, 2004; Colclough, Rose and Tembon, 2000; Hunt, 2008; Lewin, 2009; Sommer, 2010; Stambach, 2000).

Though gender parity has been achieved in primary education in Tanzania, female students have a higher risk of dropping out during the transition to secondary school and encounter more challenges in further educational advancement than their male counterparts (Okkolin et al., 2010; Okkolin, 2013; Posti-Ahokas and Palojoki, 2013; Sommer, 2010; Unterhalter et al., 2013). Thus, the Education for All target and the Millennium Development Goal for universal primary education have been reached, but achieving the goal of gender equality at all levels of education remains a challenge.

In the case of girls and women with disabilities, neither gender parity in primary school nor equality in education has been achieved. Recent research on Tanzania and other sub-Saharan African countries shows that the combination of being female with a disability multiplies the risk of marginalization (Emmett and Alant, 2006; Fleisch et al., 2012; HakiElimu, 2008; WHO and The World Bank, 2011). Due to traditional beliefs and practices and the consequent extensive social exclusion from community life and services, such as healthcare and education, girls and women with disabilities are extremely vulnerable and experience severe levels of neglect, abuse and violence (Groce and Trasi, 2004; Hanass-Hancock, 2009; Possi, 1999; Save the Children, 2011). These facts have been largely neglected in education development policies and programs and analyses on social justice in education. With reference to the three Salamanca actions, our aim is to understand the experiences of girls and women with disabilities, that is, *insiders' views*, as suggested by Njelesani et al. (2011), and include the *voices of persons who are marginalized* in education in an effort to transform policy and practise (Kiragu et al., 2011; Lehtomäki et al., 2014a).

DATA FROM FOUR GRASSROOTS COMICS WORKSHOPS

The views of girls and women with disabilities were obtained through grassroots comics workshops organized in Mwanza town, northern Tanzania, in 2010. This was most likely the first time that grassroots comics were made by persons with disabilities. The purpose of the workshops was not to collect data for research but to provide an opportunity for the participants to produce and share messages they deemed significant. The concept '*grassroots comics*' was developed by World Comics Finland, a non-governmental organization with activities around the world. According to Packalén and Sharma (2007), grassroots comics are short comics with a message that tells a story, and the goal is to make a change in the thinking and attitudes of the community. Anyone can participate, and the comics are an inexpensive way of spreading information. Only paper, pens and perhaps a photocopier are needed. The use of grassroots comics provides an empowering tool to visualize views and messages, in particular, for illiterate persons.

The umbrella organization of disabled people's organizations in the region, SHIVYAWATA Mwanza, organized the four workshops for its member organizations, CHAVITA (Tanzania Association of the Deaf), TAS (Tanzania Albino Society), CHAWATA (Tanzania Association of the Physically Handicapped) and TAMH (Tanzania Association of Mentally Handicapped).[2] The workshops in Mwanza were funded by the Abilis Foundation in Finland.[3] All the participants were persons with disabilities, except in the workshop for TAMH where most were the family members of persons with intellectual disabilities (or mentally handicapped people, as they are referred to in Tanzania) and three mentally handicapped participants. Two of them managed to finish their comics, and among the 51 participants, half were women (Table 1). The comics presented in this chapter include information about the participants, aged from 20 to 49. Some participants did not know their exact age and, therefore, age groups are used. In the workshops for CHAVITA and TAS, there were many illiterate female participants who all finished their artwork with the help of teachers who did the writing. They were also among the most motivated and successful participants; their efforts showed determination and value for learning in comics to express themselves (World Comics Finland, 2010). Edina Fidelis, the treasurer of CHAVITA, worked as a project coordinator. The teachers in the workshop were artists Sunday Ngakama and Sanna Hukkanen, from World Comics Finland,[4] and Jonathan Livingstone interpreted Tanzanian Sign Language (World Comics Finland, 2010).

Table 1. Participants in the 2010 Grassroots Comics workshops in Mwanza (World Comics Finland, 2010).

Organization	*Women*	*Men*	*Total*
CHAVITA	4	7	11
TAS	7	3	10
CHAWATA	10	8	18
TAMH	5	7	12
All total	26	25	51

In the grassroots comics workshops, the participants had the freedom to choose their topics and were given instructions on how to express their messages in the form of comics. The stories presented were mainly real life experiences of significance to the participants. According to the artists who led the workshops, most of the comics dealt with issues relating to basic rights such as education, healthcare, employment, family and relationships (World Comics Finland, 2010). The topic of education was chosen by many participants, thus suggesting that access to and participation in education were deemed important but challenging. Therefore, comics displaying learning experiences and views on education were selected for this inquiry along with discussion on the three interconnected

Salamanca Framework actions which focus on education for girls and women. Nine of the selected comics were made by women and one by a young man with a physical disability who wanted to show his observation concerning the situation of a woman with a disability.

During the grassroots comics workshops in 2010, the participants wanted to share their experiences and made a plan to distribute their comics in the Mwanza area. The comics were reproduced in wall-poster format and distributed in small groups to the places where they could best reach target groups, including schools, government and city offices, hospitals and health centers, courts, bus stops and stations, ferry terminals and markets. During the distribution, the participants collected feedback from the community. Among the interviewees, there were people from many walks of life, including doctors, teachers, city officers and ordinary passers-by. The comics drew the attention of big crowds, and the workshop participants received good feedback on their *abilities* (World Comics Finland, 2010). Henceforth, therefore, we refer to persons and women with [dis]abilities, thus emphasizing their abilities. This chapter responds to the participants' request to disseminate their messages as widely as possible. In the remainder of the chapter, the three Salamanca actions are discussed in light of the grassroots comics by the girls and women with [dis]abilities and their family members. Each comic included the title of the story, the participant's name, age group and the abbreviation of the association (see Table 1) she belonged to.

EVERY WOMAN AND GIRL WITH A DISABILITY HAS A RIGHT TO EXPRESS HER WISHES WITH REGARD TO HER EDUCATION

Several comics showed that girls and women with [dis]abilities want to go to school; however, their parents ignore these wishes and are ignorant of their right to education. In the comics, the girls and women highlight that they value education not only for improving their own socio-economic status but more as a way of helping their families and parents. Neema Kajanja describes the serious outcomes of being excluded from education, a common experience of persons with disabilities in Tanzania, in her comic titled 'Education for All' (Comic 1). The mother gives a present to one of her children but nothing to her albino child. The mother takes the 'normal' child to school and says that the sister cannot learn or study because she is an albino. The young albino girl feels sad that her sister gets to attend school but she herself has to stay at home. As an adult, she worries about how she can care for her old parents (and contribute economically) without having an education.

Comic 1: 'Education for All' by Neema Kajanja, 20–29 years, TAS.

Mother:	*My dear child, here's a gift.*
Albino daughter:	*What about me?*
Mother:	*Let's go; I will take you to school. Your sister can't learn because she is an albino.*
Albino daughter:	*Why is it that my sister is taken to school but I have to stay home?* When the albino daughter develops into an adult, she wonders '*I have no education, so how can I help my parents?*'

Similar to Neema Kajanja's comic, Selina Denis's comic (Comic 2) also emphasizes the ignorance among parents and families concerning the universal right to education. In her comic titled 'The importance of schooling,' Selina Denis reports on a mother who abandons her deaf daughter. The little child is rescued by her uncle, only to work in his house; she does not attend school even though she wants to study. As an adult, she gets married, and her husband promises to find a teacher for her to learn to read and write.

Comic 2: 'The importance of schooling' by Selina Denis, 20–29 years, CHAVITA.

The mother abandons her deaf child outdoors.
Mother: *Well, I dump this deaf one who is useless.*
Child: *Waaa*?!
The uncle rescues the deaf child and returns home with her.
Uncle: *Hush, don't cry.*
Uncle: *There is no way you can go to school. You just have to work here at home.*
Girl: *I will not learn to read and write and will not find a job.*
Woman: *I got married, but I do not know how to read.*
Husband: *Don't worry my wife, I will find you a teacher.*

SPECIAL EFFORTS TO ENCOURAGE THE PARTICIPATION OF GIRLS AND WOMEN WITH DISABILITIES

Many comics spoke clearly about the need to educate parents and families about the universal right to education and the importance of education. Those produced by TAMH members, most of whom were parents and family members of children with intellectual disabilities, explained that usually, mothers are the ones who value education and take children to school while fathers do not see the importance of schooling children with disabilities, in particular, girls. Christina Aloyce's comic titled 'Education' portrays this situation (Comic 3).

Comic 3: 'Education' by Christina Aloyce, 20–29 years, TAMH.

Anna:	*I don't know when I too will go to school.*
Man:	*Disabled children can also attend school.*
Father:	*I have a lot of work and can't take someone who can't do anything to school.*

Mother: *Hold on, I will take you to school, Anna. You get an education like other children do.*

The girl is received and starts school.

Counteracting the ignorance among parents and families is expressed in several of the comics, whereas others highlighted the significant change that has taken place in Tanzania, the increased awareness among girls and women with disabilities, their families and even in the broader community, including friends and neighbors, of the right to education and the motivation to learn and participate. In Comic 4, Stephan Protas, a young man, describes the culturally appropriate negotiation process in a family concerning the daughter's right to education.

Comic 4: 'She has the right to learn' by Stephan Protas, 30–39 years, CHAWATA.

Girl: *Mom, I would also like to go to school like my brothers.*

Mother: *Ok, I will tell your father.*

Father: *It is a good idea, but you know that our daughter is disabled.*
Mother: *Yes, but she has the right to study.*

In her comic 'My dream,' Generoza Nyamwela explains that her parents do not take her to school. Her friend responds that the parents do not respect her basic human rights and helps her to get enrolled in a school (Comic 5). The title explicitly describes the situation: 'Education remains a dream for the majority of Tanzanian girls and women with disabilities.'

Comic 5: 'My dream' by Generoza Nyamwela, 20–29 years, CHAWATA.

Mariamu: *My friend, my parents do not want to take me to school because I am disabled.*
Joyce: *Oh, my friend, they don't respect your basic human right to education. You have to be taken to school.*
Mariamu: *I would be very happy, Joyce, if you could take me to school so that I can learn and be free.*

Joyce: *Don't worry, Mariamu, tomorrow we'll go and enrol you in school so that you can study.*

The comics provided evidence of the experiences of poverty, disability and lack of education. Even those who have access to school are at risk of dropping out. In Lucia Philipo's comic 'What shall I do?' (Comic 6), a secondary school student develops cancer which results in a leg amputation. The father tells his daughter that he cannot afford to buy her crutches and a prosthesis and, therefore, she cannot continue her education. The young student cries.

Comic 6: 'What shall I do?' by Lucia Philipo, 40–49, CHAWATA.

A girl develops cancer while in her second year (Form 2) in secondary school.[5]
One of her legs had to be amputated (at the doctor's).
Father: *The prices of crutches and prosthetic legs have risen and are high.*
Father: *You have to quit school. I can't afford the price of crutches, and that of prosthetic legs have risen.*
The girl: *What shall I do?*

Barriers, such as lack of accessible communication, that hinder educational advancement are also highlighted in Edina Fidelis's comic 'A Deaf Student in Secondary School' (Comic 7). While the secondary school teacher speaks facing the chalkboard and another student responds, the deaf student experiences exclusion in communication and her learning is consequently challenged. In the special vocational school where the teacher uses Sign Language, the student understands what is taught and feels happy.

Comic 7: 'A Deaf Student in Secondary School' by Edina Fidelis, 30–39 years, CHAVITA.

A deaf student has advanced to secondary school.
Student: *The answer is ten!*
Deaf student: *What is the question?*

(The teacher speaks while facing the chalkboard, and therefore, the deaf student cannot read the teacher's lips. If the teacher had paid attention to her needs, he would have faced the students while teaching, and lip-reading would have been possible. This explanation was given by Edina Fidelis during the workshop.)

Parents' decision: *We have decided that you will study at the vocational school in Igange.*

The deaf student: *Thank you.*

(The vocational education teacher uses Sign Language.)

TRAINING AND EDUCATION FOR DEVELOPMENT

The comics emphasized that education empowers. Furthermore, they focused on the importance of learning, being capable of advocating for education, empowering others who do not yet know about their right to education and informing society in general. A state of empowerment is understood as essential for social inclusion and participation in working life and society in general. Esther Shileki's comic titled 'Education is key' (Comic 8) presents a young woman seeking funding support to pay for her tuition and materials; on the other hand, it visualizes her important role as an advocate after successfully completing her studies.

Comic 8: 'Education is key' by Esther Shileki, 20–29 years, TAMH.

Young woman: *Teacher, can I please have some financial help with my tuition and materials.*

Teacher: *Go away! There is nobody here to help with your problems.*

Man: *Take this money for the tuition and materials.*
Young woman: *Thank you very much.*
She returned to school, continued with her studies, and later, she got a job.
She went back to her village: *We should love persons with intellectual disabilities; they are like any other person, and with education, they become capable.*

Accessible communication, in particular, media and television, appeared in the comics as important means for empowering persons with disabilities and for educating parents, families and communities. Selina Denis's comic presents a deaf woman's incapacity to follow an election campaign; she goes to the television management and suggests they hire a Sign Language interpreter so that she and other deaf people could have access to the campaign discussions (Comic 9). When interpretation is available, the deaf woman watches the discussions; one of the candidates promises to build a school for deaf students, and she decides to vote for that candidate. Selina Denis herself is illiterate because school was inaccessible to her. The comics she produced depict her real life experiences (see also Comic 2).

Comic 9: 'Television campaign' by Selina Denis, 20–29 years, CHAVITA.

Election candidate on television:	*Vote for me*!
Deaf woman:	*I don't understand; I am deaf*!
Two deaf women:	*Let's go to the Star TV station*! *Ok*!
One deaf woman:	*We would like to have an interpreter on television.*
The other deaf woman:	*...so that the communication challenges of deaf people can be eliminated.*
Television station representative:	*Thank you for the advice; we will arrange it.*
One of the candidates on television:	*I will build a school for deaf persons, so vote for me.*
Deaf woman:	*Fine, I will vote.*

In the grassroots comics, the empowered are those persons who have access to information and knowledge and claim their right to participation on equal terms not only in school but also elsewhere in society, such as in the use of public transport, as Veronica Mtiro describes (Comic 10). Furthermore, empowerment has to do with collaboration and social inclusion. In Veronica Mtiro's comic, this is shown by a co-passenger who is aware and responsive and encourages and co-advocates for the right of the women with a disability to use public transport.

Comic 10: 'Transport' by Veronica Mtiro, 30–39 years, CHAWATA.

Minibus conductor:	*Let's leave her; she will just delay us.*
Co-passenger:	*Let's help her so that she can travel with us.*
Conductor:	*There is no room for a wheelchair, or she has to pay extra.*
Co-passenger:	*How could she leave her legs?*

In the evaluations of the four grassroots comics workshops, the participants depicted experiences of empowerment (World Comics Finland, 2010). In the beginning, the participants did not think that they could draw comics and found it difficult to understand the idea behind comics. After learning about drawing and comics and finally seeing their own artwork revealing powerful messages, the participants were astonished and felt a sense of pride. They valued their own work. According to the report (World Comics Finland, 2010), especially women who were illiterate showed a strong commitment to learning how to express their views and voice their thoughts. At first, when the comics were posted for exhibitions and shown in public, people did not believe that they were done by persons with [dis] abilities and their family members because the works were very good. The participants were present to explain their stories and were praised for their abilities and talents. This was an empowering experience for them. Moreover, their messages resonated (World Comics Finland, 2010).

DISCUSSION: GIRLS AND WOMEN WITH [DIS]ABILITIES CLAIM THEIR RIGHT TO EDUCATION

The grassroots comics that specifically addressed education illustrated meaningful experiences in the daily lives of girls and women with disabilities in Tanzania, such as observing others go to school, ignorance among parents and families, staying at home to run household errands and dreaming about improving their lives through education. In what follows, we discuss the experiences exemplified in the grassroots comics in the context of educational development in Tanzania and sub-Saharan Africa, including measures that are deemed necessary for meaningful change.

With reference to the Salamanca Framework for Action in 1994, according to which 'every person with disability should have a right to express their wishes with regard to their education,' the comics reveal how it feels to be ignored and excluded. In Neema Kajanja's view (Comic 1) being excluded from education has serious consequences for her and her family. Her case depicts the common situation for persons with disabilities in Tanzania and sub-Saharan Africa where being disabled doubles the risk of never attending school (UN, 2010).

According to the most accurate statistics available on disability prevalence in Tanzania, 7.8% of the population aged seven and above had some form of activity limitation due to a disability; in this group 38.4% attended school (National Bureau of Statistics, 2008). For the same year, the Ministry of Education and Culture reported a total number of 8,410,094 pupils enrolled in primary school, and among them, only 0.4% were pupils with special needs or disabilities (URT, 2008b). The situation in Tanzania is similar to the global picture of limited improvement. Based on an assessment of changes in inclusive education, Bines and Lei (2011, p. 419) conclude that 'there are many gaps in policy and provision, and disability remains a significant factor in exclusion from schooling.' Following the UN-Convention on the Rights of Persons with Disabilities, the international community has started to react (see e.g. UN, 2010; UNESCO, 2010; UNICEF, 2013), but the inclusion of persons with disabilities in education requires a considerable amount of additional work.

As described by Neema Kajanja (Comic 1) and Selina Denis (Comic 2), most girls and women with disabilities in Tanzania and sub-Saharan Africa do not attend school; consequently, they find it difficult to be self-reliant and to support their families although they are capable and would like to (see also Macha, 2002). Their desire is reality in which there is 'Education for All,' including for girls and women with [dis]abilities. While the situation of girls has improved in the last decades, girls with [dis]abilities are less likely to attend school. Already by 2000, equal numbers of boys and girls were enrolled in primary education in Tanzania (Mushi, 2009; UNESCO, 2003/2004; URT, 2008a). According to a more recent community-level survey by HakiElimu (2008), a civil society organization in Tanzania, where children with disabilities were enrolled in schools, boys (57.7%) outnumbered girls (42.3%).

In light of the grassroots comics, efforts to encourage the participation of girls and women with disabilities are urgently needed. Selina Denis's (Comic 2) comic highlights the need to inform parents and families about the right to education and the importance of schooling for girls and women. In addition, the comics by the mothers of children with intellectual disabilities depict that fathers do not understand the importance of schooling children with disabilities. This suggests that special efforts focusing on fathers and encouraging mothers to use their influence on fathers and relatives are necessary to transform current social and cultural norms. The question of domestic workload is related to the broader environment beyond the family, that is, the community level and the social understanding of girls' roles. Traditionally, girls are expected to stay at home and work in benefit of other family members while boys may be sent to school, like in Christina Aloyce's comic 'Education' (Comic 3).

Several reports on girls' education initiatives show that social and cultural changes, opening educational opportunities for girls, reducing their workload and enabling a space for learning can be successful (e.g., Kiragu et al., 2011; Unterhalter et al., 2013; Warrington and Kiragu, 2012). In the 1990s, girls' enrolment in primary education significantly increased in sub-Saharan Africa as a result of national and international agreements and special efforts (Colclough et al., 2000; UNESCO, 2003/2004; UNICEF, 2004). Yet, in 2000, more than half of the out-of-school children in the region were girls; Tanzania was, however, among those 10 countries that reported reaching gender parity[6] in primary education (UNESCO, 2003/2004; UNICEF, 2004). In order to achieve the goal of parity, global and national commitments and coordinated support were necessary, including local negotiations concerning the return of school-aged girls and a reduction of their workload (Unterhalter and North, 2011). Recently, listening to the voices of girls has proved useful in finding sustainable solutions to end their dropout from and marginalization in education (e.g. Jones, 2011; Kiragu et al., 2011; McLaughlin and Swartz, 2011; Unterhalter, 2012).

The education of persons with disabilities may still be considered a more serious challenge than that of girls. In this context, Meekosha (2011, pp. 678f.) reminds us that 'disability is not universally understood' and 'we undervalue the legacy of indigenous knowledge, including the diverse understandings of impairment and disability.' She advocates for contextualized conceptualizations in North-South dialogues which have dominated disability theorizing, defined international policy priorities and influenced local implementations. In their review of the literature on disability and rehabilitation, Njelesani et al. (2011) find that in the Tanzanian context, emphasis is placed on productivity and community integration, and therefore, disability may be understood as impinging on the realization of these social values. By emphasizing the socially constructed perceptions of impairments and disability, Njelesani et al. (2011) and Meekosha (2011), in line with Shakespeare (2006), give priority to both the prevention of impairments and the realization of the human rights of persons with disabilities. They state that there is little evidence of community-level dialogue to reach a shared understanding of impairments and disability. In this meaning-making of disability in varying social and economic conditions, including participation in education (see Lehtomäki, 2000; Ngcobo and Muthukrishna, 2008), persons with [dis]abilities need to be consulted, and among them, particular attention has to be paid to the views of girls and women with [dis]abilities.

In the 20 years since Salamanca, educational opportunities in Tanzania for girls and women with disabilities have hardly improved (Lehtomäki et al., 2014b; Okkolin et al., 2010). Marginalization and exclusion, as portrayed by Neema Kajanja (Comic 1), Lucia Philipo (Comic 6) and Edina Fidelis (Comic 7), further disable and hinder social inclusion (see Macha, 2002). A significant change in recent years, which has been depicted in the grassroots comics, is that girls and women with [dis]abilities claim their rights and are willing to travel to villages, empower others and advocate for their rights (Comics 5, 8 and 9). The comics and the report on the workshops (World Comics Finland, 2010) highlight the experiences of empowerment through participation in the learning techniques of grassroots comics and finding the means to convey strong messages in everyday social environments where information, together with shared experiences, has the power to transform perceptions of [dis]ability.

The empowering comics provide critical insights into what girls and women with [dis]abilities and their families see as 'special efforts' that are urgently needed in education development. Their case represents evidence of what Tarabini (2010, p. 211) observes: 'neither the EFA nor the MDGs include the need to reduce inequality as an explicit goal among their objectives.' Though education is seen as a key factor in reducing poverty and achieving equality, she argues that the agendas and programs have failed due to their focus on access to schooling and primary education without addressing 'the full meaning of inequality' (p. 211). Tarabini also suggests new objectives for educational development to directly address redistribution and social justice. Extending the suggestions of Tarabini, this paper advocates for collecting and understanding the experiences of those targeted by education policies, that is, *insiders' views*, as suggested by Njelesani et al. (2011), and including the *voices of persons who are marginalized* in education to transform policy and practice (Kiragu et al., 2011; Lehtomäki et al., 2014a).

There is a striking difference between the two approaches, *girls' education* and *the education of girls with [dis]abilities*. During the last two decades, concerted global and local efforts have led to remarkable improvements in girls' education while special efforts to improve educational opportunities and participation of girls and women with [dis]abilities are wanting. The time has come to revisit the Salamanca Framework for Action and to implement the recommendations. Will the next goals and steps in global development and education actions on the ground include special efforts to end extreme exclusion and marginalization and thereby respect the views and experiences of girls and women with [dis]abilities? Grassroots comics can contribute with empowering tools to uncover *abilities* and *voices*.

NOTES

1. Our thanks go to Florian Kiuppis for arranging copies of this book for each of the ten comic authors as well as for the organizations CHAWATA, CHAVITA, TAMH, TAS and World Comics Finland.
2. SHIVYAWATA, the Tanzania Federation of Disabled People's Organizations, a non-governmental federation established in 1992, is a network of ten national disabled people's organizations (DPOs), http://www.shivyawata.or.tz/
3. Abilis Foundation, Finland, http://www.abilis.fi/index.php?lang=en
4. World Comics Finland, http://www.worldcomics.fi/

5. General education in Tanzania comprises seven years of primary education (Standards 1–7) for age group 7–13, lower secondary education (Forms I–IV) for age group 14–17 and upper secondary education (Form V–VI) for age group 18–19.
6. GPI = A gender parity index of 1 indicates parity between sexes (boys and girls); a GPI that varies between 0 and 1 means a disparity in favor of boys; a GPI>1 indicates a disparity in favor of girls.

CHAPTER EIGHTEEN

Education as Liberation from Oppression:

Personal and Social Constructions of Disability

IGNACIO CALDERÓN-ALMENDROS AND CRISTÓBAL RUIZ-ROMÁN

In the last few decades, the academic discourses concerning disability have been centered on the social model of disability. These discourses are based on the understanding that all human life is equally dignified and that people with disabilities can make important contributions to the rest of society through inclusion and the acceptance of their differences (Palacios, 2008, pp. 103f.). This position is in opposition to a widely assumed conception based on functionalism. According to Abberley (1987, p. 16), "oppressive theories of disability systematically distort and stereotype the identity of their putative subjects, restricting their full humanity by constituting them only in their 'problem' aspects." Swartz and Watermeyer (2008, p. 187), for their part, considered that, at the heart of discrimination against people with disabilities, is the idea that they do not meet the necessary requirements to be considered fully human. Goffman (1963) made a similar point when he stated that "normal people" consider stigmatized persons not to be fully human. In more general terms, Freire (1972) argued that the oppressed are dehumanized insofar as they are both reified and alienated, transformed into objects by the need of the oppressor to control them.[1]

The social disability model emphasizes something that has historically constituted a boundary: the humanity of people with disabilities, insistently denied by those who, from a position of privilege, define the identity and the lives of people with disabilities as being radically separate from their own. However, the proposals made thus far have not quite yet departed from an interpretation that continues to leave them relegated to being excluded. We need theoretical tools which emanate from reality, based on the problematization of the lives of the oppressed, with the firm intention of not creating any more grounds for exclusion. The studies on disability must be necessarily founded in more generic sociological and pedagogical theories and practices, embedded in philosophies and pedagogies of difference (Skliar, 2007; Skliar and Dussel, 2011).

IDENTITY, CONFLICT AND DISABILITY

Throughout human history, women and men have felt the need to respond to the question "who am I" in order to occupy and give meaning to their existence in the world. In order to understand this process of conferring meaning on personal existence, it is necessary to take into account the experiences within the relationships with others, as well as the various contexts in which such experiences take place. As stated by Giddens (1982), our personalities and perspectives are strongly influenced by the culture and the society in which we happen to live. Each individual constructs their own patterns of interpretation and action based on others, on the culture, and on the patterns of interpretation and action legitimized by their community's culture. These do not determine personal identity, but they do have a strong influence in terms of guiding what each person values and gives meaning to in their life. Authors from various different disciplines, such as Bernstein, Bruner, Castells, Cole, Erikson, Freire, Geertz and Vygotsky, have all agreed on the importance the socio-cultural environment has in the formation of individual identity. Nevertheless, not all social systems have the same capacity to influence, or to make an impact in the same way, or encompass the same meanings, experiences, customs and rules, or value or create hierarchies in the same way.

On many occasions, educational agents hide or negate the conflicts that they have with the people that they are trying to socialize. Covering up the conflicts dilutes existing fights, forces the subject to submit to the ties of hegemonic concepts and deprives citizens of the ability for collective improvement. This is why it is necessary to make the conflict explicit and to see power as a key factor in the understanding of human relationships, as one cannot sever differences from the very inequality upon which they are conditional (Ball, 1987; Carr and Kemmis, 1986; Foucault, 1999; Tyler, 1988).

The experiences of people with disabilities are marked from an early age by this inequality, which is embodied in the conditioning exerted by the different contexts of behavior and ways of thinking about, and representing, reality. Each of these environments uses its own models of interaction and has very different motivations and values, the majority of them being processes of domination in order to achieve the integration of the individual into the system of meanings shared by the group.

People with disabilities (and especially those with cognitive disabilities) are aggressively attacked by hostile environments. The pressure that the different contexts exercise on modeling the behavior and way of thinking of the subject are grounded in strong arguments of hierarchy and domination, the former being a consequence of the latter. This constant inertia towards domination of some over others crystallizes into the construction of hierarchical systems into which the individual is integrated. All of this fits within the market-driven, utilitarian knowledge logic of neoliberal society, based on capitalist assumptions, where the value of the person depends on their economic production and not on other more specific human qualities. It is the triumph of structural functionalism: biological interpretations used to analyze human realities.

DISABILITY AND THEORIES OF REPRODUCTION AND RESISTANCE IN EDUCATION

The theories of reproduction (e.g., Bourdieu and Passeron, 1977; Bowles and Gintis, 1972; Baudelot and Establet, 1971) have played an important role in exposing the assumptions and ideological purposes hidden behind the rhetoric of neutrality and social mobility of functionalist theories (Giroux, 1988, p. 106). And, despite containing errors that have been extensively criticized, they were, and still are, highly relevant, basically because they succeeded in repositioning the problem that functional structuralism places in the individual's terrain. If, before theories of reproduction, the academic success or failure of a student was basically due to their individual characteristics and attitudes, after the theories referred to above, the issue was brought into the social, cultural and political arenas. These authors managed to show that there was no biological or natural justification for the low academic achievement of students from disadvantaged social classes.

This meant that new analyses were generated along the same lines that tried to fathom if this social division was due to, for example, gender or race. However, Barton and Oliver (1992) showed that little attention has been given to people with disabilities from the point of view of educational inequalities. Somehow it has been taken for granted that people with disabilities are not governed by similar patterns. It is assumed that they obtain the academic results that they should obtain, and the social fate that this earns them. That is, the education of people with disabilities is still largely interpreted, even within critical theory, from the parameters of structural functionalism. It still has not been assumed that, in the same way as the school legitimizes, sustains and strengthens the stratification based on social class, it also generates mechanisms that lead people with disabilities into poverty, exclusion and social devaluation.

Both the theories of reproduction and those subsequently developed by Foucault (1975, 1981, 1993), differences aside, emphasized something that goes beyond the marginalization that some groups exercise over others. As we proposed elsewhere (Calderón-Almendros, 2011; Calderón-Almendros and Habegger, 2012; Calderón-Almendros, 2014a, 2014b; Ruiz-Román, Calderón-Almendros and Torres-Moya, 2011), the school exercises the power to legitimize and justify these situations in such a penetrating way that they are finally subjectified by the individual. This is what Foucault called biopower. It endows public discourse with greater legitimacy, as the subject becomes an agent and participates in the categorization developed by the institution: the victim starts to interpret the situation as being their fault and thus the stigmatizing discourse of the school is uncritically internalized.

The theories of reproduction denied the possibility of overcoming models of domination. As an answer to this lack, resistance theories (Anyon, 1983; Willis, 1981; Apple, 2004; Giroux, 1988) have shown that students are in a continuous process of negotiation with the powers to which they are subjected, whilst the imbalance of power in these relationships often renders the fight too inefficient. All of these theories, from different perspectives, agree on the difficulty involved in truly participating in the construction of identities, these being understood as sites of hope and conflict (Freire, 1985). At the core of this approach is the attempt to understand how schools constitute subjectivities and produce meaning, and how they are linked to issues of power and control (Giroux, 2001, p. 104).

From this point of view, the structure has an important power in the construction of identities, but at the same time agency (the capacity that an agent has to act in the world) is recognized, as individual resistance operates on both individual and social levels (Freire, 1972). In all life experiences we come in contact with the structure and we act largely in accordance with its guidelines. However, we also contest such structure when we question it and/or act outside its coordinates, that is, to the extent that we problematize it (Freire, 1972). This offers a far-reaching theoretical tool, both for the analysis of social and educational reality and for the construction of counter-hegemonic proposals that question oppressive theories and allow fair and efficient action to take place.

Revealingly, the theories of resistance have not had much impact on the field of disability. Just as was the case with structuralist theories, disability issues have been excluded again from the major sociological and pedagogical theories. It was not until the paper by Gabel and Peters (2004) was published that a serious and formal way of constructing disability praxis on the basis of resistance theories was presented as a possibility. Resistance has been undervalued, particularly that emanating from people with disabilities themselves. Gabel and Peters considered resistance theory as a way of leveraging the knowledge generated by it and developing local praxis globally, since it provides a way of understanding the complex relationships and negotiations between diverging ideas that do not currently have a place in the social model of disability. In the praxis terrain, the work of Calderón-Almendros and Habegger-Lardoeyt (2012) and Calderón-Almendros (2014a) made a contribution on how families and teachers can resist exclusionary educational practices.

According to Susinos and Parrilla (2008, pp. 158f.), resistance theories recognize, beyond the impact that social structures have on people, the capacity of individuals to resist dominant discourses. Together with Gabel and Peters (2004), they see in resistance theories the possibility of understanding in a complex way how "some people with disability resist the dominant discourses of stigma, political and social exclusion and the power of experts in the lives of people with disabilities" (Susinos and Parrilla, 2008, pp. 158f.). This is a path that allows people to discover, analyze and question reality and also recognizes individual agency, thus opening a way for research through their own voices (Parilla, 2009, p. 111).

Resistance constitutes a means of opposing scholastic socialization, in which moral positions – often defensive ones – show certain lacks in a context that frequently denies the possibility of progressing and growing. The majority of these are acts of protest and complaints. They uncover latent conflict silenced by the scholastic institution, mainly due to the vast differences in the opportunities for real participation in school decision-making. These positions would only resist if they do not produce domination patterns, and their analysis contributes to the movement for the rights of people to prevail over the rights of property (Apple, 2000, p. 195). This could lead to the coming together of excluded groups and critical professionals in order to consolidate synergies as "forces for change" (Echeita et al., 2011, p. 36).

In this way the school becomes an institution that fights for democracy and justice (Giroux, 1988, 2001, 2002; McLaren, 2003; López Melero, 2004; Apple and Beane, 1999), where oppressed people can emerge. From this position, we will now make some contributions derived from a case study (Calderón-Almendros, 2014a) about the process of identity construction of a person with cognitive disability, in which it can be seen how well-constructed resistance can be transformed into inner power. Resistance, when balancing the scale, becomes resilience (Van Hove et al., 2012).

COMMUNITIES OF RESISTANCE, RESILIENT IDENTITIES

The conflict arising in the group's attempt to dominate the subject consists of two basic milestones:

1. The beginning of the conflict in a person's life occurs in two ways simultaneously. One is the *conditioning understood as a condition*, that is, as a real structure within which the subject develops. As we have said, we are all framed within a specific time and place, with certain material and symbolic conditions through which we construct our own meanings. The social structure in which a person is embedded, their public image constructed in the different contexts and the expectations placed on them, create the platform on which the subject develops, and this narrows their chances, and even their way, of understanding reality. These are the material and symbolic conditions that exist before the person becomes part of the social group. That is, culture precedes us, and this culture is imbued with social representations: "value systems, ideas and practices… which enable individuals to orientate themselves in their material and social world and to master it" (Moscovici, 1973, p. xiii). These finally become what we know as "common sense." As socialization processes are vertical and downward in nature, "common sense" finally results in an imposition of the environment, especially for certain groups and people that fare poorly in the social representations that influence them. In the case of people with cognitive disabilities, the social representations of disability are merely external constructions which the people with disability have little capacity to change (Ferreira, 2008; De la Rosa, 2008). It is for this reason that we speak of conditioning as a condition: the social system itself creates systems of meaning that the subjects have to adapt to during socialization. This adaptation implies the subjectification of a social hierarchy in which people with cognitive disabilities are perceived as being incomplete and less worthy, as well as being exempt from certain rights.

The second way in which conflict is produced is *conditioning as praxis and experience*. If conditioning as a condition refers to restrictions imposed by the "recipient" (the social, political and cultural structures, to which the individual must conform), conditioning as experience refers to the pressure that the environment exerts in its continuous interaction with the subject, in direct actions with it. The continuous pressure makes the person conform to the mold, and domination becomes evident in each given context. This is the process experienced by the person in the social group that seeks the subjectification of the referred system of meanings, which could easily be epitomized by the metaphor of the conquest.

These values, however, are partly contrasted with those explicitly sought in schools as institutions. Domination embodied in control (behavioral and symbolic) and hierarchy (centered on academic excellence and based on a meritocratic system) are revealed as fundamental aims of the school experience. In the teaching, the curriculum, the school organization, the attitude of teachers, the structure of the education system, the activities, the school's times and spaces, etc., the explicit educational goals have their place in processes to generate and maintain a way of understanding social reality: normality. All of this has its roots in the medical model, which has been passed on to the school system. Normality is constructed and maintained in the school by an obvious process of differentiation that carries with it unequal chances of success, learning, participation and recognition in the school and social spheres. Presented as being essential is a system of rewards and punishments during the schooling process, which are intended to subdue, rather than students with disabilities, their families (through classifications and other seemingly neutral forms of segregation). A double domestication is thus produced that preserves the structure of the social reality through normalization: the families submit to social representations that agree with the norm, in turn carrying out the delegated task of making the person with disability internalize, and subjectivize, the stigma.

2. The second point of the conflict is the subject's reaction, and close proximity to, social conditioning, and represents a liberation, insofar as the subject has a way out of the conflict. The most logical move is the assimilation and internalization of values that are shown in the different contexts. This adaptation is largely unconscious; it is internalized without the control of the subject and normally manifests itself in a natural way. It is precisely that unconscious element which causes the subject to embody social values and expectations, acting and responding on behalf of society, as such values and expectations become transmitted to the individual. Therefore it cannot be said that a real dynamics of liberation exists. This adaption movement is what has sometimes been identified with socialization, reducing the process to internalization and acculturation. Accordingly, families sometimes see the process that leads to the person being devalued, segregated and excluded from the educational context as something unavoidable.

This social adaptation does not seem to happen without the resistance of the person involved and of their close environment. The families partly modify the social representations on disability upon the birth of the individual (or the arrival of a disability), inasmuch as they experience the stigma. This sometimes leads to an initial interpretation of reality in terms of fairness, moved by emotion and as a result of an imbalance in the relationships that the context (mainly the school) establishes with the family. However, the roles adopted by the professionals (including those in the health sector) tend to dissolve the conflict by a process of assimilation, since the discourse is then turned back to scientific and neutral terms that dominate the rest of the social environment. Emotion is suppressed by reason. Despite this, both the individual and their family manage to preserve some of the new values that differ from the social ideal. This is a complex process, given that those values are not shared by the majority of the contexts and social groups to which they belong. Therefore, they incorporate contradictory patterns of thinking to offer, by way of exchange, what each context demands and shares.

In rare exceptions, the representations that are created in families and subjects about disability succeed in overcoming this conflict without adaptation. It is a complex resistance to the environmental pressures that pervade most social settings. When this happens, there is a new movement of the subject, that of resistance. This ultimate answer shows the dynamics towards the subjectification of the individual (in the sense that the individual becomes a subject by questioning the socialization process), who opts for a particular cultural manifestation, taking action against the movement of acculturation of the other socializing groups.

To free themselves of this typecasting, and to prevent society from imprisoning them under the "disabled" label, the individual has to seek resistance mechanisms. Mechanisms that allow the individual to escape from this "prison" so that others recognize the individual as a person. These labels limit our knowledge about the person, and their role is to give the impression of knowing what the person is like, without actually knowing that person. They constitute a type of lazy and superficial (lack of) knowledge about the person which leads people to protect themselves from the person with disability (especially if they have cognitive disabilities) even without knowing them. This predetermined knowledge (who the person is, what must be thought and known about a person that we do not know) provides a pattern of behavior applicable to the different people that we have decided to stigmatize in this way. This definitely plays the role of social control over the person so labeled. For this reason the label is a nail in the coffin that ultimately destroys the humanity of the person with a disability, their legitimacy as a subject. It is a form of domination, oppression and objectification that determines the other, and eliminates an opportunity to know them. The label objectifies because it deals with the person as if they were a thing, making it impossible to see, feel and deal with the real person, who is left unable to fulfill their wishes. The label prevents the person from being, and everyone else from establishing a non-oppressive relationship with them. The logic of power pervades the large majority of social actors around them and ends up controlling the person. Thus the stigma marks the person, wounded in their humanity and emotionally injured, in which case they can only try to shake off the yoke.

However, the answers of resistance to social impositions – relationships, the construction of hierarchies, domination – and cultural impositions – the interpretation of a partial cultural selection (to a certain extent arbitrary) in the school - are basically neutralized by bureaucratic strategies, such as increasing the level of control that institutions (especially school ones) exercise over the person and their impact on the context. This increase of control would eventually lie in discrediting the "rebellious" behavior, labeling it as "deviant," which in the case of people with cognitive disabilities strongly reinforces the stigma that the person sought to oppose. A referral to education pathways, forms of schooling and special education centers emerge as an institutional answer. They express the need to control the thoughts and ways of behaving that challenge normality as the rationale for organizing reality and, in particular, school reality. Behavioral control is thus reinforced, given the close link to the medical model still existing in special education centers.

The movements that subjects make (and often their closest environments) do not contribute to the liberation of the subject from the social norms that constrain them, against which they rebel, but rather further entangle them in their situation of oppression. Despite this, the people who try to break away from this situation that condemns them to despair do not lose everything in the process. With rebellion, individuals emerges as subjects with their own identity, gradually constructed in opposition to the values that oppress them and this constitutes an explicit attempt at liberation, even though it is mixed with escape strategies that try to avoid the problems caused by some group norms. These escape strategies fall somewhere between resistance and adaptation, as they embody a flight from confrontation but a departure from the norm, which has not been strictly abided by.

Only when this spontaneous and unreflective rebellion is transcended is it possible to generate truly resistant responses. If the person opposes the situation in the context in a more or less conscious way, and generates strategies that do not imply the strengthening of the control of their way of thinking, attitudes and behavior, only then can we speak of resistance through interpretation (Ruiz-Román et al., 2011). It is a complex process that is initially born of trust in intuition and emotions, using these to overcome the interpretations and prescriptions made by professionals, who act as agents of normality and the *status quo*. That is, part of the environment must be able to question what the institutions dictate and establish, so that the development of a relatively autonomous movement of the subject becomes possible. These conditions allow for the contrasting of ideas and the consolidation of resistance proposals through interpretation. It is not possible to fight the world alone. People need to find points of reference that rely on personal action, whom they can trust. When this happens, social blackmail loses power and the subject emerges in a process of empowerment. In this road to freedom, individuals and their supportive environment need to develop their education, since institutional control – which guards normality – increases with age and a higher status in the social pyramid. Accordingly, the established order is challenged. This is the order which perpetuates the privileged position of some groups and people, whilst at the same time oppressing others. Intuition and emotion are not enough to resist, interpret and create the future. The situation requires a systematic analysis and the design of intelligent, consistent and firm action (including all types of intelligence); a logical process that occurs when values, ideas, and ways of behaving that started the process and would have been successful are not abandoned. These constructions must shed light on the complex processes that allow the wedge-like breaking of the oppressive barriers that are stubbornly erected in our society. This wedge breaks cracks in the barriers when it remains guided by the autonomous control of personal life, when the person does not yield to the deterrent projects that the school context imposes, and when the individual asserts their dreams, although they will mostly be interpreted as obscene. Only those dreams that have not been stolen provide the necessary fuel to reach a different destination. Meanwhile, the road becomes a process of liberation: an educational process in which the oppressor and the oppressed return their humanity to each other. It is the overcoming of Freire's oppressor-oppressed contradiction (1972).

TOWARDS THE RECOVERY OF LOST HUMANITY

After what has been discussed in these pages, what needs to be reflected on is how people with disabilities could join other groups and construct in this way new possibilities for the future. Ways out of obvious social and educational harassment, which allow the construction of new life projects. But as for community life, we cannot make the mistake of focusing on that which is individual again. What we have attempted to show is precisely the round trip between the personal and the structural, which spans relationships. And this new project is based on alternative, counter-hegemonic ways of narrating and understanding life (personal, group, school and social life), which bring forth again the humanity that had been mutilated by the bureaucratic and socialization processes. These forms of resistance articulated in the collective, which endure the bouts of stigmatization and the ideology of domination, end up distilling resilient experiences: people who manage to overcome the adverse conditions of their experience without compromising their questioned humanity, thanks to a profound search for the meaning of life (Cyrulnik, 2001; Frankl, 2006; Ungar, 2012; Rutter, 1979, 1985, 1993).

Collaboration-based resistance movements enable people to heal their psychological bruises, coming back from the world of the dead (Cyrulnik, 2001) by recovering their stolen humanity. And if we are narratives, as postulated by Bruner (1991), we can create and recreate the stories of our personal and group life, and so redesign our damaged identities. That is why recovering stories of resilience makes it possible to leave the borders of normality, question the unquestioned, and create new life and social maps which are guided by our desires. There is work to be done on the unconditional support to the fight against equality (on whatever grounds); on the scientific interpretation of the legitimate voices of the people with and without disabilities; on teachers being able to accompany students as humans (but not on a therapeutic basis); and on making public the stories of resilience that succeed in questioning and moving frontiers. Those who question them can subvert power, and they are resilient because they necessarily harbor reconciliation within themselves.

NOTE

1. This paragraph may illustrate the theoretical perspective of the authors, which is slightly unorthodox in two ways. Firstly, because it is influenced not only by British, but also by American Disability Studies. And secondly, because our theoretical sources exceed the scope of Disability Studies, as they also cover critical pedagogy, theories of resistance, philosophy and pedagogy of difference, as well as cultural psychology.
2. This chapter was translated from Spanish by Julian Thomas (www.textos-academicos.com)

CHAPTER NINETEEN

Reconciling "All" with "Special"

A Way Forward Towards a More Inclusive Thinking

JUDITH HOLLENWEGER

WHAT HAPPENED SINCE SALAMANCA?

"Salamanca" stands for the event and document marking the definite arrival of "inclusive education" in national and international agendas (Hodkinson, 2012). According to Ainscow (2005, p. 13), it "places schools at the centre of analysis rather than the disability of the person." It demands capacity building to support "participation and learning of an increasingly diverse range of learners" rather than promote a few identified as being special. And it should do so through "developing practices" rather than try to mould learners to fit traditional classrooms. Schools should appreciate diversity as an engine for innovation rather than see it as a source of trouble. Learning should be understood as an adventure shared by teacher and student, rather than pre-determined steps through the curriculum. Did Salamanca initiate the necessary shifts to rethink normality as diversity? Did it help to understand learning as something happening to a community of learners rather than to isolated minds? Did it lead to an understanding of inclusive education as something created, lived and nurtured rather than ready-made? And most importantly, did Salamanca reconcile the rights and needs of "all children" with the rights and needs of "special children"?

None of these questions can unequivocally be answered in the affirmative. But it is fair to say that many international and national policy initiatives since Salamanca addressing issues like participation, social inclusion and equity were more inspired by neoliberalism than Salamanca and mainly sought to increase economic competitiveness while maintaining social peace. For example, soon after Salamanca, the UK introduced neo-liberal reforms, encouraging competition between schools and providing incentives for schools to select higher achieving students (Glennerster, 2002). Policy development was influenced by contradictory principles of economic competitiveness and personalised learning; by pairing excellence with enjoyment and at the same time moving away from a child-centred to a society-centred education (Brehony, 2005, p. 31). According to Antoniou, Dyson and Raffo (2012), despite a wide range of policies and some successes to reduce educational inequalities in England, the extent of educational inequality remains largely unchanged.

It seems that children with "special needs" were included where it suited decision makers and left behind where it did not. Sometimes children with disabilities are part of "all," sometimes not, a rather confusing fact reflected also in developments at UNESCO to be explored later. This confusion is also part of the discussions around PISA (Programme for International Student Assessment). Students with disabilities were excluded from PISA (Hörmann, 2007), but PISA results confirm Salamanca's principles in so far as equitable and "inclusive" education systems consistently outperform others. Based on the 2009 data, OECD developed two indicators of inclusiveness of education systems (vertical inclusion, horizontal inclusion; OECD, 2011, pp. 455f.). But according to these indicators, Italy, a pioneer and champion of "inclusive education," has one of the least inclusive education systems. Another example: Norway abolished its special schools, but Finland is OECD's champion of inclusive education, despite segregating four per cent of students in special settings (European Agency for Development in Special Needs Education, 2012). Norway on the other hand experienced a shock when PISA results for 2003 and 2006 dropped below OECD average (OECD, 2004, p. 52; Kjaernsli and Roe, n.d.). Teachers were found to have low expectations of disadvantaged children and as children with special needs progressed through the grades, they were more and more marginalised (Wendelborg and Tøssebro, 2010). In addition, the numbers of students identified as having "special needs" and receiving segregated provision in Norway have risen substantially since inclusive education was initiated (Nes, 2010). According to Ainscow and César, Norway's idea of a "school for all" was more about identity building than about embracing and valuing differences (2006, p. 235) and it seems that "inclusion" in Italy fails many children despite a long tradition of "inclusion."

PISA excluded children with disabilities due to their functional limitations in carrying out the test, but highlighted the precarious educational situation of many children from disadvantaged or diverse cultural backgrounds (OECD, 2010), thus drawing attention to the complex dynamics of exclusion. At the same time, OECD invested much time and effort to develop a cross-national categorisation system to make education statistics of children with disabilities more comparable internationally (for example OECD, 2007). The exercise was doomed to fail because disability categories are products of the respective school systems and often have little to do with the characteristics of a child or youth. Due to this well-known fact (see below), some countries have long before Salamanca moved away from categorical approaches, for example the United Kingdom following the recommendation of the Warnock report (1978), while in other countries, such as the United States of America, abolishing disability categories in education seems beyond the scope of the imaginable. The development of a "non-categorical approach" as requested by the Salamanca Statement (UNESCO, 1994, p. 28) has made little progress in the last twenty years. Even in the UK, it was never fully implemented (Mittler, 2002) and today categories are increasingly used again in the statement of need (Riddell, Tisdall, Kane and Mulderrig, 2006, p. 73). So what has gone wrong after Salamanca with the effort to reconciling "all" with "special" and what can we learn from it for the future? And why does the way we think about disability need to change in order to achieve "inclusive education"?

DID SALAMANCA CHANGE OUR UNDERSTANDING?

"Diversity," "participation" and "inclusive education" have become the new unifying concepts for parents, teachers, disability activists, labour market economists, international development agencies and politicians alike. The diverse agendas of ensuring access to mainstream schools for children with disabilities, of combating under-achievement of children with minority background, of improving the life situation of impoverished and vulnerable communities, of providing education to girls and of international development work—just to name a few—became evident since Salamanca (Miles and Singal, 2010; Armstrong et al., 2011; Kiuppis, 2014). Despite adopting UNESCO's agenda of "Education for All," Salamanca's version of "Inclusive Education" remained centred around certain groups, particularly students with special education needs and disabilities (Artiles et al., 2006, p. 67). Merging UNESCO's two programme tracks (Combating Exclusion in Education and Special Needs Education) in 2000 did not result in the hoped for development of a shared understanding, but rather in the neglect of the situation of persons with disabilities (Kiuppis, 2014).

Mainly due to the Convention on the Rights of Persons with Disabilities (CRPD; United Nations, 2006), disability is now back on the agenda. In 2010, for the first time "disability" appears in the Millennium Development Goals Report (United Nations, 2010; 2011). According to the report, disability should be defined "through an ecological model in which disability is seen as an evolving concept reflecting the interaction between the individual and social attitudes and the physical, economic and political environment that hinders the full and equal participation of persons with disability in society" (United Nations, 2011, p. viii). In the same year, UNESCO dedicated its annual "Education for All Global Monitoring Report" to "Reaching the marginalized." In 2011, the "World Report on Disability" was launched by the World Health Organisation and the World Bank. And more recently, UNICEF dedicated its annual report "The State of the World's Children 2013" to "Children with disabilities." Questions avoided for a long time are now again on the table: Who is disabled and how is "disability" understood in the context of education? When is "disability" something individuals bring to school or when something schools create?

Looking at "inclusive education" today, one cannot avoid the impression that it means different things to different people depending on their viewpoint, interests and motivations (Armstrong et al., 2011, pp. 30f.; Takala and Hausstätter, 2012). Rather than revolutionize the way people understood disability, rather than initiating a paradigm shift (Ainscow, 2005), Salamanca was succeeded by a diffusion of ideas and a fragmentation of concepts. Adjustments were made to present a politically correct façade (Slee, 1998) where needed. New words were introduced or new meaning given to existing words to fit ideologies (Wilson, 2000) rather than to tackle conceptual problems. Ideas from economics (e.g., capability approach), sociology (e.g., neo-institutionalism, system theory) or philosophy (e.g., theories of justice) were transposed into education to explain or prove the value of "inclusive education." As a result, a shared meaning rooted in a shared terminology was lost and with it a common language to describe, analyse and understand relevant differences in persons and systems.

Twenty years on, the need for a new approach to understand "disability" is painfully clear. A new conceptualisation of "disability" should be fluid and responsive to changes in the environment—such as good educational practice—rather than fixed in categories of defects attached to a person. It should highlight problems related to participation of all children rather than give prominence to selected disorders such as autism. The United Nations recommends the "International Classification of Functioning, Disability and Health" (WHO, 2001) as a framework and model to monitor the implementation of the CRPD, and consequently also to be used in education (Article 24; United Nations, 2006). Since the CRPD, the rights-based approach to disability is no longer just an academic notion, but something to be applied in reality—using the ICF. So far, the ICF is viewed critically by supporters of inclusive education, because it conceptualizes disability in the context of health and well-being and therefore in their eyes must be a medical model of disability. And for people who see categorisation in itself as an exercise of power and an act of oppression, any classification system has to be rejected. But denying the existence of categorization as a fundamental cognitive process and the relevance of categories as building blocks of knowledge (Hollenweger, 2013a, p. 509) will not improve understanding—just the opposite. Since Salamanca, the dilemma of categorisation and difference has been avoided by many and acknowledged by some; now it is time to overcome it.

TOWARDS A RELATIONAL UNDERSTANDING OF DISABILITY

Using labels and medical categorisation for children "having a disability" in education has been discredited as meaningless or even harmful long before Salamanca (e.g., Goffman, 1963; Warnock, 1978; Mehan et al., 1986). The CRPD defines disability as a dynamic interaction between characteristics of the person and the environment; disability describes the characteristics of a situation of a person, rather than the characteristics of a person alone. Situations can be improved and thus "disability" reduced or avoided. Presently, medical labels are on the rise again, especially Autism Spectrum Disorder, Dyslexia and Attention Deficit Hyperactivity Disorder to ensure access to services, privileges and additional support. It is therefore not surprising that children from disadvantaged backgrounds are much less likely to be identified under these labels and therefore do not gain access to such services (Froehlich et al., 2007; Begeer et al., 2009; Durkin et al., 2010). These children are overrepresented in categories (e.g., intellectual disabilities, learning disabilities) that attract less funding and more often lead to exclusion (Sullivan and Artiles, 2011). Based on these facts, it is safe to assume that the implementation of a rights-based approach without the disposal of traditional disability categories will likely aggravate social injustices rather than eliminate them.

But how could this be achieved? Firstly, all disorders have to be placed on equal footing so that the simple choice of label does not pre-determine support or placement. If at all, the focus should be on the impact of disorders on participation in education, not on the disorder itself. Focusing on participation restrictions in diverse social situations would facilitate comparisons between identified and not identified children and would provide a common metric to understand social bias leading to over- or underrepresentation of different groups. Secondly, traditional disability categories have to be disaggregated to understand the information bits they are actually representing. Disability categories are amalgamates, including information on social situations (e.g., service provision, expectations, classroom characteristics) and on the personal situation of a person (e.g., age, gender, socio-economic background, ethnicity). They include some aspects of functioning, but remain silent on others. Children with "intellectual disabilities" do not only have problems with "intellect," but likely also with communication, mobility or relationships. If problems are to be understood, they have to be linked to the situation of the child in question, not merely reflect an abstract notion of a disorder.

But even more importantly, teachers need explicit knowledge of a child's strengths. Thirdly, a better understanding has to be developed as to which aspects of "disability" are to a greater or lesser extent unchangeable across settings (e.g., being blind), which aspects of "disability" are related to specific situations or conditions (e.g., not being able to climb stairs, but use a lift; not being able to read unless the text is in Braille) and which aspects of "disability" are the result of social constructions and therefore not attributable to a person (e.g., low achievement as a result of low expectations rather than low cognitive abilities).

The ICF provides an information system with 1454 potential units to represent the different dimensions and components of "disability." These information units are organised in two parts; the first part relates to functioning and disability (body functions and structures, activities and participation) and the second part to contextual factors (environmental and personal factors). Rather than defining what disability is, the ICF provides an information system in which (diverse) data can be systematically organised and different definitions or conceptualisations of disability mapped. "Disability" is not represented by one category, but by as many as are needed to describe the situation of a person. "Disability" is understood as "an interactive and evolutionary process"; different models can be created and different aspects of this process studied (WHO, 2001, p. 18). Contextual factors can be analysed as moderating factors (e.g., assistive devices enhancing participation), as mediating factors (e.g., effect of teacher expectations on student performance) as independent factors (e.g., age) or confounded factors (e.g., socio-economic background) (Wang et al., 2006). By capturing functioning in different settings (e.g., at home, leisure, school) a better understanding can be gained of the impact of specific environmental factors, for example adult interactive styles on communication (Kossyvaki et al., 2012) or regional differences on over-all participation (Colver et al., 2011). Today's differences in definition arise from different foci (social dimension vs. biological dimension), different premises underlying the same construct as well as using different thresholds or severity levels. By providing one metric and a common framework, these differences can be better analysed and understood.

The ICF provides the tools to analyse functioning in specific environments, of individuals and through aggregation also of groups and populations, for example by asking all students of three Swiss universities about difficulties in their studies. In this study, over 20% of the students indicated problems with "focussing attention" to an extent that interfered with their studies. Only 14% of the students with this particular difficulty indicated that it was linked to a disability or chronic illness (Hollenweger et al., 2005, p. 64). In the sub-sample of students with a self-declared health problem or disability, 31% indicated having this particular difficulty (i.e., focussing attention), but only about half declared it to be linked to their health problem or disability (p. 66). Students with mental health problems were most likely to be affected, but problems with "focusing attention" were also reported by 25% of the students with musculoskeletal disorders and to a lesser degree by students with allergies or respiratory problems and students with metabolic disorders (p. 67). Students with self-declared ADHD or specific learning difficulties only made up 1% of all students with health problems or disabilities. These results illustrate the diversity of difficulties and the multi-layered relationships between disorders, impairments and participation restrictions. Such self-reported data can be compared with other data; by using different measurements and information sources, a better understanding can be gained on built-in biases (e.g., self-reported data, information provided by parents or teachers, clinical assessment). Not only is disability relative, but also the way it is measured and documented (Hollenweger, 2013b).

UNDERSTANDING PARTICIPATION AND PARTICIPATION RESTRICTIONS

Since its introduction, substantial advances have been made to use the ICF to describe functioning and disability and relevant environmental factors. Comparable and reliable descriptions are necessary to understand differences in accessibility, availability, adaptability and acceptability of diverse educational provision in diverse populations. But rights are not only about access to education, they are also about having one's rights respected in education (Tomasevski, 2001). A mere description of functioning is not very helpful in understanding the complex dynamics and interactions that lead to identification and exclusion. Why are children with minority background over-represented in services meant for children with "special needs" (Gabel et al., 2009)? Why do IQ scores of children with below average IQs (mean 73) improve significantly (to a mean 96) when given a candy for each correct answer (Clingman and Fowler, 1976; Duckworth et al., 2011)? Why are the youngest children in a grade twice as likely as their older peers to be identified as having ADHD (Elder, 2010)? And what is the dynamics behind findings showing that student achievement is influenced both by teachers' (Carugati and Selleri, 2004) and students' personal epistemologies and beliefs (Jordan and Stanovich, 2001)?

Clearly, teachers are to a large extent responsible for creating the immediate educational environment, so this could be captured by using the ICF as described above. But more importantly, they interact directly with students in these environments. It is therefore not surprising that teachers have a substantial impact on students, exceeding that of any school level factors (Hattie, 2009) which received so much attention by inclusionists. To understand differences in participation, there is a need to address both aspects: the nature and impact of educational contexts or environments as well as the nature of situations between people that are created within these contexts. The participation of teachers and the participation of students change as a function of their interaction. So rather than just concentrating on the situation of the child, we have to also be aware of the over-all social situation (see next section). "Participation" is the interface between the personal and the social and therefore a useful tool for inclusive education and ensuring the rights of individuals in social settings. It can be used to bridge different conceptual systems and epistemological traditions used in sociology, pedagogy, psychology or didactics when trying to understand the situation of vulnerable children in education. But before doing so, we need to develop a better understanding of what "participation" is and how it could be defined using the ICF.

The ICF defines participation as "involvement in a life situation" (WHO, 2001, p. 10) or the "lived experience" of a person in the actual context in which they live (p. 123), thus adopting a situational approach and a relational understanding of participation. A more elaborate and explicit definition of "participation" was developed to map not only the different aspects of being involved (behaviourally, cognitively and emotionally engaged), but also the fact that being involved in education requires settings that engage children in activities and interactions typical and meaningful for their community and age group. In addition, true participation in education also prepares for adult life; it is directed towards socially and personally meaningful goals (European Agency, 2011, pp. 28f.). Not all aspects of participation are always equally important to ensure over-all participation, and many times, trade-offs are necessary. The life domains represented in the ICF classification of activities and participation can be used to study these dynamics. The environmental factors of the ICF provide the building blocks to describe different educational contexts. Contexts are connected through time and space; therefore a relational framework is needed to help organise contexts into systems. For this purpose, a matrix was developed (Hollenweger, 2010) and used to make sense of existing indicators of participation (European Agency, 2011). The matrix helps to link micro-, meso- and macro-levels with input, process and outcome variables, thus providing a grid in which to organise, aggregate, disaggregate or compare different measures or indicators for participation at the individual level and at different levels of the education system (p. 22).

SHARED PARTICIPATION AS SOCIAL PRACTICE

But what is needed to go beyond the mere description of participation within and across settings, time and populations and to actually understand the dynamics behind changes? How can we develop a better knowledge of the ways in which people and situations create opportunities or barriers for participation? Social contexts determine—at least to a certain extent—how people are likely to act and which meaning is given to a situation by them. This has been described as the "intercontext" (Rohlfing et al., 2003) or the "social situatedness" of learning (Lave and Wenger, 1991), of activities (Engeström, 2008) or of identities (e.g., "being ADHD;" Gee, 2001, p. 99). Engeström's activity theory provides a model to explore the dynamics of participation in activity systems by extracting and organising the more durable characteristics of social interactions and shared activities. The model helps to organise and contextualise information to understand social practice. Such a model is needed to extract the environmental factors and the components of functioning that are really at work in a social context, for example the impact of teachers' beliefs related to "disability." Jordan et al. (2009) found that 55% of the teachers who participated in their studies vacillated between understanding disability as something responsive to their interventions and understanding it as a fixed trait of their students. In their view, "these mid-range beliefs reflected teachers' struggle to resolve the paradox between their beliefs and the policies and procedures" (p. 538). The ICF's information units can be used to identify and understand such contradictions around concepts of "disability" within and between the components of teachers' activity systems.

But human action is not only defined by social situations; people also act as independent agents. Each person brings their "internal milieu" or "intracontext" (Rohlfing et al., 2003) to a social situation which influences their sense-making and their actions (personal situatedness). To make sense of what a person may experience in a social situation and of what effects their participation (or lack of it) may have on their life, a personal perspective is needed that contextualises present participation in the over-all life experience of a person, her development and biography. The way in which people are involved in social situations is constantly shifting as a function of the interaction between personal and social situatedness. But as children collect relevant information from specific situations, concepts are formed which subsequently constitute the intracontext. In other words, the social becomes personal. A pre-requisite to participate in social situations is the ability to make sense of it. If children are brought up without the enjoyment of the entire scope of social activities, they will not acquire or develop the functionings necessary to fully participate. Both inner and outer determinants of situations need to be taken into account at the same time and understood together to comprehend a person's opportunities to participate, or what Amartya Sen described as "capabilities" (1992). Again, the ICF is able to capture information necessary for the analysis of interactions between the personal and the social and how this interaction changes across situations and time. Such a methodology would be useful to better understand the dynamics between factors that lead to either resilience or vulnerability.

The ICF is merely a classification system, although well organized and multidimensional. In itself it does not solve any problems. But it has the potential to become a common language that can serve as a tool to address old problems in a different way. This would be a good start to help bring about the paradigm shift announced in Salamanca so many years ago. The ICF has reconciled "all" with "special" and its relational approach sheds new light on obscure and problematic concepts such as "special needs." This essay has tried to show ways in which the ICF could be helpful to disaggregate today's disability categories and gain a better understanding of the disparate underlying concepts. This would be a first step to describe functioning and disability coherently and to understand differences, for example between self-reported data and clinical assessments or between different levels of participation in different life situations. This would help understand the impact of environments on functioning of children and help identify barriers to education. If the concept of participation—one component of the ICF—were defined as something happening in meaningful social context and directed towards meaningful goals, it would help to understand barriers and facilitators influencing the process of education as well as the interaction between them. Also, an attempt was made to bring together situational and biographical perspectives to understand "shared participation" or "social practice" and understand the impact of social practices on the development of individuals. Such an approach would help an understanding of how education affects individuals, how "functioning" turns into "functionings" and "participation" into "capabilities" (Sen, 1992)—in other words, how education contributes to people's ability to exercise their rights or opportunities in life. And ultimately, is this not what inclusive education should really be about?

CHAPTER TWENTY

Mapping the "Individual":

Invigorating Social Theories of Inclusive Education

DAN GOODLEY AND FLORIAN KIUPPIS

Disability is often understood as a problem that resides in the individual. What is "the individual" and what kinds of individual are valued by contemporary societies? How have the social and human sciences contributed to common sense understandings of what it means to be an individual? This chapter addresses these questions by considering "the individual," and particularly the distinction between average and exceptional individuals, as a problematic construct and one that is cherished and reified by capitalist societies of the Global North and needs to be challenged by Disability Studies. It reflects some deep-held concerns regarding social exclusion and educational relations in inclusive education. The chapter provides different ways of *reading* the story of an eight-year-old boy and maps out some alternative conceptions of "the individual" described therein that are more conducive to the promotion of inclusive forms of education and citizenship, including ensembled individualism, post-conventionalist rhizomes, and post-humanist connectivities.

INTRODUCTION

What might occur if we were to suggest that Western predominant assumptions about "the individual"—and the kinds of individual valued by contemporary societies, for the most part in the Global North—are the root of the problems for the enactment of inclusive education? What consequences would ensue if we accepted that the social and human sciences have contributed to these problematic common sense understandings of what it means to be "an individual"? How might normative concepts of the individual threaten to exclude disabled people in education? (Kiuppis, forthcoming). This chapter addresses these questions by critiquing predominant conceptualizations of the individual as a problematic, pesky, ubiquitous, flat-lining phenomenon, which are cherished and reified by capitalist societies of the Global North and reified through the practices of psychology. The question is raised as to how we can develop alternative notions of the individual and personhood that are potentially more commensurate with the hopes and aspirations connected with inclusive education as "multiple ways of the future" (Kiuppis, 2014a), encompassing also non-capitalist societies. Using a story of an eight-year-old boy that is being *transcribed* from an individual story to a (demedicalized) rhizomatic story (cf. Goodley, 2007a; 2007b), alternative conceptions of "the individual" are offered that are collectivist and therefore more conducive to the promotion of inclusive forms of education and citizenship, including ensembled individualism and post-conventionalist rhizomes.[1]

RE/APPRAISING PSYCHOLOGY'S INDIVIDUAL

> *An individual story: "David" is eight years old and has moderate learning disabilities and autism. He struggles to connect with other children. He enjoys math and has an obsessive interest in numbering objects. He is well behind his peers in terms of cognitive, emotional, and social development. He needs to have a teaching assistant working with him at all times. He is an isolated soul and a problem to the teachers who try to educate him. Some parents of a few of his non-disabled peers in his class recently put together a petition seeking David's exclusion from the school. It is widely reported in the school that he often disrupts the learning of the more able children in his class.*

The origin of the concept of the individual has been documented in many histories of social science and philosophical expositions of the Renaissance, imperialism, modernity, capitalism, and patriarchy. For example, Finlay and Langdridge (2007) elaborate on the Cartesian dualism that followed the work of neoclassical scholars such as the seventeenth century philosopher René Descartes, which saw human subjectivity as separate and fundamentally different from the objective world of matter and bodies, as well as of God, thereby providing an ideational basis for the notions of freedom and self-fulfillment of human beings. The mind was celebrated and considered as separate from the body, human freedom upheld, each contrasted with the unruly depths of the natural world; the individual was born. Western culture soaked up this mind-body dualism and unknowingly reproduced it. This, Finlay and Langdridge (2007, p. 15) argued, was particularly the case in social science disciplines such as psychology, in which "the psychological and social complexity" of the individual become lost. Somewhat contrarily, Gottfried Wilhelm Leibniz assumed in context of his theory of monads that there is no dualism between body and soul—the world is considered as "One"—and according to the principle of individuation, subjectivity is supported by abilities that are naturally given, However, Gilles Deleuze—who extensively incorporated Leibniz's philosophical and mathematical perspectives into his *œuvre,* and to whom we come back below when rethinking "the individual"—expressed the relationship between the body and the soul as follows: "These are not two cities, a heavenly and earthly Jerusalem, but the roof and the foundations of the same city, the two floors of the same house" (Deleuze, quoted in Dosse, 2011, p. 453).

The phenomenon of the individual has a long sociopolitical history and etymology. It is tied to the enlightenment rise of the *reasoned* individual and *his* democracy over the sovereignty of church and monarchy. The individual is also the creation of capitalism, a convenient signifier of an alienating symbolic order, which masks the inequities of social and political life. Moreover, individuals populate consumerist and marketized forms of education, work, and leisure. Those individuals able to benefit from this meritocracy flourish, whereas the less able tend to flounder. In dominant ideas of everyday life, the individual remains the key site of understanding for the etiology of disablism. As Gayatri Chakravorty Spivak (1985, p. 244) coins it, "individualism in an age of imperialism relates to the making of human beings – the constitution and interpellation of the subject not only as an individual but as individualist."

In recent and current societies, the individual is the hub around which is organized the maintenance of discipline, citizenship, rights, and responsibilities demanded of democratic governments and state institutions of school, prison, welfare institution, and workplace. Discourses of these institutions and their professionals have served the disciplining of the individual. Human and social sciences have informed their knowledge about the individual, and about the differentiation between the average individual and the exceptional individual, the latter being characterized as, for example, disabled or gifted, or having developmental delays, disabilities, or atypical behaviors. However, these sciences did not simply provide understandings of the individual, they made the individual in their own image.

Clearly, the wide range of social sciences is too much to cover in this chapter, and therefore below we turn briefly to the discipline of psychology, with a particular focus on its morphology during the 20th century, and keeping in mind our individual story of David. Whereas the historiography of psychology is full of heretical characters and dramatic fractures, some dominant stories of psychology can be identified that contribute to a distinct conceptualization of the individual. We recount some of these stories that inform an "error-laden notion of the individual as whole, complete, perfect and self-sustaining" (Davis, 2006, p. 236), an individual against whom David is contrasted as exceptional and stigmatized as a deficient other.

AVERAGE INDIVIDUALS

Psychology's history is intertwined with biomedical approaches to the mind and body, the restoration of normality, a jostling for position among the natural sciences, a key consultative role in various forms of state administrative rule, and a core discipline for the developing welfare services. Key to the formation of the psychological individual was the discovery of the norm. Davis (1995) argues that the "normal individual" (and its counterpart, the "feebleminded, parasitic and morally questionable") is part of the history of modernist progress, industrialization, and the ideological consolidation of the power of the bourgeois. "An able body," he argues, "is the body of a citizen." By contrast, "deformed, deafened, amputated, obese, female, perverse, crippled, maimed and blinded bodies do not make up the body politic" (Davis, 1995, pp. 71f.). Possessing an "undesired differentness" (Goffman, 1963, p. 5), they do not belong to those *normals* whose features and behaviors would commonly be anticipated and expected. The statistical average becomes equated with "average man"—"*L'homme moyen*" of the statistician Quetelet, who was working in the 19th century—typifying the expected and cherished norms of the ruling classes of a given time. For Davis, the attitudes of middle-class society can be characterized as a sensibility of individualism: the drama of individual attainment, exploration, and achievement over the wild savagery of nature. The achievements of average man cast him or her as a heroic character. Although it is possible to trace various civilizations' rejections of disabled bodies and minds long before the 20th century, the sensibility of the average individual, Davis argues, seeped into early 20th century pseudoscientific theories of humanity and the population to the extent that the norm and average became confused and fused as the same entity. As a result, psychological understandings of human development came to view the norm-as-average as natural.

Measuring the norm has served psychology well over the years, permitting psychologists to play an increasingly influential role in the social administration, assessment, and classification of the population in institutions such as schools and prisons as well as those related to work, welfare, and the social and health sectors. Thus, what is new in inclusive education is "the idea to continuously overcome both the categorical (classificatory) differentiation of learners according to characteristics that stick to them like attributes and the subsequent separation of the learners into groups of people with supposedly similar features" (Kiuppis, 2014a, p. 758). While special education relied heavily on medical measures, so too did the concept of education in integrated settings. Inclusive education has to tackle the dilemma of including without excluding or further marginalizing. However, in this regard, it to some extent may be helpful to recall John Rawls's "egalitarian difference principle" (Rawls, 2003 [1921], pp. 86–93), a perspective that takes into consideration the differences between people as well as their equal rights. Accordingly, specific measures that are necessary to accelerate or achieve de facto equality among people do not necessarily need to be considered discriminating, marginalizing, or excluding (cf. UN, 2006, Art. 5). Rather, *exclusive* concentration on different development potentialities, abilities, characteristics, and expectations should be understood as a prerequisite of inclusive education in any heterogeneous group of learners. However, capitalist societies have administratively separated individuals on the basis of nativist norming notions, such as ability and intelligence, also but not only in educational theory and practice. Post-war North American social psychological ideals of the individual implicitly and explicitly mirrored the values of the theorists who proffered them (Wright Mills, 1970). Social problems were understood as events and occasions that deviated from the middle-class, small-town status of their bourgeois authors. Problems were found when some individuals failed to fall in line with the stale principles of the American middle classes. Problems were marked by deviant individuals who threatened the consensual and valued idea(l)s of social theorists and their theories. The individual is closely tied to the social fabric of the status quo: a model and marker of societal progress and civilization. Individuals—like David in our story—who fall outside such an idea are dealt with accordingly. Educationally, attempts are made to diagnosis and then rehabilitate individual learners to become as near as possible to the statistical norm. Hence, tragically, there is often overemphasis on the situation of lower(or higher)-than-average children, who are stigmatized by the use of labels such as "moderate learning disabilities and autism" and surrounded by supposedly homogeneous groups of learners (see Hickman and Walter, 1995, on the "myth of homogeneity"), implying that those *abnormals* automatically have special educational needs and that children with special educational needs generally "have disabilities." Consequently, it is appalling that this tends to imply that disability is an attribute of a person, rather than considering that disabled people only have one important attribute in common, namely that they are all subject to oppression (Kiuppis, 2013, p. 154). However, while the educational approach of integration was considered a step in the right direction to overcome segregated (special) educational settings for learners with medical diagnoses, critics held against the integration approach its primary focus on and categorical ascription of special educational needs, as it perpetuated the divide between those children and others who were, mistakenly, considered as the homogenous groups into which the medically labeled individuals should be integrated. In other words, educational integration was criticized as an approach to preserve the special status of the latter group rather than to overcome it. Arguably, despite the integration of medically labeled individuals into mainstream schools, stigmatization and discrimination did not seem to cease and segregation of children with disabilities persisted within schools.

COGNITIVISM

For Lash (2001, p. 109), individualism creates the interiority of the human subject. Nowhere is this more evident than in the epistemology of *cognitivism.* From the 1950s onwards, cognitivism provided psychology with what it had been waiting for: a form of scientific and empirical psychology that assumed rational processes of thought within individual subjects who were responsive to scientific study, analysis, and treatment. The notion of the individual as cognitively abled was rapidly embraced by psychology to categorize short-term and long-term memory, to assess problem solving, and to measure levels of mental processing and conscious decision-making. Here was the all singing, all dancing rational thinker, primed and ready for investigation. Cognitivism gave a scientific language to the civilized notion of the homunculus—"little man" in Latin—that is assumed to reside in each and every individual, giving them "intelligence," "awareness," and "abilities" (Thomas and Loxley, 2001, p. 65). Applied to human beings, cognitivism and its epistemological ally positivism, enliven cognition but rarely touch on feelings and often render anonymous the very people it studies (Turner, 2008, pp. 232f.). When one holds that the primary ingredients of the mind are cognitive, it opens some doors but shuts others (Gergen, 2001, p. 808). As for David, he is given access to specialized moments of pedagogy while simultaneously being denied access to community belonging in the classroom, school, and wider community. However cognitivism's interest in David and other learners revolves around an interest in the ir/rationality of mind, a pre-occupation with early historical origins in the 18th and 19th centuries. As Davis (1995, p. 3) observes, when modernity's madhouses replaced the leper colonies, the confinement of defects of the *body* was switched to the confinement of defects of the *mind.* An age of reason and, by extension, madness was embraced. Cognitivism can be viewed as a hyper-reasoned, conscious, and reasonable conceptualization of the individual against which all individuals are universally marked and judged. It is a symptom of the modernist Cartesian distinction of the inner world of the mind and the external world of the social. Cognitivism was fit for purpose for psychology's quest for status as a functionalist science. In reality, cognitivism played handmaiden to social values (Shield, 1992, p. 102). Cognitivism celebrates and measures the occidental logocentric subject so valued by contemporary Global North societies and allows for the sorting of people in terms of their cognitive worth. Deficit thinking, as we will find in David's story, is there to be found and eradicated.

DEVELOPMENTALISM

A further under-girding assumption of psychology's individual is that of *developmentalism.* The child is measured to ensure "normal" development (Waldschmidt,

2005). When "abnormal" or "pathological" development is observed, it is classified and corrected. Walkerdine (1993) describes developmental psychology as one of the "grand meta-narratives of science"—a story where the central character is the individual child but the story is grand and totalizing, and the story of children's development is made testable. The "developing child" is not a description of a "real" entity, but a powerful discursive prescription (Walkerdine, 1993, p. 454), written onto by a host of expectations such as "meeting targets," "age-appropriate behavior," and marks of deficiency, including "educational subnormality," "special educational needs," and "below average intelligence." Following Burman (2008), children are understood through the application of developmentalist theories that promise universal progress in emotionality (self-containment), intelligence (cognitivism), independence (mastery), and rationality (reason) that meets an endpoint of normality (average man) or higher (high-functioning man). Woollet and Marshall (1997) argue that while psychologies promoted their universalized stage theories of development, in actuality those ideas were based on limited samples of people (normally white, middle-class American subjects), for whom independence, achievement, and academic attainment were seen as *the* central tasks of the development for *all* children and adolescents. Such is the seductive nature of developmentalism that Harwood and Humphrey (2008) observe that in Global North societies the new average achievement of children expected by parents, schools, and teachers is not "average man" but "gifted and talented man." This observation might help to explain the anxieties of the parents of non-disabled children in David's class.

NORMALIZATION

The process of *normalization* is of key importance to the making of a developing individual. A normalized individual is a confessional individual who is all too ready and willing to share their innermost thoughts and worries, not just with professional counselors and therapists but also in a public context that demands it. An individual wants to be normal. Whether through psychoanalytic, humanist, complementary, new age, or behaviorist psychosurgery, therapy, or self-help books, today's individual is tied to the Global North humanist myth of fullness and bliss, and of abstract individualism: "an ultimate self untied at last from dependency, a man in space" (Haraway, 1991, p. 151). This myth promotes psychological interventions to cure mental illness, improve education, reduce crime, stamp out prejudice, and create fulfilling lives (Gergen, 2001, p. 804). Although these aims seem laudable, disabled people have been subjected to a number of questionable interventions in the name of these aims. When psychologists unproblematically draw on long-established indexes (i.e., of personality traits, attitude types, and social cognitions) of people's inner worlds (i.e., their emotions and cognitions), they deem some individuals more rational and worthy of social position and wealth than others (Gergen, 2001, p. 805). A popular signifier of psychology is therapy. For disabled people, therapy equates with oppression. Reeve's (2004) critique of counseling in the lives of disabled people notes a tendency for loss models to dominate the therapeutic context—both in the therapy room and training literature—followed quickly by the associated aim of "adjustment." She observes that when disabled people do seek counseling it is automatically assumed to be because they are seeking to deal with the loss that they feel; they want to be normalized. Psychoanalysis (as part of a process of psychologization) has entered popular culture, influencing how non-disabled/disabled people make sense of themselves and others. It is therefore important that we tackle the psychoanalytic register as a key site of the constitution of the individual. In particular, a key area of analysis relates to the ways in which psychoanalytic discourses demand their subjects to occupy a peculiarly Western space of sameness and oneness: the healthy, self-conscious individual.

PSYCHOLOGIZATION

As Goodley and Lawthom (2005) have argued, the components of the individual described above capture the practices of *psychologization*: a view of the individual as a unitary, isolated, cognitively able, rational, developed, innately normed, consensual being. Psychologization reduces social problems to the level of the individual (Wright Mills, 1970, p. 69) and therefore has the potential to be:

- Individualistic—the scientific study of mind and behavior
- Bourgeois—the ideas of the majority (and ruling) are exercised over the minority
- Apolitical—changing individuals rather than society
- Professional-led—favoring experts over lay persons
- Pseudo-scientific—emphasizing science (a poor version of it)
- Normalizing—concerned with individuals adjusting to their impairment
- Oppressive—whereby disabled people are treated as mere subjects of psychology's individualizing practices.

Psychologization and its preferred individuals maintain the disabling status quo, and this has huge implications for the "disabled individual."

SELF-CONTAINED INDIVIDUALISM

Henriques et al. (1989) ask how psychology understands its subject. The answer can be traced back to modernist and renaissance roots. The core conception of psychology's subject—the *unitary rational subject*—is the sovereign self of modern individualism. As part of the modernist project, psychology became the science of the individual subject. This science functions as a discourse that participates positively in the construction of the social world and the instrumental rationality of the individual (Henriques et al., 1989, p. 122). Psychology is a science that speaks of the individual. Psychology has long-held implicit assumptions (that are then made explicit) *about* the individual and, conversely, what is *required* to be an individual. The accepted individual, whom many of us are expected to mirror, is adult, male, middle class, heterosexual, rule abiding, sane, non-disabled, and European.[2] The converse—the Other—is the unacceptable: child, female, working class, homosexual, criminal, insane, disabled, and resolutely non-European. Venn suggests that in order to promote the desired individual, an obsessional focus on the abject Other is required, normalizing and disciplining this section of the population as part of the quest for the model citizen and rational self.

The work of the American psychologist Edward Sampson has critically evaluated the individual that was created through the unholy alliance of cultural hegemony and psychological knowledge. Sampson (1977) describes our cultural ethos as the era of the *self-contained individual*. This idealized form of personhood refers to a private, egocentric, self-sufficient, independent, agentic cultural paragon who has little need for others, is antithetical to the notion of interdependence and mutuality, is inherently masculine, and suitably (com)pliant to educational, workplace, and industrial management. This ideal becomes psychology's big "discovery" and the preferred ontological destiny for all persons. Psychology holds this aloft as an ideal to be achieved,

> By ignoring the cultural and historical conditions that present this as an ideal, it fails to provide an adequate assessment of alternatives or the implications that derive from its ideal. For example, does self-contained individualism offer a reasonable way of dealing with the massive problems that confront a complex and interdependent world? (Sampson, 1977, p. 774)

The individual of post/industrial societies is a "normal" one who will contribute to the making of society as a body of functions (Michalko, 2002, p. 156). An individual is ready, able, and (preferably) willing. Such a vision of humanity threatens to individualize social life and fails to place people in their social contexts.

Sampson (1985) explains self-contained individualism through reference to popular psychological theories that helped to develop the culturally dominant idea (and psychology's idea) that order and coherence are achieved by means of personal control and mastery. For Sampson (1985, p. 1204), "to centre order within the persona is a peculiarly Western worldview" that the individual will be the main architect of order and coherence. We associate an individual with control and connect "manyness" with chaos. In a later paper, Sampson (1993) suggests that psychology's conception of human nature is primarily a white, male, and Western

"United Statesian" character. Individuals who differ in their "human nature" (or nationality) come out a poor second. The individual is self-contained in ways best suited to rich nations. However, Sampson does not stop there. As Table 1 shows, he encourages rethinking the individual, a point that we develop in the next section.

Table 1. Self-contained and ensembled individualism: an adapted version of Sampson's (1988, p. 16) two indigenous psychologies of individualism.

	Type 1 Self-contained individualism	**Type 2 Ensembled individualism**
Self/other boundary	Firm: "peculiar" and "eccentric" version of self; ideas of Western society planted early in history and developed by capitalism	Fluid: "majority world" versions of self; captured in Maori (New Zealand/Aotearoa) and Chewong (Malaysian) cultures and beliefs such as Islamic thought
Control	Personal: based on egocentric models of psychology; related to personal achievement of atomistic individuals; qualities of character	Field: based on sociocentric models; related to relational actions of communities of individuals; community cohesion
Conceptions of person/self	Excluding: an ontology of exclusion; internally directed subjectivism found in Shakespeare's time and characteristic of contemporaneous views of the person; atomistic strangers; independent and separated	Including: an ontology of inclusion; self-defined in relation to others; to be found in non-Western, majority world contexts: "I am who I am through my relations with others"; "I am completed through these relations"; interdependent and connected

RETHINKING "THE INDIVIDUAL": BECOMING RHIZOME

A rhizomatic story: David is eight years old and has an educational statement written about him that notes he has the labels of "moderate learning disabilities and autism." His presence in the classroom often creates uncertainty for the teacher and teaching assistant. Other children in the classroom are receptive to what appear to be David's preferences. They are quick to curb consistent contact, instead giving David his own space. This works well for Ruby, one of David's fellow students. She does not have a label but, like David, prefers her own company. The teaching assistant discusses an idea with the teacher. Could the "golden time" of the lesson, normally given over to group artwork, be broken into small groups and include individual creative arts? The teacher agrees. David, Ruby, and other students enjoy their art. The teacher and teaching assistant are encouraged to look at other ways of restructuring the content, order, and performance of the classroom.

Inspired by the work of Sampson, we could ask what alternative ensemble versions of the individual or personhood could we develop in ways that are responsive to the ambitions of inclusive education? An ensembled individualism views self and others as intimately related and connected. Others respond to the self in varying ways, and vice versa, to the extent that each part of the apparent binary of self-other becomes knotted in complicated web of relationships. In our second story, David's presence in the classroom can be read as a possibility: an opportunity to reconsider what can be done together in this pedagogical space.

We can explore this ensemble sense of self through what Shildrick (2009) describes as post-conventionalist theoretical writing and the use of the notion of rhizome. In a recent book by one of us (Goodley, 2014), the author seeks to celebrate the productive potentialities prompted by disabled children failing to fit the normative standards of school. One of these potentialities is revising how we understand learning as something enacted and achieved by an individual learner. Instead, and the author is guided here by Erevelles (2002a, b), when disability and education encounter one another, there is a demand for new ways of thinking about education and the individual. Disability, it is argued here, ignites debate around remapping the educational environment (Goodley, 2014). Rather, the optimism that I desire is tied to notions of becomings and rhizomatic connection developed in the work of Deleuze and Guattari (1987). Some of my own recent (collaborative) writing has drawn upon the ideas of Deleuze and Guattari to analyze the lives of disabled children and their encounters with school (Goodley, 2007a, 2007b; Goodley and Runswick-Cole, 2013). Ramlow (2006, p. 181) offers a summative account of the theoretical contribution of Deleuze and Guattari, whom he describes as "opposing an understanding of desire and subjectivity constituted on an originary lack and insufficiency, which by extension is reproduced in the normative ordering of society." Rather, Ramlow (2006, p. 181) continues, "Deleuze and Guattari cast subjectivity as machinic assemblages, and desire as productive of new and different relationships and social arrangements."

Deleuze and Guattari conceptualize desire as productive (i.e., not lacking), uncertain, and reaching out for connection with others. Goodley (2014) notes that rather than the desire to be a particular kind of individual subject (e.g., autonomous, functioning, and self-contained) they ask: What might it be like to desire becoming the other? How might we become in the company of others? What kinds of connection might we make in the process of becoming (with) other(s)? Too often, we have seen the risks created by segmenting the subject along fixed binary lines (e.g., disabled/non-disabled, stupid/clever, and included/excluded). The question, therefore, is not which subject to become but how to escape the forces of subjectification that block flows of desire and territorialize the subject with rigid segmentarities (Goodley, 2007a). We should look for those moments when, as Buchanan (1997) puts it, subjects transcend the given to become and engage with places of immanence, to create action and results rather than establish transcendentals, not being, but always becoming, as a line of flight. We can extend this notion through reference to our second concept, the *rhizome*:

> A rhizome has no beginning or end; it is always in the middle, between things, interbeing, *intermezzo*. The tree is filiation, but the rhizome is alliance, uniquely alliance. The tree imposes the verb 'to be,' but the fabric of the rhizome is the conjunction, 'and…and…and….' This conjunction carries enough forces to shake and uproot the verb 'to be.' (Deleuze and Guattari, 1987, pp. 27f., original emphases)

Rather than thinking of the dis/abled learner as a tree rooted in a particular soil giving rise to a distinct form of arborescent growth, the rhizome pitches the learner as ginger or weed: multiply rooted, expansive, difficult to pin down, and potentially everywhere. The rhizome is not singularly rooted but multiply interlinked and ever growing (Bearne, 2000). The dis/abled learner is no longer a lacking subject or a fixed entity (Goodley, 2007b): he or she is ever moving, a body no longer embodied, and a learner always plugged in to relationships with others—he or she is rhizome. This is powerful thinking, as rhizomes are constantly in the midst of being produced, constantly evolving, always becoming (Goodley, 2007b). "Rhizomatic learning," for Allan (2011, p. 156) is "always in process, having to be constantly worked at by all concerned, and never complete." This "in-betweenness," she argues, is "an inclusive space, in which everyone belongs and where movement occurs." Learning might constitute what Curti and Moreno (2010, pp. 416f.) define as "communal becomings; communities of relations, ethics and mappings of togetherness which always challenge the delimitations of borders." Rhizomatic learners constitute their own communal becomings.

In our second story of David, we read him as rhizomatic pioneer pushing at the barriers of disability and educational knowledge, and forcing educators in his midst to think again. As Goodley (2014) argues, teaching staff are equally bound up in these rhizomatic communal becomings: teacher–pupil boundaries are tested; pedagogical assumptions are revisited; and values associated with the borderlands of shared and private spaces are revised. Whereas David is very much known in our first individual story (as so typical of psychological knowledge), in this second story he refutes being settled, pinned down, or penned in. He is a pedagogical space maker and boundary breaker. To borrow from Sampson (1988), he offers an ontology of inclusion, a self defined in relation to others, and an opportunity to recast education in terms of moments of interdependence and connection. David, Ruby, and their teachers are paradigm-busters and makers of new forms of ensembled individualism.

CONCLUSION

Both David and disability contest the idealization of the individual. The truth of this individual is that it is a simulacrum: an idealized fantasy of modernity that has never existed (Hardt and Negri, 2000, p. 151). Biesta (1998, p. 13) suggests that a new attitude to the individual is required: a new style of political judgment and political imagination, related as well as to pedagogy, and more specifically to inclusive education, that should not mainly be seen as a process of the socialization of "individuals" into existing social, cultural, and political ways of doing and being. This critique is in line with his notion of "subjectification" and his differentiation between empowerment and emancipation (Biesta, 2012; Kiuppis, 2013, p. 149). An interdependent view of the individual suggests that health and illness are aspects of larger systems and are not located entirely within the single person (Sampson, 1977, p. 775). It is necessary to take seriously the psychologization of everyday life: to recognize that the individual valued by contemporary society is a complex phenomenon made by long histories of oppression and domination of medicalization, colonization, patriarchy, and heteronormativity. Shepherd (1966, pp. 61f.) argues:

> Are any of us independent? Are we not all interdependent? … The norm is the man with a house, family, garden, job and a car at the gate … we have grown up with a great belief in the virtue of endless activity … the belief that it is better to do something active badly, rather than something more contemplative well, is almost universally accepted in Europe, if not in Asia.

How, then, can we incorporate the mandates of Article 24 of the UN-Convention on the Rights of Persons with Disabilities, which came into force in 2008 and which states parties shall ensure that: "Persons with disabilities can access an inclusive, quality and free primary education and secondary education on an equal basis with others in the communities in which they live" (UN, 2006, 2b) and "Effective individualized support measures are provided in environments that maximize academic and social development, consistent with the goal of full inclusion" (2e) (see Kiuppis and Peters, 2014)? Disability may find more answers to the question of emancipation through the interdependent relationships as mapped out in this chapter.

NOTES

1. Dan Goodley would like to acknowledge and thank Sage Publications Ltd for granting permission to draw upon material from Chapter 5, "De-psychologising disability studies" from Goodley (2011). Florian Kiuppis thanks Waxmann Publishing Co. for permission to include elements of Kiuppis (2014b).

2. Weiss (1999, p. 164), following Rosi Braidotti (1994), suggests that in actuality the big subject is reasonable man: "man-white-western-male-adult-reasonable-heterosexual-living-in-towns-speaking-a-standard-language."

SECTION FOUR

Beyond Salamanca

CHAPTER TWENTY-ONE

Working for Inclusive Education by 2030

PETER MITTLER

INTRODUCTION: A PERSONAL JOURNEY

This contribution will summarize the opportunities and resources which are now available not only to achieve but to transcend the goals of the Salamanca Declaration to enable children and young people with disabilities to become contributing citizens in their local communities. But since inclusion is fundamentally about personal values and social justice, it seems appropriate to begin with some contextual background to my own journey towards education as a fundamental human right (Mittler, 2010; 2013).

My professional career as a clinical psychologist in the UK began at a time when children with intellectual disabilities were still excluded from education as 'ineducable'; little was expected of those who went to special schools and nothing from the majority who had been sent to residential institutions. Dissatisfaction with the quality of services for people with intellectual and developmental disabilities soon led me to join others in advocacy for changes in policy and practice.

My later university work involved research relevant to children, parents and practitioners, as well as courses for teachers and other professionals. I learned about the difficulties of translating research to practice but it took me some time to understand that staff training achieves little without organizational commitment to the management of change. Experience as a ministerial adviser also taught me that neither sound policies nor legislation benefit people with disabilities if they are not properly implemented or monitored.

The Salamanca conference was a major landmark on my journey because it established the right of children with disabilities to be included in the UN Education for All (EFA) movement, alongside others excluded from education by poverty or gender. I remain proud of what was achieved there and of my contribution in drafting the Final Report and chairing the concluding session, which adopted the Action Plan and Framework for Action. But although many more children with disabilities are now attending ordinary schools, they were overlooked in the EFA plans of most of the 94 governments represented at Salamanca.

My commitment to the human rights of disabled people was stimulated by regular contacts, as the representative of Inclusion International, with the leaders of Disabled Peoples' International (DPI) and other international disability NGOs who met regularly with United Nations officials and professionals to plan the 1981 International Year of Disabled Persons and subsequent regional Decades, the World Programme of Action and the Standard Rules on the Equalization of Opportunities (Mittler, 2005). This commitment was strengthened by becoming the parent of a child with physical and communication impairments and by later experience of my own age-related impairments.

From the early 1980s, there was increasing pressure from DPI for the human rights of peoples with disabilities to be grounded in international law, in parallel with other groups experiencing discrimination (Driedger, 1989). In the wake of a major UN World Conference on human rights and the adoption of the Vienna Declaration in 1993, the UN General Assembly voted in 2001 to set up a drafting committee for an international Convention in which Disabled Persons' Organizations (DPOs) worked in close partnership with government representatives and specialists to create the Convention on the Rights of Persons with Disabilities which has now been ratified by most of the world's governments. A newly published book provides detailed accounts from a wide spectrum of civil society representatives of the complex negotiations that culminated in the adoption of the CRPD and remains highly relevant to the new challenge of its implementation (Sabatello and Schulze, 2014). Chapters by Lansdown (2014) on rights involving birth registration, sterilization, play, family life, consultation, protection from violence and access to justice and by Shaw (2014) on the specific difficulties of securing agreement on inclusive education remain highly relevant in the implementation of the Convention at national level.

RESOURCES FOR ADVOCACY

At least five powerful sets of resources for action and advocacy have become available since Salamanca, all of which need to be used to achieve change.

1) Support from UN-Agencies

The adoption of the Convention has led to a system-wide recognition of the rights of people with disabilities across all UN agencies, as well as by key international development agencies such as the World Bank (Mittler, 2012). For example, WHO's comprehensive *World Report on Disability* (WHO and World Bank, 2011) and UNICEF's (2013a) *State of the World's Children: Children with Disabilities* provide strong foundations for national CRPD implementation plans by summarizing current knowledge and highlighting examples of good practice, particularly in low and middle income countries. Information relevant to UN actions and opportunities is also regularly updated in monthly newsletters on the main UN Enable website (http://www.un.org/disabilities). Most of the guidance documents for governments and NGOs can be downloaded from the internet.

Despite the general perception that UN agencies are centralized in New York, Geneva and Vienna, some of its most effective work, particularly in relation to education and disability, is taking place at regional level in its Economic and Social Commissions for Africa (Addis Ababa), Asia and Pacific (Bangkok), Europe (Geneva), Latin America and Caribbean (Santiago) and Western Asia (Beirut). For example, the Asia Pacific region has just embarked on its Third Decade of Disabled Persons, played a major part in the drafting of the Convention and is providing detailed information on its implementation (Economic and Social Commission for Asia and the Pacific, 2010). UNESCO's regional bureau in Latin America which has given strong support to inclusive education over several decades is now developing detailed indicators for monitoring educational outcomes (UNESCO, 2011).

The European Union has its own Human Rights Convention and Court and is the only regional organization to have formally ratified the Convention. It is now mainstreaming disability rights into its own agencies and seeking to persuade its member states to do so. It earlier helped to fund the European Agency for Development in Special Needs Education (EADSNE), a consortium of government officials and civil society representatives which has produced detailed reports on each country and a stream of informative publications on policy and practice (http://www.european-agency.org/). More recently, the EU funded the Academic Network of European Experts in Disability (ANED) to create a comprehensive online database on CRPD implementation for every European country (http://www.disability-europe.net). Its report on developments in education (Ebersold, 2011) provides an example of its regular thematic analyses and recommendations.

2) Post-2015 Development Goals

The Convention now needs to be set in the broader context of a clear UN commitment that the new post-2015 Development Goals will be based on fundamental principles of human rights and focus on the reduction of inequalities arising from disability as well gender, ethnicity, age and location (UN Secretary-General, 2013).

The universal goals for education now being developed for 2030 will prioritize the nature and quality of what children learn and how long they remain in school. Furthermore, education is no longer defined only in terms of schooling but as a lifelong process, which begins in infancy and continues in the home and local community during childhood and adolescence and beyond (UNESCO, 2013; Commonwealth Secretariat, 2012). These are also the goals clearly identified in Article 24 of the CRPD.

Whether these recommendations are translated into action now depends, as does the Convention, on advocacy by Disabled Persons Organizations and civil society in putting pressure on their national governments to implement this commitment.

3) The Disability Movement

The CRPD is the first Convention to include representatives of potential beneficiaries as equal partners with governments in negotiating each of its principles and Articles. Their participation is clearly reflected in the application of the social model of disability to identify obstacles to the expression of human rights and in recommendations on how these can be overcome. DPI's commitment to 'Nothing About Us Without Us' has been endorsed at the highest level.

The International Disability Alliance is a consortium of international disability NGOs whose members were equal partners with the UN in the drafting of the Convention and who continue to have a catalytic role in its implementation by providing relevant information and support for advocacy at national and local level. IDA's regular newsletters (http://www.internationaldisabilityalliance.org) are an indispensable source of information, as are those of NGOs focusing on people with specific impairments, such as intellectual disability (http://www.inclusion-europe.org). Other valuable resources for inclusive education include the Enabling Education Network (http://www.eenet.org.uk), Leonard Cheshire Disability (2013) (http://www.lcdisability.org/international), and the International Disability and Development Consortium (2013), which has published excellent guidelines for teacher education (http://www.iddcconsortium.net).

Some national DPOs have created similar coalitions and alliances in order to speak with a single voice to their own government and to the UN Human Rights monitoring bodies. For example, the Japanese Disability Forum persuaded its government to delay ratification until it had first completed a radical programme of harmonization of existing legislation with the CRPD. DPOs chaired the Prime Minister's Committee set up for this purpose, made up half its membership and also became paid staff members of the Secretariat which achieved many of these changes in a short period of time (Osamu, 2013).

4) Advocacy by Internet

The rapid development of the internet, the social media and the mobile phone has opened a new chapter in the history of democracy by providing immediate access to information to enable citizens to communicate with each other to advocate for change.

The CRPD is the first human rights treaty to include representatives of potential beneficiaries as equal partners with governments in negotiating each of its principles and Articles. It has also been described by the UN Secretary General as 'the first human rights treaty to emerge from lobbying conducted extensively through the Internet' (cited by MacKay, 2014). Furthermore, the internet enabled members of civil society organizations who could not afford to travel to New York to confer amongst themselves and submit their conclusions to the appropriate person or committee (Sabatello and Schulze, 2014). The internet had also been used to great effect by the UN in partnership with NGOs to enable tens of thousands of people from all parts of the world to participate in a series of global discussion groups on priorities for the post-2015 goals. Internet forums such as The World We Want, Tackling Inequalities and the Global Education Forum have had a significant impact on the UN system-wide decision to include disability as a cross-cutting issue in policy and monitoring.

A recent example of global advocacy is provided by an internet petition following the attempted assassination of Malala Yousafzai and calling for education for the world's out of school children from the 35 million world-wide membership of Avaaz (http://www.avaaz.org) and presented to the President of Pakistan by Gordon Brown as UN Global Education Envoy. The President responded by signing an order to fund school places for three million out of Pakistan's 5.5 million out of school children. Because the internet now provides the means to hold his government accountable for implementing this policy, a vigilant disability lobby might have used this opportunity to press for the inclusion of children with disabilities in this policy, as well as in a similar commitment by Nigeria which has more than ten million out of school children, despite being rich in oil resources.

5) Achievements since Salamanca

Developments in inclusive education during the last 20 years have laid strong foundations for the new opportunities now presented by the Convention and the post-2015 Development Goals.

There are lessons to be learned from many projects over the last 20 years in countries as diverse as Lesotho, Vietnam, Lao PDR, Hong Kong and South

Africa, sometimes with the active participation of international NGOs such as Save the Children (Mitchell, 2005; UNICEF, 2007; Alur and Timmons, 2009). Although most pilot projects produced positive outcomes both for children with disabilities and their classmates, and many other schools followed their example, they were not as systematically scaled up from the original pilots to regional or national level as originally intended.

- The most recent comprehensive study of inclusive education projects has been carried out in Commonwealth countries by Richard Rieser, a disabled teacher who was a member of the UN committee that drafted the Convention and is now a powerful advocate for its implementation (Rieser, 2012). Based on visits and training workshops in many countries at different levels of development, his report makes clear recommendations on ways in which Article 24 of the CRPD (see Appendix B) can be implemented internationally, nationally, at provincial, regional and district levels and above all at the level of schools and classrooms and in the initial and continuing professional development of teachers.
- The 3rd edition of the *Index for Inclusion* (Booth and Ainscow, 2011) which has been translated into 37 languages has been highly influential in helping schools 'to adopt a self-review approach to analyze their cultures, policies and practices and to identify the barriers to learning and participation that may occur within each of these areas; to decide their own priorities for change and evaluate their progress and as an integral part of existing development policies, encouraging a wide and deep scrutiny of everything that makes up a school's activities' (Introduction).[1]
- Classroom practice and teacher education are also the focus of a recent manual based on wide international experience but concentrating primarily on developments in Tanzania, Kenya and Lesotho (Mariga et al., 2014). It complements an earlier toolkit of five pamphlets on inclusive classroom practice from the Asia Pacific region (UNESCO, 2009b).
- *What Really Works in Inclusive and Special Needs to match reference Education* (Mitchell, 2013) describes and evaluates 24 different teaching strategies that have been successfully used in inclusive classrooms in many different countries.
- Amongst UNESCO's numerous publications, the *Open File on Inclusive Education* (UNESCO, 2001) provides detailed guidelines for planners and policy makers on moving towards more inclusive practice under nine topic headings: managing the transition; professional development; assessment; organizing support; families and communities; developing an inclusive curriculum; resourcing and funding; managing transitions throughout education; and working with schools (see also UNESCO, 2009a for Asia-Pacific perspectives compiled by Penelope Price).

MONITORING CRPD IMPLEMENTATION

An immediate priority for civil society in every country is to take advantage of the opportunities now available to monitor the action taken by governments to implement the Convention Article by Article and to report their conclusions to the CRPD Committee of the UN Office of the High Commission on Human Rights (OHCHR) based in Geneva (http://www.ohchr.org).

The 150 governments that have so far ratified the Convention are required to submit a detailed progress report to the CRPD Committee after two years and then every four years on actions taken to implement the General Principles and specific Articles of the Convention. Guidelines for the submission of reports by governments make it clear that national implementation plans must specify action under each Article, identify responsible actors and be linked to measurable objectives within a stated time frame (OHCHR, 2009). In recognition of the reality of each country having a different starting point for implementation, the Convention requires ratifying governments to provide concrete evidence of *progressive realization* of a national plan of action over a given period of time. A parallel toolkit for DPOs and other civil society organizations provides detailed training modules on the preparation of evidence, as well as suggestions for follow-up actions at national level (OHCHR, 2012). An excellent training manual focusing on implementing the rights of children with disabilities has been drawn up by Gerison Lansdown (2009) for Save the Children.

The CRPD Committee consists of 18 elected members, of whom 17 are currently persons with disabilities. After making a detailed study of relevant information from all available sources, a committee member designated as Country Rapporteur draws up a 'list of issues' which require further explanation or information from the government. The full Committee then engages in 'constructive dialogue' with the government delegation and later publishes its Concluding Observations and Recommendations on the OHCHR website.

Examination of the Committee's reports on the countries where its work has been completed confirms that the most successful civil society submissions have come from a national coalition of DPOs but with specialist support where needed. Independent reports from Australia, Austria, Hong Kong, Hungary and Spain provide particularly instructive examples of such coalitions. Moreover, the Committee does not mince its words. In response to the Austrian government's somewhat complacent report on inclusive education, it expressed its concern that 'progress towards inclusive education in Austria is stagnant...the number of children in special schools is increasing and...insufficient efforts are being made to support inclusive education of children with disabilities' (OHCHR CRPD Committee, 2013).

An essential advocacy opportunity for civil society is provided by the Optional Protocol to the Convention which requires separate ratification. This enables individuals who complain of infringement of their rights to make direct representations to the CRPD Committee. It follows that a high priority for DPOs is to ensure that the 62 governments that have so far failed to ratify the Optional Protocol as well as the Convention should be put under pressure to do so (listed in http://www.un.org/disabilities).

Although Article 24 focuses on education, the rights of children, young people and families are fundamental to all the Articles of the Convention (Lansdown, 2014). One of its General Principles concerns 'respect for the evolving capacities of children with disabilities and their right to preserve their identities' (Article 3h). Other relevant Articles focus on their right to life (10) and self-expression (7); freedom from torture or cruel, inhuman or degrading treatment or punishment (15) and exploitation, violence or abuse (16); right to a name, nationality, birth registration, to know and be cared for by their parents (18); respect for home and family and right to a family life and to retain their fertility (23); habilitation and rehabilitation from early life (26) and participation in play, recreation and leisure (30). Furthermore, implementation of Article 19 on Independent Living depends on foundations being laid in childhood by parents and by an education system that enables its students to participate in decision-making and express their views (Mittler, 2001).

Disability is now included in the remit of all other OHCHR Human Rights Committees such as the Convention on the Rights of the Child, as well as in the Commission's regular Universal Periodic Reviews of all human rights at national level. The UN also hosts an annual conference for governments that have ratified the Convention. All these events provide opportunities for civil society to make representations and to submit independent reports. A recent guide to the work of the OHCHR for civil society includes many examples drawn from its work on the CRPD (OHCHR, 2013).

Because all documentation on the work of the OHCHR is available on the internet and some of its sessions can be watched live, the Committee's proceedings and conclusions can be used to generate public debate and to put pressure on governments to act on its recommendations. Civil society can ensure that its criticisms of national policy and practice are widely disseminated by the media. Government representatives can also be held to account by vigilant DPOs for not following up on commitments made in UN meetings.

A ROAD MAP TO 2030

An essential starting point for a road map to 2030 and beyond is reliable data about all children and young people in every country and community. UNESCO's annual EFA Global Monitoring Reports provide a baseline for reaching the new education goals in the next 15 years (UNESCO, 2012; 2014).

- Since 2000, the total number of out of school children has fallen from 102 million to 57 million, of whom at least a third are children with disabilities (Balescut and Eklindh, 2006).
- 47 out of every 100 out of school children are reported by their governments as 'unlikely ever to attend school.' Although girls from very poor families living in rural areas are known to be at greatest risk of exclusion, no comparable data exist for children with disabilities.
- 250 million primary age children are not learning basic educational skills, whether in school or not.
- Although the gender gap has narrowed to two to three per cent in many countries, there are still 17 countries where fewer than nine girls for every ten boys are attending school.
- 123 million young people aged 15 to 24 lack basic reading and writing skills; 61 per cent are women.

DEARTH OF DISABILITY DATA

The shortage of relevant data on people with disabilities in many countries now constitutes a major obstacle to monitoring the implementation of the CRPD and the post-2015 Development Goals. People with disabilities are often not included in national Household Surveys and Censuses which are used by all UN and international agencies, nor can they be counted if they lack a birth certificate or are excluded from school or community services. It is already clear from OHCHR reports that governments in all regions have been unable to respond to the CRPD requirement to provide disability-disaggregated data in reporting progress in implementing the Convention. Not to be counted can be considered a fundamental human rights abuse.

Although several research groups are collecting essential data on disabled children in a number of low and middle income countries, the measures were not originally designed for monitoring and would need to be scaled up at least regionally for monitoring the Convention and assessing progress towards the post-2015 goals. Examples include the well-established work of the UN Washington Group on Disability Statistics (United Nations Economic Council, 2012) and the UNICEF-supported MICS (Multiple Indicator Cluster Surveys) (Gottlieb, Maenner, Cappa and Durkin 2009; Llewellyn, Emerson, Madden, and Honey, 2012).

The Statistics for Inclusive Development Section of the UN Enable website provides a recent progress report on the work of these organizations on two modules to be incorporated in national surveys and censuses in 2015. The first extends earlier MICS studies on activity limitations in speech and language, hearing, vision, mobility, and motor skills to include learning, emotions and behavior. A new module will measure the barriers and facilitators to education by children with and without disabilities and will cover attitudes, accessibility, getting to school and affordability (http://www.un.org/disabilities).

The UNESCO regional office for Latin America and the Caribbean (UNESCO, 2011) is developing 23 quantitative and 19 qualitative indicators under category headings which include 'attention to diversity; accessibility/adaptability; support services; equal opportunities; socio-demographic disparities; access and completion of studies; teachers; paths through education and institutional management.' Proposals for inclusive education indicators were also made by the European Agency for Development in Special Needs Education prior to the present discussions on post-2015 goals (Kyriazopoulou and Weber, 2009) but their present status is not clear.

A recent submission by Commonwealth Ministers of Education on the monitoring of post-2015 Development Goals is one of the few to suggest quantitative indicators for achievement levels in National Learning Assessments at grades 1, 6, 9 and 12 disaggregated by special needs, as well as wealth quintile, location, gender, age and social group (Commonwealth Secretariat, 2012). An interim report from the Learning Metrics Task Force (2013) also refers to the need to include children who are out of school, under-achieving or disabled.

These are all promising developments but there is little evidence of coordination with other groups developing post-2015 indicators to ensure that disability-relevant data are collected. Furthermore, despite the consensus that the post-2015 Goals should be based on human rights, there is no evidence of a working partnership with the UN Human Rights bodies which already undertake detailed and highly critical scrutiny of all Conventions.

PRIORITY FOR TEACHER TRAINING AND SUPPORT

In order to provide all children with basic education by 2030, the world will need an additional 3.3 million primary teachers and 5.1 million lower secondary teachers (UNESCO, 2014).

Because progress towards inclusive education depends first and foremost on the skills and commitment of millions of teachers world-wide, every country needs to ensure that existing and planned teacher education programmes at all levels are based on agreed principles and practice of inclusive education. Unfortunately, this issue has so far received relatively little attention in the implementation of the Convention or in the global discussions of post-2015 goals for education.

Although there have been many positive developments in inclusive teacher education in the last 20 years (Forlin, 2010), the first reports from the CRPD Committee reflect major shortcomings in teacher education even in countries where relatively good progress is being made towards inclusive education. This is consistent with the conclusions of a detailed survey by the European Agency for Development in Special Needs Education that 'teacher educators lacked knowledge, understanding, commitment and experience to teach about inclusive education' (EADSNE, 2011).

An immediate priority is to create the nucleus of a national task force for training teachers and other educators in the principles and practice of inclusive education, using a systematic 'training of trainers' structure, in which those who are trained enter into a contractual commitment to train others. Its work should be based on consultation and consensus on what constitutes good practice in the training of educators, with the aim of providing guidance on the design and delivery of inclusive teacher education consistent with the CRPD. Once agreed, guidelines should be accessible on the internet and through distance education courses. Evidence that such a system was in place could count as evidence of the 'progressive realization' of the right to education required by the Convention.

Because training for inclusion must itself be inclusive, it needs to be incorporated in all courses and modules of initial and continuing teacher education. Where specialist tutors are available, their dual role is to work through their mainstream colleagues and to provide support where specialist knowledge and experience are essential—for example in facilitating access to the curriculum for children with severe sensory or intellectual impairments. This is an example of the 'twin track' approach, in which 'teachers (and those who train and employ them) need to embrace inclusive beliefs and practices that *generally support all learners* and make education a welcoming and positive experience for all but also need to be sufficiently confident and skilled to *meet the specific learning needs of students with disabilities*' (IDDC, 2013, original italics).

A recent major global review of teacher education commissioned by UNICEF (2013b) and led by Richard Rieser concludes that the skills necessary for inclusive teaching are not 'special' but depend on basic teaching competencies. The report's recommendations are relevant to all teachers.

- All teacher trainers must demonstrate their understanding of inclusive education of children with disabilities
- All teachers need to develop a child-focused pedagogy
- All pre-service teachers should be given grounding in the principles and practice of inclusive education, while elective impairment-specific skills courses for 10–20% of pre-service teachers are needed

- Serving teachers' education about children with disabilities should be addressed through in-service training, continuing education and support, while diploma and masters level qualifications on inclusion should also be made widely available
- Tailored training and support are needed for school principals who are key catalysts for school improvement" (pp. 30f.).

The report also recommends that specific monitoring indicators consistent with Article 31 of the CRPD on data collection need to be developed. These include the proportion of pre-service teachers who have received training on the inclusion of children with disabilities and of in-service teachers who have undertaken courses for the inclusion of children with disabilities for 5 days, 20 days, 90 days and 1 year.

CONCLUSIONS

Limited or tokenistic responses by governments, combined with apathy and a 'business as usual' mentality among professionals, could easily nullify the Convention and may already have done so in some countries.

Using the resources now available to overcome obstacles to change calls for a coordinated commitment and action plan not only by governments and Disabled Persons Organizations but by service planners and providers, members of professional and voluntary organizations, the academic and research community and in the last analysis by society at large.

Because the biggest single obstacle to accepting this challenge may lie in our values and priorities as individuals and as members of our own professional cultures, each of us might make a start by taking a hard look at our own attitudes to change at this critical juncture in the human rights of people with disabilities.

The final word therefore belongs to Gerard Quinn, one of the pioneers who put disability rights on the global agenda:

> The United Nations Convention on the Rights of Persons with Disabilities is a mirror to society; it makes us face up to our own values and it forces us to acknowledge the large gap that still exists between the 'myth system' (i.e. our own values) and the 'operations system' (i.e. how these values are dishonoured in daily practice).
>
> —(Quinn, 2009, p. 246)

NOTE

1. http://www.csie.org.uk/resources/inclusion-index-explained.shtml#intro

CHAPTER TWENTY-TWO

Another Salamanca?

ROGER SLEE

Ten years after the *Salamanca Statement on Principles, Policy and Practice in Special Needs Education* together with its *draft Framework for Action* appeared on the international education landscape (compare Appendix A), Ainscow and César (2006) reflected upon its significance for the movement for inclusive education as follows:

> Arguably the most significant international document that has ever appeared in the field of special education, the Salamanca Statement argues that regular schools with an inclusive orientation are "the most effective means of combating discriminatory attitudes, building an inclusive society and achieving education for all" [Salamanca Statement, p.iv]. Furthermore, it suggests that such schools can "provide an effective education for the majority of children and improve the efficiency and ultimately the cost-effectiveness of the entire education system" [ibid.].
>
> —(Ainscow and César, 2006, p. 231)

Alan Dyson (1999, p. 37) had previously observed that:

> The Salamanca Statement is currently proving extremely powerful as a means of stimulating educational change. Even the UK Government, not noted for looking beyond its national boundaries for educational policies, nor, indeed, for subscribing readily to international publications, has recently declared its support for Salamanca, and announced a policy of inclusion.
>
> —(Dyson, 1999, p. 37)

The Salamanca Statement may well be described as an international touchstone for a wide movement of educators (general and special), policy-makers, and disability activists seeking to advance their rendition of inclusive education. Indeed, the Salamanca Statement has become default vocabulary for educational reform pursuant to more inclusive schooling for students with disabilities. The framing of the statement by the conferees in Salamanca is laudable and ongoing reference to it some twenty years hence signifies its enduring influence.

Notwithstanding this influence, it is important to remember that the statement is a product of time and place, and that as such it warrants reconsideration in new times. The corrosive effects of the passage of time on progress towards inclusive education warrant fresh local and international analyses and the composition of a similarly powerful agreement capable of similar reception, influence and impact may well be necessary. In this respect Edward Said's (2000) offering of *travelling theories* is instructive. Once radical forces for change that originate within an incubator of specific conditions of time, place, political economy, culture and institutional organization tend to lose their analytic acuity and insurrectionary verve as they travel across time and place. Change forces are tamed, popularized and domesticated. New orthodoxies and attendant dogmas quash the original political intent. This cooption of inclusive education into neo-political discourse is apparent across jurisdictions (Slee, 2006; Thomas and Loxley, 2007; Brantlinger, 2006). This chapter will consider recent manifestations of inclusive education as a potential, if not actual, collaborator with educational exclusion.

The aim of this chapter is threefold. First I will foreground my discussion by briefly describing the origin and content of the Salamanca Statement. This section is deliberately brief as there are contributors to this collection of chapters who were active in the framing and dissemination of the Salamanca Statement. Second I will suggest significant social and education policy changes that strengthen the force and reach of educational exclusion at this point in time. This section is indicative rather than exhaustive. It is offered as a prompt for further analyses of extremely complex issues. Third I will attempt to sketch how we might frame a statement for our times. I employ "sketch" quite deliberately as this thinking is preliminary not complete, tentative not confident.

BACKGROUND

Endorsed by the United Nations Educational, Scientific and Cultural Organisation (UNESCO), the United Nations Development Programme (UNDP), The United Nations Fund for Population Activity (UNFPA), the United Nations International Children's Emergency Fund (UNICEF) and the World Bank, representatives from 155 countries and 150 organisations met in 1990 at a world conference entitled

Education for All (EFA) in Jomtien, Thailand. Six education goals were endorsed by the Education for All world conference:

- Expand and improve comprehensive early childhood care and education, especially for the most vulnerable and disadvantaged children.
- Ensure that by 2015 all children, particularly girls, those in difficult circumstances and those belonging to ethnic minorities have access to complete, free and compulsory primary education of good quality.
- Ensure that the learning needs of all young people and adults are met through equitable access to appropriate learning and life-skills programs.
- Achieve a 50 % improvement in adult literacy by 2015, especially for women, and equitable access to basic and continuing education for all adults.
- Eliminate gender disparities in primary and secondary education by 2005, and achieve gender equality in education by 2015, with a focus on ensuring girls' full and equal access to and achievement in basic education of good quality.
- Improve all aspects of the quality of education and ensure the excellence of all so that recognized and measurable learning outcomes are achieved by all, especially in literacy, numeracy and essential life skills (UNESCO, 1990).

Taking a lead from the Jomtien proclamation on Education for All (EFA), the World Conference on Special Needs Education: Access and Quality held in the city of Salamanca in Spain in June 1994 brought together delegates from ninety-two governments and twenty-five organisations. The conference culminated in the production of the now famous Salamanca Statement and Framework for Action on Special Needs Education. Turning to the statement itself, the following beliefs and proclamation was set out:

- Every child has a fundamental right to education, and must be given the opportunity to achieve and maintain an acceptable level of learning.
- Every child has unique characteristics, interests, abilities and learning needs,
- Education systems should be designed and educational programmes implemented to take into account the wide diversity of these characteristics and needs.
- Those with special educational needs must have access to regular schools which should accommodate them within a child centred pedagogy capable of meeting these needs.
- Regular schools with this inclusive orientation are the most effective means of combating discriminatory attitudes, creating welcoming communities, building an inclusive society and achieving education for all; moreover, they provide an effective education to the majority of children and improve the efficiency and ultimately the cost-effectiveness of the entire education system.

Brahm Norwich (2008, p. 20) observes tensions within the Salamanca Statement proclamations:

> Though the Salamanca Statement about inclusive education makes strong statements about inclusive schooling, it only asserts the fundamental right to education, not to an inclusive education.

The Salamanca Statement is enlisted to support both those who argue for what is clumsily referred to as "full inclusion" and also by those who frame conditions around the inclusion of the child into the regular school. Full inclusion is a spurious proposition (Slee, 2010, p. 117). Cascade models (Deno, 1970) reinforce the enduring assumptions and contingencies that surround neo-special educational renditions of inclusion. Tenure is conditional for children who are seen as defective and a burden to the work of ordinary schools who educate ordinary children.

> One is included or one is not included. Fractions of inclusion time or place are vulgar fractions.
>
> —(Slee, 2010, p. 117)

Full inclusion falls into the same special educational lexicon that offers "reverse inclusion" as an inclusive educational initiative. Reverse inclusion refers to the placement of so-called normal children in a special class with disabled students. They may be correct—children who are escorted to the segregated setting to do their community service may learn about exclusion and realise how distorted our view of the world and human identity has become. Like Sally Tomlinson (1982), I am more inclined to believe that the blanket of benevolence that propels such initiatives will smother the possibility for critical engagement.

Together with Daniels and Garner (1999, p. 4), Artiles and Dyson (2005, p. 39) claim that the extraordinary power and worldwide influence of the Salamanca Statement comes from its "ability to deal in absolutes." The Salamanca Statement, they argue, progresses from a reliance on declarations of human rights to assertions about the uniqueness of individual needs, "and thence into assertions that education systems should be designed around uniqueness" and "that children with special educational needs must attend regular schools" (2005, p 40). The regular school will then achieve wider educational and social benefits for all. Where the Statement falls silent is in the detail to suggest the reforms required for regular schooling to become more inclusive. The Salamanca Statement, and the successive activity under the Education for All banner, has provided a platform for educators, civil servants, activists and researchers to adopt the discourse of inclusive education. The Salamanca Statement has been supported and elaborated through local legislation and jurisdictional regulations as well as through international covenants such as Article 24 of the United Nations Convention on the Rights of Persons with Disability (compare Appendix B) and Optional Protocol adopted by the General Assembly of the United Nations in 2006.

EDUCATIONAL EXCLUSION—A STUBBORN FOE

Twenty years on from the declaration of the Salamanca Statement in 1994 we can certainly point to some authentic gains for inclusive education across jurisdictions, schools and classrooms. The chronicling of these compelling stories offers inspiration and strategic instruction to the next generation of social and education reformers and hope for people with disability, their carers and their advocates (Alur and Bach, 2010; Carrington and Macarthur, 2012). Less recognized is the contribution of inclusive education for the improvement in the quality of educational experiences and outcomes for all students. Inclusive schooling, based on principles of universal design, enlarges education to allow students to occupy and appreciate the world of diversity that really exists rather than the fabricated world of the traditional regular or special school. Segregation is an effective incubator for ignorance, mythology and social dysfunction. Of course, this underlines the oft-made point that inclusion is not simply what is done to and for children with disabilities; it is as Julie Allan (2005; 2008) reminds us, following Foucault, an ethical project on ourselves.

The stories of exclusion are also compelling and instructive. They too should be documented and meticulously analysed to develop ameliorative strategies consistent with changing contexts. Previously I have argued that the interrogation and dismantling of the structures and cultures of exclusion may be more productive than the endless pursuit of securing an agreed definition of inclusive education (Slee, 2010). In this section of this essay I want to consider two areas of education change since the drafting of the Salamanca Statement that have enlarged the scope for educational exclusion. This discussion will be set against an introductory backdrop of broader social changes that frame education movements. The areas that I consider are:

- The growth of a high stakes accountability ethos for school performance and student achievement.
- The multiple impacts of hyper-awareness of behaviour and attention disorders on the treatment of disengaged and disruptive students.

Of course, this discussion acknowledges the importance of the specific cultural, religious, geographic, political, economic and structural contingencies of divergent international contexts, of global divergences and convergences (Singal and Muthukrishna, 2014). It is important to acknowledge that this essay is dominated by and limited to an Anglo-centric view (Connell, 2007).

Delivering the *Castle Lectures in Ethics, Politics and Economics* at Yale University in 2004 Richard Sennett (2006) spoke of *The Culture of New Capitalism.* Half a century of wealth creation, he suggests, had produced greater economic inequality and social instability. Increasing globalization of markets underpinned by profound changes in technology forms new loose structures and relations of production. Labour is sought from its cheapest supply points. Industries, information, capital and people are detached from traditional notions of nation-state and community. Old crafts and skills are rendered redundant and people's lives alter radically. They must continually remake their knowledge, skills and occupational identity to chase down new occupations. People become increasingly mobile, detached from familial and social ties; dwelling and workplace are separated by commutes. People move on rather than stay. Detachment replaces former attachments. Solidarity gives way to fluidarity (McDonald, 2006). Vulnerability is enlarged as redundancies and unemployment increases. People live in fear of the *spectre of uselessness* (Sennett, 2006, p. 86) in a condition of collective indifference (Slee, 2010).

Under these conditions of increasing competition, as Bauman (1997; 2004) reminds us, the fear of *strangers* intensifies and we distance ourselves from those who are the collateral casualties of the new ethics of production and consumption (Bauman, 2008). The increasing numbers of those excluded by the quicksand of poverty (Dorling, 2010; Wilkinson and Pickett, 2009) become loathsome *human waste* (Bauman, 2004). They are a threat to our own material prosperity. In Australia, the Abbott Liberal (read conservative) Government refers to a society of *leaners and lifters* as it strives to diminish the reach of the welfare state or social safety net. Politicians speak of the virtues of drug testing welfare recipients as a means of determining their real need and willingness to join the ranks of the *lifters.*

Bauman describes the way in which the forces of exclusion are depersonalized and discursively shifted from decisions by human actors to technical events:

> … the production of human waste has all the markings of an impersonal, purely technical issue. The principal actors in the drama are 'terms of trade,' 'market demands,' 'competitive pressures,' 'productivity' or 'efficiency' requirements, all covering up or explicitly denying any connection with the intentions, will, decisions and actions of real humans with names and addresses.
>
> —(BAUMAN, 2004, p. 40)

While political, and educational rhetoric, is replete with homage to diversity and multiculturalism, the reality is that we live in a state of ambient fear. *Mixaphobia* (Bauman, 1997, p. 81; Bauman and Mazzeo, 2012) is a more precise representation of our regard for the *other*. Anti-immigration platforms and protection from incursions by people displaced by conflict, natural disasters and poverty is a widespread and increasingly acceptable political disposition. The recourse to panic and fortification of privilege is routine (Aubenas, 2011; Marr, 2011). Inclusion is conditional.

Let us make some bold observations about education against this political backdrop. I want to suggest that while the volubility of inclusive education and of the value of diversity and difference is more frequent and shrill across education jurisdictions, the risk of exclusion remains intractable.

Inclusion in an age of neo-liberal accountabilities

The discourse of inclusion sits alongside a more strident discourse of improving standards. Standards are measured through national and international testing programmes and schools are adjudicated according to the performance of students on these tests. Rather than rehearse the extensive literature on the impact of high stakes accountability on schooling (Thrupp and Willmot, 2003; Apple, 2006; Ball, 2013; Stobart, 2008; Rizvi and Lingard, 2010; Ravitch, 2011), I will simply offer the following observations on specific effects for vulnerable students.

First, the ranking of schools according to student examination and test performance increases risk aversion and the exercise of greater scrutiny over their actual and potential enrolment for academic prognosis. Students are reduced to the status of bearers of results. Competitive individualism is a hallmark of school organisation. Gillborn and Youdell (1999) have charted the practice of *educational triage* as schools determined which students were more and less likely to progress or regress their table standings and, accordingly, where efforts should be made for best returns. High stakes testing has increased in-school stratification of students and the consolidation of privilege and disadvantage (Oakes, 2005; Gamoran, 2010). As has been established by empirical research, failure is not random. Poverty and race are reliable predictors of academic underperformance and educational exclusion (Tomlinson, 1982; Connell, 2007, Gillborn, 2008). Under these conditions particular profiles such as students with disabilities, children from indigenous populations, those with diminished access to educational resources and the accoutrements of cultural capital, traveller and refugee children are increasingly vulnerable.

Second, education jurisdictions and schools have been positioning themselves according to the education marketplace (Ball, 1990; 2007; 2013). Schools, as we have noted, market themselves to population segments. Often described in terms of choice, this segmentation of schooling reinforces educational and social hierarchies (Teese, 2013). While some schools are positioned to guide their students through to higher education and wider vocational opportunity, others contain disengaged or difficult to teach young people (Slee, 1994; Parsons, 2009). The growth in alternative educational provision has continued in correspondence to erratic and high levels of suspension, exclusion and educational disengagement (te Riele, 2007).

Arne Duncan (2014), Secretary of Education in the US, in a speech at the Frederick Douglass High School in Baltimore on January 8th, 2014, reflected upon the excessive use of suspensions and expulsions across US education jurisdictions. "Unfortunately today," he declares,

> suspensions and expulsions are not primarily used as a last resort for serious infractions.... Over time, the overreliance on exclusionary discipline has gotten much worse.
>
> —(DUNCAN, 2014)

Over the past four decades exclusionary discipline sanctions in the US have increased by 40%. He cites data from the State Department for Education's Civil Rights Data Collection to report that schools in South Carolina suspended 12.7% of their students in the 2009–2010 school year. This accounts for about one in eight students and contrasts with North Dakota where 2.2% or one in fifty of their students were suspended.

> That huge disparity is not caused by differences in children; it's caused by differences in training, professional development, and discipline policies. It is adult behavior that needs to change.
>
> —(DUNCAN, 2014)

Duncan, like Parrish (2002), acknowledges the disproportionate suspension and expulsion of students of color and students with disabilities.

Behaviour disorders; endemic or pandemic?

The move to include students with disabilities in their neighbourhood schools has prompted education jurisdictions to formulate models for allocating resources to students with disabilities and special educational needs. Predictably, these models often proceeded from the diagnosis of the nature and the seriousness of a student's impairment or deficit. Following the logic, attempts were then made to calculate the quantum of resources—personnel, adjustments for access, curriculum materials and other supports—needed for the student to be able to participate in the class. Such models generate perverse effects. The seriousness of the disability might be overstated to secure greater levels of funding. Inclusion is treated as a case-by-case challenge to accommodate individual children rather than as a project of school reform and educational capacity building. Under such conditions schools and teachers scrutinised student cohorts for additional candidates for support. In other words the funding model encouraged the calibration of student populations.

Education jurisdictions are reporting increased prevalence of behaviour disorders (Harwood and Allan, 2014). Disengagement and disruption is often considered to represent disordered genetic structures (Barkley, 2006; Cooper, 2008). Accordingly increasing numbers of students who show symptoms of inattention, defiance, disorganisation, disengagement and withdrawal are diagnosed with a range of disorders described in the *Diagnostic and Statistical Manual of Mental*

Disorders—DSMV (American Psychiatric Association, 2012). These include conditions such as Attention Deficit-Hyperactivity Disorder (ADHD), Oppositional Defiance Disorder (ODD) and Autistic Spectrum Disorders (ASD). Following the diagnosis of the student, the school may apply a series of interventions to both manage and support the student with a view to improving their access to the curriculum, educational experience and academic success. Seeing the disaffected pupil as a product of impaired pathology unlocks a range of additional resources to assist in the development of a revised education or regulatory strategy.

Inclusive education programmes encouraged departments of education to calibrate the student population more extensively in order to provide a model for the allocation of resources and the design of interventions to improve the educational chances of students with disabilities or special educational needs. It is important to note in this discussion that while the prevalence of disabilities such as physical, cognitive and sensory conditions has remained relatively stable, there have been dramatic increases in the diagnosis and classification of students with behavioural and emotional disabilities. This invites the question: how might we explain the incidence of this new wave of *disaffected pupils* in the twenty-first century?

Nikolas Rose (2007) draws on the work of Ludwik Fleck (1979) to consider the ebb and flows of *thought collectives* that build authority and political momentum around sets of knowledge. Hilary Rose and Steven Rose (2013) offer a salutary account of the genome project and bioethics and question the authority of the so-called truths of brain science (Rose, 2005) and pharmacological and therapeutic practices it generates. The progress of sciences of the brain linked to the genome project has transformed fledgling understandings of cognitive disorders, inattention, hyperactivity and disruptive behaviour. "Brain science" is a commonplace reference in popular education writing, policy pronouncements and rationales for innovative pedagogy. The genetic architecture of the child and its relationship with the quality of their behaviour and learning dispositions fuels scientific enquiry in scholarly journals, heated exchanges on media talk-shows, school staffroom discussions and car-park conjecture amongst parents waiting to pick up their children. Absent from this discussion of brain science is an acknowledgement of the arguments lurking within a broad and divided multi-disciplinary project (Rose, 2005; Greenberg, 2013; Rose and Rose, 2013). On offer it seems are more sophisticated tools with which to diagnose, treat and ameliorate cognitive and behavioural disorders. Brain science of varying veracity saturates information networks that are now widely accessible through the worldwide web and social media and often indiscriminately quoted. In this climate of hyper-awareness underachieving and noncompliant children are susceptible to the diagnostic gaze.

Debates that surround "sluggish cognitive tempo" disorder (Whitehouse, 2014; Schwarz, 2014) illustrate the construction of childhood disorders and the calibration of school populations. Hyper-awareness of behaviour disorders and mental illness leads to mass adoption of symptomologies and treatments and an accompanying inexpert and reductive attribution of causation. Data from the Australian Institute of Health and Welfare (2011) reports that one in four young people experience mental illness and this has been used to explain student under-achievement and disengagement. Mental illness is in danger of becoming a proxy for difficulties in school.

Successive editions of the *Diagnostic and Statistical Manual of Mental Disorders —DSM* (American Psychiatric Association, 2013), the fifth edition of which is also available as an App for iOS and Android devices, catalogues a growing and more finely calibrated and contestable (Greenberg, 2010; 2013; Kutchins and Kirk, 1997; Rose, 2005; Rose, 2007) array of disorders and syndromes. This knowledge of behaviour provides influential accounts of what lies behind intractable problems for schools: inattention, disaffection and disruption. DSM is used as an evolving diagnostic tool and there are well-documented (Kutchins and Kirk, 1997; Whitaker, 2002; 2010) disputes over what disorders or syndromes should be excluded from or included in successive editions. The syndromes in DSM are codified for health insurance purposes, making it a particularly powerful catalogue of human identity.

The pervasive availability of information fuels thought collectives around particular health and behavior identities. The claim for additional and specialised treatments in education is illustrative. Whitaker (2010) is amongst others (e.g. Rose, 2005; Rose, 2007) to critically consider the history and the political and economic influence of the science of Attention Deficit-Hyperactivity Disorder (ADHD). The manufacturer of Ritalin, commonly used to treat ADHD, Ciba-Geigy, assisted in establishing Children and Adults with Attention Deficit Hyperactivity Disorder (CHADD). CHADD is a community organisation of 12,000 members; including 2,000 clinicians treating attention disorders, across 194 local affiliates in forty-one states of the US. It has an information, broadcasting (Attention Radio) and accredited training arm, hosts frequent seminars, workshops and training programmes across the U.S., hosts *Attention Magazine and blogs Attention Radio*, awards science prizes and boasts an impressive annual international conference with over 1200 registered delegates (Slee, 2010, p. 136).

Sally Tomlinson (2012) recently reflected upon an apparent paradoxical rise in the size and influence of the "special education industry" at a time of "worldwide movement towards the inclusion of populations of young people who would previously have been wholly excluded." She continues:

> Yet governments of all political persuasions, bowing to a variety of economic, professional and parental vested interests, have acquiesced in the expansion of the SEN industry, implicitly conceding its importance in dealing with potential groups who, while being offered some education and training, appear increasingly surplus in 'knowledge economies' and/or are in need of social control from an early age.
>
> —(TOMLINSON, 2012)

My point is not to deny childhood disorders and mental illness and the profound challenges that they present to people. Rather I am cautioning against the way in which so-called inclusive education practices can become forces for exclusion or mechanisms for calibrating and regulating school populations to maintain institutional and cultural rigidities.

ANOTHER SALAMANCA?

Yes, the *Salamanca Statement* has been an important and influential resource with which to advocate for inclusive education for students with disabilities. Its significance has had global reach. It will continue to be influential and an acknowledged important historical point of reference. In Australia in 2012 three important documents were published that persuade us of the need for a reassessment of inclusive education policies and programmes. Each illuminates general and specific limitations of the educational provision for students with disabilities. In June 2012 the Department of Education, Employment and Workplace Relations published the findings of the *Review of Disability Standards for Education 2005* (DEEWR, 2012). The report highlights seven thematic areas that reflect fundamental problems for the implementation of the Disability Standards for Education:

- o Awareness
- o Clarity and definitions
- o Access and participation
- o Discrimination
- o Complaints, accountability and compliance
- o Contemporary education context
- o Resources

The sixth theme, *Contemporary education context*, is apposite in its acknowledgement that education policies, cultures and practices place students with disability at greater risk of educational and social exclusion.

Soon after, the Victorian Auditor-General's Office (VAGO, 2012) published its report on *Programmes for Students with Special Learning Needs* in the Legislative Assembly of Victoria (Australia) on August 29th, 2012. The report is not flattering for the Department for Education and Early Childhood Development. The Executive Summary states that:

> Since 2006, DEECD (Department of Education and Early Childhood Development) has distributed more than $2.6 billion to schools through PSD (Programmes for Students with Disabilities). However, DEECD does not have the information it needs to determine whether PSD funding is being used efficiently and effectively. Concerns raised about this

> by VAGO (Victorian Auditor General's Office) in 2007 still have not been adequately addressed and instead of having five years worth of high quality data about the programme, the department still knows very little about its impact on the educational outcomes of supported students.
>
> —(VAGO, 2012, p. viii)

Following the report from VAGO, The Victorian Equal Opportunity and Human Rights Commission (September, 2012) published *Held Back,* which reports on the experiences of students with disabilities in Victorian schools. Data was collected from 1,827 educators, students with disabilities and their parents. The report provides an account of the experiences of students with disabilities that are less than inclusive and it reminds us that the prospects for students with disabilities in Australia do not match those not designated as disabled.

I suspect that there is international convergence. Stories abound about schools that have worked with their communities to build inclusive cultures and practices. Parents will talk of the positive experiences of their children in inclusive classrooms and schools. Still, all too often the reportage is otherwise where exclusion is set in the fabric of school cultures and practices. More particularly education systems struggle to see inclusive education as an opportunity for systemic reform to build capacity of schools to benefit from the differences within their student cohorts. The challenges are great.

Another Salamanca-like conference and statement may be useful. My hunch is that it should not be a gathering of former Salamanca Statement drafters charged with updating the document. Sustainability requires the next generation of activists to engage in the process guided by enduring principles adapted to changing contingencies. The next gathering requires new questions arising from the analyses of a range of data that place the issues of disablement and capacity building into the larger agenda of reorganising education for the twenty-first century. Decoupling disability for consideration apart from school reform writ large returns us to a compensatory mind-set. Salamanca II needs to be a document that takes up the ethical project of interrogating the world we want to live in and devising education standards capable of achieving that world-vision. A new set of performance indicators could reasonably start with indicators of inclusion and exclusion. In this respect I suspect there may be more benefit in fusing the projects of Jomtien and Salamanca. This could be emblematic of the need to not separate students with disabilities as a special case for inclusion, of the requirement to build the capacity of schools, teachers and communities to embrace difference and diversity as a resource for learning how to live together (Touraine, 2000).

CRITICAL AFTERWORD

From Salamanca to the United Nations Convention on the Rights of Persons with Disabilities and Beyond

TARA FLOOD

History tells us that the Salamanca Statement published in 1994, and signed by the 'great and the good,' encouraged a change in attitude and thinking either at the frontline or at policy level among those working in education.

The key sentence in the Salamanca Statement states 'Regular schools with an inclusive orientation are the most effective means of combating discriminatory attitudes, creating welcoming communities, building an inclusive society and achieving education for all.'

However, for disabled people, particularly those who were and remain active in the global disabled rights movement, the Salamanca Statement was only the start, and did not go far enough—it still allowed for some disabled children and young people to be segregated into special education. Many activists felt (and still do) that this weakened the possibility of the Salamanca Statement having any real and lasting impact in terms of the ending of segregated education as well as the capacity building of mainstream education to welcome the inclusion of disabled children and young people.

It could be argued that the Salamanca Statement missed an opportunity to advocate the ending of segregation and the development of education systems worldwide because of the Salamanca conference organizers' obsession with producing a document that all participants could sign. I would argue that the commitment to full inclusion was weakened by the dominance of education professionals who have traditionally 'medicalized' the education of disabled learners and by the lack of disabled people's voices at the Salamanca conference.

Disabled people had to wait 10 years before the language of inclusive education as a right would start to be embedded in a global human rights treaty. There had been many earlier attempts by disabled people to persuade the United Nations and the global community to recognize that the situation for disabled people around the globe was critical in all aspects of life. There were early signs of change in 1985, when former United Nations Secretary General Perez de Cuellar described the situation of disabled people worldwide as 'the silent emergency.'

In 2001 the UN accepted a motion from the Mexican government that a human rights treaty was required in recognition of the particular situation of disabled people. Prior to then, disabled people had been considered as included in 'and others' descriptions in existing treaties—a dehumanizing label by anyone's standard.

The UN-Convention on the Rights of Persons with Disabilities (UNCRPD), as it is now known, was negotiated during eight sessions of an Ad Hoc Committee of the General Assembly held between 2002 and 2006, making it the fastest negotiated human rights treaty thus far.

The UNCRPD was a first for the UN for two reasons: it was the first human rights treaty of the 21st century, and it was the first human rights treaty to involve civil society representation at every stage of the discussions. Disabled people were present either as representatives of civil society or as members of governmental delegations.

The UNCRPD text includes 50 Articles, 32 of which cover specific areas such as the Right to Life, Accessibility, Independent Living, Access to Justice, Communication, Family Life, and Education. No new rights are included but the UNCRPD provides clarity and recognition that any existing human and civil rights apply equally to disabled people.

There are a number of differences between the Salamanca Statement and the UNCRPD position on education, and I consider that the UNCRPD significantly improves on the 1994 lukewarm commitment to inclusive education. Firstly, in Article 24 the right to inclusive education is unequivocal—there are no exceptions, and there is no mention of segregated or special education, only the setting out of obligations to meet the needs of all disabled learners to enable them to fully participate in a mainstream learning environment. Secondly, there is a UNCRPD scrutiny process, although in terms of education change is not required immediately because Article 24 is one of the UNCRPD rights subject to the 'progressive realization' principle. However, governments that do ratify the Convention must demonstrate how they are progressing towards the development of an inclusive education system that welcomes all disabled learners. Third, and lastly, the language and tone of the UNCRPD reflects a Social Model of Disability approach to change, where the responsibility lies firmly with society to change its practices, processes, and policies to ensure that disabled people are treated equally as human beings, in contrast to the traditional approach to disability that sees the disabled person as the medical problem to be fixed. Disabled people believe that the language of special educational needs has its roots in this Medical Model of Disability approach.

The UK position on the UNCRPD is interesting. The UK government was one of the first to sign the Convention and ratified the text in June 2009. UK government's expediency can be explained as due to unrelenting lobbying from disabled people and our allies. My organization, the Alliance for Inclusive Education (www.allfie.org.uk), which is run and controlled by disabled people, campaigned for ratification alongside many others because we saw, and continue to see, the huge potential opportunity that the UNCRPD presented.

The priority now for disabled people and civil society is to be an effective voice of challenge in the implementation of the UNCRPD, wherever we are in the world and to raise awareness of the potential, protection and aspiration for change the Convention brings for all disabled people.

From my perspective as a disabled person and an activist, the UNCRPD is as clear and strong in its provision for the protection of disabled people's human rights and their aspirations because disabled people were there at the negotiating table—their presence secured a living, breathing blueprint for the paradigm shift required to make real for and with disabled people wherever they are located in the world.

"Nothing About Us Without Us"

Appendices

APPENDIX A

The Salamanca Statement on Principles, Policy and Practice in Special Needs Education

(Adopted by the "World Conference on Special Needs Education" in Salamanca, Spain, 7–10 June 1994)

Reaffirming the right to education of every individual, as enshrined in the 1948 Universal Declaration of Human Rights, and renewing the pledge made by the world community at the 1990 World Conference on Education for All to ensure that right for all regardless of individual differences.

Recalling the several United Nations declarations culminating in the 1993 United Nations Standard Rules on the Equalization of Opportunities for Persons with Disabilities, which urges States to ensure that the education of persons with disabilities is an integral part of the education system, noting with satisfaction the increased involvement of governments, advocacy groups, community and parent groups, and in particular organizations of persons with disabilities, in seeking to improve access to education for the majority of those with special needs still unreached; and recognizing as evidence of this involvement the active participation of high level representatives of numerous governments, specialized agencies and inter-governmental organizations in this World Conference.

1. We, the delegates of the World Conference on Special Needs Education representing ninety-two governments and twenty-five international organizations, assembled here in Salamanca, Spain, from 7–10 June 1994, hereby reaffirm our commitment to Education for All, recognizing the necessity and urgency of providing education for children, youth and adults with special educational needs within the regular education system, and further hereby endorse the Framework

for Action on Special Needs Education, that governments and organizations may be guided by the spirit of its provisions and recommendations.

2. We believe and proclaim that:

- every child has a fundamental right to education, and must be given the opportunity to achieve and maintain an acceptable level of learning,
- every child has unique characteristics, interests, abilities and learning needs,
- education systems should be designed and educational programmes implemented to take into account the wide diversity of these characteristics and needs,
- those with special educational needs must have access to regular schools which should accommodate them within a child-centred pedagogy capable of meeting these needs,
- regular schools with this inclusive orientation are the most effective means of combating discriminatory attitudes, creating welcoming communities, building an inclusive society and achieving education for all; moreover, they provide an effective education to the majority of children and improve the efficiency and ultimately the cost-effectiveness of the entire education system.

3. We call upon all governments and urge them to:

- give the highest policy and budgetary priority to improve their education systems to enable them to include all children regardless of individual differences or difficulties,
- adopt as a matter of law or policy the principle of inclusive education, enrolling all children in regular schools, unless there are compelling reasons for doing otherwise,
- develop demonstration projects and encourage exchanges with countries having experience with inclusive schools,
- establish decentralized and participatory mechanisms for planning, monitoring and evaluating educational provision for children and adults with special education needs,
- encourage and facilitate the participation of parents, communities and organization of persons with disabilities in the planning and decision-making processes concerning provision for special educational needs,
- invest greater effort in early identification and intervention strategies, as well as in vocational aspects of inclusive education,
- ensure that, in the context of a systemic change, teacher education programmes, both pre-service and in-service, address the provision of special needs education in inclusive schools.

4. We also call upon the international community; in particular we call upon:

- governments with international cooperation programmes and international funding agencies, especially the sponsors of the World Conference on Education for All, the United Nations Educational, Scientific and Cultural Organization (UNESCO), the United Nations Children's Fund (UNICEF), United Nations Development Programme (UNDP), and the World Bank:
  - to endorse the approach of inclusive schooling and to support the development of special needs education as an integral part of all education programmes;
  - the United Nations and its specialized agencies, in particular the International Labour Office (ILO), the World Health Organization (WHO), UNESCO and UNICEF:
  - to strengthen their inputs for technical cooperation, as well as to reinforce their cooperation and networking for more efficient support to the expanded and integrated provision of special needs education;
- non-governmental organizations involved in country programming and service delivery:
  - to strengthen their collaboration with the official national bodies and to intensify their growing involvement in planning, implementation and evaluation of inclusive provision for special educational needs;
- UNESCO, as the United Nations agency for education:
  - to ensure that special needs education forms part of every discussion dealing with education for all in various forums,
  - to mobilize the support of organizations of the teaching profession in matters related to enhancing teacher education as regards provision for special educational needs,
  - to stimulate the academic community to strengthen research and networking and to establish regional centres of information and documentation; also, to serve as a clearinghouse for such activities and for disseminating the specific results and progress achieved at country level in pursuance of this Statement,
  - to mobilize funds through the creation within its next Medium-Term Plan (1996–2002) of an expanded programme for inclusive schools and community support programmes, which would enable the launching of pilot projects that showcase new approaches for dissemination, and to develop indicators concerning the need for and provision of special needs education.

5. Finally, we express our warm appreciation to the Government of Spain and to UNESCO for the organization of the Conference, and we urge them to make every effort to bring this Statement and the accompanying Framework for Action to the attention of the world community, especially at such important forums as the World Summit for Social Development (Copenhagen, 1995) and the World Conference on Women (Beijing, 1995).

Adopted by acclamation, in the city of Salamanca, Spain, on this 10th of June, 1994.

APPENDIX B

Convention on the Rights of Persons with Disabilities, Art. 24

(United Nations 2006)

EDUCATION

1. States Parties recognize the right of persons with disabilities to education. With a view to realizing this right without discrimination and on the basis of equal opportunity, States Parties shall ensure an inclusive education system at all levels and life long learning directed to:

   a. The full development of human potential and sense of dignity and self-worth, and the strengthening of respect for human rights, fundamental freedoms and human diversity;
   b. The development by persons with disabilities of their personality, talents and creativity, as well as their mental and physical abilities, to their fullest potential;
   c. Enabling persons with disabilities to participate effectively in a free society.

2. In realizing this right, States Parties shall ensure that:

   a. Persons with disabilities are not excluded from the general education system on the basis of disability, and that children with disabilities are not excluded from free and compulsory primary education, or from secondary education, on the basis of disability;

b. Persons with disabilities can access an inclusive, quality and free primary education and secondary education on an equal basis with others in the communities in which they live;
c. Reasonable accommodation of the individual's requirements is provided;
d. Persons with disabilities receive the support required, within the general education system, to facilitate their effective education;
e. Effective individualized support measures are provided in environments that maximize academic and social development, consistent with the goal of full inclusion.

3. States Parties shall enable persons with disabilities to learn life and social development skills to facilitate their full and equal participation in education and as members of the community. To this end, States Parties shall take appropriate measures, including:

a. Facilitating the learning of Braille, alternative script, augmentative and alternative modes, means and formats of communication and orientation and mobility skills, and facilitating peer support and mentoring;
b. Facilitating the learning of sign language and the promotion of the linguistic identity of the deaf community;
c. Ensuring that the education of persons, and in particular children, who are blind, deaf or deafblind, is delivered in the most appropriate languages and modes and means of communication for the individual, and in environments which maximize academic and social development.

4. In order to help ensure the realization of this right, States Parties shall take appropriate measures to employ teachers, including teachers with disabilities, who are qualified in sign language and/or Braille, and to train professionals and staff who work at all levels of education. Such training shall incorporate disability awareness and the use of appropriate augmentative and alternative modes, means and formats of communication, educational techniques and materials to support persons with disabilities.

5. States Parties shall ensure that persons with disabilities are able to access general tertiary education, vocational training, adult education and lifelong learning without discrimination and on an equal basis with others. To this end, States Parties shall ensure that reasonable accommodation is provided to persons with disabilities.

List of Contributors

Mel Ainscow
Mel Ainscow is Professor of Education and Co-director of the Centre for Equity in Education at the University of Manchester. He is also Adjunct Professor at Queensland University of Technology. Previously a head teacher, local education authority inspector and lecturer at the University of Cambridge, his work focuses on ways of making school systems effective for all children and young people. Currently he is leading Schools Challenge Cymru, the Welsh Government's multi-million pound flagship programme to accelerate the rate of improvement across the country's schools. In the Queen's 2012 New Year honours list he was awarded a CBE for services to education.

Julie Allan
Julie Allan is Professor of Equity and Inclusion and Head of the Department of Disability, Inclusion and Special Needs at the University of Birmingham, UK and Visiting Professor at the University of Borås in Sweden. Her work encompasses inclusive education, disability studies and children's rights and she has been advisor to the Scottish Parliament, the Welsh Assembly, the Dutch and Queensland Governments and Council of Europe. Her most recent books include *Psychopathology at School: Theorizing Mental Disorders in Education* (with Valerie Harwood) and *Social Capital, Children and Young People* (with Ralph Catts).

Susan Baglieri

Susan Baglieri, Ed.D., is Associate Professor in the Department of Secondary and Special Education at Montclair State University, New Jersey, USA. She joined MSU after serving on the faculty at Long Island University, Brooklyn, New York City. She was on the Board of Directors of the Society for Disability Studies from 2008–2011 and has served as an assistant editor for *Disability Studies Quarterly*. Baglieri seeks to advance theory and practice in Disability Studies in Education through scholarship on universal curriculum design and teacher education. She is co-author of the book *Disability Studies and the Inclusive Classroom*.

Dóra S. Bjarnason

Dóra S. Bjarnason is Professor at the University of Iceland, School of Education. She was educated as a sociologist in the UK and as a teacher at the Icelandic University College of Education. She has worked as a teacher and visiting scholar in universities in several countries around the world and as a tenured professor in the University College of Education, later the University of Iceland since the early 1990s. She obtained her master's degree at Keel University in the UK, was a Morris Ginnsberg fellow at the LSE for a time, and obtained her Doctor Phil. Degree from Oslo University. She taught sociology at Icelandic Universities and directed the MEd and MA programs for special needs/inclusive education teachers for over a decade. Research interests include inclusive education policy and practice, school development, voices of disabled children and youth, and families of disabled children and youth. She is the author of several books and articles in her field. Homepage: http://vefir.hi.is/dsb/.

Alicia A. Broderick

Alicia A. Broderick, PhD, is an Associate Professor of Education in the Inclusive Education graduate programs of the College of Education and Human Services at Montclair State University, New Jersey, USA. Broderick's program of research aims to explore the implications for teacher education of Disability Studies in Education (DSE) work, as well as to engage in DSE scholarship through a specific exploration of the workings of ableism in media and cultural representations of autism. She is also particularly interested in exploring dis/ablement in the context of unschooling.

Ignacio Calderón-Almendros

Ignacio Calderón-Almendros, PhD in Education, is Associate Professor in the Department of Theory and History of Education (University of Malaga-Spain). He is a member of the Education Theory and Social Education Research Group (Regional Ministry of Economy, Innovation, Science and Employment of Andalusia), and he has collaborated with different Research Groups and universities in Europe and Latin America. His research interests are educational exclusion and inclusion, disability and socio-cultural disadvantage, which analyses through the educational experience.

Colette Chabbott

Dr. Colette Chabbott is an adjunct faculty member in the International Education Program at George Washington University in Washington, DC, and consults on international development and education. Since 2006, she has worked with, among others, the Hewlett Foundation, the Research Triangle Institute, UNICEF, Save the Children, and BRAC on improving the quality of primary education in South Asia and the Middle East, particularly as it relates to gender, early grades reading, social mobilization, and alternative primary schools. Previously she served at the (U.S.) National Research Council, Stanford University (1996–1999), and USAID (1984–1992). Her latest publication is *Institutionalizing Health and Education for All: Global Goals, Innovations, and Scaling Up* New York: (Teachers' College Press 2014).

Scot Danforth

Scot Danforth is Professor of Education at San Diego State University. His books include *Becoming a Great Inclusive Educator* (2014), *The Incomplete Child: An Intellectual History of Learning Disabilities* (2009), *Disability and the Politics of Education: An International Reader* (2008, with Susan Gabel), *and Vital Questions Facing Disability Studies in Education* (2007, with Susan Gabel). For six years, he served (with Brenda Jo Brueggemann) as co-editor of *Disability Studies Quarterly*.

Markus Dederich

Markus Dederich currently works as a Full Professor at the University of Cologne (Germany), Faculty of Human Science, Department of Special Education and Rehabilitation since 2011. After his graduation as MA in Sociology, Philosophy, and Musicology and PhD in Philosophy he worked as Research Assistant until 2002 before becoming a Full Professor for Theory of Special Education at the Technical University of Dortmund. His main areas of research are ethical and anthropological issues and disability studies.

Tara Flood

Tara Flood is a disability rights activist and has been the Director at the Alliance for Inclusive Education since April 2006. Tara has been involved with the disability rights movement at a grassroots level, for the last 14 years, and she is committed to creating social and political change that will deliver equality for all disabled people at a local, regional, national, European and international level.

Tara was involved in the discussions at the United Nations in the development of the new UN-Convention on the Rights of Persons with Disabilities and is now working to get the Convention fully implemented.

Tara works with organisations led by disabled people, allied organisations, children's rights organisations, statutory agencies and Government departments, both in a personal and professional capacity, and is committed to the voices and experiences of ALL disabled people being at the heart of discussions and decision making about our lives.

Tara is a Sheila McKechnie Foundation campaigning award winner (2008) for her work on social inclusion.

Tara is a disabled person and a 'special' school survivor.

Lani Florian

Lani Florian is a Professor and Bell Chair of Education at the University of Edinburgh. She is an Academician of the Academy of Social Sciences (UK). Her research interests include models of provision for meeting the needs of all learners, and inclusive pedagogy. She is editor of the *Sage Handbook of Special Education* now in its second edition and co-author of *Achievement and Inclusion in Schools*, winner of the 2008 NASEN/Times Education Supplement academic book award. She has consulted on special needs education and inclusion for a number of international organizations including Open Society Foundations, UNICEF, and the OECD.

Dan Goodley

Dan Goodley is Professor of Disability Studies and Education at the University of Sheffield, England. He is the author of numerous books on critical disability studies and has recently combined an analysis of disablism with a focus on the practices of ableism. Publications include *Disability Studies* (Sage, 2010) and *Dis/ability Studies* (Routledge, 2014). His work combines theoretical resources from sociology, psychology and education and recent research projects with colleagues including Rebecca Lawthom and Katherine Runswick Cole include 'Big Society? Disabled People with Learning Disabilities and Civil Society' and 'The Interconnections of Disabled Childhoods, Post-Blair' (both funded by the Economic and Social Research Council). Dan is also the father to two young women and a Nottingham Forest Football Club fan.

Rune Sarromaa Hausstätter

Rune Sarromaa Hausstätter is an Associate Professor at Lillehammer University College (Norway), Faculty of Education and Social Studies. Hausstätter has a PhD from the University of Helsinki. Main research areas are inclusive education, theories of special education and comparative special educational research.

Judith Hollenweger

Judith Hollenweger is head of the priority area "Inclusive Education" and professor at the Zurich University for Teacher Education. She serves as the president of the Swiss Accreditation Commission for diplomas in the area of special needs education and is the Swiss member of the Representative Board of the European Agency for Special Needs and Inclusive Education. In addition, she is a consultant to UNICEF and the World Health Organization (WHO) and involved in developing applications of the International Classification of Functioning, Disability and Health, Version for Children and Youth (ICF-CY) for education systems.

Sanna Hukkanen

Sanna Hukkanen is an artist, illustrator and comics activist from Joensuu, Finland. She has organized and tutored several grassroots comics workshops for different NGOs in cooperation with World Comics Finland. Among them were workshops for four DPOs in Tanzania in 2009–2010 where she worked as a facilitator for the Finnish Abilis Foundation and the Tanzanian DPO umbrella organization SHIVYAWATA. Hukkanen's own art work has a strong focus in human rights, social justice and environment. She has made comics about racism, street children, environmental issues, etc. She has also illustrated guide books for people with disabilities.

Markku Jahnukainen

Dr Markku Jahnukainen is a Professor and Director of Special Teacher Education at the Department of Teacher Education, University of Helsinki, Finland. He is also an Adjunct Professor at the University of Alberta, Canada, and served as Fritz Karsen Visiting Research Chair in Comparative Inclusive and Special Education Research at Humboldt University in Berlin, Germany (2013–14). In addition to his interest in comparative and international educational research, he has been working with life-course studies among young people in vulnerable life situations. His current research project about the educational trajectories of immigrant youth in Finland is funded by the Academy of Finland (2014–18).

Florian Kiuppis

Florian Kiuppis received his PhD in Comparative Education at Humboldt University, Berlin, and is Associate Professor at Lillehammer University College, Faculty of Education and Social Studies, responsible for the courses in Disability Studies. Florian is a member of the Editorial Advisory Board of the *International Journal of Inclusive Education*. From 2011 to 2014, he served as the chairperson of the 'Special Interest Group Inclusive Education' within the Comparative and International Education Society (CIES) and is currently leading the Teacher Preparation Working Group as part of the Task Force Inclusive Education, led by

UNICEF and UNESCO, in context of the Global Partnership on Children with Disabilities.

Elina Lehtomäki

Elina Lehtomäki is a researcher activist, Adjunct Professor in Education at the University of Helsinki and Senior Researcher, PhD, at the University of Jyväskylä in Finland. Her research interests include participation in education, meaning of education and learning, life course of persons with disabilities and international education development. For years she has worked and collaborated with organizations of persons with disabilities, colleagues and partner universities in several African countries and UN agencies. Together with the University of Dar es Salaam in Tanzania her team conducted a research project 'Educated Girls and Women in Tanzania: Sociocultural interpretations of the meaning of education.' Elina Lehtomäki has been a visiting scholar at the Global Partnership for Education in Washington DC, Centre for Research and Interdisciplinarity in Paris and at the UNESCO Headquarters.

Gretar L. Marinósson

Gretar L. Marinósson is Professor emeritus at the University of Iceland, School of Education. He was educated as an educational psychologist in the UK and as a teacher and worked as a teacher and school psychologist in England and in Iceland for a number of years before entering academia in Reykjavík. He obtained his master's and doctoral degrees in Manchester and London, respectively. He directed the education of special needs teachers, and was Dean of research and director of the Research Centre at the Iceland University of Education. Research interests include special and inclusive education, social interaction and school development.

Jerome Mindes

Jerome Mindes is a Managing Project Specialist with the American Institutes for Research, where he has responsibility for project management, technical assistance, and business development for its International Development, Evaluation and Research Program. From 1997 to 2002, he served as the founding Coordinator of the International Working Group on Disability and Development, a consortium of disability and development assistance organizations and professionals working to elevate disability issues on the global development assistance agenda. He has worked to advance disability rights and access in the United States and over 25 developing nations.

Peter Mittler

Peter Mittler is Emeritus Professor of Special Needs Education and a former Dean of the Faculty of Education at Manchester University where he established the Hester Adrian Research Centre in 1968. He has undertaken a range of consultancies for

UN agencies, was rapporteur for the Salamanca conference and chaired the session which adopted the Declaration and Framework for Action. He is a former President of Inclusion International which he represented at UN meetings.

Within the UK he has been ministerial adviser on intellectual disability and chaired a working party making recommendations to government on the professional training and development of all teachers for inclusive education.

Sigamoney M. Naicker

Sigamoney M. Naicker is Chief Director of Inclusive Education in Cape Town, South Africa. He was appointed by President Nelson Mandela to the National Commission for Education Support Services in South Africa. When the country became a democracy, Sigamoney was the first National Director of Inclusive Education. He is the author of *Curriculum 2005, A Space for All: An Introduction to Inclusive Education* and co-editor of *Inclusive Education in Action in South Africa*. Sigamoney was appointed extra-ordinary Associate Professor at the University of Western Cape and Professor of Practice in Curriculum Studies and Educational Management at the University of Venda.

John Parry

John Parry is a Lecturer in Education (Early Years and Inclusion) at the Open University in the UK. He has many years experience as a practitioner working in the early years sector, primarily as a teacher and co-ordinator of educational support services for pre-school children. From 2003 until 2009 he was chairperson of the National Portage Association in the UK. His research interests are the development of inclusion in schools and early years provision; early intervention; and peer relationships in inclusive settings.

Xavier Rambla

Xavier Rambla is Associate Professor of sociology at the Univ. Autònoma de Barcelona (ESP), and was lecturer at the Univ. Vic (ESP, 1995–2001). He has led research projects on Education for All in Latin America (2009–2011), as well as on education and anti-poverty policies in the Southern Cone (2006–2008). He has also collaborated in projects on education and social cohesion in Europe (2003–2005), and critical co-educational action-research in several regions in Spain (1995–2000).

As a visiting lecturer, Dr. Rambla has taught education, globalization and inequalities in a number of European and Latin American universities for short periods.

At the Faculty of Political Science and Sociology (UAB), he has been responsible for strategic planning (2006–2008) and the Bachelor's Degree in Sociology (2009–2011), and has convened a mixed commission in charge of creating the students' council (2009–2010).

He has also contributed to connecting academic research with professional practitioners by collaborating as a consultant with some civil society organizations.

Jonathan Rix

Jonathan Rix is a Senior Lecturer in Inclusion, Curriculum and Learning at the Open University in the UK. He has worked as a teacher and writer in a wide range of educational and community settings. His extensive publications concern policies, practices and language associated with inclusion; capturing diverse perspectives; and developing models to facilitate our thinking about the form and function of education. He has a particular personal and professional interest in issues relating to learning difficulties. He research has included projects funded by the British Academy, the National Council of Special Education in Ireland and the Training and Development Agency for Schools in England.

Cristóbal Ruiz-Román

Cristóbal Ruiz-Román, PhD in Education, is Associate Professor in the Department of Theory and History of Education (University of Malaga-Spain). He is a member of the Education Theory and Social Education Research Group (Regional Ministry of Economy, Innovation, Science and Employment of Andalusia). His research interests are resilience and socio-cultural and race disadvantage in children and youth at social risk, which analyses through the educational experience.

Lena Saleh

Lena Saleh is a former UNESCO Senior Education Specialist (1979–1999) and was head of the section on Special Needs and Inclusive Education. From 1977 to 1978 she was Consultant to the Ministry of Labour and Social Development in Jordan and helped in establishing the Section for Rehabilitation and Special Needs Education. From 1974 to 1976 she worked in Lebanon, first as Director of St Luke's Centre for children with intellectual disabilities, and later as Executive Director of the Lebanese Association (parents) for Children with Intellectual Disabilities. During the period of 1972 to 1984 she was a member of the Executive Board of Inclusion International (previously known as ILSMH) and was its Vice-President for the last four years. She is a graduate of Teachers College, Columbia University (1963) with an MA in Special Needs Education; she holds a BA in Child Development from the Lebanese American University (former Beirut College for Women). Lena started her professional career as a teacher educator with UNRWA in Palestine.

Roger Slee

Roger Slee is the Founding Director of The Victoria Institute for Education, Diversity and Lifelong Learning at Victoria University (Australia). He is also the

Founding Editor of the International Journal of Inclusive Education and held the Chair of Inclusive Education at the Institute of Education – University of London before returning to Australia. Roger was also the Deputy Director-General of the Queensland Ministry of Education. Roger is holds an honorary Chair in Education at The University of Auckland in New Zealand and is a Visiting Professorial Fellow at the Institute of Education. Roger's most recent book is *The Irregular School.*

Emily Vargas-Barón

Emily Vargas-Barón directs The RISE Institute, a leading global authority on policy development in early childhood intervention (ECI) and early childhood development (ECD). She has a PhD in Anthropology from Stanford University, with a specialization in international educational planning. She has assisted over 20 countries to develop their national policies and strategic plans for ECD and/or ECI, and she helped Belarus, Bosnia and Herzegovina, and Georgia to design their national ECI systems and program policies and procedures. She developed and led an ECI program in the US for 15 years. She has published several books and journal articles on ECI and ECD.

Siri Wormnæs

Siri Wormnæs is professor emeritus at University of Oslo, Department of Special Needs Education. Her work has included research, lecturing, and student supervision. She has collaborated with persons, organizations and universities in several countries. In addition to working as a special teacher in Norway in the early days of inclusion, she has worked as a teacher in Norway and Pakistan, and has headed competence building projects in Egypt, Palestine, Uganda, Kenya and Tanzania. For three years she co-chaired the UNESCO Education for All Flagship entitled "The Right to Education for Persons with Disabilities: Towards Inclusion."

References

FOREWORD

Ball, J. (2011). *Enhancing Learning of Children from Diverse Language Backgrounds: Mother Tongue-Based Bilingual or Multilingual Education in the Early Years*. Paris, France: UNESCO.

Vargas-Barón, E. (2013). "Building and Strengthening National Systems for Early Childhood Development," in *Handbook of Early Childhood Development Research and Its Impact on Global Policy*. New York, NY: Oxford University Press and Society for Research in Child Development.

Vargas-Barón, E., Janson, U., and Mufel, N. (2009). *Early Childhood Intervention, Special Education and Inclusion: a Focus on Belarus*. Geneva, Switzerland: UNICEF

CHAPTER 1

Ainscow, M. (2012). Moving knowledge around: Strategies for fostering equity within educational systems. *Journal of Educational Change*, 13(3), 289–310.

Ainscow, M., and César, M. (2006). Inclusive education ten years after Salamanca: Setting the agenda. *European Journal of Psychology of Education*, 21(3), 231–238.

Artiles, A.J., Kozleski, E.B., and Waitoller, F.R. (2011). *Inclusive education: Examining equity on five continents*. Cambridge, MA: Harvard Education Press.

Baglieri, S., Bejoian, L.M., Broderick, A.A., Connor, D.J., and Valle, J. (2011). [Re]Claiming 'Inclusive Education' toward cohesion in educational reform: Disability Studies unravels the myth of the normal child. *Teachers College Record*, 113(10), 2122–2154.

Ballard, K. (Ed) (1999). *Inclusive education: International voices on disability and justice*. London, UK: Routledge.

Booth, T. (1996). A perspective on inclusion from England. *Cambridge Journal of Education*, 26(1): 87–99.

Brantlinger, E. (1997). Using ideology: Cases of nonrecognition of the politics of research and practice in Special Education. *Review of Educational Research*, 67(4): 425–459.

Dyson, A., and Millward, A. (2000). *Schools and special needs: Issues of innovation and inclusion.* Thousand Oaks, CA: Sage.

Hausstätter, R.S. (2013). In Support of Unfinished Inclusion. *Scandinavian Journal of Educational Research*. doi: 10.1080/00313831.2013.773553

Hinz, A. (2004). From segregation to inclusion in Germany. In: V. Heung and M. Ainscow (Eds.), *Inclusive education: A framework for reform?* (pp. 135–145). Hong Kong: Hong Kong Institute of Education.

Kiuppis, F. (2013). "Pedagogikkens pentagon" revis(it)ed – Considerations on emancipation from a disability studies and inclusive education perspective. In: J. Steinnes and S. Dobson (Eds.), *Pedagogikk under livets tre* (pp. 147–160). Trondheim, Norway: Akademika.

Kiuppis, F. (2014a). Why (not) associate the principle of inclusion with disability? Tracing connections from the start of the 'Salamanca Process.' *International Journal of Inclusive Education*, 18(7), 746–761.

Kiuppis, F. (2014b). *Heterogene Inklusivität, inklusive Heterogenität.* Münster/New York: Waxmann.

Kiuppis, F. (forthcoming). Bridging Continents, Cultures, and Crip Theories: Comparative and International Disability Studies in Education and Sociology. In: *Disability Studies Quarterly.* Spring 2015, special issue: Interventions in Disability Studies Pedagogy.

Kiuppis, F. and Peters, S. (2014). Inclusive education for all as special interest within the comparative and international education research community. *Annual Review of Comparative and International Education 2014*, Volume 25, 53–63.

Miles, S. (2002). Learning about inclusive education: The role of EENET in promoting International Dialogue. In: P. Farrell and M. Ainscow (Eds.), *Making special education inclusive* (pp. 51–62). New York: David Fulton Publishers.

Mittler, P. (2010). *Thinking globally acting locally: A personal journey.* Milton Keynes: AuthorHouse.

OECD (Organization for Economic Cooperation and Development) (2007). *No more failures: Ten steps to equity in education.* Paris, France: OECD.

Riehl, C.J. (2000). The principal's role in creating inclusive schools for diverse students: A review of normative, empirical, and critical literature on the practice of educational administration. *Review of educational research*, 70(1), 55–81.

Rieser, R. (2012). *Implementing inclusive education: A Commonwealth guide to implementing Article 24 of the UN-Convention on the Rights of Persons with Disabilities.* 2nd ed. London, UK: Commonwealth Secretariat.

Westwood, P. (2013). *Inclusive and adaptive teaching: Meeting the challenge of diversity in the classroom.* New York: Routledge.

Westwood, P. (2007). *Commonsense methods for children with special educational needs.* New York: Routledge.

CHAPTER 2

Abbott, A. (1988). *The system of professions: An essay on the division of expert labor.* Chicago: University of Chicago Press.

Black, M. (1986). *The children and the nations: The story of UNICEF.* Sydney, Australia: P.I.C. Pty Ltd.

Black, R.E., Morris, S.S., and Bryce, J. (2003). Child survival I: Where and why are 10 million children dying every year? *Lancet*, 361(9376), 2226–2234.

Brunsson, N. (1989). *The organization of hypocrisy: Talk, decisions and action in organizations*. New York: John Wiley.

Chabbott, C. (2003). *Constructing education for development: International organizations and Education for All*. New York: RoutledgeFalmer.

Chowdhury, A.M.R., Choudhury, R.K., and Nath, S.R. (Eds.) (1999). *Hope, not complacency: State of primary education in Bangladesh*. Dhaka, Bangladesh: University Press, Limited.

Cole, W.M., and Ramirez, F.O. (2013). Conditional decoupling: Assessing the impact of national human rights institutions, 1981–2004. *American Sociological Review*, XX(X), 24.

Coombs, P.H. (1968). *The world educational crisis: A systems analysis*. New York: Oxford University Press.

Ferguson, J. (1990). *The anti-politics machine: "Development," depoliticization, and bureaucratic power in Lesotho*. New York: Cambridge University Press.

Frank, D., Hironaka, A., Meyer, J., Schofer, E., and Tuma, N. (1998). The rationalization and organization of nature in world culture. In J. Boli and G. Thomas (Eds.), *World polity formation since 1875*. Stanford: Stanford University Press.

Haggis, S.M. (1992). *Education for all: Purpose and context* (World Conference on Education for All Monograph No. I). Paris: UNESCO.

Inter-Agency Commission (1990). *Final report: Meeting basic learning needs*. New York: Inter-Agency Commission of the World Conference on Education for All.

Jones, P. (2005). *The United Nations and education: Multilateralism, development and globalisation*. New York: Routledge Falmer.

Lumsdaine, D.H. (1993). *Moral vision in international politics: The foreign aid regime, 1949–1989*. Princeton: Princeton University Press.

Rohde, J.E. (1982). *Why the other half dies: The science and politics of child mortality in the Third World. The Leonard Parsons Memorial Lecture, University of Birmingham, UK, 15 March*. Paris: UNESCO Unit for Co-operation with UNICEF and World Food Programme.

Rohde. (2008). Alma Ata: Rebirth and revision at 30. *Lancet*, 372(9642): 950–961.

Social Watch (1996). *Social watch: The starting point*. Montevideo, Uruguay: Instituto del Tercer Mundo.

Steiner-Khamsi, G., and Stolpe, I. (2006). *Educational import: Local encounters with global forces in Mongolia*. New York: Palgrave Macmillan.

UNESCO and Government of Spain. Ministry of Education and Science. (1994, June). *World Conference on Special Needs Education: Final report*. Paper presented at the World Conference on Special Needs Education, Salamanca, Spain.

UNICEF. (2013). *Children with disabilities* (Annual). New York: UNICEF.

Watkins, K. (2000). *Education now: Break the cycle of poverty*. London: Oxfam.

CHAPTER 3

UNESCO (1993). *Teacher Education Resource Pack: Special Needs in the Classroom*. Paris, France: UNESCO.

UNESCO (1994). *Final report: World Conference on Special Needs Education: Access and Quality*. Paris, France: UNESCO.

UNESCO (1995). *Review of the Present Situation in Special Education*. Paris, France: UNESCO.

UNESCO (1998). *Inclusive Schools and Community Support Programmes, Phase I, 1996–1997*. Paris, France: UNESCO.

UNESCO (1999a). *Salamanca Five Years On: A review of UNESCO Activities in the Light of the Salamanca Statement and Framework for Action*. Paris, France: UNESCO.

UNESCO (1999b). *Welcoming Schools: Students With Disabilities in Regular Schools*. Paris, France: UNESCO.

World Education Forum (2000). Thematic Studies—Education For All, 2000 Assessment, Dakar, Senegal. Paris, France: UNESCO.

UNESCO (2002). *Inclusive Schools and Community Support Programmes, Phase II, 1998–2001*. Paris, France: UNESCO.

CHAPTER 4

Ainscow, M. (1994). *Special needs in the classroom: A teacher education guide*. London, UK: Jessica Kingsley/UNESCO.

Ainscow, M. (1999). *Understanding the development of inclusive schools*. London, UK: Routledge.

Ainscow, M. (2005). Developing inclusive education systems: What are the levers for change? *Journal of Educational Change*, 6, 109–124.

Ainscow, M. (2006). From special education to effective schools for all: A review of progress so far. In L. Florian (Ed.) *The Sage handbook of special education* (pp. 146–159). London, UK: Sage.

Ainscow, M. (2008). Teaching for diversity. In M. Connelly, M.F. He, and J. Phillion (Eds.), *The Sage handbook of curriculum and instruction* (pp. 240–259). London, UK: Sage.

Ainscow, M. (2010). Achieving excellence and equity: Reflections on the development of practices in one local district over 10 years. *School Effectiveness and School Improvement*, 21 (1), 75–91.

Ainscow, M. (2012). Moving knowledge around: Strategies for fostering equity within educational systems. *Journal of Educational Change*, 13(3), 289–310.

Ainscow, M. (2013). Developing more equitable education systems: Reflections on a three-year improvement initiative. In V. Farnsworth and Y. Solomon (Eds.), *What works in education? Bridging theory and practice in research* (pp. 77–89). London, UK: Routledge.

Ainscow, M., Booth, T., and Dyson, A. (2004). Understanding and developing inclusive practices in schools: A collaborative action research network. *International Journal of Inclusive Education*, 8(2), 125–139.

Ainscow, M., Booth, T., and Dyson, A. (2006). Inclusion and the standards agenda: Negotiating policy pressures in England. *International Journal of Inclusive Education*, 10(4–5), 295–308.

Ainscow, M., Booth, T., and Dyson, A., with Farrell, P., Frankham, J., Gallanaugh, F., Howes, A., and Smith, R. (2006). *Improving schools, developing inclusion*. London, UK: Routledge.

Ainscow, M., Dyson, A., Goldrick, S., and West, M. (2012a). *Developing equitable education systems*. London. UK: Routledge.

Ainscow, M., Dyson, A., Goldrick, S., and West, M. (2012b). Making schools effective for all: Rethinking the task. *School Leadership and Management*, 32(3), 1–17.

Ainscow, M., and Howes, A. (2007). Working together to improve urban secondary schools: A study of practice in one city. *School Leadership and Management*, 27, 285–300.

Ainscow, M., and Kaplan, I. (2005). Using evidence to encourage inclusive school development: Possibilities and challenges. *Australasian Journal of Special Education*, 29(2), 12–21.

Ainscow, M., Muijs, D., and West, M. (2006). Collaboration as a strategy for improving schools in challenging circumstances. *Improving Schools*, 9(3), 192–202.

Ainscow, M., Nicolaidou, M., and West, M. (2003). Supporting schools in difficulties: The role of school-to-school cooperation. *NFER Topic*, 30, 1–4.

Ainscow, M., and West, M. (Eds.) (2006). *Improving urban schools: Leadership and collaboration.* Maidenhead, UK: Open University Press.

Ainscow, M., West, M., and Nicolaidou, M. (2005). Putting our heads together: A study of headteacher collaboration as a strategy for school improvement. In: C. Clarke (Ed.) *Improving schools in difficult circumstances* (pp. 117–136). London, UK: Continuum.

Argyris, C., and Schon, D. (1996). *Organisational Learning II: Theory, method and practice.* Reading, MA: Addison-Wesley.

Ball, S.J. (2010). New class inequalities in education. *International Journal of Sociology and Social Policy*, 30(3/4), 155–166.

Blair, T. (2005). Higher standards: Better schools. Speech on education at 10 Downing Street 24.10.05. (Accessed at http://www.pm.gov.uk/output/Page8363.asp).

Booth, T. (1995). Mapping inclusion and exclusion: concepts for all? In C. Clark, A. Dyson and A. Millward (Eds.) *Towards inclusive schools?* (pp. 96–111). London, UK: Fulton.

Booth, T., and Ainscow, M. (2011). *The index for inclusion*, 3rd ed. Bristol, UK: Centre for Studies on Inclusive Education.

Brighouse, T. (2007). The London Challenge—A personal view. In T. Brighouse and L. Fullick (Eds.), *Education in a global city* (pp. 71–94). London, UK: Institute of Education Bedford Way Papers.

Clark, C., Dyson, A., Millward, A., and Robson, S. (1999). Theories of inclusion, theories of schools: Deconstructing and reconstructing the 'inclusive school.' *British Educational Research Journal*, 25(2), 157–177.

Clarke, P., Ainscow, M., and West, M. (2005). Learning from difference: Some reflections on school improvement projects in three countries. In A. Harris (Ed.), *International developments in school improvement* (n.p.). London, UK: Continuum.

Dyson, A., Gallannaugh, F., and Millward, A. (2003). Making space in the standards agenda: Developing inclusive practices in schools. *European Educational Research Journal*, 2(2), 228–244.

Dyson, A., Kerr, K., Raffo, C., and Wigelsworth, M. (2012). *Developing children's zones for England.* London, UK: Save the Children.

Dyson, A., and Millward, A. (2000). *Schools and special needs: Issues of innovation and inclusion.* London, UK: Paul Chapman.

Giroux, H.A., and Schmidt, M. (2004). Closing the achievement gap: A metaphor for children left behind. *Journal of Educational Change*, 5, 213–228.

Hiebert, J., Gallimore, R., and Stigler, J.W. (2002). A knowledge base for the teaching profession: What would it look like and how can we get one? *Educational Researcher*, 31(5), 3–15.

Howes, A., and Ainscow, M. (2006). Collaboration with a city-wide purpose: Making paths for sustainable educational improvement. In M. Ainscow and M. West (Eds.), *Improving urban schools: Leadership and collaboration* (pp. 104–116). Maidenhead, UK: Open University Press.

Howes, A., Booth, T., Dyson, A., and Frankham, J. (2003). Teacher learning and the development of inclusive practices and policies: Framing and context. *Research Papers in Education*, 20(2), 131–146.

Howes, A., Frankham, J., Ainscow, M., and Farrell, P. (2004). The action in action research: Mediating and developing inclusive intentions. *Educational Action Research*, 12(2), pp. 239–257.

Huberman, M. (1993). The model of the independent artisan in teachers' professional relationships. In J.W. Little and M.W. McLaughlin (Eds.), *Teachers' work: Individuals, colleagues and contexts.* (pp. 11–50). New York: Teachers College Press.

Hutchings, M., Hollingworth, S., Mansaray, A., Rose, R., and Greenwood, C. (2012). *Research report DFE-RR215: Evaluation of the City Challenge programme.* London, UK: Department for Education.

Kenway, J. (2013). Challenging inequality in Australian schools: Gonski and beyond. *Discourse: Studies in the Cultural Politics of Education* accessed at (http://dx.doi.org/10.1080/01596306.2013.770254).

Lo, M.L., Yan, P.W., and Pakey, C.P.M. (2005) (Eds.). *For each and everyone: Catering for individual differences through learning studies.* Hong Kong, China: Hong Kong University Press.

Messiou, K., Ainscow, M. et al. (in press). Learning from differences: A strategy for teacher development in respect to student diversity. *School Effectiveness and School Improvement.*

Miles, S., and Ainscow, M. (2011). *Responding to diversity in schools.* London, UK: Routledge.

Muijs, D., Ainscow, M., Chapman, C., and West, M. (2011). *Collaboration and networking in education.* London, UK: Springer.

Muijs, D., West, M., and Ainscow, M. (2010). Why network? Theoretical perspectives on networking. *School Effectiveness and School Improvement,* 21(1), 5–26.

Mulford, B. (2007). Building social capital in professional learning communities: Importance, challenges and a way forward. In L. Stoll and L.K. Seashore (Eds.), *Professional learning communities: Divergence, depth and dilemmas* (pp. 166–180). London, UK: Open University Press.

OECD (2007). *No more failures: Ten steps to equity in education.* Paris, France: OECD.

Riehl, C.J. (2000). The principal's role in creating inclusive schools for diverse students: A review of normative, empirical, and critical literature on the practice of educational administration. *Review of Educational Research,* 70(1), 55–81.

Stigler, J., and Hiebert, J. (1999). *The teaching gap: Best ideas from the world's teachers for improving education in the classroom.* New York: Free Press.

Talbert, J.E., Mileva, L., Chen, P., Cor, K., and McLaughlin, M. (2010). *Developing school capacity for inquiry-based improvement: Progress, challenges, and resources.* Stanford, CA: Stanford University, Center for Research on the Context of Teaching.

UNESCO (2009). *Guidelines for inclusion: Ensuring access to education for all.* Paris, France: UNESCO.

CHAPTER 6

Dalen, M., and Wormnæs, S. (2003). The relationship between disability, gender and education in the Norwegian context. Background paper commissioned for *The Education for All Global Monitoring Report 2003/4 Gender and Education for All: The Leap to Equality.* Retrieved from http://databank.worldbank.org/data/home.aspx.

Hawley, T.S., Crowe, A.R., and Brooks, E.W. (2012). Where do we go from here? Making sense of prospective social studies teachers' memories, conceptions, and visions of social studies teaching and learning. *Teacher Education Quarterly,* 39(3), 63–83.

International Disability Rights Monitor (IDRM) (2004). *Regional report of the Americas. IDRM,* Washington D.C.: Center for International Rehabilitation.

Lortie, D.C., (1975). *Schoolteacher: A sociological study.* Chicago: The University of Chicago Press.

Mewborn, D.S. and Tyminski, A.M. (2006). Lortie's apprenticeship of observation revisited. *For the Learning of Mathematics,* 26(3), 30–33.

Mindes, J. (2001). UNESCO Director General establishes Flagship on "Education for All and Disabilities." *Disability World*, 10(September–October), http://disabilityworld.org/09–10_01/news/flagship.shtml.

Ojok, P. and Wormnæs, S. (2012). Inclusion of pupils with intellectual disabilities: Primary school teachers' attitudes and willingness in a rural area in Uganda. *International Journal of Inclusive Education*, 17(9), 1003–1021.

UNESCO (1990). *World declaration on education for all and framework for action to meet basic learning needs. Jomtien, Thailand.* Paris, France: UNESCO.

UNESCO (1994). *The Salamanca Statement and framework for action on special needs education.* Paris, France: UNESCO.

UNESCO (2000). *The Dakar framework for action: Education for all—meeting our collective commitments. World Education Forum, Dakar, Senegal.* Paris, France: UNESCO.

UNESCO (2002). EFA Global Monitoring Report 2002. *Is the world on track?* Paris, France: UNESCO.

UNESCO (2003a). EFA Global Monitoring Report 2003/4: *Gender and education for all—the leap to equality*. Paris, France: UNESCO.

UNESCO (2003b). *Overcoming exclusion through inclusive approaches in education: A challenge and a vision*. Paris, France: UNESCO.

UNESCO (2004a). *EFA Flagship initiatives. Multi-partner collaboration mechanisms in support of EFA goals.* Paris, France: UNESCO.

UNESCO (2004b). Conceptual paper. *The right to education for persons with disabilities: Toward inclusion. An EFA Flagship*. Paris, France: UNESCO.

UNESCO (2005). EFA Global Monitoring Report 2005. Education for All global monitoring report. *Education for all. The quality imperative*. Paris, France: UNESCO.

UNESCO (2013). *UNESCO education. Policy and planning*. Retrieved from http://www.unesco.org/new/en/education/themes/planning-and-managing-education/policy-and-planning/.

WHO (2001). *ICF—International classification of functioning, disability and health*. Geneva, Switzerland: WHO.

Wormnæs, S. (2004). *Quality of education for persons with disabilities*. Background paper commissioned for EFA Global Monitoring Report 2005.

Wormnæs, S., and Olsen, M. (2009). Mothers' hearts speaking: Education enlightens, empowers and protects girls with disabilities. *International Journal of Special Education*, 24(1), 64–74.

CHAPTER 7

Acedo, C., Ferrer, F., and Pàmies, J. (2009). Inclusive education: Open debates and the road ahead, *Prospects*, 39: 227–238.

Acedo, C., and Opertti, R. (2012). Educación Inclusiva: De focalizar grupos y escuelas a lograr una educación de calidad como el corazón de una Educación para Todos. [Inclusive Education: from targeting groups and schools to providing quality Education for All]. In *La Educación para Todos en América Latina. Estudios sobre las desigualdades y la agenda política en educación* [Education for All in Latin America. Studies on inequalities and the political agenda in education] (pp. 23–44). Buenos Aires: Miño y Dávila, OEI-UNESCO.

Ainscow, M. (2005). Developing inclusive education systems: What are the levers for change? *Journal of Educational Change*, 6, 109–124.

Ainscow, M. (2010). Achieving excellence and equity: Reflections on the development of practices in one local district over 10 years. *School Effectiveness and School Improvement*, 21(1), 75–92.

Ainscow, M. (2012). Moving knowledge around: Strategies for fostering equity within educational systems. *Journal of Educational Change*, 13, 289–310.

Ainscow, M., and César, M. (2006). Inclusive education ten years after Salamanca: Setting the agenda. *European Journal of Psychology of Education*, XXI (3), 231–238.

Ainscow, M., Dyson, A., Goldrick, S., and West, M. (2012). Making schools effective for all: Rethinking the task. *School Leadership and Management*, 32(3), 1–17.

Ainscow, M., and Miles, S. (2008). Making Education for All inclusive: Where next? *Prospects*, 38, 15–34.

Ainscow, M., and Sandill, A. (2010). Developing inclusive education systems: The role of organisational cultures and leadership. *International Journal of Inclusive Education*, 14(4), 401–416.

Asian Development Bank (ADB). (2010). *Strengthening inclusive education*. Mandaluyong City, Philippines: Asian Development Bank.

Booth, T. (2011). The name of the rose: Inclusive values into action in teacher education. *Prospects*, 41, 303–318.

Booth, T., and Ainscow, M. (2002). *Index for inclusion: Developing learning and participation in schools*. Bristol, UK: Centre for Studies on Inclusive Education.

Curcic, S., Gabel, S.L., Zeitlin, V., Cribaro-DiFatta, S., and Glarner, C. (2011). Policy and challenges of building schools as inclusive communities. *International Journal of Inclusive Education*, 15(1), 117–133.

Florian, L., and Black-Hawkins, K. (2011). Exploring inclusive pedagogy. *British Journal of Educational Research*, 37(5), 813–828.

Florian, L., Young, K., and Rouse, K. (2010). Preparing teachers for inclusive and diverse educational environments: Studying curricular reform in an initial teacher education course. *International Journal of Inclusive Education*, 14(7), 709–722.

Jakobi, A.P. (2012). Facilitating transfer. International organisations as central nodes for policy diffusion. In G. Steiner-Khamsi and F. Waldow (Eds.), *Policy borrowing and lending in education* (pp. 391–407). London and New York: Routledge.

Kamp, A., and Mansouri, F. (2010). Constructing inclusive education in a neo-liberal context: Promoting inclusion of Arab-Australian students in an Australian context. *British Educational Research Journal*, 36(5), 733–744.

Klugman, B. (2011). Effective social justice advocacy: A theory-of-change framework for assessing progress. *Reproductive Health Matters*, 19(38), 146–162.

Lalvani, P. (2013). Privilege, compromise, or social justice: Teachers' conceptualizations of inclusive education. *Disability and Society*, 28(1), 14–27.

Ligero, J.A. (2011). Dos métodos de evaluación: Criterios y teoría del programa [Two methods of evaluation: Criteria and theories of change]. *Documentos de trabajo. Serie CECOD [Working Papers. CECOD Series]*, 15, 1–30.

Marchesi, A. (2009). Las metas educativas 2021. Un proyecto iberoamericano para transformar la educación en la década de los bicentenarios [An Ibero-American project for transforming education in the decade of the bicentenaries]. *Revista CTS [CTS Review]*, 12(4), 87–157.

Mayne, J. (2008). Contribution analysis: An approach to exploring cause and effect. *ILAC Brief*, 16, 1–20.

Mullick, J. (2013). Development of the distributed leadership practice for inclusive education (DLPIE) scale. *Asian Journal of Inclusive Education*, 1(1), 31–46.

Murillo, F.J., and Duk, C. (2010). Editorial. Escuelas inclusivas para la justicia social. [Editorial. Inclusive schools for social Jjustice] *Revista Latinoamericana de educación inclusiva* [Latin American Journal of Inclusive Education], 4(1), 11–13.

OEI (Organización de Estados Iberoamericanos) The organization of Ibero-American States. (2010). *Metas educativas 2021: La educación que queremos para la generación de los bicentenarios. Documento final* [Educational Goals 2021: The education we want for the generation of the bicentenaries]. Madrid, Spain: OEI y CEPAL.

Pawson, R. (2006). *Evidence-based policy. A realist perspective.* London, UK: Sage.

Pawson, R. and Tilley, N. (2004). *Realist evaluation* (Report prepared for the British Cabinet Office [online], http://www.communitymatters.com.au/RE_chapter.pdf, accessed 10 June 2014.

Polat, F. (2011). Inclusion in education: A step towards social justice. *International Journal of Educational Development*, 31, 50–58.

Purdue, K., Gordon-Burns, D., Gunn, A., Madden, B., and Surtees, N. (2009). Supporting inclusion in early childhood settings: Some possibilities and problems for teacher education. *International Journal of Inclusive Education*, 13(8), 805–815.

Rambla, X. (2012). 'Soft power,' educational governance and political consensus in Brazil. *International Studies in Sociology of Education*, 22(3), 191–212.

Rambla, X., Ferrer, F., Tarabini, A., and Verger, A. (2008). Inclusive education and social inequality: An update of the question and some geographical considerations. *Prospects*, 38, 65–76.

Sharma, U., Forlin, C., Deppeler, J., and Guang-Xue, Y. (2013). Reforming teacher education for inclusion in developing countries in the Asia-Pacific region. *Asian Journal of Inclusive Education*, 1(1), 3–16.

Slee, R. (2008). Beyond special and regular schooling? An inclusive education reform agenda. *International Studies in Sociology of Education*, 18(2), 99–116.

Steiner-Khamsi, G. (2004). Blazing a trail for policy theory and practice. In G. Steiner-Khamsi (Ed.), *The global politics of educational borrowing and lending* (pp. 201–220). New York and London: Columbia University, Teachers College Press.

UNESCO. (2009). *Policy guidelines on inclusion in education.* Paris, France: UNESCO.

Verger, A., Novelli, M., and Altinyelken, H.K. (2012). *Global education policy and international development.* London, UK: Bloomsbury.

White, H., and Phillips, D. (2012). Addressing attribution of cause and effect in small n impact evaluations: Towards an integrated framework. *3IE Working Paper*, 15, 1–20.

CHAPTER 8

Ainscow, M. (1999). *Understanding the development of inclusive schools.* London: Falmer.

Ainscow, M. and Sandill, A. (2010): Developing inclusive education systems: The role of organisational cultures and leadership, *International Journal of Inclusive Education*, 14(4), 401–416.

Allan, J. (2008) *Rethinking inclusive education—The philosophers of difference in practice.* Dordrecht, The Netherlands: Springer.

Armstrong, D., Armstrong, A. and Spandagou, I. (2011). Inclusion: By choice or by chance? *International Journal of Inclusive Education*, 15(1), 29–39.

Beach, D. and Sernhede, O. (2011). From learning to labour to learning for marginality: School segregation and marginalization in Swedish suburbs. *British Journal of Sociology of Education*, 32(2), 257–274.

Booth, T. (2011). The name of the rose: Inclusive values into action in teacher education, *Prospects*, 41(3), 303–318.

CREDO (Center for Research on Education Outcomes) (2009). *Multiple Choice: Charter School Performance in 16 States*. Palo Alto, CA: CREDO, Stanford University.

CREDO (2013). *National charter school study*. Palo Alto, CA: CREDO, Stanford University.

Department for Children, Schools and Families (DCSF) (2009) Schools, Pupils and Their Characteristics: January 2009, Statistical First Release (provisional) [online], http://webarchive.nationalarchives.gov.uk/20130401151655/http://www.education.gov.uk/researchandstatistics/statistics/allstatistics/a00196015/schools-pupils-and-their-characteristics, accessed 10 June 2014.

Department for Education (DfE) (2011a). Statistical first release: Special educational needs in England, January 2011 [online], https://www.gov.uk/government/publications/special-educational-needs-in-england-january-2011, accessed June 10 2014.

Department for Education (DfE) (2011b). *Support and aspiration: A new approach to special educational needs and disability*. London, UK: Department for Education.

Department for Education and Employment (DfEE) (1998) *Statistical Bulletin Number 9/98 Special Educational Needs in England: January 1998*, London, UK: The Stationery Office.

Dyson, A. and Gallanaugh, F. (2007). National policy and the development of inclusive school practices: A case study. *Cambridge Journal of Education*, 37(4), 473–488.

Florian, L. and Black-Hawkins, K. (2011). Exploring inclusive pedagogy. *British Educational Research Journal*, 37(5), 813–828.

Galvin, R. (2003). The paradox of disability culture: The need to combine versus the imperative to let go. *Disability and Society*, 18(5), 675–690.

Hart, S. (2010). Learning without limits. In J. Rix, M. Nind, K. Sheehy, K. Simmons, J. Parry, and R. Kumrai (Eds.), *Equality, participation and inclusion 2: Diverse contexts* (pp. 253–267). Oxon: Routledge.

Kiuppis, F. (2014). Why (not) associate the principle of inclusion with disability? Tracing connections from the start of the 'Salamanca Process.' *International Journal of Inclusive Education*, 18(7), 746–761.

Kivirauma, J. and Kivinen, O. (1998). The school system and special education: Causes and effects in the twentieth century. *Disability, Handicap and Society*, 3(2), 153–165.

Laluvein, J. (2010). School inclusion and the 'community of practice.' *International Journal of Inclusive Education*, 14(1), 35–48.

McLeskey, J., and Waldron, N.L. (2011). Learning disabilities practice educational programs for elementary students with learning disabilities: Can they be both effective and inclusive ? *Exceptional Children*, 26(1), 48–57.

Miles, S., and Singal, N. (2010). The Education for All and inclusive education debate: Conflict, contradiction or opportunity? *International Journal of Inclusive Education*, 14(1), 1–15.

Naraian, S. (2011). Seeking transparency: The production of an inclusive classroom community. *International Journal of Inclusive Education*, 15(9), 955–973.

Northern Ireland Statistics and Research Agency (2012). Enrolments at grant-aided schools 2012/13 [online] http://www.deni.gov.uk/enrolments_at_grant-aided_primary_and_post-primary_schools_2012_13_-_basic_statistics_-_final_version.pdf (accessed 10 June 2014).

Parry, J., Rix, J., Sheehy, K., and Simmons, K. (2013). The journey travelled: A view of two settings a decade apart. *British Journal of Educational Studies* (online) http://www.tandfonline.com/doi/full/10.1080/00071005.2013.819411.

Peters, S.J. (2007). Education for all: A historical analysis of international inclusive education policy and individuals with disabilities. *Journal of Disability Policy Studies*, 18(2), 98–108.

Richardson, J., and Powell, J.W. (2011). *Comparing special education: Origins to contemporary paradoxes*. Stanford, CA: Stanford University Press.

Rix, J. and Sheehy, K. (2013). Nothing special—The everyday pedagogy of teaching. In L. Florian (Ed.), *The Sage handbook of special education* (2nd ed.). London, UK: Sage.

Rix, J., Sheehy, K., Fletcher-Campbell, F., Crisp, M., and Harper, A. (2013). *Continuum of education provision for children with special educational needs: Review of international policies and practices* (Volumes 1 and 2). Trim, UK: National Council for Special Education.

Rustemier, S. (2002). *Social and educational justice—the human rights framework for inclusion*. Bristol, UK: Centre for Studies on Inclusive Education.

Scull, B.J., and Winkler, A.M. (2011). *Shifting trends in special education*. Ohio: The Thomas B. Fordham Institute.

Slee, R. (2008). Beyond special and regular schooling? An inclusive education reform agenda. *International Studies in Sociology of Education*, 18(2), 99–116.

The Scottish Government (2012a). *Pupil Census 2012 supplementary data* [online], http://www.scotland.gov.uk/Topics/Statistics/Browse/School-Education/dspupcensus/pupcensus2012 (Accessed 10 June 2014).

The Scottish Government (2012b). *Pupils—Pupil numbers* [online] http://www.scotland.gov.uk/Topics/Statistics/Browse/School-Education/TrendPupilNumbers (Accessed 10 June 2014)

Tomlinson, S. (2012). The irresistible rise of the SEN industry. *Oxford Review of Education*, 38(3), 267–286.

UNESCO (1994). *The Salamanca Statement and framework for action on special needs education*. Paris: UNESCO.

Utdanningsdirektoratet (2008). *Equity in education for all—Understanding Central Concepts*, (accessed at http://www.udir.no/Stottemeny/English/Equity-in-Education-for-all-understanding-central-concepts/). 10 June 2012.

Veck, W. (2009). From an exclusionary to an inclusive understanding of educational difficulties and educational space: Implications for the Learning Support Assistant's role. *Oxford Review of Education*, 35(1), 41–56.

Waitoller, F.R. and Kozleski, E. B.(2015) No Stone Left Unturned: Exploring the Convergence of New Capitalism in Inclusive Education in the U.S. *Education Policy Analysis Archives, 23* (18).

Welsh Government (2012). *Pupils with Statements of Special Educational Needs: January 2012* [online], http://wales.gov.uk/statistics-and-research/pupils-statements-special-educational-needs/?lang=en, accessed 10 June 2014).

CHAPTER 9

Act on the Amendment of the Basic Education Act 642/2010 (2010). Helsinki: Government Printing Office.

Bachman, K. and Haug, P. (2006). *Forskning om tilpassa opplæring* [Research on adapted education]. Volda: Høgskulen i Volda.

Biesta, G. (2004). Against learning. Reclaiming a language for education in an age of learning. *Nordisk Pedagogikk*, 24(1), 70–82.

Biesta, G. (2010). *Good education in an age of measurement. Ethics, politics, democracy*. London: Pluto Press.

Danforth, S. (2009). *The incomplete child: An intellectual history of learning disabilities*. New York: Peter Lang.

Gallagher D.J., Heshusius L., Iano, R.P., and Skrtic, T.M. (2004). *Challenging orthodoxy in special education: Dissenting voices*. Denver: Love Publishing.

Graham. L.J., and Jahnukainen, M. (2011). Wherefore art thou, inclusion? Analysing the development of inclusive education in New South Wales, Alberta and Finland. *Journal of Education Policy*, 26 (2), 261–286.

GSI (2014). https://gsi.udir.no, accessed 20 September 2014.

Haug P. (2003a). Har spesialundervisninga ein plass i skulen for alle? [Can we have special teaching in a school for all?] *Nordisk tidsskrift for spesialpedagogikk*, 2, 86–94.

Haug, P. (2003b). Qualifying teachers for the school for all. In K. Nes, M. Strømstad, and T. Booth (Eds.). *Developing inclusive teacher education*. New York: Routledge.

Hausstätter, R.S. (2011). *The traditionalism-inclusionism controversy in special education: A conceptual analysis* Research Report University of Helsinki. PhD thesis.

Hausstätter, R.S. (2013). In support of unfinished inclusion. *Scandinavian Journal of Educational Research* (6 March 2013), 1–11.

Hausstätter, R.S. and Takala, M. (2011). Can special education make a difference? Exploring the differences of special educational systems between Finland and Norway in relation to the PISA results. *Scandinavian Journal of Disability Research*, 13(4) 271–281.

Hernes, G. (1974). Om ulikhetens reproduksjon. Hvilken rolle spiller skolen? [On the reproduction of difference: What is the role of the school?] In Mortensen, M.S. (Ed.), *I forskningens lys* (pp. 147–170). Oslo: NAVF.

Itkonen, T., and Jahnukainen, M. (2010). Disability or learning difficulty? Politicians or educators? Constructing special education in Finland and the United States. *Comparative Sociology*, 9(2), 182–201.

Jahnukainen, M. (2011). Different strategies, different outcomes? The history and trends of the inclusive and special education in Alberta (Canada) and in Finland. *Scandinavian Journal of Educational Research*, 55(5), 489–502.

Jahnukainen, M., Pösö, T., Kivirauma, J. and Heinonen, H. (2012). Erityisopetuksen ja lastensuojelun kehitys ja nykytila [The current state and development of the special education and child welfare]. In M. Jahnukainen (Ed.) *Lasten erityishuolto ja -opetus Suomessa* [Children's special care and special education in Finland]. 13. Ed. The Central League of Child Welfare. Tampere: Vastapaino, 15–54.

Jauhiainen, A., Kivirauma J. (1997). Disabling school? Professionalisation of special education and student welfare in the Finnish compulsory school. *Disability and Society*, 12(4), 623–641.

Kirjavainen, T., Pulkkinen, J. and Jahnukainen, M. (2014). Perusopetuksen erityisopetusjärjestelyt eri ikäryhmissä vuosina 2001–2010 [Special education arrangements in basic education for different age cohorts in years 2001–2010]. *Kasvatus – The Finnish Journal of Education*, 45(2), 152–166.

Kirkebæk, B. (1993). *Da de åndssvage blev farlige* [When the mentally disabled became dangerous]. Holte: Socpol.

Kiuppis, F. (2011). Mer enn én vei til framtiden: Om ulike tolkninger av inkluderende opplæring. [More than one way to the future: On different interpretations of inclusive education]. *Norsk Pedagogisk Tidsskrift*, 2, 91–100.

Kivirauma, J. (2002). Erityisopetuksen historialliset kehityslinjat Suomessa [The historical development of special education in Finland]. In M. Jahnukainen (Ed.), *Lasten erityishuolto ja -opetus Suomessa* [Childrens' special care and special education in Finland] (pp. 23–33). Helsinki: Central Union for Child Welfare.

Kivirauma J. and Ruoho, K. (2007). Excellence through special education? Lessons from the Finnish School Reform. *Review of Education*, 53(3), 283–302.

Nordahl, T. and Hausstätter, R.S. (2009). *Spesialundervisningens forutsetninger, innsatser og resultater. Situasjonen til elever med særlige behov under Kunnskapsløftet* [The role of special education under the Knowledge Promotion Reform]. Høgskolen i Hedmark: Utdanningsdirektoratet.

OECD 2011. *Strong performers and successful reformers in education*. Lessons from PISA for the United States. OECD Publishing, http://dx.doi.org/10.1787/9789264096660-en, accessed 10 June 2014.

Official Statistics of Finland (OSF) (2010a). *Special education* [e-publication]. Appendix Table 1. Comprehensive school pupils transferred to special education in 1995–2010. Helsinki: Statistics Finland [referred: 4.6.2014]. Access method: http://www.stat.fi/til/erop/2010/erop_2010_2011–06–09_tau_001_en.html, 4 June 2014.

Official Statistics of Finland (OSF) (2010b). *Special education* [e-publication]. Appendix Table 5. Comprehensive school pupils receiving part-time special education in the academic year 2009–2010 by primary reason for special education. Helsinki: Statistics Finland [referred: 4.6.2014]. Access method: http://www.stat.fi/til/erop/2010/erop_2010_2011–06–09_tau_005_en.html.

Powell, J.J.W. (2011). *Barriers to inclusion. Special Education in the United States and Germany*. Boulder, CO: Paradigm.

Richardson J.G. and Powell, J.J.W. (2011). *Comparing special education. Origins to contemporary paradoxes*. Stanford: Stanford University Press.

Rytivaara, A., Pulkkinen, J. and Takala, M. (2012). Erityisopettajan työ: opettamista yksin ja yhdessä [The work of a special teacher: Teaching alone and together]. In M. Jahnukainen (Ed.) *Lasten erityishuolto ja—opetus Suomessa* [The special care and education in Finland], 13th ed. (pp. 333–352). Tampere: Vastapaino.

Sabel, C., Saxenian, A., Miettinen, R., Kristensen, P.H. and Hautamäki, J. (2011). *Individualized service provision in the new welfare state: Lessons from special education in Finland.*_Sitra Studies 62. Helsinki: Sitra.

Sebba, J. and Ainscow, M. (1996). International developments in inclusive schooling: Mapping the issues. *Cambridge Journal of Education*, 26(1), 5–18.

Simons, M. and Masschelein, J. (2005). Inclusive education for exclusive pupils: A critical analysis of the government of the exceptional. In: S. Tremain (ed.) *Foucault and the government of disability*. Ann Arbor: University of Michigan Press, 208–228.

Takala, M. and Hausstätter, R.S. (2012), Effects of history and culture on attitudes toward special education: A comparison of Finland and Norway. *ISRN Education*. Article ID 161039.

Tetler, S. (2000). *Den inluderende skole-fra vision til virkelighed* [The inclusive school. From utopian idea to reality]. Copenhagen: Gyldendal.

Thuen, H. (2013). Kjærligheten til en fremmed. Spesialpedagogikkens utspring [Love to a stranger: The start of special education]. In S. Dobson and J. Steinnes (Eds.), *Pedagogikkens pentagon. Festskrift for Øivind Haaland*. Trondheim: Akademika forlag.

Tøssebro, J. (2010). *Hva er funksjonshemming* [What is disability?]. Oslo: Universitetsforlaget.

Tuunainen, K. (1994). Country briefing: Special education in Finland. *European Journal of Special Needs Education, 9*, 189–198.

Vislie, L. (1995). Integration policies, school reforms and the organisation of schooling for handicapped pupils in Western societies. In: C. Clark, A. Dyson and A. Milward (Eds.), *Towards inclusive schools?* London: David Fulton, 42–53.

Vislie, L. (2003). From integration to inclusion: Focusing on global trends and changes in the western European societies. *European Journal of Special Needs Education*, 18(1), 17–35.

CHAPTER 10

Allan, J. (2012). The sociology of disability and the struggle for inclusive education. In M. Arnot (Ed.), *The sociology of disability and inclusive education. A tribute to Len Barton*, (pp. 75–91). Abingdon, Oxon: Routledge.

Armstrong, D., Armstrong, A.C., and Spandagou, I. (2011). Inclusion: By Choice or by Chance? *International Journal of Inclusive Education*, 15(1), 29–39.

Axelsdóttir, K. (2012). Aðeins orð á blaði? Um sýn reykvískra grunnskólakennara á menntastefnuna skóli margbreytileikans [Only words on paper? On the vision of Reykjavik compulsory school teachers with regard to the educational policy of the school of diversity]. M.Ed. thesis, University of Iceland.

Bjarnason, D.S. (1995). Frá samskipan og blöndun til lifandi menningarsamfélags [From mainstreaming and integration towards a fully inclusive learning society]. *Glæður, tímarit um uppeldis- og skólamál*, 5(1), 41–56.

Bjarnason, D.S. (1996). Iceland: from institutions to normalisation? Changes in policy and practice of Icelandic welfare services for the intellectually disabled 1960–1995. In J. Tössebro, A. Gustavsson and G. Dyrendahl (Eds.), *Intellectual disabilities in the Nordic Welfare States. Policies and everyday life* (pp. 91–105). Oslo: HöyskoleForlaget.

Bjarnason, D.S. (2004). *New voices from Iceland: Disability and young adulthood.* New York: Nova Science Publishers.

Bjarnason, D.S. (2010). Gjenom labyrinten: Hva er (special) pedagogikk I et includerende miljö? [Through the maze: What is (special) education in inclusive settings?]. In S. Reindahl and R.S. Hausstatter (Eds.), *Spesialpedagogikk og etikk: Kollective ansvar og individuelle rettigheder* [Special education and ethics: Collective responsibility and individual rights]. Lillehammer, Norway: Höjskoleforlaget.

Björnsson, K. (1991). *Sálfræðiþjónusta skóla: þáttur hagnýtrar sálfræði.* Reykjavík: Iceland University Press in collaboration with Reykjavík Education Office.

D.E.S. (1978). *Special educational needs (The Warnock report).* London: Department of Education and Science (DES).

Ferguson, D.L. (1995). The real challenge of inclusion. Confessions of a "rabid inclusionist." *Phi Delta Kappan*, 77, 43–49.

Ferguson D.L. (2006). International trends in inclusive education: The continuing challenge to teach each one and everyone. *European Journal of Special Needs Education*, 23(2), 109–120.

Fræðslumiðstöð Reykjavíkur [Reykjavík Education Office]. (2000). *Stefna í málefnum barna með íslensku sem annað tungumál í grunnskólum Reykjavíkur* [Policy on the teaching of children with Icelandic as second language]. Accessed 10 June 2014, http://www.grunnskolar.is/fraedslumidstodin.

Fréttablaðið. (2014). *Verkefni kennara orðin of mörg* [Teachers' tasks too numerous]. Feb. 15th 2014. http://www.visir.is/menntun,-rettlaeti-og-starf-kennarans

Garðarsdóttir, Ó. (2008). Félagskerfi skólans [The school's social order]. In L. Guttormsson (Ed.), Almenningsfræðsla á Íslandi 1880–2007. Skólahald í bæ og sveit [bls. 247–262] [Public education in Iceland 1880–2007. Vol I: Schooling in town and country] [pp. 247–262]. Reykjavík: University of Iceland Press.

Gunnþórsdóttir, H. (in press). The teacher in an inclusive school: Influences on the ideas of Icelandic and Dutch compulsory school teachers. In B. Boufoy-Bastich (Ed.) *International cultures of educational inclusion.* Strasbourg: Analytrics.

Gunnþórsdóttir, H. and Bjarnason, D.S. (2014). Conflicts in teachers' professional practices and perspectives about inclusion in Icelandic compulsory schools. *European Journal of Special Needs Education*. DOI: 10.1080/08856257.2014.933543

Guttormsson, L. (Ed.) (2008). *Almenningsfræðsla á Íslandi 1880–2007. Skólahald í bæ og sveit* [Public education in Iceland 1880–2007. Vol I: Schooling in town and country]. Reykjavík: University of Iceland Press.

Jóhannesson, I.Á. (2006). Strong, independent, able to learn more: Inclusion and the construction of school students in Iceland as diagnosable subjects. *Discourse*, 27(1), 103–119.

Jónasson, J.T. (2008a). Grunnskóli verður til [Compulsory school in the making]. In L. Guttormsson (Ed.), *Almenningsfræðsla á Íslandi 1880–2007. Síðara bindi: Skóli fyrir alla 1946–2007* (bls. 102–117) [Public education in Iceland 1880–2007, Vol. II, School for all 1947–2007 (pp. 102–117)]. Reykjavík: Iceland University Press.

Jónasson, J.T. (2008b). Skóli fyrir alla? [School for all?]. In L. Guttormsson (Ed.). *Almenningsfræðsla á Íslandi 1880–2007. Síðara bindi: Skóli fyrir alla 1946–2007* (bls. 272–291) [Public education in Iceland 1880–2007, Vol. II, School for all 1947–2007 (pp. 272–291)]. Reykjavík: Iceland University Press.

Kiuppis, F. (2011). Mer enn én vei til framtiden: Om ulike tolkninger av inkluderende Opplæring [More than one way to the future: On different interpretations of inclusive education]. *Norsk Pedagogisk Tidsskrift*, 2, 91–100.

Kozleski, E.B., Artiles, A.J., and Waitoller, F.R. (2011). Introduction: Equity in inclusive education. Historical trajectories and theoretical commitments. In A.J. Artiles, E.B. Kozleski and F.R. Waitoller (Eds.), *Inclusive education. Examining equity on five continents* (pp. 1–14). Cambridge, MA: Harvard Education Press.

Lög um aðstoð við þroskahefta, nr. 47 (1979). [Law on support for the intellectually disabled no.47/1979]. Reykjavík: Ministry of Social Affairs.

Lög um fræðslu barna, nr. 34 (1946). [Education Act nr. 34/1946]. Reykjavík: Ministry of Education.

Lög um fræðslu barna, nr. 59 (1907). [Education Act nr. 59/1907]. Reykjavík: Ministry of Education.

Lög um framhaldsskóla, nr. 92 (2008). [Education Act. Upper secondary schools]. Reykjavík: Ministry of Education, Science and Culture.

Lög um grunnskóla, nr. 64 (1974). [Education Act. Compulsory schools]. Reykjavík: Ministry of Education.

Lög um grunnskóla, nr. 66 (1995). [Education Act. Compulsory schools]. (1995). Reykjavík: Ministry of Education.

Lög um grunnskóla, nr. 91 (2008). [Education Act. Compulsory schools]. Reykjavík: Ministry of Education, Science and Culture.

Lög um leikskóla, nr. 90 (2008). [Education Act. Pre schools]. Reykjavík: Ministry of Education, Science and Culture.

Lög um málefni fatlaðra, nr. 59 (1992). [Law on the affairs of people with disabilities]. Reykjavík: Ministry of Social Affairs.

Margeirsdóttir, M. (2001). *Fötlun og samfélag. Um þróun í málefnum fatlaðra* [Disability and society. On the development of the affairs of people with disabilities]. Reykjavík: Iceland University Press.

Marinósson, G.L. (1979). School Psychological Service in Iceland. In: C. D. Catterell: *Psychology in the schools in international perspective*. Columbus, OH: Catterell.

Marinósson, G.L. (Ed.). (2007). *Tálmar og tækifæri. Menntun nemenda með þroskahömlun á Íslandi* [Obstacles and opportunities. The education of students with intellectual disability in Iceland]. Reykjavík: Iceland University Press.

Marinósson, G.L. (2011). *Responding to diversity at school. An ethnographic study.* Saarbrücken, Deutschland: LAP Lambert Academic Publishing.

Marinósson, G.L. and Bjarnason, D.S. (2007). Making sense of the educational contexts of students with intellectual disability in Icelandic mainstream schools. Paper presented at the European Conference on Educational Research, Ghent, Belgium.

Marinósson, G.L. and Bjarnason, D.S. (2011). Þróun náms í sérkennslufræðum við H.Í. [The development of post-graduate programmes in special needs education at the University of Iceland]. *Glæður*, 21(1), 34–40.

Matthiasdóttir, R.K., Björnsdóttir, A. and Bjarnason, D.S. (2013). Skóli án aðgreiningar. Viðhorf sérkennara í grunnskólum til stefnunnar skóli án aðgreiningar [Inclusive education. The perspectives of special educators on the policy and practice]. *Glæður*, spring: 58–68.

Mýrdal, S., Jóhannesson, I.Á., Geirsdóttir, G., and Finnbogason, G.E. (2001). Icelandic educators interviewed about governance and integration/exclusion. In S. Lindblad and T.S. Popkewitz (Eds.), *Listening to education actors on governance and social integration and exclusion* (pp. 207–238). Uppsala Reports on Education 37. Uppsala, Sweden: Uppsala University [EGSIE Work Package 4].

Ólafsdóttir, Á.K. (2008). Brotið á fötluðum börnum [The rights of children with disabilities violated]. *Vísir.is.* http://www.visir.is/brotid-a-fotludum-bornum.

Ólafsdóttir, Á.K. (2013). Oddný í Undralandi [Oddný in Wonderland]. *Vísir.is.* http://www.visir.is/oddny-i-undralandi.

Ragnarsdóttir, H. (2008). *Collisions and continuities. Ten immigrant families and their children in Icelandic society and schools.* Saarbrücken, Germany: VDM Verlag Dr. Müller.

Reglugerð um kennslu á fávitastofnunum nr. 199 (1972). [Ordinance on teaching in institutions for imbeciles nr. 199/1972]. Reykjavík: Ministry of Education.

Reglugerð um nemendur með sérþarfir í grunnskóla nr. 585 (2010). [Ordinance on students with special needs in Compulsory Schools nr. 585/2010]. Reykjavík: Ministry of Education, Science and Culture.

Reglugerð um sérkennslu nr. 270 (1977). [Ordinance on special education nr. 270/1977]. Reykjavík: Ministry of Education.

Reykjavíkurborg (2002). *Stefna fræðsluráðs Reykjavíkur um sérkennslu* [The policy of Reykjavík Educational Board on special education]. Accessed 10 June 2014, http://www.reykjavik.is/Portaldata/1/Resources/menntasvid/skjol/stefna_um_serkennslu_lokaskjal.pdf

Reykjavíkurborg (2005). *Sérkennslukönnun í almennum grunnskólum vorið 2005* [Special education in regular compulsory schools in the spring of 2005]. Accessed 10 June 2014, http://www.reykjavik.is/Portaldata/1/Resources/skjol/svid/menntasvid/pdf_skjol/utgafur

Reykjavíkurborg (2007). *Vinnustaðagreining á grunnskólum og fræðslumiðstöð Reykjavíkur.* Unnið af Capacent Gallup [Analysis, by Capacent Gallup, of work conditions in compulsory schools and Reykjavik Education Office]. Reykjavik: Reykjavik City.

Reykjavíkurborg (2012). *Stefna skóla og frístundaráðs Reykjavíkurborgar. Skóli án aðgreiningar og sérstakur stuðningur við nemendur í grunnskólum* [The policy of Reykjavík School and Leisure Board: Inclusive education and special support for students]. Reykjavík: Author.

Richardson, J.G. and Powell, J.J.W. (2011). *Comparing special education. Origins to contemporary paradoxes.* Stanford, CA: Stanford University Press.

Salamanca yfirlýsingin og rammaáætlun um aðferðir vegna nemenda með sérþarfir [The Salamanca declaration and a plan of action for students with special needs]. (1995). Reykjavík: Ministry of Education, Science and Culture.

Sigurðsson, Þ. (1993). *Þættir úr sögu sérkennslunnar* [Strands from the history of special education]. Reykjavík: Þórsútgáfan.

Slee, R. (2011). *The irregular school. Exclusion, schooling and inclusive education.* Oxon: Routledge.

Statistics Iceland [Hagstofan]. (2013). Grunnskólinn. Nemendur sem njóta sérkennslu eða stuðnings [Compulsory schools. Students receiving special education or support] (accessed at, http://www.hagstofa.is/?PageID=2604&src=https://rannsokn.hagstofa.is/, 10 June 2014).

Þjóðviljinn [Will of the nation], daily newspaper (March 23, 1975). Ríkið leigir Kjarvalshús [The state hires Kjarvalshús] (accessed at http://timarit.is).

Thomas, G. and Loxley, A. (2001). *Deconstructing special education and constructing inclusion.* Buckingham, England: Open University Press.

Umbætur og nýskipan í ríkisrekstri [Reform and innovation in state management] (1993). Reykjavík: Ministry of Finance.

UNESCO (1994). *Final report. World Conference on Special Needs Education: Access and Quality.* Salamanca, Spain: UNESCO and the Ministry of Education and Science, Spain.

CHAPTER 11

Ainscow, M., Booth, T., and Dyson, A. (2006). *Improving schools, developing inclusion.* New York: Routledge.

Alliance for Inclusive Education (2014). *Integration is not inclusion* (accessed at, http://www.allfie.org.uk/pages/useful%20info/integration.html, 10 June 2014).

Apple, M.W. (2004). Creating difference: Neo-liberalism, neo-conservatism and the politics of educational reform. *Educational Policy,* 18(1), 12–44.

Artiles, A.J., Harris-Murri, N. and Rostenberg, D. (2006). Inclusion as social justice: Critical notes on discourses, assumptions, and the road ahead. *Theory into Practice*, 45(3), 260–268.

Ballard, K. (Ed.) (1999). *Inclusive education: International voices on disability and justice.* London, UK: Routledge.

Bell, D. (1973). *The coming of post-industrial society: A venture in social forecasting.* New York: Basic Books.

Black-Hawkins, K. and Florian, L. (2012). Classroom teachers' craft knowledge of their inclusive practice. *Teachers and Teaching,* 18(5), 567–584.

Centeno, M.A. (1993). The new Leviathan: The dynamics and limits of technocracy. *Theory and Society*, 22(3), 307–335.

Clarence, E. (2002). Technocracy reinvented: The new evidence-based policy movement. *Public Policy and Administration*, 17(3), 1–11.

Cremin, L. (1961). *The transformation of the school: Progressivism in American education, 1876–1957.* New York: Alfred A. Knopf.

Danforth, S. (in press). Social justice and technocracy: Tracing the narratives of inclusive education in the United States. *Discourse: Studies in the Cultural Politics of Education.*

Dudley-Marling, C. and Baker, D. (2012). The effects of market-based school reforms on students with disabilities. *Disability Studies Quarterly*, 32(2).

Elledge, A., Le Floch, K.C., Taylor, J. and Anderson, L. (2009). *State and local implementation of the "No Child Left Behind Act." Volume V—Implementation of the 1 percent rule and 2 percent interim policy options.* Washington, DC: United States Department of Education.

Fierros, E.G., and Conroy, J.W. (2002). Double jeopardy: An exploration of restrictiveness and race in special education. In D. Losen and G. Orfield (Eds.), *Racial inequity in special education* (pp. 39–70). Cambridge, MA: Civil Rights Project at Harvard University and Harvard Education Press.

Fischer, F. (1990). *Technocracy and the politics of expertise.* Thousand Oaks, CA: Sage.

Fleischer, D.Z. and Zames, F. (2011). *The disability rights movement: From charity to confrontation* (updated edition). Philadelphia, PA: Temple University Press.

Florian, L. (2006). Teaching strategies: For some or all? *Kairaranga*, 7, 24–27.

Florian, L. and Black-Hawkins, K. (2011). Exploring inclusive pedagogy. *British Educational Research Journal,* 37(5), 813–828.

Green, J.L., Camilli, G. and Elmore, P.B. (Eds.) (2006). *Handbook of complementary methods in education research.* Washington, DC: American Educational Research Association; Mahwah, NJ: Erlbaum.

Guba, E. (1990). *The paradigm dialog.* Newbury Park, CA: Sage.

Gunnell, J.G. (1982). The technocratic image and the theory of technocracy. *Technology and Culture,* 23(3), 392–416.

Hardman, M.L. and Dawson, S. (2008). The impact of federal public policy on curriculum and instruction for students with disabilities in the general classroom. *Preventing School Failure*, 52(2), 5–11.

Hehir, T. (2005). *New directions in special education: Eliminating ableism in policy and practice.* Cambridge, MA: Harvard Education Press.

Individuals with Disabilities Education Act Data (2012). Washington, DC: U.S. Department of Education.

Kanigel, R. (1997). *The one best way: Frederick Winslow Taylor and the enigma of efficiency.* New York: Viking.

Kleinert, H., Kearns, J., and Kennedy, S. (1997). Accountability for all students: Kentucky's Alternate Portfolio system for students with moderate and severe cognitive disabilities. *Journal of the Association for Persons with Severe Handicaps*, 22(2), 88–101.

Kimura, A.H. (2010). Between technocracy and democracy: An experimental approach to certification of food products by Japanese consumer cooperative women. *Journal of Rural Studies*, 26, 130–140.

Lipsky, D.K. and Gartner, A. (1996). Inclusion, school restructuring, and the remaking of American society. *Harvard Educational Review*, 66(4), 762–797.

Meynaud, J. (1969). *Technocracy.* New York: Free Press.

Nagle, K., Yunker, C. and Malmgren, K.W. (2006). Students with disabilities and accountability reform: Challenges identified at the state and local levels. *Journal of Disability Policy Studies,* 17(1), 28–39.

Nisbet, J. (2004). Commentary: Caught in the continuum. *Research and Practice for Persons with Severe Handicaps*, 29(4), 231–236.

Osgood, R.L. (2005). *The history of inclusion in the United States.* Washington, DC: Gallaudet University Press.

Pelka, F. (1997). *The ABC-CLIO companion to the disability rights movement.* Santa Barbara, CA: ABC-CLIO.

Phillips, D.C. (1983). After the wake: Postpositivistic educational thought. *Educational Researcher*, 12(5), 4–12.

Phillips, D.C. and Burbules, N.C. (2000). *Postpositivism and educational research.* Lanham, MD: Rowman and Littlefield.

Putnam, R.D. (1977). Elite transformation in advanced industrial societies: An empirical assessment of the theory of technocracy. *Comparative Political Studies*, 10, 383–412.

Ravitch, D. (2010). *The death and life of the great American school system: How testing and choice are undermining education*. New York: Basic Books.

Ridley, F.F. (1966). French technocracy and comparative government. *Political Studies*, 14(1), 34–52.

Sapon-Shevin, M. (1999). *Because we can change the world: A practical guide to building cooperative, inclusive classroom communities*. Boston: Allyn and Bacon.

Scott, H. (1933). *Introduction to technocracy*. New York: John Day.

Shapiro, J.P. (1994). *No pity: People with disabilities forging a new civil rights movement*. New York: Times Books.

Smith, J. and Heshusius, L. (1986). Closing down the conversation: The end of the quantitative-qualitative debate among educational inquirers. *Educational Researcher*, 15(1), 4–12.

Stroman, D. (2003). *The disability rights movement: From deinstitutionalization to self-determination*. Lanham, MD: University Press of America.

Taylor, S.J. (1988). Caught in the continuum: A critical analysis of the principle of the Least Restrictive Environment. *Journal of the Association for Persons with Severe Handicap*, 13(1), 41–53.

U.S. Department of Education (2004). Twenty-Sixth Annual Report to Congress on the Implementation of the Individuals with Disabilities Education Act (p. F–140). Washington, DC: U.S. Department of Education.

Vislie, L. (2003). From integration to inclusion: Focusing global trends and changes in the western European societies. *European Journal of Special Needs Education*, 18(1), 17–35.

Wong, K.K. (2008). Federalism, equity, and accountability in education. In B.S. Cooper, J.G. Cibulka and L.D. Fusarelli (Eds.), *Handbook of education politics and policy* (pp. 19–29). New York: Routledge.

Ysseldyke, J., Dennison, A. and Nelson, R. (2004). *Large-scale assessment and accountability systems: Positive consequences for students with disabilities* (Synthesis Report 51). Minneapolis: University of Minnesota, National Center for Educational Outcomes.

CHAPTER 12

Behr, A.L. (1980). *New perspectives in South African education*. Durban and Pretoria: Butterworths.

Department of Education (2010). *Screening, identification, assessment and support* (SIAS). Pretoria: Government Printer.

Department of Basic Education (2011a). *ANA national assessments 2011: A guideline for the interpretation and use of ANA results*. Cape Town: Government Printer.

Department of Basic Education (2011b). *Action plan to 2014: Towards the realisation of Schooling 2025*. Pretoria: Department of Basic Education.

Department of Basic Education (2012a). *Framework for development of teachers in inclusive education*. Specialisation Area: Visual Impairment. Pretoria: Government Printer.

Department of Basic Education (2012b). *Framework for the development of teachers in inclusive education*. Specialisation Area: Deaf and hard of Hearing. Pretoria: Government Printer.

Department of Basic Education (2012c). *Presentation to standing committee*. Pretoria: South Africa Department of Basic Education.

Department of Education (1997). *Quality education for all. Report of the National Commission for Special Education Needs and Training and National Committee for Education Support Services*. Pretoria: South Africa Department of Education.

Special needs education: Building an inclusive education and training system follow with (Education White Paper 6)

Department of Education (2007). *Guidelines to ensure quality education and support in special schools and special schools as resource centres*. Pretoria: Government Printer.

Department of Education (2008). *National strategy on screening, identification, assessment and support*. Pretoria: Government Printer.

Department of Education and Training (1979). *Handbook for education*. Pretoria: South Africa Department of Education.

Fulcher, G. (1989). *Disabling policies? A comparative approach to education policy and disability*. London: Falmer Press.

Naicker, S.M. (1999). *Curriculum 2005: A space for all: An introduction to inclusive education*. Cape Town: Tafelburg.

Naicker, S.M. (2005). An emerging pedagogy of possibility. In D. Mitchell (Ed.), *Contextualizing inclusive education* (pp. 230–251). London. Routledge.

National Education Policy Investigation (1992). *National education policy investigation: Education support services*. Cape Town: Oxford University Press.

CHAPTER 13

Allan, J. (2008). *Rethinking inclusive education: The philosophers of difference in practice*. Dordrecht, Netherlands: Springer.

Allen, R. (2010). Replicating Swedish '*free school*' reforms in England. Bristol, UK: University of Bristol. http://www.bristol.ac.uk/cmpo/publications/allen10.pdf, accessed 10 June 2014.

Apple, M. (2008). Foreword. In J. Allan and R. Slee (Eds.), *Doing inclusive education research*. Rotterdam, Netherlands: Sense.

Beckett, S. (1993). *Waiting for Godot*, edited by J. Knowlson and D. MacMillan. New York: Grove Press.

Bergh, A. (2011). Why quality in education and what quality? A linguistic analysis of quality in Swedish government texts. *Education Inquiry*, 2(4), 709–723.

Böhlmark, A., and Lindahl, M. (2008). Does school privatization improve educational achievement? Evidence from Sweden's voucher reform (IZA Discussion Paper No. 3691).

Booth, T., and Ainscow, M. (2011). *The index for inclusion: Developing learning and participation in schools*. Bristol, UK: Centre for Studies in Inclusive Education.

Brantlinger, E. (2006). The big glossies: How textbooks structure (special) education. In E. Brantlinger (Ed.), *Who benefits from special education? Remediating (fixing) other people's children* (pp. 45–76). Mahwah, NJ/London: Lawrence Erlbaum Associates.

Buber, M. (1997). *Israel and the world: Essays in a time of crisis*. Syracuse: Syracuse University Press.

CSIE (Centre for Studies in Education) (2005). *News digest* (June) (accessed at, http://inclusion.uwe.ac.uk/csie/june05.htm, 1 May 2007).

Connor, D. (2012). Common confusions with inclusion. In M. Strax, C. Strax, and B. Cooper (Eds.), *Kids in the middle: The micropolitics of special education* (pp. 101–122). Plymouth, UK: Rowman and Littlefield Education.

Council of Europe (2010). *Policies and practices for teaching sociocultural diversity: A framework of teacher competences for engaging with diversity*. Strasbourg, France: Council of Europe.

DfE (2011). *Support and aspiration: A new approach to special educational needs and disability*. London, UK: The Stationery Office.

DfE. (2012). *The Green Paper on special needs and disability.* SN/SP/5917 House of Commons Library <http://www.parliament.uk/briefing-papers/SN05917>, accessed 10 June 2014.

Ferri, B. (2012). Undermining inclusion? A critical reading of response to intervention (RTI). *International Journal of Inclusive Education*, 16(8), 863–880.

Ferri, B., Gallagher, D., and Connor, D. (2011). Pluralizing methodologies in the field of LD: From 'what works' to what matters. *Learning Disability Quarterly*, 34(3), 222–231.

Gallagher, D. (2010). Educational researchers and the making of normal people. In C. Dudley-Marling and A. Gurn (Eds.), *The myth of the normal curve* (pp. 25–38). New York: Peter Lang.

Göransson, K., Nilholm, C., and Karlsson, K. (2011). Inclusive education in Sweden? A critical analysis. *International Journal of Inclusive Education,* 15(5), 541–555.

Gresham, F.M. (2007). Evolution of the response-to-intervention concept: Empirical foundations and recent developments. In S.R. Jimerson, M.K. Burns and A.M. van der Heyden (Eds.), *Handbook of response to intervention: The science and practice of assessment and intervention* (pp. 10–24). New York: Springer.

Haug, P. (2006). Formulation and realization of social justice: The compulsory school for all in Sweden and Norway, *European Journal of Special Needs Education,* 14(3), 231–239.

House of Commons Select Committee on Education and Skills (2006). *Third Report.* http://www.publications.parliament.uk/pa/cm200506/cmselect/cmeduski/478/47807.htm, accessed 10 June 2014.

House of Commons Select Committee on Education and Skills (2011). *Fifth Report.* http://www.publications.parliament.uk/pa/cm200405/cmselect/cmeduski/86/8605.htm#a2, accessed 10 June 2014.

Knowlson, J., and MacMillan, D. (1993). *The theatrical notebooks of Samuel Beckett: Waiting for Godot.* London, UK: Faber and Faber.

Macintyre, A. (1998). Notes from the moral wilderness. In K. Wright (Ed.), *The Macintyre reader.* Cambridge, UK: Polity Press.

Maclure, M. (2005). Clarity bordering on stupidity: Where's the quality in systematic review? *Journal of Education Policy,* 20(4), 393–416.

Nusche, D., Halász, G., Looney, J., Santiago, P., and Shewbridge, C. (2011). *OECD review of evaluation and assessment in education in Sweden.* Paris, France: OECD.

Palast, G. (2009). 'No child's behind left' <http://www.gregpalast.com/no-childs-behind-left-2/>, accessed 10 June 2014.

Paley, A.R. (2007). Key initiative of 'no child' under federal investigation: Officials profited from reading first program. *Washington Post*, A01, April 21. http://www.washingtonpost.com/wp-dyn/content/article/2007/04/20/AR2007042002284.html, accessed 10 June 2014.

Persson, B. (2003). Exclusive and inclusive discourses in special education research in Sweden, *International Journal of Inclusive Education,* 17(3), 271–280.

Persson, B. (2006). *Inclusive education in the Nordic welfare state: Obstacles, dilemmas and opportunities.* Paper presented at the European Conference on Educational Research, Geneva, 11–15 September.

Persson, B. (2012). *Teacher education for inclusion* (Country report for Sweden, accessed at, <http://www.european-agency.org/agency-projects/Teacher-Education-for-Inclusion/country-info/country-information#country-reports>, 10 June 2014).

Persson, E. (2012). Raising achievement through inclusion. *International Journal of Inclusive Education* (accessed at, <http://dx.doi.org/10.1080/13603116.2012.745626>, 10 June 2014).

Pestalozzi, H. (1951). *The education of man: Aphorisms* (translated by H. Norden and R. Norden). New York: Philosophical Library.

Putnam, R. (2007). *E pluribus unum:* Diversity and community in the twenty-first century. The 2006 Johan Skytte Prize Lecture. *Scandinavian Political Studies*, 30(2), 137–174.

P2i. (2012). Analysis of the use and value of the index for inclusion (Booth and Ainscow, 2011) and other instruments to assess and develop inclusive Education Practice in p2i Partner Countries, <www.icevi-europe.org/enletter/issue51–09EASPD3.pdf>, accessed 10 June 2014.

Riedel, M. (1990). Preface. In G.C. Fiumara, *The other side of language: A philosophy of listening.* London, UK: Routledge.

Rousseau, J.-J. (2000) [1762]. *Emile* (translated by B. Foxley). London, UK: Everyman.

Rönnberg, L. (2011). Exploring the intersection of marketisation and central state control through Swedish national school inspection. *Education Inquiry*, 2(4), 695–713.

Slee, R. (2011). *The irregular school.* London, UK: Routledge.

Sleeter, C. (2008). Equity, democracy and neoliberal assaults on teacher education. *Teaching and Teacher Education*, 24(8), 1947–1957.

Thomas, G. (2007). Theory and the construction of pathology. Paper presented at the American Educational Research Association, New York, 24–28 March.

Thomas, G. (2013). A review of thinking and research about inclusive education policy, with suggestions for a new kind of inclusive thinking. *British Journal of Educational Research*, 39(3), 473–490.

Tomlinson, S. (2012). The irresistible rise of the SEN industry. *Oxford Review of Education,* 38(3), 267–286.

Training and Development Agency (2012). ITT trainees: The pillars of inclusion. Inclusive teaching and learning for pupils with special educational needs (SEN) and/or disabilities. Training Toolkit <https://www.european-agency.org/agency-projects/Teacher-Education-for-Inclusion/country-study-visits-2011/london-uk-england/ITT-trainees-the-pillars-of-inclusion.pdf>, accessed 10 June 2014.

Täljedal, I. (2011). Reform and reaction in teacher education at Umeå University. *Education Inquiry*, 2(2), 319–329.

Veck, W. (2012). Martin Buber's concept of inclusion as a critique of special education. *International Journal of Inclusive Education*, 17(6), 614–628.

Warnock, M. (2010). Special educational needs: A new look. In L. Terzi (Ed.), *Special educational needs: A new look* (pp. 11–45). London, UK: Continuum.

CHAPTER 14

Adorno, T.W. (1997). *Negative Dialektik* [Negative dialectics]. Frankfurt/M., Germany: Suhrkamp.

Bedorf, T. (2011). *Andere. Einführung in die Sozialphilosophie* [Others. An Introduction to Social Philosophy]. Bielefeld, Germany: Transcript.

Bedorf, T. (2012). Emmanuel Levinas – Der Leib des Anderen [Emmanuel Levinas – The Body of the Other]. In E. Alloa (Ed.), *Leiblichkeit* (pp. 68–80). Tübingen, Germany: Mohr-Siebeck.

Biewer, G. (2009). *Grundlagen der Heilpädagogik und Inklusiven Pädagogik* [Foundations of special and inclusive education]. Bad Heilbrunn, Germany: Klinkhardt.

Dederich, M. (2013). *Philosophie in der Heil- und Sonderpädagogik* [Philosophy in special education]. Stuttgart, Germany: Kohlhammer.

Fornefeld, B. (1995). *Das schwerstbehinderte Kind und seine Erziehung. Beiträge zu einer Theorie der Erziehung* [The severely disabled child and its education. Contributions to a theory of education]. Heidelberg, Germany: Winter.

Ganslandt, H. (2004). Gleichheit (sozial) [Equality (Social)]. In J. Mittelstraß (Ed.), *Enzyklopädie Philosophie und Wissenschaftstheorie* [Encyclopedia of philosophy and philosophy of science], Vol. 2 (pp. 778–780). Stuttgart, Germany: Metzler.

Gosepath, S. (2010). Gleichheit/Ungleichheit [Equality/Inequality]. In H.-J. Sandkühler (Ed.), *Enzyklopädie Philosophie* [Encyclopedia of Philosophy], Vol. 1 A-H (pp. 919–924). Hamburg, Germany: Felix Meiner.

Hinz, A. (1993). *Heterogenität in der Schule. Integration – Interkulturelle Erziehung – Koedukation* [Heterogeneity in schools. Integration – intercultural education – coeducation]. Hamburg, Germany: Curio.

Levinas, E. (1988). *Eigennamen* [Proper Names]. *Meditationen über Sprache und Literatur.* Munich, Germany and Vienna, Austria: Hanser.

Levinas, E. (1995). *Zwischen uns. Versuche über das Denken des Anderen* [Entre Nous. Thinking of the Other]. Munich, Germany and Vienna, Austria: Hanser.

Levinas, E. (2011). *Jenseits des Seins oder anders als Sein geschieht* [Otherwise Than Being: Or Beyond Essence], 4th printing, Freiburg/Munich, Germany: Alber.

Liebsch, B. (1999). *Moralische Spielräume. Menschheit und Anderheit, Zugehörigkeit und Identität* [Moral Scopes. Humanity and Otherness, Belonging and Identity]. Göttingen, Germany: Wallstein.

Liebsch, B. (2000). Politische und ethische Differenzsensibilität [Political and Ethical Sensibility for Diversity]. In E. Escoubas and B. Waldenfels (Eds.): *Phénemenologie Francaise et Phénomenologie Allemande [French and German Phenomenology]* (pp. 397–425). Paris, France: L'Harmattan.

Liesen, C. (2006). *Gleichheit als ethisch-normatives Problem der Sonderpädagogik: Dargestellt am Beispiel ‚Integration'* [Equality as Ethical and Normative Problem in Special Education. The Example of 'Inclusion']. Bad Heilbrunn, Germany: Klinkhardt.

Lutz, H. and Wenning, N. (2001). Differenzen über Differenz – Einführung in die Debatten [Differences about Difference – An Introduction into the Debates]. In H. Lutz and N. Wenning (Eds.), *Unterschiedlich verschieden. Differenz in der Erziehungswissenschaft* [Differently Different. Diversity in Educational Studies] (pp. 11–24). Opladen, Germany: Leske and Budrich.

Prengel, A. (1995). *Pädagogik der Vielfalt. Verschiedenheit und Gleichberechtigung in Interkultureller, Feministischer und Integrativer Pädagogik* [Pedagogy of Diversity. Difference and Equality in Intercultural, Feminist and Inclusive Education], 2nd printing, Opladen, Germany: Leske and Budrich.

Schnell, M.W. (2008). *Ethik als Schutzbereich. Kurzlehrbuch für Pflege, Medizin und Philosophie [Ethics as a Domain of Protection. A Short Textbook for Nursing, Medicine and Philosophy].* Bern, Switzerland: Huber.

Stinkes, U. (1993). *Spuren eines Fremden in der Nähe. Das ‚geistig behinderte' Kind aus phänomenologischer Sicht* [Traces of a Stranger Nearby. The 'Intellectually Disabled Child' in Phenomenological Perspective]. Würzburg, Germany: Königshausen and Neumann.

Waldenfels, B. (1987). *Ordnung im Zwielicht* [Order in Twilight]. Frankfurt/M., Germany: Suhrkamp.

Waldenfels, B. (2006). *Grundmotive einer Phänomenologie des Fremden [Basic Motives of a Phenomenology of the Other].* Frankfurt/M., Germany: Suhrkamp.

Weisser, J. (2005). *Behinderung, Ungleichheit und Bildung. Eine Theorie der Behinderung* [Disability, Inequality and Education. A Theory of Disability]. Bielefeld, Germany: Transcript.

Welsch, W. (1991). *Unsere postmoderne Moderne* [Our Postmodern Modernity], 3rd printing. Weinheim, Germany: VHC.

CHAPTER 15

Aronowitz, S. (2008). *Against schooling: For an education that matters.* Boulder, CO: Paradigm Publishers.

Baglieri, S., Bejoian, L.M., Broderick, A.A., Connor, D.J., and Valle, J.W. (2011). [Re]claiming "Inclusive Education" Toward Cohesion in Educational Reform: Disability Studies Unravels the Myth of the Normal Child. *Teachers College Record*, 113(10), 2122–2154.

Baglieri, S., and Shapiro, A. (2012). *Disability studies and the inclusive classroom: Critical practices for creating least restrictive attitudes*. New York: Routledge.

Baker, B. (2002). The hunt for disability: The new eugenics and the normalization of school children. *Teachers College Record*, 104, 663–703.

Broderick, A.A., and Ne'eman, A. (2008). Autism as metaphor: Narrative and counter narrative. *International Journal of Inclusive Education*, 12(5–6), 459–476.

Brown, L. (n.d.). *Identity-first language.* On Autistic Self Advocacy Network website: http://autisticadvocacy.org/identity-first-language/. Accessed 10 June 2014.

Campbell, F. (2009). *Contours of ableism: The production of disability and abledness.* New York: Palgrave Macmillan.

Charlton, J. (1998). The dimensions of disability oppression: An overview. In J. Charlton (Ed.), *Nothing about us without us: Disability oppression and empowerment* (pp. 21–36). Berkeley, CA: University of California Press.

Davis, L. (2002). *Bending over backwards: Disability, dismodernism, and other difficult positions.* New York: New York University Press.

Edyburn, D.L. (2010). Would you recognize universal design for learning if you saw it? Ten propositions for new directions for the second decade of UDL. *Learning Disability Quarterly*, 33(1), 33–41.

Graham, L. and Slee, R. (2008). An illusory interiority: Interrogating the discourse/s of inclusion. *Educational Philosophy and Theory*, 40(2), 277–293.

Gray, P. and Riley, G. (2013). The challenges and benefits of unschooling, according to 232 families who have chosen that route. *Journal of Unschooling and Alternative Learning*, 7(14), 1–27.

Hall, T.E., Meyer, A., and Rose, D.H. (Eds.) (2012). *Universal design for learning in the classroom: Practical applications.* New York: Guilford Press.

Higher Education Opportunity Act (2008), 122 U.S.C. § 3078.

Holt, J. (1976/2004). *Instead of education: Ways to help people do things better.* Boulder, CO: Sentient Publications.

Illich, I. (1970). *Deschooling society*. London, UK: Marion Boyers.

Individuals with Disabilities Education Improvement Act of 2004 (2004), 20 U.S.C. § 1400.

No Child Left Behind Act of 2001 (2003), 20 USCA § 6301 et seq.

Prakash, M.S., and Esteva, G. (2008). *Escaping education: Living as learning with grassroots cultures.* New York: Peter Lang.

Ravitch, D. (2010). *The life and death of the great American school system: How testing and choice are undermining education*. New York: Basic Books.

Ravitch, D. (2013). *Reign of error: The hoax of the privatization movement and the danger to america's public schools.* New York: Random House.

Rose, D.H., and Meyer, A. (2002). *Teaching every student in the digital age: Universal design for learning.* Alexandria, VA: Association for Supervision and Curriculum Development.

Swann, M., Peacock, A., Hart, S., and Drummond, M.J. (2012). *Creating learning without limits.* Maidenhead: Open University Press.

Taylor, S.J. (1988). Caught in the continuum: A critical analysis of the principle of the least restrictive environment. *Journal of the Association for Persons with Severe Handicaps (JASH)*, 13(1), 41–53.

Technology-Related Assistance for Individuals with Disabilities Act of 1988 § 2201 29 *U.S.C.* (1988).

UNESCO (1994). *Final report: World Conference on Special Needs Education: Access and Quality*. Paris, France: UNESCO.

UNESCO (2013). *Flexible learning strategies for out-of-school children and youth* (Brochure). Bangkok: UNESCO Bangkok.

Valle, J.W., Connor, D.J., Broderick, A.A., Bejoian, L.M., and Baglieri, S. (2011). Creating alliances against exclusivity: A pathway to inclusive educational reform. *Teachers College Record*, 113(10), 2283–2308.

Wheatley, K. (2009). Unschooling: An oasis for development and democracy. *Encounter: Education for Meaning and Social Justice*, 22(2), 27–32.

CHAPTER 16

Abberley, P. (1987). The concept of oppression and the development of a social theory of disability. *Disability, Handicap and Society*, 21, 5–19.

Ainscow, M. (Ed.) (1991). *Effective schools for all.* London, UK: David Fulton Publishers.

Ainscow, M., and Miles, S. (2008). Making Education for All inclusive: Where next? *Prospects*, 37(1), 15–34.

Alexander, R. (2004). Still no pedagogy? Principle, pragmatism and compliance in primary education. *Cambridge Journal of Education*, 34(1), 7–33.

Allan, J. (2006). The repetition of exclusion. *International Journal of Inclusive Education*, 10(2–3), 121–133.

Black-Hawkins, K., **and** Florian, L. (2012). Teachers' craft knowledge of their inclusive practice. *Teachers and Teaching: Theory and Practice*, 18(5), 567–584.

Black-Hawkins, K., Florian, L., and Rouse, M. (2007). *Achievement and inclusion in schools*, London, UK: RoutledgeFalmer.

Blanton, L.P., Pugach, M.C., and Florian, L. (2011). *Preparing general education teachers to improve outcomes for students with disabilities* (White Paper). Washington, DC: American Association of Colleges for Teacher Education and National Center for Learning Disabilities.

Daniels, M. (2001). *Dancing with words: Signing for hearing children's literacy.* Westport, CT: Bergin and Garvey.

European Agency for Development in Special Needs Education (2011). *Teacher education for inclusion across Europe: A synthesis of policy and practice in 25 countries.* Odense, Denmark: European Agency for Development in Special Needs Education.

Florian. L. (2010). The concept of inclusive pedagogy. In G. Hallett and F. Hallett (Eds.), *Transforming the role of the SENCO* (pp. 61–72). Buckingham, UK: Open University Press.

Florian, L. and Black-Hawkins, K. (2011) Exploring Inclusive Pedagogy. *British Educational Research Journal*, 37(5), 813–828.

Florian, L. and Kershner, R. (2009). Inclusive Pedagogy. In H. Daniels, H. Lauder and J. Porter (Eds.), *Knowledge, values and educational policy: A critical perspective* (pp. 173–183). London, UK: Routledge.

Florian, L. and Spratt, J. (2013). Enacting inclusion: A framework for interrogating inclusive practice. *European Journal of Special Needs Education,* 28(2), 119–135.

Fulcher, G. (1989). Integrate and mainstream? Comparative issues in the politics of these policies. In L Barton (Ed.), *Integration: Myth or reality?* Lewes, UK: Falmer Press.

Gallagher, D. (2014). Challenging orthodoxy in special education: On longstanding debates and philosophical divides. In L. Florian (Ed.), *The sage handbook of special education,* 2nd ed. (pp. 819–840). London, UK: Sage Publications.

Hart, S., Dixon, A., Drummond, M.J., and McIntyre, D. (2004). *Learning Without Limits.* Maidenhead, UK: Open University Press.

Norwich, B. (1993). Ideological dilemmas in special needs education: Practitioners' views. *Oxford Review of Education*, 19(4), 527–545.

Norwich, B. (2008). *Dilemmas of difference: International perspectives and future directions.* London, UK: Routledge.

Ofsted (2000). *Evaluating Educational Inclusion Guidance for inspectors and schools.* London, UK: Ofsted.

Opertti, R. and Brady, J. (2011). Developing inclusive teachers from an inclusive curricular perspective. *Prospects*, 41(3), 459–472.

Peters, S. (2003). *Inclusive education: An EFA strategy for all children.* Washington, DC: The World Bank.

Ravet. J. (2011). Inclusive/exclusive? Contradictory perspectives on autism and inclusion: The case for an integrative position. *International Journal of Inclusive Education*, 15(7), 667–682.

Skrtic, T.M. (1986). The crisis in special education knowledge: A perspective on perspective. *Focus on Exceptional Children*, 18(7), 1–16.

Skrtic, T.M. (1991). *Behind special education: A critical analysis of professional culture and school organisation.* Denver, CO: Love Publishing.

Slee, R. (2010). *The irregular school: Exclusion, schooling and inclusive education.* London, UK: Routledge.

Tomlinson, S. (1982). *A sociology of special education.* London, UK: Routledge and Kegan Paul.

UNESCO (1994). *The Salamanca Statement and Framework for Action on Special Needs Education.* Paris, France: UNESCO.

Vaughn, S., and Linan-Thompson, S. (2003). What is special about special education for students with learning disabilities? *The Journal of Special Education*, 37(3), 140–147.

Winzer, M.A. (2014). Confronting difference: A brief history of special education. In L. Florian (Ed.), *The sage handbook of special education*, 2nd Ed. (pp. 21–33). London, UK: Sage.

Ysseldyke, J.E. (2001). Reflections on a research career: Generalizations from 25 years of research on assessment and instructional decision making. *Exceptional Children*, 67(3), 295–309.

CHAPTER 17

Bines, H., and Lei, P. (2011). Disability and education: The longest road to inclusion. *International Journal of Educational Development*, 31, 419–424.

Burke, K., and Beegle, K. (2004). Why children aren't attending a school: The case of Northwestern Tanzania. *Journal of African Economies*, 13(2), 333–355.

Colclough, C., Rose, P., and Tembon, M. (2000). Gender inequalities in primary schooling: The roles of poverty and adverse cultural practice. *International Journal of Educational Development,* 20(1), 5–29.

Croft, A. (2013). Promoting access to education for disabled children in low-income countries: Do we need to know how many disabled children there are? *International Journal of Educational Development*, 33(3), 233–243.

Emmett, T., and Alant, E. (2006). Women and disability: Exploring the interface of multiple disadvantage. *Development Southern Africa*, 23(4), 445–460.

Fleisch, B., Shindler, J., and Perry, H. (2012). Who is out of school? Evidence from the Statistics South Africa Community Survey. *International Journal of Educational Development*, 32, 529–536.

Groce, N.E., Trasi, R. (2004). Rape of individuals with disability: AIDS and the folk belief of virgin cleansing. *The Lancet*, 363, 1663–1664.

HakiElimu (2008). *Do children with disabilities have equal access to education? A research report on accessibility to education for children with disabilities in Tanzanian schools*. Dar es Salaam, Tanzania: HakiElimu.

Hanass-Hancock, J. (2009). Interweaving conceptualizations of gender and disability in the context of vulnerability to HIV/AIDS in KwaZulu-Natal, South Africa. *Sexuality and Disability*, 27, 35–47.

Hunt, F. (2008). Dropping out from school: A cross-country review of literature. CREATE, Pathways to Access No. 16. Consortium for Research on Educational Access, Transitions and Equity: University of Sussex, UK. http://www.create-rpc.org/pdf_documents/PTA16.pdf, accessed 10 June 2014.

Jones, S.K. (2011). Girls' secondary education in Uganda: Assessing policy within the women's empowerment framework. *Gender and Education*, 23(4), 385–413.

Kiragu, S., Swartz, C., Chikovore, J., Lukalo, F., and Oduro, G.Y. (2011). Agency, access, silence and ethics: How young people's voices from Africa can contribute to social and educational change in adult-dominated societies. In C. Day (Ed.), *International handbook of teacher and school development* (pp. 254–263). London, UK: Routledge.

Lehtomäki, E. (2000). The meaning of education from policy to practice: Including people with hearing impairment in Mozambique and Tanzania. In L.-E. Malmberg, S.-E. Hansén and K. Heino (Eds.), *Basic Education for All, A global concern for quality*. Report from the 1999 (pp. 267–281) NASEDEC Conference, Vasa, Sweden, May 6–8, 1999. Turku, Finland, Åbo Akademi University, Faculty of Education.

Lehtomäki, E., Janhonen-Abruquah, H., Tuomi, M.T., Okkolin, M.A., Posti-Ahokas, H., and Palojoki, P. (2014a). Research to engage voices on the ground for educational development. *International Journal of Educational Development*, 35, 2014, 37–43.

Lehtomäki, E., Tuomi, M.T., and Matonya, M. (2014b). Educational research from Tanzania 1998–2008 concerning persons with disabilities: What can we learn? *International Journal of Educational Research*, 64, 32–39.

Lewin, K.M. (2009). Access to education in Sub-Saharan Africa: Patterns, problems and possibilities. *Comparative Education*, 45(2), 151–174.

Lewis, I., and Little, D. (2007). Report to NORAD on desk review of inclusive education policies and plans in Nepal, Tanzania, Vietnam and Zambia, http://www.eenet.org.uk/resources/docs/Policy_review_for_NORAD.pdf, accessed 10 June 2014.

Macha, E. (2002). *Gender, disabilities and access to education in tanzania*. PhD diss. University of Leeds, UK, http://etheses.whiterose.ac.uk/282/, accessed 10 June 2014.

McLaughlin, C., and Swartz, S. (2011). Can we use young people's knowledge to develop teachers and HIV-related education? *Prospects* 41(3), 429–444.

Meekosha, H. (2011). Decolonising disability: Thinking and acting globally. *Disability and Society*, 26(6), 667–682.

Mushi, P. (2009). *History and development of education in Tanzania*. Dar es Salaam, Tanzania: Dar es Salaam University Press.

National Bureau of Statistics (2008). Tanzania 2008 Disability Survey Report. Retrieved from http://nbs.go.tz/tnada/index.php/catalog/5, accessed 10 June 2014.

Ngcobo, J., and Muthukrishna, N. (2008). Teachers' dominant discourse on disability and inclusive education: A case study at a semi-rural township school in the province of KwaZulu-Natal, South Africa. In S.L. Gabel and S. Danforth (Eds.), *Disability and the politics of education: An international reader* (pp. 19–40). New York: Peter Lang.

Njelesani, J., Couto, S., and Cameron, D. (2011). Disability and rehabilitation in Tanzania: A review of the literature. *Disability and Rehabilitation*, 33(23/24), 2196–2207.

Okkolin, M.A. (2013). *Highly educated women in Tanzania – Constructing educational well-being and agency*. Phd. diss., University of Jyväskylä. Jyväskylä, Finland (Jyväskylä Studies in Education, Psychology and Social Research, 483 (accessed at https://jyx.jyu.fi/dspace/handle/123456789/42370, 10 June 2014).

Okkolin, M.A., Lehtomäki, E., and Bhalalusesa, E. (2010). The successful education sector development in Tanzania – comment on gender balance and inclusive education. *Gender and Education*, 22(1), 63–71.

Packalén, L., and Sharma, S. (2007). *Grassroots comics – A development communication tool*. Helsinki, Finland: Ministry for Foreign Affairs of Finland.

Possi, M.K. (1999). Culture and disability: Superstitious behaviour towards people with disabilities in Coastal Tanzania. *African Journal of Special Needs Education*, 1, 22–35.

Posti-Ahokas, H., and Palojoki, P. (2013). Navigating transitions to adulthood through secondary education: Aspirations and value of education for Tanzanian girls. *Journal of Youth Studies*. DOI: 10.1080/13676261.2013.853871.

Posti-Ahokas, H., and Lehtomäki, E. (forthcoming). Female students speaking back to education policy: Exploring student voice work in Tanzania. *Gender and Education*.

Save the Children (2011). *Out from the shadows: Sexual violence against children with disabilities*. London: Save the Children UK, accessed at http://www.savethechildren.org.uk/resources/online-library/out-shadows-sexual-violence-against-children-disabilities

Sayed, Y., Soudien, C. and Carrim, N. (2003). Discourses of exclusion and inclusion in the South: Limits and possibilities. *Journal of Educational Change*, 4, 231–248.

Shakespeare, T. (2006). *Disability rights and wrongs*. London: Routledge.

Sommer, M. (2010). Where the education system and women's bodies collide: The social and health impact of girls' experiences of menstruation and schooling in Tanzania. *Journal of Adolescence*, 33, 521–529. DOI: 10.1016/j.adolescence.2009.03.008

Stambach, A. (2000). *Lessons from Mount Kilimanjaro: Schooling, community, and gender in East Africa*. New York, NY: Routledge.

Sumra, S. (2003). *Implementation of the Primary Education Development Plan: Voices from the Community*. Dar es Salaam, Tanzania: Haki Elimu.

Tarabini, A. (2010). Education and poverty in the global development agenda: Emergence, evolution and consolidation. *International Journal of Educational Development*, 30, 204–212.

Tikly, L., and Dachi, G., (2009). Social justice in African education in the age of globalisation (pp. 120–137). In W. Ayers, T. Quinn, D. Stovall (Eds.), *Handbook of social justice in education*. New York: Routledge.

UN (2006). Convention on the Rights of Persons with Disabilities, opened for signatures 30 March 2007, entered into force 3 May 2008.

UN (2010). *Disability and the Millennium Development Goals* (A review of the mdg process and strategies for inclusion of disability issues in millennium development goal efforts) accessed at http://www.un.org/disabilities/documents/review_of_disability_and_the_mdgs.pdf.

UNESCO (2003/2004). *EFA global monitoring report*. Gender and education for all, the leap for equality. Paris, France: UNESCO.

UNESCO (2010). *Global EFA monitoring report: reaching the hard to reach*. Paris, France: UNESCO.

UNICEF (2004). *Changing the lives of girls: evaluation of the african girls' education initiative* (accessed at http://www.ungei.org/resources/index_579.html).

UNICEF (2013). *The State of the Worlds Children 2013: Children with disabilities*. http://www.unicef.org/sowc2013/

Unterhalter, E. (2012). Inequality, capabilities and poverty in four African countries: Girls' voice, schooling, and strategies for institutional change. *Cambridge Journal of Education*, 42(3), 307–325.

Unterhalter, E., Heslop, J. and Mamedub, A. (2013). Girls claiming education rights: Reflections on distribution, empowerment and gender justice in Northern Tanzania and Northern Nigeria. *International Journal of Educational Development* (accessed at http://dx.doi.org/10.1016/j.ijedudev.2013.05.007).

Unterhalter, E. and North, A. (2011). Girls' schooling, gender equity and the global education and development agenda: Conceptual disconnections, political struggles, and the difficulties of practice. *Feminist Formations*, 23(3), 1–22.

URT (United Republic of Tanzania) (2008a). *Report on the development of education* (accessed at http://www.ibe.unesco.org/National_Reports/ICE_2008/tanzania_NR08.pdf).

URT (United Republic of Tanzania) (2008b). *Dar es Salaam*: Tanzania: Education Sector Development Committee. Education Sector Performance Report 2007/2008. Education Sector Development Committee.

URT (United Republic of Tanzania) (2011). *Basic education statistics* in Tanzania 2007–2011. National data. Dar es Salaam: The Ministry of Education and Vocational Training.

Warrington, M. and Kiragu, S. (2012). It makes more sense to educate a boy: Girls 'against the odds' in Kajiado, Kenya. *International Journal of Educational Development*, 32(2012), 301–309.

World Comics Finland (2010). *Grassroots Comics by Disabled People*, (Report January-February 2010. accessed at http://comics-with-attitude.blogspot.fr/2012/01/v-behaviorurldefaultvmlo_03.html).

World Health Organization (WHO) and The World Bank (2011). *World report on disability* (accessed at http://whqlibdoc.who.int/publications/2011/9789240685215_eng.pdf).

CHAPTER 18

Abberley, P. (1987). The concept of oppression and the development of a social theory of disability. *Disability, Handicap and Society*, 2(1), 5–19.

Anyon, J. (1983). Intersections of gender and class: Accommodation and resistance by working-class and affluent females to contradictory sex-role ideologies. In S. Walker and L. Barton (Eds.), *Gender, class, and education*. Barcombe, UK: Falmer.

Apple, M.W. (2000). *Teoría crítica y educación* [Critical theory and education]. Madrid, Spain/Buenos Aires, Argentina: Miño y Dávila.

Apple, M.W. (2004). *Ideology and curriculum.* New York/London, UK: Routledge Falmer.

Apple, M.W., and Beane, J.A. (Eds.) (1999). *Democratic schools.* Buckingham, UK: Open University Press.

Ball, S.J. (1987). *The micro-politics of the school: Towards a theory of school organization.* New York: Methuen.

Barton, L. and Oliver, M. (1992). Special needs: Personal trouble or public issue? In M. Arnot and L. Barton (Eds.), *Voicing concerns. Sociological perspectives on contemporary education reforms* (pp. 67–87). Wallingford, Oxfordshire, UK: Triangle Books.

Baudelot, C. y Establet, R. (1971). *L'école capitaliste en France* [The capitalist school in France]. Paris, France: Éditions Maspero.

Bourdieu, P., and Passeron J.C. (1977). *Reproduction in education, society, and culture.* London, UK: Sage.

Bowles, S., and Gintis H. (1972). IQ in the *United States class structure.* Social Policy, 3, 4f.

Bruner, J. (1991). *Acts of meanings.* London, UK: Harvard University Press.

Calderón-Almendros, I. (2011). Breaking away to find a way: Poverty and school failure in a Spanish adolescent life-history. *British Journal of Sociology of Education*, 32(5), 745–762.

Calderón-Almendros, I. (2014a). *Educación y esperanza en las fronteras de la discapacidad. Estudio de caso único sobre la construcción creativa de la identidad.* [Education and hope in the boundaries of disability. A single case study on creative identity construction]. Madrid, Spain: CERMI.

Calderón-Almendros, I. (2014b). *Sin suerte pero guerrero hasta la muerte. Educación, pobreza y exclusión en la vida de Medina* [Down on luck but will fight to the death. Education, poverty and exclusion in Medina's life history]. Granada, Spain: Octaedro.

Calderón-Almendros, I., and Habegger-Lardoeyt, S. (2012/Forthcoming). *Educación, hándicap e inclusión. Una lucha familiar contra una escuela excluyente* [Education, handicap and inclusion. A family struggle against an excluding school]. Granada, Spain: Octaedro/Rotterdam: Sense Publishers.

Carr, W., and Kemmis, S. (1986). *Becoming critical: Education, knowledge and action research.* London, UK: Falmer Press.

Cyrulnik, B. (2001). *Les vilains petits canards.* París, France: Odile Jacob.

De la Rosa, L. (2008). *La historia de vida de Ángel. Parálisis cerebral, normalidad y comunicación* [The story of Angel's life. Cerebral palsy, normality, and communication]. Madrid, Spain: La Muralla.

Echeita, G., Parrilla, Á., and Carbonell, F. (2011). La educación especial a debate [The debate on special education]. *Revista Ruedes de la Red Universitaria de Educación Especial,* 1(1), 35–53.

Ferreira, M.A.V. (2008). A sociological approach to disability based on the social model: Some characteriological sketches. *Revista Española de Investigaciones Sociológicas*, 12, 141–174.

Foucault, M. (1975). *Surveiller et punir.* Paris, France: Gallimard.

Foucault, M. (1981). *The hermeneutics of the subject.* New York: Picador.

Foucault, M. (1993). *Microfísica del poder* [Microphysics of power]. Madrid, Spain: La Piqueta.

Foucault, M. (1999). *Estrategias de poder* [Power strategies]. Barcelona, Spain: Paidós.

Frankl, V. (2006). *Man's search for meaning. An introduction to logotherapy,* Boston: Beacon Press.

Freire, P. (1972). *Pedagogy of the oppressed.* Harmondsworth, UK: Penguin.

Freire, P. (1985). *The politics of education: Culture, power, and liberation.* Westport, CT: Bergin and Garvey Publishers.

Gabel, S. and Peters, S. (2004). Presage of a paradigm shift? Beyond the social model of disability toward resistance theories of disability. *Disability and Society*, 19(6), 585–600.

Giddens, A. (1982). *Sociology: a brief but critical introduction*. London, UK: Macmillan.

Giroux, H.A. (1988). *Teachers as intellectuals: toward a critical pedagogy of learning*. New York: Bergin and Garvey Publishers.

Giroux, H.A. (2001). *Theory and resistance in education: Towards a pedagogy for the opposition*. South Hadley, MA: Bergin and Garvey.

Giroux, H.A. (2002). Repensando la política de resistencia. Notas sobre una teoría crítica de la lucha educativa [Rethinking the politics of resistance. Notes on a critical theory of educational struggle]. *Barbecho, Revista de Reflexión Socioeducativa*, 2, 17–25.

Goffman, E. (1963). *Stigma: Notes on the management of spoiled identity*. Englewood Cliffs, NJ: Prentice-Hall.

López-Melero, M. (2004). *Construyendo una escuela sin exclusiones. Una forma de trabajar en el aula con proyectos de investigación*. [Building an inclusive school. One way to work in the classroom with research projects]. Málaga, Spain: Aljibe.

McLaren, P. (2003). Pedagogía crítica en la época de la resignación [Critical pedagogy in the resignation era]. *Barbecho, Revista de Reflexión Socioeducativa*, 2, 8–12.

Moscovici, S. (1973). On social representation. In J.P. Forgas (Ed.), *Social cognition. Perspectives in everyday life*. London, UK: Academic Press.

Palacios, A. (2008). *El modelo social de discapacidad: Orígenes, caracterización y plasmación en la Convención Internacional sobre los Derechos de las Personas con Discapacidad* [The social model of disability: its origins, characterization and embodiment in the international convention on the rights of persons with disabilities]. Madrid, Spain: CERMI.

Parrilla, A. (2009). What if research on inclusion were not inclusive? Reflections from a biographical-narrative research. *Revista de Educación (Madrid)*, 349, 101–117.

Ruiz-Román, C., Calderón-Almendros, I., and Torres-Moya, F.J. (2011). Constructing identity in the margins of globalisation: Education, participation and learning. *Cultura y Educación*, 23(4), 589–599.

Rutter, M. (1979). Protective factors in children´s responses to stress and disadvantages. In M.K. Kent and J.E. Rolf (Eds.), *Primary prevention of psychopathology* (pp. 49–74). Hanover, NH: University Press of New England.

Rutter, M. (1985). Resilience in the face of adversity: Protective factors and resistance to psychiatric disorder. *British Journal of psychiatric*, 147, 598–611.

Rutter, M. (1993). Resilience: Some conceptual considerations. *Journal of Adolescent Health*, 14, 626–631.

Skliar, C. (2007). *¿Y si el otro no estuviera ahí? Notas para una pedagogía (improbable) de la diferencia* [If the other would not be there? Notes for a pedagogy of difference]. Buenos Aires, Argentina: Miño y Dávila.

Skliar, C. and Dussel, I. (2011). From equity to difference: Educational legal frames and inclusive practices in Argentina. In A.J. Artiles, E.B. Kozleski, and F.R. Waitoller (Eds.), *Inclusive education. Examining equity on five continents* (pp. 185–200). Cambridge, MA: Harvard Education Press.

Susinos, T. and Parrilla, A. (2008). Dar la voz en la investigación inclusiva. Debates sobre inclusión y exclusión desde un enfoque biográfico-narrativo [Giving people a voice in inclusive research. Debates about inclusion and exclusion from a biographical-narrative approach]. *Revista Electrónica Iberoamericana sobre Calidad, Eficacia y Cambio en Educación*, 6(2), 157–169.

Swartz, L. and Watermeyer, B. (2008). Cyborg anxiety: Oscar Pistorius and the boundaries of what it means to be human. *Disability and Society*, 23(2), 187–190.

Tyler, W. (1988). *School organization: a sociological perspective*. Kent, UK: Croom Helm Ltd.

Ungar, M. (Ed.) (2012). *The social ecology of resilience: A handbook*. New York, NY: Springer.

Van Hove, G., Gabel, S.L., De Schauwer, E., Mortier, K., Van Loon, J., Loots, G., Devlieger, P., Roets, G., Claes, L. (2012). Resistance and resilience in a life full of professionals and labels: Narrative snapshots of Chris. *Intellectual and Developmental Disabilities*, 50(5), 426–435.

Willis, P. (1981). *Learning to labour: How working class kids get working class jobs.* New York: Columbia University Press.

CHAPTER 19

Ainscow, M. (2005). Understanding the development of inclusive education system. *Electronic Journal of Research in Educational Psychology*, 7(3), 5–20.

Ainscow, M., and César, M. (2006). Inclusive education ten years after Salamanca. Setting the agenda. *European Journal of Psychology of Education*, 21(3), 231–238.

Antoniou, L., Dyson, A., and Raffo, C. (2012). Policy interventions to reduce educational inequalities – The case of England 1997–2010. In M. Demeuse, D. Frandji, D.Greger and J.-Y. Rochex (Eds.), *Educational Policies and Inequalities in Europe* (pp. 23–54). New York: Palgrave Macmillan.

Armstrong, D., Armstrong, A.C., and Spandagou, I. (2011). Inclusion: By choice or by chance? *International Journal of Inclusive Education*, 15(1), 29–39.

Artiles, A.J., Kozleski, E.B., Dorn, S. and Christensen, C. (2006). Learning in inclusive education research: re-mediating theory and methods with a transformative agenda. *Review of Research in Education*, 30, 65–108.

Begeer, S., El Bouk, S., Boussaid, W., Terwogt, M.M., and Koot, H.M. (2009). Underdiagnosis and referral bias of autism in ethnic minorities. *Autism and Developmental Disorders*, 39, 142–148.

Brehony, K.J. (2005). Primary schooling under new labour: the irresolvable contradiction of excellence and enjoyment. *Oxford Review of Education*, 31(1), 29–46.

Carugati, F., and Selleri, P. (2004). Intelligence, educational practices and school reform: Organisations change, representations persist. *European Journal of School Psychology*, 2(1), 149–167.

Clingman, J., Fowler, R.L. (1976). The effects of primary reward on the I.Q. performance of grade-school children as a function of initial I.Q. level. *Journal of Applied Behaviour Analysis*, 9(1), 19–23.

Colver, A.F., Dickinson, H., Parkinson, K., Arnaud, C., Beckung, E., Fauconnier, J., Marcelli, M., McManus, V., Michelsen, S.I., Parkes, J., and Thyen, U. (2011). Access of children with cerebral palsy to the physical, social and attitudinal environment they need: A cross-sectional European study. *Disability and Rehabilitation*, 33(1), 28–35.

Duckworth, A.L., Quinn, P.D., Lynam, D.R., Loeber, R., Stouthamer-Loeber, M. (2011). Role of test motivation in intelligence testing. *Proceedings of the Academy of Sciences*, 108(19), 7716–7720.

Durkin, M.S., Maenner, M.J., Meaney, J., Levy, S.E., DiGuiseppi, C., Nicholas, J.S., Kirby, R.S., Pinto-Martin, J.A., and Schieve, L.A. (2010). Socioeconomic inequality in the prevalence of autism spectrum disorder. Evidence from a U.S. Cross-sectional Study. *PLoS ONE*, c5(7), e11551.

Elder, T.E. (2010). The importance of relative standards in ADHD diagnoses: Evidence based on exact birth dates. *Journal of Health Economics*, 29(5), 641–656.

Engeström, Y. (2008). *From teams to knots. Activity-theoretical studies of collaboration and learning at work.* Cambridge, UK: Cambridge University Press.

European Agency for Development in Special Needs Education (2011). *Participation in inclusive education. A framework for developing indicators.* Brussels, Belgium/Odense, Denmark: European Agency for Development in Special Needs Education.

European Agency for Development in Special Needs Education (2012). *Special needs education. Country data 2012.* Odense and Brussels: European Agency for Development in Special Needs Education.

Froehlich, T.E., Lamphear, B.P., Epstein, J.N., Barbaresi, W.J., Katusic, S.K., and Kahn, R.S. (2007). Prevalence, recognition and treatment of attention-deficit/hyperactivity disorder in a national sample of US children. *Archives of Pediatrics and Adolescent Medicine*, 161, 857–864.

Gabel, S.L., Curcic, S., Powell, J.J.W., Khader, K. and Albee, L. (2009). Migration and ethnic group disproportionality in special education: An exploratory study. *Disability and Society*, 24(5), 625–639.

Gee, J.P. (2001). Identity as an analytic lens for research in education. *Review of Research in Education*, 25, 99–125.

Glennerster, H. (2002). United Kingdom Education 1997–2001. *Oxford Review of Economic Policy*, 18(2): 120–136.

Goffman, E. (1963). *Stigma: notes on the management of spoiled identity.* Englewood Cliffs, NJ: Prentice-Hall.

Hattie, J. (2009). *Visible learning. A synthesis of over 800 meta-analysis relating to achievement.* London, UK and New York: Routledge.

Hodkinson, A. (2012). Illusionary inclusion – what went wrong with New Labour's landmark educational policy? *British Journal of Special Education*, 39(1), 4–11.

Hollenweger, J. (2010). MHADIE's matrix to analyse the functioning of education systems. *Disability and Rehabilitation*, 32, 116–124.

Hollenweger, J. (2013a). Beyond categories and labels: Knowledge to support assessment for learning. 'Disability'—A Problem Well Put? In L. Florian (Ed.), *The Sage handbook of special education.* Los Angeles, London: Sage, 507–522.

Hollenweger, J. (2013b). Developing applications of the ICF in education systems: Addressing issues of knowledge creation, management and transfer. *Disability and Rehabilitation*, 35(13), 1087–1091.

Hollenweger, J., Keck, A., and Gürber, S. (2005). *Menschen mit Behinderungen an Schweizer Hochschulen. Befunde und Empfehlungen.* Zurich, Switzerland: Rüegger Verlag.

Hörmann, B. (2007). Disappearing students: PISA and students with disabilities. In S. T. Hopmann, G. Brinek, and M. Retzl (Eds.), *PISA according to PISA: Does PISA keep what it promises?* Münster, Germany: LIT Verlag.

Jordan, A., Schwartz, E., and McGhie-Richmond, D. (2009). Preparing teachers for inclusive classrooms. *Teaching and Teacher Education*, 25, 535–542.

Jordan, A., and Stanovich, P. (2001). Patterns of teacher-student interaction in inclusive elementary classrooms and correlates with student self-concept. *International Journal of Disability, Development and Education*, 48(1), 33–52.

Kiuppis, F. (2014). Why (not) associate the principle of inclusion with disability? Tracing connections from the start of the 'Salamanca Process.' *International Journal of Inclusive Education*, 18(7), 746–761.

Kjaernsli, M. and Roe, A. (n.d.). On the right track. Norwegian students' proficiency in reading, mathematics and science literacy in the PISA Assessment 2009 [online], http://www.pisa.no/pdf/publikasjoner/Short_version_in_English_PISA2009_Norway.pdf, accessed 10 June 2014.

Kossyvaki, L., Jones, G., and Guldberg, K. (2012). The effect of adult interactive style on the spontaneous communication of young children with autism at school. *British Journal of Special Education*, 39(4), 173–184.

Lave, J. and Wenger, E. (1991). *Situated learning: legitimate peripheral participation.* Cambridge, UK: Cambridge University Press.

Mehan, H., Hertweck, A., and Meihls, J.L. (1986). *Handicapping the handicapped: decision making in students' educational careers*. Palo Alto, CA: Stanford University Press.

Miles, S. and Singal, N. (2010). The education for all and inclusive education debate: Conflict, Contradiction or Opportunity? *International journal of inclusive education*, 14(1), 1–15.

Mittler, P. (2002). Educating pupils with intellectual disabilities in England: Thirty years on. *International Journal of Disability, Development and Education*, 49(2), 145–160.

Nes, K. (2010). The first decade of the 21st century: A backlash for inclusion in Norwegian Schools. *Zeitschrift für Inklusion*, 2, Available at: http://www.inklusion-online.net/index.php/inklusion/article/view/57/61, accessed 10 June 2014.

OECD (2004). *Equity in education. Thematic review. Norway*. Paris, France: OECD.

OECD (2007). *Students with disabilities, learning difficulties and disadvantages. Policies, statistics and indicators*. Paris, France: OECD.

OECD (2010). *PISA 2009 results: Overcoming social background – equity in learning opportunities and outcomes*, Vol. II. Paris, France: OECD.

OECD (2011). *Education at a glance*. Paris, France: OECD.

Riddell, S., Tisdall, K., Kane, J., and Mulderrig, J. (2006). *Literature review of educational provision for pupils with additional support needs*. Edinburgh, UK: Scottish Executive Social Research.

Rohlfing, K.J., Rehm, M., and Geocke, K.U. (2003). Situatedness: The interplay between context(s) and situation. *Journal of Cognition and Culture*, 3(2), 132–156.

Runswick-Cole, K. (2011). Time to end the bias towards inclusive education? *British Journal of Special Education*, 38(3), 112–119.

Sen, A. (1992). *Inequality reexamined*. Cambridge, MA: Harvard University Press.

Slee, R. (1998). The politics of theorising special education. In C. Clark, A. Dyson, A. Millward (Eds.), *Theorising special education* (pp. 125–135). London, UK: Routledge.

Sullivan, A.L. and Artiles, A.J. (2011). Theorizing racial inequality in special education: applying structural inequity theory to disproportionality. *Urban Education*, 46(6), 1526–1552.

Takala, M. and Hausstätter, R.S. (2012). Effects of history and culture on attitudes toward special education: a comparison of finland and norway. *International Scholarly Research Network*. Article ID 161039. Available at: http://www.hindawi.com/isrn/education/2012/161039/, accessed 10 June 2014.

Tomasevski, K. (2001). *Human rights obligations: Making education available, accessible, acceptable and adaptable* (Right to Education Primers, no. 3). Gothenburg, Sweden: Novum Grafiska AB. Available online at http://www.right-to-education.org/index.html, accessed 10 June 2014.

UNESCO (1994). *Salamanca Statement and Framework for Action on Special Needs Education*. Paris: UNESCO. Available at: http://unesdoc.unesco.org/images/0009/000984/098427eo.pdf, accessed 10 June 2014.

United Nations (2006). *UN-convention on the rights of persons with disabilities*. New York: United Nations.

United Nations (2010). *The Millennium Development Goals Report*. New York: United Nations.

United Nations (2011). *Disability and the Millennium Development Goals*. A Review of the MDG Progress and Strategies for Inclusion of Disability Issues in Millennium Development Goals Efforts. New York: United Nations (accessed at: http://www.un.org/disabilities/documents/review_of_disability_and_the_mdgs.pdf, accessed 10 June 2014).

Wang, P.P., Badley, E.M., and Gignac, M. (2006). Exploring the role of contextual factors in disability models. *Disability and Rehabilitation*, 28, 135–140.

Warnock, H.M. (1978). *The Warnock report. Special educational needs. Report of the committee of enquiry into the education of handicapped children and young people*. London, UK: HMSO.

Wendelborg, C. and Tøssebro, J. (2010). Marginalisation processes in inclusive education in Norway: A study of classroom participation. *Disability and Society*, 25(6), 701–714.

Wilson, J. (2000). 'Learning Difficulties,' 'Disability' and 'Special Needs': Some problems of partisan conceptualisation. *Disability and Society*, 15(5), 817–824.

WHO (World Health Organisation) (2001). *International classification of functioning, disability and health (ICF)*. Geneva, Switzerland: World Health Organisation.

CHAPTER 20

Allan, J. (2011). Complicating, not explicating: Taking up philosophy in learning disability research. *Learning Disability Quarterly*, 34(2), 153–161.

Bearne, G.C. (2000). Differentiating Derrida and Deleuze. *Continental Philosophy Review*, 33, 441–465.

Biesta, G. (1998). Pedagogy without humanism: Foucault and the subject of education. *Interchange*, 29(1), 1–16.

Biesta, G. (2012). Philosophy of education for the public good: Five challenges and an agenda. *Educational Philosophy and Theory*, 44(6), 581–593.

Braidotti, R. (1994). *Nomadic subjects: Embodiment and sexual difference in contemporary feminist theory*. New York: Columbia University Press.

Buchanan, I. (1997). Deleuze and cultural studies. *The South Atlantic Quarterly*, 96(3), 483–497.

Burman, E. (2008). *Developments: Child, image, nation.* London: Routledge.

Curti, G.H., and Moreno, M. (2010). Institutional borders, revolutionary imaginings and the becoming-adult of the child. *Children's Geographies*, 8(4), 413–427.

Davis, L.J. (1995). *Enforcing normalcy: Disability, deafness, and the body*. New York: Verso.

Davis, L.J. (2006). The end of identity politics and the beginning of dismodernism. On disability as an unstable category. In L. Davis. (Ed.), *The disability studies reader* (2nd ed.) (pp. 231–242). New York: Routledge.

Deleuze, G., and Guattari, F. (1987). *A thousand plateaus: Capitalism and schizophrenia*. London: Continuum.

Dosse, F. (2011). *Gilles Deleuze and Félix Guattari: Intersecting lives*. New York: Columbia University Press.

Erevelles, N. (2002a). Voices of silence: Foucault, disability, and the question of self-determination. *Studies in Philosophy and Education*, 21(1), 17–35.

Erevelles, N. (2002b). Cognitive disability, race, and the politics of citizenship. *Disability, Culture and Education*, 1(1), 5–25.

Finlay, L., and Langdridge, D. (2007). Embodiment. In W. Hollway, H. Lucey, and A. Phoenix (Eds.), *Social Psychology Matters* (pp. 9–23). Maidenhead: Open University Press / Milton Keynes: The Open University.

Gergen, K. (2001). Psychological science in a postmodern world. *American Psychologist,* 56(10), 803–813.

Goffman, E. (1963). *Stigma – Notes on the management of spoiled identity*. Englewood Cliffs, NJ: Prentice Hall.

Goodley, D. (2007a). Towards socially just pedagogies: Deleuzoguattarian critical disability studies. *International Journal of Inclusive Education,* 11(3), 317–334.

Goodley, D. (2007b). Becoming rhizomatic parents: Deleuze, Guattari and disabled babies. *Disability and Society, 22*(2), 145–160.

Goodley, D. (2011). *Disability studies: An interdisciplinary introduction*. London: Sage.

Goodley, D. (2014). *Dis/ability studies: Theorising disablism and ableism.* Abingdon and New York: Routledge.

Goodley, D., and Lawthom, R. (2005). Disability studies and psychology: New allies. In D. Goodley and R. Lawthom (Eds.), *Psychology and disability: Critical introductions and reflections* (pp. 1–16). London, UK: Palgrave.

Goodley, D., and Runswick-Cole, K. (2013). The body as disability and possibility: Theorising the "leaking, lacking and excessive" bodies of disabled children. *Scandinavian Journal of Disability Research,* 15(1), 1–19.

Haraway, D. (1991). *Simians, cyborgs and women: The reinvention of nature*. London: Free Association Books.

Hardt, M., and Negri, A. (2000). *Empire.* Cambridge, MA: Harvard University Press.

Harwood, V., and Humphrey, N. (2008). Taking exception: Discourses of exceptionality and the invocation of the ideal. In S. Gabel and S. Danforth (Eds.), *Disability and the international politics of education* (pp. 371–384). New York: Peter Lang.

Henriques, J., Hollway, W., Urwin, C., Venn, C., and Walkerdine, V. (1989). *Changing the subject: Psychology, social regulation and subjectivity*. London: Methuen.

Hickman, M.J., and Walter, B. (1995). Deconstructing whiteness: Irish women in Britain. *Feminist Review*, 50, 5–19.

Kiuppis, F. (2013). "Pedagogikkens pentagon" revis(it)ed – Considerations on emancipation from a disability studies and inclusive education perspective. In J. Steinnes and S. Dobson (Eds.), *Pedagogikk under livets tre* (pp. 147–160). Trondheim, Norway: Akademika.

Kiuppis, F. (2014a). Why (not) associate the principle of inclusion with disability? Tracing connections from the start of the 'Salamanca Process.' *International Journal of Inclusive Education*, 18(7), 746–761.

Kiuppis, F. (2014b). *Heterogene Inklusivität, inklusive Heterogenität.* Münster/New York: Waxmann.

Kiuppis, F. (2014c). Zusammenhänge zwischen der Bedeutungsrelativität der Beschreibung eines Einzelfalls im Kontext von Behinderung und der Bewertungsrelativität seiner Auslegung. *EthikJournal*, 2(1).

Kiuppis, F. (forthcoming). Bridging continents, cultures, and crip theories: comparative disability studies in education. In: *Disability Studies Quarterly.* Spring 2015, special issue: Interventions in Disability Studies Pedagogy.

Kiuppis, F. and Peters, S. (2014). Inclusive education for all as special interest within the comparative and international education research community. *Annual Review Of Comparative and International Education 2014*, Volume 25, 53–63.

Lash, S. (2001). Technological forms of life. *Theory, culture and society,* 18(1), 105–120.

Michalko, R. (2002). *The difference that disability makes.* Philadelphia: Temple University Press.

Ramlow, T.R. (2006). Bodies in the borderlands: Gloria Anzaldua's and David Wojnarowicz's mobility machines. *MELUS,* 31(3), 169–187.

Rawls, J. (2003) [1921]. The principles of justice. In J. Rawls (Ed.), *A theory of justice* (pp. 47–101). Cambridge, MA: Harvard University Press.

Reeve, D. (2004). Counselling and disabled people: Help or hindrance? In J. Swain, S. French, C. Barnes, and C. Thomas (Eds.), *Disabling barriers, enabling environments* (2nd ed.) (pp. 233–238). London: Sage.

Sampson, E.E. (1977). Psychology and the American ideal. *Journal of Personality and Social Psychology,* 35(11), 767–782.

Sampson, E.E. (1985). The decentralisation of identity: Toward a revised concept of personal and social order. *American Psychologist,* 40(11), 1203–1211.
Sampson, E.E. (1988). The debate on individualism: Indigenous psychologies of the individual and their role in personal and societal functioning. *American Psychologist,* 43(1), 15–22.
Sampson, E.E. (1993). Identity politics: Challenges to psychology's understanding. *American Psychologist,* 48(12), 1219–1230.
Shepherd, A. (1966). One body. In P. Hunt (Ed.), *Stigma: The experience of disability* (pp. 57–66). London: Geoffrey Chapman.
Shield, S.A. (1992). Functionalism, Darwinism and the psychology of women: A study in social myth. In J. S. Bohan (Ed.), *Seldom seen, rarely heard* (pp. 79–106). Boulder, CO: Westview Press.
Shildrick, M. (2009). *Dangerous discourses of disability, subjectivity and sexuality.* Basingstoke, New York: Palgrave Macmillan.
Spivak, G.C. (1985). Three women's texts and a critique of imperialism. *Critical Inquiry,* 12(1), 243–261.
Thomas, G., and Loxley, A. (2001). *Deconstructing special education and constructing inclusion.* Buckingham: Open University Press.
Turner, B. (2008). *The body and society.* (3rd ed.). London: Sage.
UN (2006). *Convention on the rights of persons with disabilities.* New York: UN.
Waldschmidt, A. (2005). Who is normal? Who is deviant? "Normality" and "risk" in genetic diagnostics and counseling. In S. Tremain (Ed.), *Foucault and the government of disability* (pp. 191–207). Ann Arbor, MI: University of Michigan Press.
Walkerdine, V. (1993). Beyond developmentalism. *Theory and Psychology* 3(4), 451–469.
Weiss, G. (1999). The duree of the techno-body. In E. Grosz (Ed.), *Becomings: Explorations in time, memory and futures* (pp. 161–175). New York: Cornell University Press.
Woollet, A., and Marshall, H. (1997). Young women's accounts of their bodies in relation to autonomy and independence. In K. Davis (Ed.), *Embodied practices: Feminist perspectives on the body* (pp. 27–40). London: Sage.
Wright Mills, C. (1970). *The sociological imagination.* Oxford: Oxford University Press.

CHAPTER 21

Alur, M., and Timmons, V. (Eds.) (2009). *Inclusive education across cultures: Crossing boundaries, sharing ideas.* New Delhi, India, and London, UK: Sage Publications.
Balescut, J., and Eklindh, K. (2006). Literacy and persons with developmental disabilities: Why and how? Internal paper cited in *Literacy for Life* (EFA Global Monitoring Report). Paris, France: UNESCO.
Booth, T., and Ainscow, M. (2011). *Index for Inclusion: Developing learning and participation in schools,* 3rd ed. Bristol, UK: Centre for Studies in Inclusive Education.
Commonwealth Secretariat (2012). *Commonwealth recommendations for the post-2015 Development Framework for Education.* London, UK: Commonwealth Secretariat.
Driedger, D. (1989). *The last civil rights movement: A history of Disabled Peoples' International.* London, UK: Hurst.
Ebersold, S. with Schmitt, M.J., and Priestley, M. (2011). *Inclusive education for young and disabled people in Europe: Trends, issues and challenges: a synthesis of evidence from ANED country reports and additional sources.* Leeds, UK: University of Leeds, Centre for Disability Studies.

Economic and Social Commission for Asia and the Pacific (2010). *Disability at a glance 2010: A profile of 36 countries and areas in Asia and the Pacific.* Bangkok, Thailand: United Nations Social Development Division.

European Agency for Development in Special Needs Education (2011). *Teacher education for inclusion across Europe – challenges and opportunities.* Odense, Denmark: European Agency for Development in Special Needs Education.

Forlin, C. (2010). *Teacher education for inclusion: Changing paradigms and innovative approaches.* Oxford, UK: Routledge.

Gottlieb, C., Maenner, M., Cappa, C., and Durkin, M. (2009). Child disability screening, nutrition, and early learning in 18 countries with low and middle incomes: Data from the third round of UNICEF's Multiple Indicator Cluster Survey (2005–06). *Lancet*, 374, 1831–1839.

International Disability and Development Consortium (2013). *Teachers for All: Inclusive teaching for children with disabilities.* Brussels, Belgium: IDDC.

Kyriazopoulou, M., and Weber, H. (Eds.) (2009). *Development of a set of indicators for inclusive education in Europe.* Odense, Denmark: European Agency for Development in Special Needs Education.

Lansdown, G. (2009). *See me, hear me: A guide to using the UN-Convention on the Rights of Persons with Disabilities to promote the rights of children.* London, UK: Save the Children.

Lansdown, G. (2014). Children with disabilities. In M. Sabatello, and M. Schulze, (Eds.) *Human rights and disability advocacy* (pp. 97–112). Philadelphia: University of Pennsylvania Press.

Learning Metrics Task Force (2013). *Towards universal learning: What every child should learn.* Paris, France: UNESCO Institute of Statistics and Brookings Institute.

Leonard Cheshire Disability (2013). *Inclusive education: an introduction.* London, UK: siLCI.

Llewellyn, G., Emerson, E., Madden, R., and Honey, A. (2012). *The well-being of children with disabilities in the Asia-Pacific Region: An analysis of UNICEF MICS 3 survey data from Bangladesh, Lao PDR, Mongolia and Thailand.* Sydney, Australia: University of Sydney, Centre for Disability Research and Policy.

MacKay, D. (2014). Foreword. In: Sabatello, M. and Schulze, M. (Eds.) (2014) *Human rights and disability advocacy* (pp. xi-xiii). Philadelphia: University of Pennsylvania Press.

Mariga, L., McConkey, R., and Myezwa, H. (2014). *Introducing inclusive education in low income countries: A resource book for teacher educators, parent trainers and community development workers.* Cape Town, South Africa: Atlas Alliance and Disability Innovations Africa.

Mitchell, D. (Ed.) (2005). *Contextualising inclusive education.* London, UK: Routledge.

Mitchell, D. (2013). *What really works in inclusive and special needs education* (2nd. edition). London: Routledge.

Mittler, P. (2001). Preparing for self-advocacy. In B. Carpenter, R. Ashdown and K. Bovair (Eds.), *Enabling access: Effective education for pupils with learning difficulties*, 2nd ed. London, UK: Fulton.

Mittler, P. (2005). The role of the United Nations. In D. Mitchell (Ed.), *Contextualising inclusive education* (pp. 22–36). London, UK: Routledge.

Mittler, P. (2010). *Thinking globally: Acting locally: A personal journey.* Bloomington, IN and Milton Keynes: Authorhouse.

Mittler, P. (2012). It's our Convention: Use it or lose it? *Development, CBR and Inclusive Development*, 23(2), 7–21.

Mittler, P. (2013). *Overcoming exclusion: Social justice through education.* London, UK: Routledge World Educator Series.

Office of the High Commission on Human Rights (2009). *Guidelines on treaty specific documents to be submitted by States Parties under Article 35, Paragraph 1 of the Convention on the Rights of Persons with Disabilities.* Geneva, Switzerland: OHCHR (CRPD/C/2/3).

Office of the High Commission on Human Rights (2012). *Convention on the Rights of Person with Disabilities: Training guide* (Professional Training Series 19). New York and Geneva, Switzerland: OHCHR.

Office of the High Commission on Human Rights (2013). *How to follow up on United Nations Human Rights recommendations: A practical guide for civil society*. Geneva, Switzerland: OHCHR.

Office of the High Commissioner on Human Rights CRPD Committee (2013). *Concluding observations on the initial report of Austria, adopted by the Committee at its tenth session* (report CRPD/C/AUT/CO/1, 2–13 September 2013). Geneva, Switzerland: OHCHR.

Osamu, N. (2013). Challenges of the harmonisation and ratification of the Convention on the Rights of Persons with Disabilities by Japan. *Journal of Policy and Practice in Intellectual Disabilities*, 10(2), 93–95.

Quinn, G. (2009). Bringing the UN-Convention on rights for persons with disabilities to life in Ireland. *British Journal of Learning Disabilities*, 37, 245–249.

Rieser, R. (2012). *Implementing inclusive education: a commonwealth guide to implementing article 24 of the UN-convention on the rights of persons with disabilities* (2nd ed.). London, UK: Commonwealth Secretariat.

Sabatello, M. and Schulze, M. (Eds.) (2014) *Human rights and disability advocacy*. Philadelphia: University of Pennsylvania Press.

Shaw, B. (2014). Inclusion or choice? Securing the right to inclusive education for all. In Sabatello, M. and Schulze, M. (Eds.) (2014), *Human Rights and Disability Advocacy* (pp. 58–69). Philadelphia: University of Pennsylvania Press.

UNESCO (2001). *Open file on inclusive education*. Paris, France: UNESCO.

UNESCO (2009a). *Embracing diversity: Toolkit for creating inclusive-friendly environments*. Bangkok, Thailand: UNESCO.

UNESCO (2009b). *Towards inclusive education for children with disabilities: A guideline*. Bangkok, Thailand: UNESCO.

UNESCO (2011). *Regional education system on students with disabilities: Methodological proposal*. Santiago, Chile: Regional Bureau of Education.

UNESCO (2012). *Youth and skills: Putting education to work* (Education for All Global Monitoring Report). Paris, France: UNESCO.

UNESCO (2013). *Proposed post-2015 education goals: Emphasizing equity, measurability and finance*. Education for All Global Monitoring Report. Paris: UNESCO.

UNESCO (2014). *Teaching and learning: achieving quality for all* (Global Monitoring Report) 2013/2014. Paris, France: UNESCO.

United Nations Economic Council (2012). *Report of the Washington Group on disability statistics* [E/CN.3/2012/21]. New York: UN Statistical Commission.

United Nations Secretary-General (2013). *Report of the High Level Meeting on Disability and Development in the realisation of the Millennium Development Goals for Persons with Disabilities* (General Assembly Resolution A/68/L.1). New York: United Nations.

UNICEF (2007). *Promoting the human rights of children with disabilities*. Florence, Italy: UNICEF, Innocenti Digest 13.

UNICEF (2013a). *State of the world's children: Children with disabilities*. New York: UNICEF.

UNICEF (2013b). *Educating teachers for children with disabilities: Mapping, scoping and best practices exercise in the context of developing inclusive education* (UNICEF Rights, Education and Protection Project (REAP). Working Document). New York: UNICEF and Australian Government (Consultant: Richard Rieser).

World Health Organisation and World Bank (2011). *World report on disability*. Geneva: WHO.

CHAPTER 22

Ainscow, M. and César, M. (2006). Inclusive education ten years after Salamanca: Setting the agenda. *European Journal of Psychology of Education,* XXI(3): 231–238.

Allan, J. (2005). Inclusion as an ethical project. In S. Tremain (Ed.), *Foucault and the government of disability* (pp. 281–297). Ann Arbor, The University of Michigan Press).

Allan, J. (2008) *Rethinking inclusive education: The philosophers of difference in practice.* Dordrecht, Springer.

Alur, M., and Bach, M. (2010) *The journey for inclusive education in the Indian sub-continent.* London, Routledge.

American Psychiatric Association (2013). *Diagnostic and statistical manual of mental disorders: DSM-5.* Arlington, VA: American Psychiatric Association.

Apple, M.W. (2006). *Educating the "right" way: Markets, standards, God, and inequality.* New York: Routledge.

Artiles, A., and Dyson, A. (2005). Inclusive education in the globalization age: The promise of a cultural-historical analysis. In D. Mitchell (Ed.) *Contextualizing inclusive education* (pp. 37–62). London, Routledge.

Aubenas, F. (2011). *The night cleaner.* Cambridge, UK: Polity Press.

Australian Institute of Health and Welfare (2011) Young Australians: Their health and wellbeing 2011. Canberra, Australian Institute of Health and Welfare.

Ball, S.J. (1990). *Politics and policy making in education: Explorations in policy sociology.* London, UK: Routledge.

Ball, S.J. (2007). *Education plc: Understanding private sector participation in public sector education.* Abingdon, Routledge.

Ball, S.J. (2013). *The education debate.* Bristol, UK: The Policy Press.

Barkley, R.A. (2006). *Attention-deficit hyperactivity disorder: A handbook for diagnosis and treatment.* New York: Guilford.

Brantlinger, E.A. (2006). *Who benefits from special education? Remediating (fixing) other people's children.* London, UK: Lawrence Erlbaum Associates.

Bauman, Z. (1997). *Postmodernity and its discontents.* Cambridge, UK: Polity.

Bauman, Z. (2004). *Wasted lives: Modernity and its outcasts.* Cambridge, UK: Polity.

Bauman, Z. (2008). *Does ethics have a chance in a world of consumers?* Cambridge, MA: Harvard University Press.

Bauman, Z., and Mazzeo, R. (2012). *On education: Conversations with Riccardo Mazzeo.* Cambridge, UK, Polity Press.

Carrington, S., and Macarthur, J. (Eds.) (2012). *Teaching in inclusive school communities.* Milton, Queensland: Wiley.

Connell, R.W. (2007). *Southern theory. The global dynamics of knowledge in social science.* Cambridge, UK: Polity Press.

Cooper, P. (2008). Like alligators bobbing for poodles? A critical discussion of education, ADHD and the biopsychosocial perspective. *Journal of Philosophy in Education, 42,* 457–474.

Daniels, H. and Garner, P. (Eds.) (1999). *Inclusive education: Supporting inclusion in education systems.* London, UK: Kogan Page.

Deno, E. (1970). Special education as developmental capital. *Exceptional Children,* 37(3), 229–237.

Department for Education, Employment and Workplace Relations (2012). *Review of disability standards for education 2005* (Report for Department for Education, Employment and Workplace Relations). Canberra, Australia: Australian Government Printer.

Dorling, D. (2010). *Injustice. Why social inequality persists.* Bristol, UK: The Policy Press.

Duncan, A. (2014). *Rethinking school discipline.* Press Release January 8th, 2014, Washington DC: State Department of Education, http://www.ed.gov/news/speeches/rethinking-school-discipline, accessed 10 June 2014.

Dyson, A. (1999). Inclusion and inclusions: Theories and discourses in inclusive education. In H. Daniels and P. Garner (Eds.), *Inclusive education: World yearbook of education.* London, UK: Kogan Page.

Fleck, L. (1979). *Genesis and development of a scientific fact.* Chicago: University of Chicago Press.

Gamoran, A. (2010). Tracking and inequality: New directions for research and practice. In M.W. Apple, S.J. Ball, and L.A. Gandin (Eds.), *The Routledge international handbook of the sociology of education* (pp. 213–228). Abingdon, UK: Routledge.

Gillborn, D. (2008). *Racism and education: Coincidence or conspiracy?* London, UK: Routledge.

Gillborn, D. and Youdell, D. (1999). *Rationing education: Policy, practice, reform, and equity.* Buckingham, UK: Open University Press.

Greenberg, G. (2010). *Manufacturing depression: The secret history of a modern disease.* New York: Simon and Schuster.

Greenberg, G. (2013). *The book of woe: The DSM and the unmaking of psychiatry.* New York: Blue Rider Press.

Harwood, V., and J. Allan (2014). *Psychopathology at school.* Abingdon, UK: Routledge.

Kutchins, H. and Kirk, S.A. (1997). *Making us crazy: DSM: The psychiatric bible and the creation of mental disorders.* New York: Free Press.

Marr, D. (2011). *Panic.* Collingwood, Victoria: Black Inc.

McDonald, K. (2006). *Global movements: Action and culture.* Oxford: Blackwell.

Norwich, B. (2008). *Dilemmas of difference, disability and inclusion: International perspectives and future directions.* London, UK: Routledge.

Oakes, J. (2005). *Keeping track: How schools structure inequality.* New Haven, CT: Yale University Press.

Onaga, E.E. and Martoccio, T.L. (2008). Dynamic and uncertain pathways between early childhood, inclusive policy and practice. *International Journal of Child Care and Education Policy,* 2(1), 67–75.

Parrish, T. (2002). Racial disparities in the identification, funding and provision of special education. In D. Losen and G. Orfield (Eds.) *Racial inequality in special education* (pp. 15–38). Cambridge, MA: Harvard Education Press.

Parsons, C. (2009). *Strategic alternatives to exclusion from school.* Stoke on Trent, UK: Trentham.

Ravitch, D. (2011). *The death and life of the great American school system: How testing and choice are undermining education.* New York: Basic Books.

Rizvi, F., and Lingard, B. (2010). *Globalizing education policy.* Abingdon, UK: Routledge.

Rose, N. (2007). *The politics of life itself. Biomedicine, power and subjectivity in the twenty-first century.* Princeton, NJ: Princeton University Press.

Rose, H., and Rose, S. (2013). *Genes, cells and brains.* London, UK: Verso.

Rose, S. (2005). *The 21st century brain. Explaining, mending and manipulating the mind.* London, UK: Vintage.

Said, E.W. (2000). *Reflections on exile and other essays.* Cambridge, MA: Harvard University Press.

Schwarz, A. (2014). Idea of new attention disorder spurs research and debate. *The New York Times,* April 11th. http://www.nytimes.com/2014/04/12/health/idea-of-new-attention-disorder-spurs-research-and-debate.html?_r=2, accessed 10 June 2014.

Sennett, R. (2006). *The culture of the new capitalism.* London, UK: Yale University Press.

Singal, N., and Muthukrishna, N. (2014). Introduction: Education, childhood and disability in countries of the South – Re-positioning the debates. *Childhood*, 1–15.

Slee, R. (1994). *Changing theories and practices of discipline*. London, UK: Falmer.

Slee, R. (2006). Limits to and possibilities for reform. *International Journal of Inclusive Education*, 10(2), 109–119.

Slee, R. (2010). *The irregular school: Exclusion, schooling, and inclusive education.* London, UK: Routledge.

Stobart, G. (2008). *Testing times: The uses and abuses of assessment.* Abingdon, UK: Routledge.

Teese, R. (2013). *Academic success and social power: Examinations and inequality*. North Melbourne, Australia: Scholarly Press.

te Riele, K. (2007). Educational alternatives for marginalised youth. *The Australian Educational Researcher*, 34(3), 56–68.

Thomas, G., and Loxley, A. (2007). *Deconstructing special education and constructing inclusion. (Second Edition)*. Maidenhead, UK: Open University Press.

Thrupp, M., and Willmott, R. (2003). *Education management in managerialist times: Beyond the textual apologists.* Buckingham, UK: Open University Press.

Tomlinson, S. (1982). *A sociology of special education.* London, UK: Routledge and Kegan Paul.

Tomlinson, S. (2012). The irresistible rise of the SEN industry. *Oxford Review of Education*, 38(3), 267–286.

Touraine, A. (2000). *Can we live together? Equality and difference.* Oxford, UK: Polity.

UNESCO (1990). *World declaration on education for all.* Geneva, Switzerland: United Nations. http://www.unesco.org/education/efa/ed_for_all/background/jomtien_declaration.shtml, accessed 10 June 2014.

Victorian Auditor-General's Office (2012). *Programmes for students with special learning needs.* Melbourne, Australia: Victorian Auditor-General's Office.

Victorian Equal Opportunity and Human Rights Commission (2012). *Held back.* Melbourne, Australia: VEO and HRC.

Whitaker, R. (2002). *Mad in America: Bad science, bad medicine, and the enduring mistreatment of the mentally ill.* Cambridge, MA: Perseus Publishers.

Whitaker, R. (2010). *Anatomy of an epidemic: Magic bullets, psychiatric drugs, and the astonishing rise of mental illness in America.* New York: Crown Publishers.

Whitehouse, A. (2014). Is sluggish cognitive tempo a valid new childhood disorder? *The Conversation*, 30th April: *http://theconversation.com/is-sluggish-cognitive-tempo-a-valid-new-childhood-disorder-25646?utm_medium=email&utm_campaign=Latest+from+The+Conversation+for+30+April+2014&utm_content=Latest+from+The+Conversation+for+30+April+2014+CID_5050feaa4ce0b39ba419bbe588841171&utm_source=campaign_monitor&utm_term=Is%20sluggish%20cognitive%20tempo%20a%20valid%20new%20childhood%20disorder*, accessed 10 June 2014.

Wilkinson, R., and Pickett, K. (2009). *The spirit level. Why more equal societies almost always do better.* London, UK: Penguin.

Disability Studies in Education

GENERAL EDITORS: SUSAN L. GABEL & SCOT DANFORTH

The book series Disability Studies in Education is dedicated to the publication of monographs and edited volumes that integrate the perspectives, methods, and theories of disability studies with the study of issues and problems of education. The series features books that further define, elaborate upon, and extend knowledge in the field of disability studies in education. Special emphasis is given to work that poses solutions to important problems facing contemporary educational theory, policy, and practice.